Finance for Non-Financial Managers

3rd Edition 1997

A.H. Millichamp
B.A., M.Soc.Sc., F.C.A., F.C.C.A.

Alan Millichamp is a former lecturer at the University of Wolverhampton. He has many years experience in teaching accounting to student accountants and to managers. His current activities include tutoring managers in accounting at the Open University Business School.

CONTINUUM
London and New York

Acknowledgements

A CIP catalogue record for this book can be obtained from the British Library

Continuum

ISBN 0 8264 5739 1

Copyright A.H. Millichamp © 1992

Continuum

The Tower Building, 11 York Road, London, SE1 7NX

370 Lexington Avenue, New York, NY 10017 - 6550

First edition 1992

Reprinted 1993

Second Edition 1995

Third Edition 1997

Reprinted 1998, 2000, (twice)

Typeset by: KAI Typesetters, Nottingham

Printed in Great Britain by: Ashford Colour Press, Gosport, Hants

Preface

1. Aim

The aim of this book is to provide an approach to learning which actively involves the student. It will be found most useful on those courses where students are encouraged to be active participants in the learning process. However, it can equally well be used on more conventional courses and by students pursuing a private course of study.

Typical courses on which it can be used include D.M.S., M.B.A., Edexcel (BTEC), Certified Diploma in Accounting and Finance, Degree courses in which accounting and finance is a part and all courses (eg engineering, personnel, marketing, purchasing, catering, tourism etc) on which students need an understanding of accountancy in order to communicate with accountants and implement necessary financial plans and controls as part of their management role.

2. Scope

In line with current employment trends, this new edition contains much more emphasis on service industries and the not-for-profit sectors while not forgetting that the roots of accounting and finance lie in manufacturing and trading.

3. The structure of the book

The book contains nineteen units, each of which deals with selected related topics in finance and accounting. The units progress from the elementary to the relatively advanced and ideally will be taken in sequence. However, individual tutors can easily use selected units to suit their courses or take them in a different order.

Each Unit contains:

a.   A part of the growth of a company — Martin Padlocks Ltd — from its small beginnings until it becomes a multi-national. Numerous accounting and financial problems are encountered on the way. The owner is not an accountant but has to learn to understand and use financial accounts, management accounts and financial management techniques in order to successfully manage his company.

   You are presented with the problems as seen through the eyes of the owner and, via tackling and solving the tasks, discover as he does, the accountancy and financial knowledge and skills required of non-accountant managers. Answers to tasks are provided in Appendix C.

   The ongoing saga of Martin Padlocks appears between bold rules in the text. Each instalment of the saga has a number of scenarios to set the scene, a number of tasks and some quick answer questions. The quick answer questions are to make you think and to revise knowledge gained earlier. The answers to the quick answer questions are in Appendix D.

b.   A full and well-illustrated exposition of the relevant financial accounting, management accounting and financial management principles and practice.

c.   A summary of the Unit.

d. Exercises and assignment/case studies. There are now over 220 exercises and assignments. There are answers to selected exercises (those marked with an asterisk) in Appendix A. In addition there six assignments in Appendix E. Each of these covers several Units.

Notes to the third edition

I have taken the opportunity to:

❒ Revise and update it.

❒ Change the layout so that there is now only one section and the exercises follow the text in each Unit.

❒ Add more material on the service and not-for-profit sectors.

Note for lecturers

Using the book

This book may be used in a number of ways. For example, as a classroom workbook, as a basis for directed but unsupervised learning, as a conventional textbook, as a follow up of formal teaching or a mixture of these methods. Plenty of examples are included for classroom teaching and as homework and assignments.

Lecturers' supplement

A comprehensive Lecturers' supplement is available on disk to help those lecturers using the book as a course text. Application should be made to the publisher on departmentally headed paper.

The supplement contains:

❒ Templates of all numerical problems, set up in Excel (easily transportable to other spreadsheets).

❒ Answers to numerical problems, set up in Excel.

❒ Answers to written problems .

❒ Suggestions for role play, group work, further reading etc.

❒ Additional exercises and assignments.

Appendices

There are three appendices:

A. Answers to selected exercises (those marked *).

B. Glossary of accounting terms.

C. Answers to tasks.

D. Answers to Quick Answer Questions.

E. Six Assignments.

Suggestions and criticisms

I have had many suggestions and criticisms (and some compliments!) on the first two editions. I would welcome many more on the third edition. Please write to me via the publishers.

Alan Millichamp, April 1997

Contents

Contents

Martin plans to float his company on the Stock Exchange and finds out the
benefits and disadvantages of being a quoted company. He finds that the
Stock Exchange is a fascinating place with all sorts of investors and investment media. We meet the Alternative Investment market and we encounter
some theories including the Efficient Market Hypothesis and the Capital
Asset Pricing model.

Martin becomes involved in a local club and finds that accounting, both
financial and management, apply to the not-for-profit as well as to profit
seeking enterprises. We explore financial and management accounting in
charities, the Health Service and in education.

Martin enters the takeover market, meets the Cash Flow Statement, discovers
residual profit, ponders over transfer pricing and finally examines segmental
reporting.

Introduction – how to use the Units

The main part of this book consists of nineteen Units, each containing several single story line scenarios. Each Unit illustrates some managerial problem or need or practice from which you can discover a part of the theory and practice of Financial Accounting, Management Accounting or Financial Management.

Each Unit has:

- ❐ Scenarios
- ❐ Quick answer questions (QAQs)
- ❐ Tasks
- ❐ Study text and summaries
- ❐ Exercises and Case-Studies/Assignments.

Scenarios

The scenarios describe the experiences of Martin who has set up a business initially to wholesale padlocks. He is faced with the problems of cash flow forecasting, understanding Profit and Loss Accounts and Balance Sheets, budgeting, pricing his products, investment appraisal and many others.

We follow his experiences over ten years as he expands, moves into manufacturing, takes over other businesses, and finally floats his company on the Stock Exchange. On the way he encounters other people's problems in manufacturing, service industries and not-for-profit enterprises.

Quick Answer Questions

These are questions which draw your attention to key features of the Scenarios. Always make some attempt at the Quick Answer Questions before looking at the answers. The answers will be found in Appendix D.

Tasks

There are several Tasks within each Unit. These define the core knowledge, understanding and skills which practical managers need in accounting. To deal with them you will most likely need to study the text in each Unit. Answers to these tasks are provided in Appendix C.

Discovery and learning

The Quick Answer Questions and the Tasks are vital parts of the discovery and learning process. They should not be ignored or skimped.

The Units and Scenarios have been arranged in a sequence which progressively develops your knowledge, understanding and skills. They should preferably be worked on in sequence and not in a haphazard fashion.

Happy learning!

1 Starting a new business: cash flow forecasting

1. Objectives

The objective of this first Unit is to introduce three of the financial matters found on starting a new business. These are the provision of capital, cash flow forecasting and the acquisition of fixed assets.

SCENARIO 1 — Martin plans to start a business

Martin is a production control manager of a department of Stubbykey plc a large firm manufacturing padlocks. Stubbykey are suffering from a reduction in demand for their products and, in a cost reduction exercise, Martin is made redundant. He is given some £10,000 severance pay which he invests in a deposit account at the Mudland Bank. He is unable to get a new well-paid job and determines instead to start a business buying or making padlocks and selling them to small hardware and security shops.

He talks over his intentions with his friend Ted, a manufacturers' agent who tells him the main problem with new businesses is the need for capital. Martin considers his private affairs and realises that, in addition to his severance pay, he has some £5,000 of savings invested in the Impeccable Building Society.

Quick Answer Questions 1.1

1. How much capital has Martin got?
2. In what form does Martin hold his capital?
3. Why does Martin's new business need capital?

Note: Answers to Quick Answer Questions (QAQs) are in Appendix D. Always make an attempt at the QAQs before looking at the answers.

SCENARIO 2 — Martin prepares a cash flow forecast

Martin decides to go ahead with starting the business but takes advice from Anne whom he appoints as his accountant and auditor. Anne suggests that he forms a company to operate the business and agrees to form it for him. The company is to be called Martin Padlocks Limited. She suggests that he should begin by preparing a cash flow forecast as it will be necessary to make arrangements to open a bank account – and bank managers need a cash flow forecast.

To this end he thinks hard, makes some informed guesses and estimates and sets out the following set of facts about the company's first six months: (the company will begin on January 1st 19x1).

a. He can sell his padlocks at cost + 50%. He reckons that the market will allow him to make sales at this price.

b. He should be able to make sales as follows:

	Jan	Feb	Mar	Apr	May	Jun	Jul
Sales in £'000	6	9	15	15	18	18	18

His customers will on average pay in the second month following delivery. For example, sales in January will result in the receipt of cash in March.

c. He will need to acquire an immediate stock to cost £8,000 and increase this by £1,000 every month, beginning in February, till the end of June as he will need a good stock to be able to satisfy customers' needs. In addition he will need to buy in each month sufficient stock to meet the following month's sales.

Thus in February he will need to buy £1,000 + £10,000 (because £10,000 + 50% = £15,000, the estimated sales for the following month) = £11,000 of stock. He will pay for his stock purchases in the month following each purchase.

d. Anne will charge him £500 for forming the company, preparing the cash flow forecast and general advice. This will be paid in March.

e. He will need a computer (£1,000), a second hand van (£5,000) and some stacking equipment (£3,000). These sums need to be paid in January.

f. He needs to pay for a small workshop: 6 months' rent in advance payable in January £2,000; rates £750 for the period to September payable in May; electricity £220 payable in April; stationery payable in January £240; advertising payable in March and June £600 each.

g. Van running expenses payable as incurred at £200 a month.

h. Wages to his two assistants will be payable monthly and will be £900 a month to Lucy and Tom £600.

i. A salary to himself £700 a month which is low but he wants to keep his drawings low to start with in order to build up the business.

j. He will put his £15,000 into the company in January and will be issued with £1 shares in exchange.

Task 1

What would you expect his cash flow forecast for the first six months to look like?

Note that you can prepare a cash flow forecast:

i.   On any piece of paper

ii.   Using a form supplied for this purpose by any branch of a high street bank

iii. Using a spreadsheet programme on a computer.

Note. Help in answering tasks is provided in the text immediately following tasks and/or will have been previously covered in the text.

---

2. Introduction

We have begun this book with cash flow forecasting because this tends to be both the easiest accounting idea to grasp and because new businesses need to get to grips with cash flow forecasting straight away. In the second Unit we will consider profit in detail but the important point to grasp is that businesses must be both profitable and have well managed cash flows. We will begin by considering the need for profit and then extend to the need for cash flow management and forecasting.

Every business needs to make a profit. In the short term (for example for one year) a business can make a loss but in the long run a business must be profitable to survive.

Further, withdrawals from a business by its owner must be less than profits. Again, in the short term, a proprietor of a business can continue to draw from the business which is making losses or profits less than the drawings. But in the long term profits must exceed drawings. In companies, withdrawals by the proprietors are called dividends and these can also in the short term be paid even when the company has made a loss or has made a profit which is less than the dividend. However in the long term, companies must make profits which exceed dividends to survive. In fact company law prohibits a company from paying dividends except out of profits. This restriction does not apply for any one year but means that a dividend in a year can only be paid to the amount that total profits since the formation of the company exceed total dividends already paid.

However even profitable companies can fail if they do not manage their cash flow satisfactorily. A simple example:

Simon starts a business with £100. He buys stock, paying the supplier £100. He sells the stock for £200 and the customer will pay him in three months. He borrows £100 from the bank and buys £200 more stock from a supplier agreeing to pay £100 now and £100 one month later.

He is now in a position where he has:

Assets:		Liabilities:	
Stock	£200	Bank	£100
Debt	£200	Creditor	£100
	£400		£200

His business now has net assets of £400 – £200 = £200.

This came from £100 original investment and £100 profit.

However he has no cash and if his debtor delayed payment he would be unable to repay the bank and pay his creditor.

This scenario happens continually with numerous businesses which are profitable but which run out of cash. The effect is often bankruptcy, receivership or liquidation.

The need is for a business to manage its cash flows. It can only easily do this by:

❐ forecasting cash flows

❐ identifying likely shortages

❐ arranging finance to eliminate the revealed shortages

❐ continually reviewing the current and future cash position.

Indeed before lending to a business, the bank always requires a cash flow forecast. There are many advantages to this:

❐ the bank can see that the business will be able to survive

❐ the bank can see that the business can pay interest and repay the loan as agreed

❏ the business owners have the importance of cash flow management impressed upon them.

3. Constructing cash flow forecasts

The easiest way to construct a cash flow forecast is to use one of the forms supplied by the bank. The following is a slightly abbreviated example:

Month	Jan		Feb	
	Budget	Actual	Budget	Actual

Receipts

1. Sales — cash
2. — debtors
3. Loans received
4. Capital introduced
5. Disposal of assets
A. Total receipts

Payments

6. Cash purchases
7. Payments to creditors
8. Principals remuneration
9. Wages/salaries
10. PAYE/NHI
11. Capital items
12. Transport/packaging
13. Rent/rates
14. Services
15. Loan repayments
    HP/leasing payments
16. Interest
17. Bank/finance charges
    Professional fees
    Advertising
18. VAT
19. Corporation/income tax
20. Dividends
B. Total payments
C. Opening bank balance
D. Closing bank balance

All that is necessary is to fill in the form with appropriate figures. In practice this is difficult because:

❏ business people do not understand all the terms and concepts used

❏ forecasting is virtually impossible especially with a new business.

However, forcing a new businessperson to think and plan and forecast is highly desirable.

An explanation of some of the terms is:

Line

1. Sales — Cash. Some businesses sell on *credit* where the sale takes place and the invoice is sent on one day and then payment is received at a *later* date. The later date can be anything from a few days to many months. It is often very difficult to forecast. Some businesses sell for cash at point of sale. Examples are retail shops, bus companies and cinemas. Some businesses are fortunate enough to receive money in advance of providing the service. An example is a travel agency. Line 1 requires a forecast of all cash to be received in each month.

2. Where sales are made on credit, it is necessary to forecast:

    ❐ how much will be sold on credit in each month

    ❐ when the customers will pay.

    In practice people who set up businesses are often surprised to find how long customers wait before paying. The worst offenders are large firms.

3. Loans received. This row will only be filled in if loans have been negotiated. At least there is a reasonable degree of certainty over this row.

4. Capital introduced. The proprietor(s) of the business will normally introduce actual money into the business at its beginning. Banks normally expect proprietors to introduce money and not rely solely on bank finance. In the case of companies, capital introduced is usually to pay for shares in the company. However many company founders also make loans to the company in addition to buying shares. Note that only money is included in a cash flow forecast. Many new business founders introduce other assets (goodwill, motor vehicles, tools, initial stock etc) but these do not go on a cash flow forecast or statement.

5. Disposal of assets. This is unlikely in a new business. If it does occur include only the actual proceeds of sale.

6, Purchases. Just as sales can be made for cash or on credit so purchases can be made
7. for cash or on credit.

    These can more easily be forecast since they are under the control of the business. However payments later than desired often occur if the business finds itself short of cash.

8. Principal(s) remuneration. A person who starts a new business usually has to rely on the business for his living expenses. He thus has to make cash drawings from the business. In a company these drawings are usually called directors' salaries or directors' emoluments as technically a director is an employee of the company.

9, Wages/salaries. Most employees are paid weekly or monthly and are paid net of
10. PAYE and National Insurance. Technically the sums deducted together with employer's national insurance are payable in the month following the pay to which they relate. It is highly desirable to keep to this requirement.

11. Capital items. These are items such as the purchase of buildings, plant, machinery and vehicles. These things are called fixed assets. Fixed assets are assets which are

bought for use in the business and not for resale. They have a useful life extending over more than one year. The term capital expenditure is used for the acquisition of fixed assets. Such expenditure is especially likely in new businesses. In cash flow forecasts, enter only the cash payable for them. Note that if the capital items are acquired by leasing or on HP, they go in row 15.

12. Transport/packing. Note that a new vehicle will go into row 11. This row is for running expenses. Remember that some items are purchased on credit (eg a garage bill paid the month following the repair) and the payment in its appropriate month is what goes in the forecast.

13. Rent/rates. These are obvious. However new businesses in new premises often find that there is a long delay before rates bills are assessed and agreed.

14. Services. These may include telephone, gas, electricity and water. Remember that they are payable usually after consumption.

15. Loan repayments. Profits have to be large enough to allow for drawings and dividends and loan repayments.

16. Interest. Banks sometimes charge interest monthly and sometimes quarterly. Amounts are surprisingly large.

17. Bank/finance charges. Banking is not free to commercial customers and again bank charges are often considerable. They are however negotiable.

18. Value added tax. This is usually payable quarterly although there are other schemes. VAT is a subject of remarkable complexity and I shall not pursue it here.

19. Corporation/income tax. Taxes are inevitable even with expert advice. Companies pay corporation tax on their profits about nine months after the conclusion of the year in which the profits were earned. The proprietors of unincorporated businesses pay income tax on the profits of the businesses. The timing and amount of corporation tax, advance corporation tax and income tax is a knotty subject and professional advice is essential. Sufficient to say that most new businesses will not pay any such taxes until eighteen months or so after the commencement of the business.

20. Dividends. Companies can pay dividends to their shareholders. It is unlikely that a new company will declare and pay a dividend until at least the first year is over.

Having entered the forecast payments and receipts month by month, it is necessary to total the amounts in rows A and B. Then the opening balance at bank is entered in the first column in row C and the month end balance computed by adding row A and deducting row B to give the month end balance which goes in row D and then into the second month of row C.

4. An example of a cash flow forecast

Federico intends to start in business on 1 January 19x2 as a wholesaler of decorative tiles. He will sell some tiles retail to local customers.

Details about his intentions are: (note that I have confined this example to three months. Most forecasts cover twelve months)

❑ He has acquired the lease of a small warehouse paying £5,000 at the beginning of January and an annual rent of £2,400 payable on the usual quarter days in arrears.

❏ Gas and electricity will cost £500 in January, £600 in February and £550 in March. These are payable in the month following consumption.

❏ He will buy £12,000 of tiles in January, £8,000 in February and £8,000 in March. His supplier expects payment in the month after supply.

❏ He will also buy about £400 a month of tiles locally for cash.

❏ He has arranged to borrow £5,000 in January from his mother repayable at £1,000 a year on December 31 each year. There is no interest on this loan.

❏ He will put in £4,000 from his own savings, his old van worth £1,500 and his collection of tiles valued at £2,500.

❏ He hopes to sell £800 a month for cash and credit sales of £4,000 in January, £14,000 in February and £16,000 in March. He estimates that payment will be 50% in the month following sale and 50% in the month after that.

❏ Federico intends to draw £400 a month for himself.

❏ He will employ Maria who will earn £300 a month less £60 tax and insurance. Employers national insurance will be £30 a month.

❏ He will need some shelving which will be delivered and paid for in January and cost £7,000. This should last 10 years.

❏ He will lease a car for himself at a cost of £250 a month.

❏ He will have to pay professional fees re the warehouse lease purchase and the cash flow forecast of £600 in February.

❏ Advertising will be payable in advance at £180 a month. The first adverts will appear in February and be paid for in January.

❏ We will ignore VAT and any other payments.

Federico

Cash flow forecast for the first quarter of 19x2

	Jan	Feb	Mar	Total
Receipts:				
Loan — mother	5,000			5,000
Capital introduced	4,000			4,000
Cash sales	800	800	800	2,400
Credit sales		2,000	9,000	11,000
Total	9,800	2,800	9,800	22,400
Payments:				
Lease	5,000			5,000
Rent			600	600
Gas and electricity		500	600	1,100
Creditors		12,000	8,000	20,000
Cash purchases	400	400	400	1,200
Drawings	400	400	400	1,200

	Jan	Feb	Mar	Total
Wages	240	240	240	720
PAYE/NHI		90	90	180
Shelving	7,000			7,000
Lease of car	250	250	250	750
Professional fees		600		600
Advertising	180	180	180	540
Total	13,470	14,660	10,760	38,890
Opening balance	0	(3,670)	(15,530)	0
Closing balance	(3,670)	(15,530)	(16,490)	(16,490)

Federico takes this forecast to his bank and asks for an overdraft facility of £20,000 as he foresees that he will need £16,490 according to his forecast but would like more to cover things not going according to plan. The bank manager refuses to offer more than £10,000 and asks Federico to reconsider his proposals to keep the overdraft under £10,000.

Possible actions are:

❐ put in more capital himself, perhaps by second mortgaging his house
❐ obtain a special loan secured on the lease
❐ reduce or delay some of his purchases
❐ negotiate more credit from his supplier
❐ attempt to buy the shelving on hire purchase or lease it.

The advantage of a forecast is that it enables cash flow difficulties to be seen in advance and action taken to avoid disaster.

SCENARIO 3 — Martin reviews his cash flow forecast

The cash flow forecast (Task 1) that was actually prepared looked like this:

Martin Padlocks Ltd Cash Flow Forecast for the six months to June 19x1

	Jan £	Feb £	Mar £	Apr £	May £	Jun £	Total £
Receipts:							
Customers			6,000	9,000	15,000	15,000	45,000
Capital	15,000						
Total	15,000		6,000	9,000	15,000	15,000	60,000
Payments:							
Suppliers		14,000	11,000	11,000	13,000	13,000	62,000
Anne			500				500
Computer	1,000						1,000
Van	5,000						5,000
Equipment	3,000						3,000
Rent	2,000						2,000

	Jan	Feb	Mar	Apr	May	Jun	Total
Rates					750		750
Electricity				220			220
Stationery	240						240
Advertising			600			600	1,200
Van Expenses	200	200	200	200	200	200	1,200
Wages	1,500	1,500	1,500	1,500	1,500	1,500	9,000
Martin	700	700	700	700	700	700	4,200
Total	13,640	16,400	14,500	13,620	16,150	16,000	90,310
B/F (a)	0	1,360	−15,040	−23,540	−28,160	−29,310	0
C/F (b)	1,360	−15,040	−23,540	−28,160	−29,310	−30,310	−30,310
	(c)	(d)					(e)

Note:

a) B/F stands for Brought Forward and indicates the balance at the beginning of the month which is nil at the 1st January 19x1.

b) C/F stands for Carried Forward and indicates the balance at the end of the month.

c) At the end of January the balance in the bank will be Receipts £15,000 less Payments £13,640.

d) At the end of February the Balance will be £1,360 − £16,400 = £15,040 overdrawn. All the overdrawn balances have a minus sign −.

e) The total column forms a check on the detail columns.

After preparing the cash flow forecast Martin and Anne sit down to review it. They find that the balances at the bank at the end of each month are likely to be:

	Jan £	Feb £	Mar £	Apr £	May £	Jun £
In the bank	1,360					
Overdrawn		15,040	23,540	28,160	29,310	30,310

Martin is horrified to realise that, despite putting £15,000 of his capital into the company, a large overdraft would be necessary.

Quick Answer Questions 1.2

1. Summarise the principal reasons why payments will greatly exceed receipts in the first six months of trading.

2. What would happen if Martin wanted to make payments and the bank overdraft was at or over its limit?

SCENARIO 4 — Martin sees his bank manager

Martin arranges an appointment with the manager of his local branch of the Mudland Bank plc and takes Anne with him. The manager agrees to grant the company an overdraft facility of £15,000 as he does not wish to invest more in the company than Martin. This is insufficient as £30,000 is needed but Anne suggests some ways that the extra can be found. These are:

a. agreeing with his suppliers that he will receive two months' credit instead of one month for a period of six months;

b. leasing the van for £200 a month instead of paying for it outright.

Tasks 2

1. Recast the cash flow forecast to take into account the changes suggested by Anne.

2. List the fixed assets which Martin's company intend to buy.

Tasks 3

1. Continue the cash flow forecast for the second six months on the assumptions:
    - ❏ Sales will stabilise at £18,000 a month
    - ❏ Stock will stabilise at the end of June
    - ❏ Rent will be £2,000 payable in July and rates will be £500 in October
    - ❏ Electricity will be £300 in July and £300 in October
    - ❏ Stationery will be £200 in August
    - ❏ Advertising will be £600 in September and December
    - ❏ Wages and Martin's salary will continue at the same amount.

2. Explain why the overdraft steadily diminishes.

3. Put the forecast on a spreadsheet.

5. Feedback on cash flow forecasting

Virtually all new businesses prepare a cash flow forecast on a monthly basis for the first year's trading. They do this primarily because the bank require it before granting loan or overdraft facilities. Subsequently the bank monitor the state of the overdraft by simply ensuring that the amount overdrawn does not exceed the facility. The bank will also required financial statements in the form of a Trading and Profit and Loss Account and Balance Sheet. Usually annual accounts are sufficient but in some cases quarterly or half yearly accounts are required. Existing businesses are also usually required by their bankers to produce cash flow forecasts when negotiating a renewal or an increase in an overdraft facility.

The firm may also prepare a forecast for its own purposes and this is now more commonly done as businessmen play with spreadsheets on their personal computers. Spreadsheets seem to be designed for the purpose of doing cash flow forecasts.

An obvious requirement of a forecast is that it is reasonably accurate. The ability to do anything is much enhanced by having feedback on actual performance and forecasting is no exception. A cash flow forecaster who is given detailed feedback on actual outcomes can determine where the forecast was wrong and why. Hopefully she will learn by this to forecast better and her next attempt will be more reliable.

A problem in practice is that feedback is not normally given to forecasters. The reason is that data necessary to verify the assumptions of the forecast are not collected by the bookkeeping systems of most firms.

For example:

❐ cash collected from customers is recorded but is not related to particular months' sales. Consequently no feedback is available on the pattern of payment by customers.

❐ cash paid to suppliers is recorded but is not related to particular months' purchases. Consequently no feedback is available on the pattern of payments to suppliers. In practice the timing of payments to suppliers is a complex business and account is usually taken of: the state of the overdraft, the availability of settlement discounts, the degree of pressure applied by a supplier and other factors.

❐ the relationship of sales, purchases and stocks is often obscure and the bookkeeping system certainly does not keep information which would give any enlightenment.

In 1991 a new Financial Reporting Standard was issued. This is FRS 1 on Cash Flow Statements. A revised version appeared in 1996. This does not require but recommends collection and reporting of:

Cash received from customers

Cash payments to suppliers

Cash paid to and on behalf of employees

Other cash payments relating to operating activities

If companies adopt this recommendation then at least some extra feedback may be available to cash flow forecasters.

The branches and subsidiary companies owned by large groups are often required to forecast their cash flows. Head office can then budget the overall finances of the group. The branches and subsidiaries are then required to supply Head Office with periodic statements of *actual* cash flows and to offer explanations for deviations from the budgets. This practice of forecasting with feedback is useful in that it enables learning both by the forecasters in the branches and subsidiaries and by Head Office staff. It also encourages good cash flow management but will cause much anxiety in the branches and subsidiaries!

Note:

1. The supply of fixed assets, goods for resale and expenses can be maintained without payment as long as credit can be obtained from suppliers of these things.

2. Sales do not immediately lead to an inflow of cash if sales are on credit.

3. The trick is to collect debts as fast as possible while keeping creditors waiting a reasonable time.

6. Problems in cash flow forecasting

Cash flow forecasting is not intrinsically difficult but there are some pitfalls:

❐ Include only cash flows. Remember that depreciation is not a cash flow.

❐ Be careful about tax flows — VAT, PAYE and NHI. Professional advice is desirable.

❐ Customers are likely to pay more slowly than expected.

❐ Allow for bad debts and disputes with customers that may slow payment.

❐ Allow for all expenses. It is easy to omit some. Provide a sum for contingencies like repairs.

- ❐ Do not forget that the proprietor must make drawings to live on.
- ❐ Loans and overdrafts require interest to be paid. With fixed term loans interest payments are usually determinable. However the amount of interest payable on an overdraft is difficult to forecast. Consult with the bank manager.

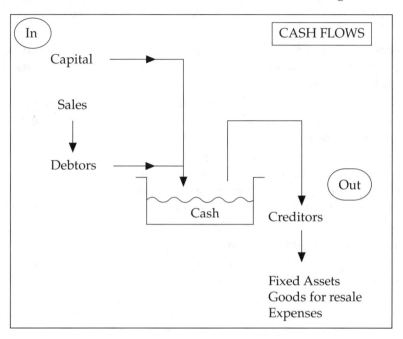

7. Summary of Unit 1

- ❐ Businesses must, in the long term, earn profits which are greater than drawings and dividends.
- ❐ Businesses must also manage their cash flows to ensure that payments can always be made when they fall due.
- ❐ Not-for-profit undertakings also need to manage their affairs so that income matches expenditure and that cash flows are managed such that payments can be made when they fall due.
- ❐ Cash flow forecasting is desirable at all times and is an essential requirement for enterprises requesting loan or overdraft facilities.
- ❐ Cash flow forecasts usually cover twelve months and each month has a column for the forecast, and for the actual flows which are of course filled in after the event. A total column is useful to check accuracy.
- ❐ If a cash flow forecast shows a cash flow problem is possible, action (such as fixing up a loan) can be taken to avert the difficulty.
- ❐ Professional advice on the forecast by an accountant is usually sought by people who intend to start a business.
- ❐ The modern way of preparing a cash flow forecast is to use a computer spreadsheet package.

- ❏ A cash flow forecast should not include non-cash flows like depreciation but should include all costs including taxes, drawings and interest.

- ❏ Capital is a technical term for all the resources invested in an enterprise by its owners.

- ❏ Capital expenditure is the acquisition of fixed assets. Fixed assets are long lived assets such as land, buildings, plant, machinery and vehicles.

- ❏ Forecast cash payments must include outgoings for capital expenditure. Capital expenditure may be made by outright purchase with payment or may be made by using financing methods such as hire purchase or leasing.

- ❏ Forecast cash receipts must include cash put into the business by the owners. In general banks do not like lending to a business a greater amount of money than has been put into the business as capital by the owners.

- ❏ Some businesses just begin with no formalities. Some are formed as limited companies as is Martin Padlocks Ltd. A limited company has to be registered with the Registrar of Companies. Formation can be effected by accountants, lawyers or on a do-it-yourself basis using company formation agents who advertise in the business press.

- ❏ Trading on credit allows customers to delay payment and while delaying payment to suppliers can compensate, it can cause problems with the supplier — like the supplier cutting off supplies or putting in the bailiffs.

- ❏ Cash flow forecasts are frequently prepared but statements of actual cash flows in the same form as the original forecast are more rarely done. If they were more frequently prepared cash flow forecasts would tend to be more accurate. Cash Flow Statements are often produced under FRS 1 but these are in a different format.

Note: All the exercises on cash flow forecasting are eminently suitable for working on a spreadsheet.

Exercise 1

Dymphna has a business buying and selling special steels. She runs a large overdraft and is regularly required to provide a cash flow forecast when her overdraft facility comes up for renewal each year. She has half yearly accounts produced and sends copies to the bank for them to review.

Required:

a. What is meant by cash in cash flow forecasting?

b. The bank do not always grant her the facility she would like (not all banks listen or like to say yes!). Explain how she can try out various strategies (eg paying her suppliers more slowly) and see how they affect her cash flows and hence her overdraft requirement. Suggest some suitable strategies.

c. Summarise the data that might be recorded in Dymphna's bookkeeping system to give her feedback on her ability to forecast.

Exercise *2

Ludwig intends to start a business on January 1st as a hairdresser. He intends to rent a property and initially he has to pay £500 for a quarter's rent in advance and pay £4,000 for the necessary equipment (furniture, hairdryers, a cash register etc). He also thinks he needs to spend some £1,000 immediately on advertising and publicity.

How much capital will he need to start the business? How much will he spend on fixed assets?

He forecasts his first three months' receipts and payments as:

Sales — January £2,000, February and March £2,500 each

Materials etc 20% of sales in each month, payable in the month following purchase

Wages £350 a month

Sundry overheads £200 a month

Drawings for personal expenditure £600 a month.

Required:

a. Prepare a cash flow forecast for his first three months. Note that his actual capital (all his savings) at the beginning was only £3,000. He needs to borrow from his bank.

b. Change the forecast by inputting sales at

(a) 20% less and

(b) 20% more.

Calculate the percentage change in maximum overdraft requirement as a result of (a) and (b).

Exercise 3

Philip begins his studies at Sheinton University on 1 October 19x1. Being a thoughtful but impecunious student, he forecasts his cash flows for the first term of three months. Probable data are:

Grant—	£200 receivable in October
Parental gift —	£300 in each month
Part time work —	£100 a month but he can make an additional £50 in December
Books —	£200 in October, £50 in December
Accommodation —	£150 a month
Meals —	£120 a month
Beer, concerts etc —	£80 a month
Transport —	£80 a month + an additional £20 in November.
Clothing —	£100 in November

a. Prepare a cash flow forecast for Philip for his first term.

b. Philip can borrow to make up any deficiency but would prefer not to. He feels he has two alternatives to borrowing:

— doing more work

— eating cheaper food.

Calculate how much more monthly income from work is required or how much less expenditure is required on food, to just breakeven and not have to borrow.

Exercise 4

Willa intends to start her catering business from 1 January 19x2:

Her forecast is:

❑ She will put £2,000 into a business bank account from her savings.

❑ She will rent a small workshop at a rent of £3,000 a year payable on usual quarter days in arrear.

❑ She will have to pay rates of £1,200, payable £380 in March and £820 in September.

❑ She will equip the workshop at a cost of £6,400 payable in February.

❑ She hopes to make cash sales and credit sales of:

Quarter	March	June	Sept	Dec
	£	£	£	£
Cash	3,000	4,000	5,000	7,000
Credit	6,000	8,000	9,000	10,000

She expects 30% of credit sales in a quarter to be outstanding at the end of a quarter.

❑ Materials will cost 30% of the sales in a quarter. She expects to still owe 25% of her purchases in a quarter at the end of the quarter.

❑ Labour will cost £1,200 a month.

❑ She will draw £400 a month.

❑ She will spend about £300 a month on other expenses (advertising, energy etc).

❑ She will buy an estate car to use in the business. This will cost £6,000 and will be financed by trading in her old car at £2,000 and the rest by hire purchase with 36 instalments at £165 a month beginning in February.

Required:

a. Prepare a cash flow forecast for Willa for the four quarters of 19x2.

b. Should she ask her bank for an overdraft or a long term loan?

c. Vary the forecast by reversing the cash and credit sales figures and by any other changes you can think of. Note their effects.

Exercise 5

Giles has been made redundant from his job as a driver with a local firm of agricultural wholesalers and intends to start a business buying produce from local farmers and selling it to supermarkets. He intends to start on 1 January 19x3 with £2,500 of his savings and his van worth £2,000.

❑ He will sell on credit to the supermarkets who will, he hopes, pay him 50% in the month following a sale and 50% in the month after that.

❑ He will have to pay cash to the farmers.

❑ He will add 50% to the cost of purchases in fixing his selling prices to supermarkets.

❑ He does not intend to carry any stock.

Expected income and expenditure for the first six months are:

	Jan £	Feb £	Mar £	Apr £	May £	Jun £
Sales	4,000	6,000	8,000	9,000	9,000	9,000
Wages	840	840	900	900	1,050	1,050
Drawings	700	700	700	700	700	700
Advertising	500	500	500	200	200	200
Motor Expenses	300	400	300	750	300	300
Other expenses	200	250	250	250	300	300

Note that wages is gross + employers national insurance contributions. You can assume that 1/3 of the cost will be paid in the month after the wages are earned.

Ignore VAT.

Required:

a. Prepare a cash flow forecast for the first six months.

b. How much overdraft should Giles ask for?

Exercise 6

Champ commenced in business on 1 January 19x2 to trade in widgets. She prepared a cash flow forecast for the first six months for the bank and recorded the actual outcome. The forecast and actual are:

Forecast:	Jan £	Feb £	Mar £	Apr £	May £	Jun £
Receipts:						
Introduced	6,000					
Customers		2,500	5,500	7,000	9,000	10,000
Payments:						
Suppliers		6,500	4,000	5,000	5,000	5,000
Overheads	2,000	2,000	2,000	2,000	2,000	2,000
Fixed Assets	10,000					
Overdraft:						
Beginning		6,000	12,000	12,500	12,500	10,500
End	6,000	12,000	12,500	12,500	10,500	7,500

Champ agreed an overdraft limit at £14,000 with her bank manager.

The actual outcome was:

	Jan £	Feb £	Mar £	Apr £	May £	Jun £
Receipts:						
Introducd	6,000					
Customers		2,000	5,000	7,500	8,500	11,000
Payments:						
Suppliers		7,000	3,300	2,200	5,600	7,800
Overheads	2,200	1,900	2,600	3,100	2,900	3,200
Fixed Assets	10,000			2,200		

Overdraft:

Beginning		6,200	13,100	14,000	14,000	14,000
End	6,200	13,100	14,000	14,000	14,000	14,000

The forecast was based on sales and purchases as:

Sales	5,000	6,000	8,000	10,000	10,000	10,000
Purchases	6,500	4,000	5,000	5,000	5,000	5,000

The actual sales and purchases were:

Sales	5,000	7,000	8,500	12,000	13,000	16,000
Purchases	7,000	4,000	6,200	6,000	8,000	5,500

Champ expects to make a gross profit of 50% of sales.

Required:

a. Deduce the assumptions Champ made in preparing the cash flow forecast.

b. Write a report detailing why the actual turned out to be different from the forecast.

c. Assess the difficulties of cash flow forecasting and how well Champ succeeded in her forecasting.

Exercise 7

The Telford branch of the Supranational Child Health Charity is required to submit a cash flow forecast for 19x7 to Head Office in London. The treasurer gathered the following data from the local committee:

a. The house to house collection will probably make £2,500 in June. The annual draw will make £3,000 gross in September and the Christmas Fayre will gross about £1,400. In addition, about £1,200 is usually received randomly through the year from donations.

b. The branch buys T-shirts and other saleable items from a local supplier who gives them one month's credit. These are sold at twice cost price and sales are expected to be £400 a month cash but with some months may total more (June £800, September £1,000, December £700). The branch have enough stock for January sales but will need to purchase stock each month sufficient for forecast sales the following month.

c. Expenses are forecast as: secretarial etc £100 a month, draw costs and prizes £1,050, Fayre costs £280. Advertising £90 a month.

The balance in the bank is sent monthly to Head Office.

Required:

a. A cash flow forecast for the branch on a monthly basis.

b. Why is this forecast useful to Head Office?

c. Would a monthly actual cash flow summary be useful?

The actual cash flows turned out like this:

	Jan £	Feb £	Mar £	Apr £	May £	Jun £	Jul £	Aug £	Sept £	Oct £	Nov £	Dec £
Inflows												
Collection						2,800						
Draw gross									2,400			
Fayre												1,680
Donations	80	125	300	70	69	152	48	120	95	105	73	64
Sales	450	320	354	402	267	760	370	427	903	380	430	800
Outflows												
Purchases	200	200	200	200	200	300	200	600		200	300	400
Secretarial	180	135	202	130	96	102	54	120	241	54	76	64
Draw								430	570			
Fayre												420
Advertising	80	90	280	65	130	120	97	103	201	56	60	140

Required:

Complete the summary and then write a commentary on what occurred as far as this can be deduced. Finally discuss the effect of the outcome on Head Office.

Case Study

Lionel has a business wholesaling souvenirs and has had an overdraft for the five years of the life of the business. Each year he negotiates an increased facility with the bank but always finds that he has to pay his suppliers later than he (or they) would like. At each renewal he produces a cash flow forecast.

He feels that his forecast cannot be accurate and worries that the bank will realise this and consequently not grant him his renewal.

Suggest reasons why his forecasts are never accurate and how feedback might improve his forecasting ability.

2 The end of the first year: the Profit and Loss Account

1. Objectives

The objective of this unit is to introduce one of the two principal financial statements — the Profit and Loss Account. The other is the Balance Sheet which is dealt with in Unit 3. We will see how the Profit and Loss Account measures the profit made by the business over a period (usually one year). The conventions used in constructing it will be discovered and some of these may surprise you! Note that not-for-profit enterprises produce a similar document called the Income and Expenditure Account.

SCENARIO 1 — Martin looks at a Profit and Loss Account

Martin's company has just completed its first year and Martin has asked Anne to prepare and audit the Accounts which he understands have to be produced. She spends some two weeks on this and finally presents Martin with what she calls the draft Profit and Loss Account. This is it:

Martin Padlocks Ltd
Trading and Profit and Loss Account for the year ending 31 December 19x1

	£	£
Sales		212,400
Less: Cost of Goods Sold:		
Opening Stock	–	
Purchases	160,730	
Less Closing Stock	14,730	146,000
Gross Profit		66,400
Less: Expenses:-		
Rent	4,000	
Rates	1,120	
Electricity	900	
Printing and Stationery	630	
Advertising	1,180	
Van Expenses	2,712	
Wages	18,000	
Director's Remuneration	9,600	
Employers' National Insurance	2,542	
Company Formation	250	
Audit and Accountancy	1,300	
Sundries	764	
Lease of van	2,400	
Bank Interest and Charges	2,990	
Depreciation	1,100	49,488
Net Profit		16,912

Quick Answer Questions 2.1

Compare these figures with those you produced in your Cash Flow Forecast (Extended Task 1 in Unit 1).

1. Are the figures as expected?
2. Are there any expenses not forecast?
3. Is the stock as expected?

SCENARIO 2 — Martin sets down to detail in his Profit and Loss Account

Martin is pleased with the profit shown but Anne tells him that an important expense — depreciation — has been included on a provisional basis. He agrees to wait for Unit 4 before going into detail on depreciation in the final Profit and Loss Account. However we make a start on it in Scenario 3 later in this Unit.

In the meantime he has a host of questions to ask Anne about the Profit and Loss Account.

Tasks 1

1. Why are the words 'Trading and' included in the heading?
2. The business sold a parcel of padlocks on credit to Hubert on 31 December. These were invoiced at £620 and delivered all on that date. Hubert has not yet paid for them but he will do so eventually. Is this sale included in the figure of *sales*?
3. Why is there no opening stock?
4. The company bought a consignment of padlocks from Brassbits Ltd on December 28th and this arrived on that date together with the invoice for £405. Martin has not yet paid for these. Are these included in the figure for purchases? Also does 'Purchases' include the purchase of stationery £28 in March?
5. Martin was asked to count his stock at 31 December and to value it at the prices at which the company had been invoiced. This had been done and the final result included as *closing stock* £14,730. Why was the stock valued at the cost to the company?
6. The company paid rates £740 for the half year to 31 March 19x2. How much of this is included?
7. The company paid £1,200 for the computer. Why is this not included?
8. The company sells its padlocks at cost + 50%. The *gross profit* does not seem to agree with this. Why might this be?
9. The company finished the year with a large overdraft. If it made a *profit* of £16,912 surely we should find cash in the bank of £16,912 somewhere. Why is this not so?

2. Introduction

At the end of each financial year, all businesses (and other enterprises like local government, clubs and societies) produce financial statements to report their activities in the year in financial terms. One of these financial statements is the *Profit and Loss Account*.

In the case of not-for profit enterprises the financial statement is called the *Income and Expenditure Account.*

The Profit and Loss Account measures and demonstrates the profit or loss achieved during the year. A year is the usual period as it is required by statute for organisations such as limited companies and building societies and for all enterprises for tax purposes. Many enterprises also produce Profit and Loss Accounts for shorter periods.

The *year end date* chosen is at the choice of the enterprise. Nearly all choose a month end which may be the calendar year end or the government's year end (31 March) or the month end nearest the date of formation of the business or it may be a date which is convenient for stocktaking. Once selected most businesses stay with the same year end but it can be changed. For example, many colleges moved their year end from 31st March to July 31st, when they gained their independence.

For retailing, wholesaling and manufacturing enterprises the full statement is usually called the *Trading and Profit and Loss Account.*

Financial statements are always *formal documents* with proper *headings* and *formats* which conform to accepted practice although several formats can be regarded as acceptable.

For retail and wholesale enterprises the format might be as shown on the following page.

You will see that profit is measured by beginning with the total sales or *turnover* achieved in the period. From this figure, successive deductions are made. The first deduction is the *cost of the goods sold* and this is derived by a calculation. A builders' merchant makes a profit by selling goods at a price which is greater than the price at which they were purchased. The difference between sales and the cost of the goods sold is called the *gross profit* and the whole section (d) to (i) is called the trading account.

Having measured the gross profit, deductions from it are made to derive the net profit. These further deductions are the *expenses* incurred in running the business. These may be called the *overhead expenses.*

a)		**Evelyn Babel — builders' merchant**	
b)		**Trading and Profit and Loss Account**	
c)		**For the year ending 31 January 19x2**	
		£	£
d)	Sales		872,000
e)	Less cost of goods sold:		
f)	Opening stock	54,300	
g)	Purchases	571,000	
		625,300	
h)	Less closing stock	63,900	561,400
i)	Gross profit		310,600
j)	Less expenses:		
k)	Rent	30,000	
	Rates	26,500	
	Insurances	7,800	

		£	£
l)	Wages and salaries	104,500	
m)	Sundry other expenses	72,000	
n)	Depreciation	23,000	263,800
o)	Net profit		46,800

I will now comment in detail on the content of the Trading and Profit and Loss Account:

a) The name of the enterprise must always be given.

b) The title of the financial statement must be given in full.

c) The period of time must be made clear.

d) Sales is the total amount of sales invoiced in the period. It is also termed the turnover. Note that it does not include VAT.

If a sale has been made in the period then it will be included in this figure even if the cash relating to the sale is received in another period. For example if Babel made a sale of bricks on 28 January 19x2 on credit to Aztecan Pyramids Ltd for £200 then the £200 is included in the sales for the year ending 31 January 19x2. This is so despite the fact that Aztecan did not pay until 14 April 19x2, that is, in the following financial year.

This idea that all sales are included in a year if they are made in that year, irrespective of the date of payment, is called the *realisation convention*.

e) The sales made are of specific goods and the cost of these specific goods is matched against the sales to determine the gross profit. The idea is that each sale generates a profit which equals the sale price less the input cost. The total gross Profit for the year is the total of such profits. This cost is not usually measured directly but is implied by the calculation (f) to (h).

f) Firstly the stock of goods for sale at the beginning of the period viz at 1 February 19x1 is considered. This total will have been arrived at by counting the goods and valuing them at *input cost* (this can be modified but is a complication we will ignore for the moment).

g) Then the total amount of goods for resale purchased in the year is added. All such goods purchased in the year are included irrespective of the date of payment.

This gives the total of goods in stock at the beginning and of goods added to stock in the year (£625,000). This is the total input cost of goods which could be sold in the year.

h) However not all such goods were sold and the unsold ones are counted and valued at input cost and deducted from the goods that could be sold to give the cost of the goods that actually were sold in the year. It should be noted that some goods will be included that were not sold. They may have been lost through other causes — theft, breakage, evaporation, mice etc. They are still included under the heading cost of goods sold although strictly speaking they were not sold. They do of course diminish profit.

i) The *gross profit* represents the profits made (that is sale price less input cost) on all sales made in the period. It is much used as an indicator of achievement both by itself and as a ratio to sales.

The ratio is easy to calculate as:

$$\text{Gross profit to sales ratio (as a percentage)} = \frac{\text{Gross profit}}{\text{Sales}} \times 100$$

In the case of Babel, the ratio is $\dfrac{£310,600}{£872,000} \times 100 = 35.6\%$

It is also possible to calculate the average mark up. This is the amount (as a percentage) which is added to the cost of goods to find the selling price. It is calculated by:

$$\text{Average mark-up (as a percentage)} = \frac{\text{Gross profit}}{\text{Cost of goods sold}} \times 100$$

In the case of Babel, the ratio is $\dfrac{£310,600}{£561,400} \times 100 = 55.3\%$

j) Clearly all businesses have overhead expenses and these are explored next. The expenses are listed by suitable *categories* and the amounts expended in the year are calculated. The categorisation is according to taste. Some businesses may have a dozen categories and some may use more and some may use less.

k) Rent is a common expense. The rent for the year will be in accordance with the lease and the amount included reflects the exact period not the amounts paid in the period. For example:

Rent was £28,000 a year up to 31 July 19x1 and was increased to £32,000 from that date. Rent is supposed to be paid quarterly in advance.

In fact payments were:

Jan 29	19x1 —	for the quarter to 30.4.19x1	£7,000
May 6	19x1 —	for the quarter to 31.7.19x1	£7,000
Aug 3	19x1 —	for the quarter to 31.10.19x1	£8,000
Nov 25	19x1 —	for the quarter to 31.1.19x2	£8,000
			£30,000
Jan 29	19x2 —	for the quarter to 30.4.19x2	£8,000

You will see that the true cost of rent for the year is £30,000 and that is the amount which is regarded as the expense for the year ending 31 January 19x2.

Part of this was paid in the previous year (on Jan 29 19x1) and a payment for the following year (on Jan 29 19x2) was made in the year. However accountants go to some trouble to measure the cost of the resource (eg occupation of the premises) actually consumed in the period. Dates of payment are irrelevant.

This measurement of the cost of the resource actually consumed is called the *accruals convention*.

l) Wages and Salaries includes the wage and salary cost of employing the staff in the year. It is usually calculated as gross remuneration payable + employer's national insurance and pension contributions. Like the rent and all other expenses, placing expenditure in the right year is important. For example if the firm pay a week in arrear such that the wages (£2,040) for the week ending 31 January 19x2 are paid on 7 February 19x2 then the £2,040 would be included in the total for the year ending 31 January 19x2 ignoring the date of actual payment.

m) I have included a bulk expense to avoid cluttering the Profit and Loss Account with more categories. In practice there would be more categories. All would be calculated in accordance with the accruals convention.

n) *Depreciation* on *fixed assets* is dealt with later.

o) Finally the net profit (or loss) in the period is calculated. You may hear talk of '*the bottom line*' meaning the profit.

Students often have difficulty in appreciating why two money columns are used. Note that the extreme right column is a summary:

Sales less cost of goods sold = gross profit which less expenses = net profit.

The left hand of the two columns is used for detail.

Some items are *not* included in the Profit and Loss Account. These include:

i) *Drawings*. Babel may take cash (or goods) out of the business for her private purposes. This is why people have businesses — so that they may draw money etc from the business to spend on their private purposes. The reason why the business can stand money being drawn from it is that it makes a profit. Clearly, in the long term, a business where drawings exceed profits is going to go bust. It makes sense therefore for the business profit to be measured to enable the proprietor to see how much he can draw. Some proprietors talk about their 'wages' from the business. These are drawings and not wages in the Profit and Loss Account sense.

ii) *Capital expenditure*. Capital expenditure is expenditure on the acquisition of fixed assets. Fixed assets are things (eg plant, machinery, vehicles etc) which last a long time and cost more than a trivial amount. Buying a new machine for £10,000 in the year ending 31 January 1991 does not reduce the profit for that year by £10,000 but does reduce the profit for the whole five years (say) in which the machine will be in use. Thus there is a reduction of profit in the year:

$$\frac{£10,000}{5} = £2,000$$

which is known as depreciation. More of this later.

iii) *Receipt* and *repayment of loans*. These do not affect profit. However any interest will do so.

SCENARIO 3 — Martin prepares a forecast Profit and Loss Account

Anne then asks him how long he thinks his fixed assets will last. He thinks and then replies:

The Computer – two years

the Stacking Equipment – 5 years

In that case, Anne says, I have computed the depreciation correctly for each year as:

Computer   £500

Equipment £600

and so we put depreciation in the Profit and Loss Account as an expense at £1,100.

Martin is quite excited at understanding how a profit and loss is constructed and decides to plan his second year by *forecasting* the Profit and Loss Account for 19x2 in the same way.

He makes a note of all the necessary data:

a. Sales should be £290,000

b. Goods will be sold at cost + 45% on average

c. Stock at the end of the year will be about one tenth of total annual purchases. As this is uncertain Martin thinks this should be rounded to the nearest £'000.

d. Rent will be as in 19x1

e. Rates will be as already paid for the first quarter and the rates for the year to 31 March 19x3 should be £2,000

f. Electricity, printing and stationery, and advertising will be as 19x1 but plus 20%, as will van expenses.

g. Wages will be as 19x1 but plus 30% but the *director's remuneration* will double. We can assume that the employer's *national insurance* will be 10% of the employees' and director's remuneration.

h. Audit and Accountancy will be £1,600 and Sundries about £1,000.

i. Bank Interest and charges may well be only half of that in 19x1.

j. Redecoration of the premises will occur in the last month of 19x2 at a cost of £2,500 and Martin will pay half of this in 19x2 and half in February 19x3.

k. Depreciation will be as in 19x1.

Tasks 2

1. Prepare a forecast Profit and Loss Account for the year 19x2.

2. Prepare a memo for Martin on the following topics:

   a. Why the sales will include all sales made in 19x2 even though the cash was not received for some of them in 19x2.

   b. The treatment of some padlocks which Martin expects to be ordered and paid for by an overseas customer in December 19x2 in the sum of £800. These will be delivered in January 19x3. Martin thinks they should be excluded from stock as he will have packed them by December 31st although he will not have sent them off. They cost £550 to make.

3. Martin is considering buying a second hand lathe in 19x2 for £5,000. It would last about 10 years. If he buys it, how would the profit be affected?

4. Explore the effect on profit of:

   ❐ buying £2,000 more goods in the year and still having them in stock at the year end

❏   selling his goods at an average mark up of 50% instead of 45%.

5.   If the forecast 19x2 profit is insufficient, suggest feasible ways in which the profit might be improved.

6.   Set up the Profit and Loss Account on a spreadsheet and explore the effects on profit of changes such as:

❏   a 5% change in sales (but with the same *mark-up*)

❏   a 5% change in mark-up (eg from 45% to 42.75%)

❏   a 5% change in wages.

SCENARIO 4 — Martin finds out about accounting conventions and compares profit with cash flows

Martin discusses the profit with Anne and comes to realise that he has earned £9,600 from the business in 19x1 and that the business has earned £16,000 or so on top of that. He has really made more than £25,000 which compares well with his earnings when he worked with Stubbykey PLC. However there are differences:

a.   All his earnings were paid to him by Stubbykey albeit after deducting PAYE and National Insurance.

b.   He has actually been paid only £9,600 by his own company and Tax and Insurance have been deducted from that.

c.   The profits made by the company belong to him but are *retained* in the company. Martin is richer in that the company has made a profit and has gained value but being richer has not resulted in any extra spending money for Martin.

d.   The company will have to pay some *Corporation Tax* on the profits in due course.

Martin is intrigued that the measurement of profit is not simple and that it is subject to certain conventions. Some of the conventions seem to be surprising, at least at first sight.

Tasks 3

1.   Explain why the profit and cash flows in the year are not the same and why it is necessary to both make a profit and control cash flows.

2.   In what ways is the Profit and Loss Account subject to accounting *conventions*. You should discuss the *entity, periodicity, money measurement, realisation, matching* and *accruals* conventions.

3. Profit and cash flows

People usually think that if a business has made a profit as measured in the Profit and Loss Account then the business will have cash somewhere of the amount of the profit. Surprisingly this is not so. The reason is that a Profit and Loss Account measures the profit, and, profit is not cash.

To see that profit made in a period is not equivalent to net cash receipts in a year, consider:

a)   Sales are included when invoiced and not when the cash was received.

b) Purchases are included when invoiced and not when the cash was paid.

c) Expenses are exactly related to the time of consumption and not to the time of payment.

d) Payments for fixed assets are excluded from the Profit and Loss Account although part will be included in depreciation.

e) Payments for drawings and dividends are excluded.

As profit is not cash then what is it?

This is not easy to answer. It can be described, not as an increase in cash, but as an increase in net assets. Net assets are assets less liabilities. Understanding the concept of profit is difficult and you will take a little while before you fully grasp it.

4. Inputs and outputs

One approach to profit measurement and understanding is to consider the idea of *input* and *output*.

The outputs of a business are the goods or services that it sells to its customers. On a Profit and Loss Account this is represented by the turnover. This may help you to see that the inclusion of all goods sold in a period, irrespective of date of payment, correctly gives the outputs of the business in the period.

The inputs are the things that the business has consumed in achieving the outputs. These include materials from which the outputs are composed (cost of goods sold), human labour (wages), use of a property (rent, rates, insurances etc), use of fixed assets (depreciation), use of money (interest) and many other things.

If the business finds that, in a period, the value of the outputs exceeds the value of the inputs then the business has made a profit. An excess of inputs over outputs is a loss.

You can now see that a Profit and Loss Account begins at the top with the outputs (turnover) and that then successive inputs are taken off. The bottom line is then the profit or the loss.

The concept of input and output works well for profit seeking businesses but less well for not-for-profit enterprises. See later in this Unit.

5. Accounting conventions

The measurement of profit in the Profit and Loss Account and the measurement of capital employed in the Balance Sheet has developed over the last century and a half in a largely pragmatic way. Only in the last few decades has development been regulated or planned.

Accounting was taught until at least the 1960s in a totally prescriptive way. Students were told that this or that was the way to do it. This approach meant that when new business developments required new developments in accounting no body of theory was available to assist accountants.

The body of theory was developed by academic accountants observing the way profit and capital measurement was carried out in practice and trying to deduce any common rules which were normally followed. This led to the discovery that there were a number of conventions that were normally adhered to.

In the 1970s in the UK (and much earlier in the USA) accounting development became more regulated by the formation by the professional accounting bodies of the accounting standards committee which produced a series of Statements of Standard Accounting Practice (SSAPs). This committee was replaced in 1990 by an independent body with statutory backing — the Accounting Standards Board. This Board has accepted the existing SSAPs and at the time of writing had issued the first eight of its Financial Reporting Standards.

In addition statutory recognition was given to accounting conventions in the Companies Act 1981 and to SSAPs in the Companies Act 1989. Also the Companies Act 1981 introduced mandatory formats for company financial statements which implicitly recognised the conventions and contemporary practice in accounting measurement.

An actual list of accounting conventions with definitions has not yet emerged and writers tend to disagree on the detail. You may read a slightly different list in other texts but the fundamentals do now seem to have achieved general acceptance.

Some of the conventions may seem strange and perhaps would not be adopted if accounting had to start again on a green field site. Many can be explained by historical circumstances. The driving force was often the conventions of double entry book-keeping which was developed in renaissance Italy.

Below are some of the conventions which affect the Profit and Loss Account and Income and Expenditure Account. There are others and we will explore them as we come to them.

Business entity

The business is seen as an entity separate from its owner(s) or proprietor(s).

The justification for this convention is that the proprietor and other interested parties (eg lenders, taxman etc) are concerned to know the profit earned by and the capital employed in the business or each business if the proprietor has more than one. Essentially the focus is on the business and not on the owner.

Money measurement

Transactions are recorded in money terms and financial statements are drawn up with assets, liabilities, revenues and expenses expressed in money terms.

The justification for this may seem obvious and in fact the objective is to report results using a common unit of measurement — money.

Realisation convention

The profit on any given transaction is included in the accounts of a period when the profit is realised. Realisation means when a transaction has occurred which gives legal rights to the receipt of money. What this means is that profit is counted on the sale of a good and not on payment. So if goods are sold on 12 December 19x2 the profit is earned in the year to 31 December 19x2 even though the goods were not paid for until 19 January 19x3.

The justification for this convention include:

❑ The critical event principle. The hard part of business is to make a sale and collecting the cash afterwards is relatively easy (credit controllers might disagree!).

Thus the profit should be considered to be earned when the hard bit has been concluded.

❑ The certainty principle. At the point of a sale it is known that a profit has been made and precisely how much it is.

❑ The asset transfer principle. On the sale the goods cease to be the property of the trader and become the property of his customer. The trader ceases to own the goods and instead has a debt due to him.

Among the consequences of this convention is that unrealised holding gains are ignored. A profit is not recognised until a sale is made.

Two problems occur with this convention:

i) Goods are often sold subject to reservation of title which means that ownership of the goods does not in law pass until payment has been made. A reservation of title clause in a contract is often known as a Romalpa clause after the case which established its legal validity. In profit measurement the reservation of title is ignored and the realisation convention is followed.

ii) In civil engineering, shipbuilding and other long term contracting the precise point of a sale of a product is not really determinable and usually profit is deemed to be earned over the course of the contract. The realisation convention is thus ignored in such cases.

Accruals

This is somewhat similar to the realisation convention. Revenues and costs are recognised and included in the Profit and Loss Account as they are accrued (= earned or incurred) not as they are paid or received.

The justification of this convention is that receipts and payments are to a degree random as to timing, whereas the earning of a revenue (eg a rent) or the consumption of a resource (eg electricity) can be accurately related to specific time periods.

The drawbacks to this convention include:

❑ the work required to apportion expenses to time periods.

❑ financial statements become more complex (than say cash flow accounting) with a consequent loss of intelligibility to the layman.

Periodicity convention

This is simply the convention which says that profits and capital should be measured regularly for distinct periods of time. The usual time interval is one year but many companies produce accounts on a monthly, quarterly or half yearly basis.

Matching convention

The matching convention requires that in an accounting period, costs are matched with related income. Where costs have been incurred and there is no related income in the period or in future periods, with which the costs can be matched, they are treated as an expense of the accounting period.

An example

Penn writes a book in 19x2 and incurred research costs of £5,000 related to the book and £2,200 related to a book he decided not to write. He has the book typeset in 19x2 at a cost of £3,000 and has 5,000 copies printed at a cost of £5 each. He sells 1,000 copies in 19x2 at £11 each. What is his profit in 19x2?

Revenue is clearly $1,000 \times £11 = 11,000$.

Costs to be matched against it are:

❏   printing costs $1,000 \times £5 = £5,000$

❏   research costs: $\dfrac{1,000}{5,000} \times £5,000 = £1,000$.

❏   typesetting costs $\dfrac{1,000}{5,000} \times £3,000 = £600$

Some of the remaining costs can be matched against future revenue in future years. These are the remainder of the associated research costs (£5,000 — £1,000) and typesetting costs (£3,000 — £600).

The unrelated research costs cannot be matched against revenues in this or any future year so they are treated as an expense of 19x2.

The profit will thus be:

$$£11,000 - (£5,000 + £1,000 + £600 + £2,200) = £2,200.$$

SCENARIO 5 — Martin prepares a simple Profit and Loss Account

Martin feels that he now understands the measurement of profit and would like to try out his new found knowledge on a simple business. His cousin Ralph, who was redundant at the same time as Martin, has started in business as a window cleaner. Ralph agrees to tell Martin the figures for his first year and Martin then tries to prepare a Profit and Loss Account for him. The figures for the year ending 31 December 19x1 are:

❏   Cash sales for cleaning windows £18,000. In addition Ralph won a contract to clean the windows of a company and the charges invoiced for cleaning windows in the year 19x1 were £4,600. All except the last month's work, amounting to £620, was paid in 19x1. The £620 was paid in 19x2. All sums received were paid into the business bank account and all expenses were paid out of it.

❏   Expenses included Printing handbills etc £240, Advertising £300, Van running expenses (tax, insurance, repairs, petrol etc) £1,290, Cleaning materials £280 (of these, some £80 at cost was unused in 19x1and will be used in 19x2), Insurance £640 (this is all for 19x1 except £200 for a liability policy which was for the year ending 31 March 19x2).

❏   He purchased a van at the beginning of 19x1 at a cost of £2,400. He reckons it will be scrapped at the end of three years.

❏   He paid his friend George £320 to canvass householders to get business. Some of this canvassing resulted in obtaining regular clients but much of it turned out to be in areas where there was insufficient business to justify travelling to these areas.

❏   He opened a bank account in the business name on 2 January 19x1 with his savings £3,000 and the bank charged him £74 as charges in the year. He drew a total of £14,200 from the account for his housekeeping and personal expenditure in 19x1.

Tasks 4

1. Calculate the balance in the bank at the end of 19x1.
2. Prepare a Profit and Loss Account for the first year.
3. Comment on the application of the accounting conventions to this Profit and Loss Account.
4. Comment in detail on how the movement in the bank account compares with the figures in the Profit and Loss Account.

6. Service industries

Service industries such as transport, professional services etc also produce Profit and Loss Accounts but omit the gross profit stage. As an example:

Example

K. Nain — veterinary surgeon
Profit and Loss Account
for the year ending 28 February 19x4

	£	£
Fees receivable		62,000
Drugs etc:		
Opening stock	890	
Purchases	4,320	
	5,210	
Less closing stock	770	
	4,440	
Wages	12,810	
Rent and rates	4,900	
Accountant's fee	1,000	
Bank interest and charges	2,480	
Advertising	1,300	
Depreciation	5,600	
Other overheads	12,200	44,730
Net profit		17,270

It is not possible to calculate a gross profit since the fees (= sales in a trading business) are for the supply of drugs *and* the supply of professional services such as consultations, inspections, surgical operations etc.

The accounting conventions apply to service industries in just the same way as they do to businesses that trade in goods. The matching convention is especially important to service industries. Note that this means that revenues and associated costs are matched together in each year. However costs that cannot be related to particular revenues are included in the Profit and Loss Account in the year in which they were incurred using the accruals convention.

7. The not-for-profit sector

Accounting evolved in trading, that is buying and selling, enterprises. Later it spread to other activities — manufacturing, extraction, construction, agriculture and services. Most textbooks on accounting until quite recently covered mainly trading and manufacturing with a digression on clubs and societies. In recent years employment has changed so that in 1995 employment in the UK (which is fairly typical of advanced countries) is:

	Percentage	Percentage
Manufacturing	18	
Mining, energy and water supply	1	
Other industries	5	24
Wholesale and retail	17	
Public administration, social work etc	15	
Health	7	
Education	8	
Hotels and restaurants	6	
Financial services	4	
Other services	19	76
		100

Consequently, it is now felt that an accounting text should reflect more closely the balance of employment in the different sectors. Clearly this may mean a textbook would have excessive length if detailed account was taken of every sector. In practice, accounting follows similar rules in all sectors and with a little help a student familiar with the rules for trading and manufacture can soon learn how to account for the other sectors. In this book we will look at intervals at other sectors and we begin with a fictitious government agency: the Banana Plant Development Agency. This agency is charged with promoting the planting of banana plants on UK farms. It was set up under the Banana Plant Act 1994. Its annual Income and Expenditure Account for the year ending 31 March 19x6 showed:

Expenditure	£'000	Income	£'000
Salaries	976	Government grant	4000
Establishment costs	235	Grants from banana	
Grants	2600	trading companies	1000
Publicity	876	Fees charged to growers	554
Sundry overheads	419	Sundry income	324
	5106		
Surplus for the year	772		
	5878		5878

What information is given by this account?

The agency receives its income from four main sources — directly from the government, from banana trading companies, from fees charged to growers and from sundry other sources.

Costs are salaries, establishment costs (these are the costs of running the headquarters and regional buildings, i.e. rent, heating, lighting etc), grants to growers and others, publicity (this is the cost of promoting the agency's activities to farmers and the public) and sundries.

Both income and expenditure are included and calculated on the accruals principle.

It is possible to see these accounts as a reflection of the input and output process whereby inputs are gathered and transformed into outputs. This does not work quite as well as it does with trading companies as you can see. However it is possible to see the outputs as first, intangible benefits which the government and the banana trading companies consider worth paying for, and secondly as tangible benefits which are sold to growers.

8. Published Profit and Loss Accounts

All organisations produce annual Profit and Loss Accounts. In the case of non-profit organisations like clubs and societies the Profit and Loss Account is called the *Income and Expenditure Account*.

Students of accounting should try to see as many Profit and Loss Accounts and Income and Expenditure Accounts as possible. You can obtain them from friends and relatives who own shares in public companies, from building society offices and from the treasurers of clubs, societies and churches and charities.

Note that some treasurers do not understand accounting sufficiently well to apply accrual accounting and produce simply a summary of receipts and payments.

Try to make sense of any accounts that you find.

Most sets of accounts are *audited*. See if there is an *auditor's report* and determine the qualifications, if any, of the auditor.

9. Summary of Unit 2

❏ Financial statements are produced for all businesses for each financial year.

❏ One of the financial statements is the Profit and Loss Account which measures and demonstrates the profit or loss earned during the period. In not-for-profit enterprises the equivalent statement is the Income and Expenditure Account.

❏ The Profit and Loss Account may also be called the Trading and Profit and Loss Account in which case a gross profit will be calculated as well as a net profit.

❏ The Trading and Profit and Loss Account will have the format:

Sales	X
Less cost of goods sold	X
Gross profit	X
Less overhead expenses	X
Net profit	X

❐ Sales will include all sales invoiced in the period irrespective of year of payment by the customers.

❐ Cost of goods sold should be the cost of goods actually sold in the year + the cost of goods lost due to other causes such as theft and destruction.

❐ Overhead expenses will include the exact cost of the resource consumed in the year, again irrespective of year of payment.

❐ Overheads will include depreciation but will exclude drawings, capital expenditure and loan receipts and repayments.

❐ The essence of profit computation is the placing of revenues (eg sales) and expenses in the right year.

❐ Profit is not cash.

❐ If the business does not trade in goods (eg a *service industry*) then the format may be:

Sales (or other form of *revenue* eg fees or fares)	x
Itemised expenses	x
Net Profit	x

❐ In most businesses the profit depends on a measurement of stocks (raw materials, goods for resale and work in progress). This is valued at the *input cost* to the business (or sometimes less).

❐ Expenses also include depreciation of fixed assets and we will deal with this later.

❐ Business managers often see the Profit and Loss Account as a *model* of the business and producing forecast Profit and Loss Accounts is a useful adjunct to the *planning* and *budgeting* process.

❐ The accounting conventions were deduced by academic accountants from observations of what accountants actually do.

❐ They now have recognition from the Accounting Standards Board and from the Companies Act.

❐ The conventions pertinent to the Profit and Loss Account are:

Business entity	— the business is seen as separate from its owner;
Money measurement	— transactions and financial statements are drawn up in money terms;
Historical cost	— assets and expenses are entered into the records at their cost to the business;
Realisation	— profit is deemed to be earned at the point of sale not the point of payment;
Accruals	— revenues and costs are recognised and included in financial statements as they are earned or incurred not as they are received or paid;
Matching	— costs are matched with related income in each successive accounting period. But costs which cannot be related to income are included in the accounting period in which they are incurred;

Periodicity — accounts are prepared at regular intervals.

There are yet more conventions and some are also pertinent to the Profit and Loss Account. We will meet them in later Units.

❑ It is possible to view business activity as inputs transformed into outputs. Then a Profit and Loss Account of a trading or manufacturing company represents an output (sales turnover) less inputs being cost of goods sold and the various expenses. This sees the enterprise as having a single output — the goods or services sold. All the inputs are expended or consumed to provide that output. This concept works well with profit seeking enterprises but less well with not-for-profit undertakings.

Accounting conventions and the Profit and Loss Account			
Entity convention	**Martin Padlocks Ltd**		
Periodicity convention	**Profit and Loss Account for the year ending 31 Dec 19xx**		
Money measurement			£
Realisation convention	Sales		210,000
Matching convention	Less: Cost of Sales:		
	Opening stock	–	
	Purchases	160,730	
		160,730	
	Less: Closing Stock	14,730	146,000
	Gross profit		64,000
Accruals convention	Expenses		45,988
	Net Profit		18,012

Exercise *1

Given the following separate sets of data for 19x2, calculate the gross profit:

Business	A	B	C
Cash Sales in 19x2	540,000	6,000	3,000
Sales on credit in 19x2	1,200	543,000	231,000
Cash received from customers in 19x2	540,950	521,000	236,000
Purchases in 19x2	412,000	490,000	134,000
Cash paid to suppliers in 19x2	398,000	502,000	139,000
Stock at end of 19x1	32,000	160,000	3,700
Stock at end of 19x2	38,000	152,000	3,900

One of these businesses is a supermarket and two are wholesalers of which one is in fresh fish and the other in expensive imported furniture. Which is the retailer and which is the fresh fish wholesaler?

Exercise *2

Given the following separate sets of data for 19x2, calculate the missing item:

Business	D	E	F	G
Sales in 19x2	450,000	?	980,000	28,000
Stock at end of 19x1	?	36,000	120,000	6,000
Purchases in 19x2	390,000	98,000	650,000	?
Stock at end of 19x2	76,000	?	230,000	7,400
Cost of goods sold	?	93,700	?	15,890
Gross Profit	80,000	31,000	?	?

Exercise 3

Tingle has a shop selling souvenirs. He is trying to forecast the elements of his trading account for 19x3 and thinks that total sales will be about £75,000. His stock at the end of 19x2 had cost £4,000 but he intends to increase that and by the end of 19x3 it should be double the 19x2 stock. He adds 50% to the cost of his goods in setting his selling prices.

a. Prepare a forecast trading account for 19x3 based on these figures.

He feels the gross profit could be more if his prices were lower. He reckons that every 5% reduction in price will bring a 10% increase in sales volume up to a maximum of double his present sales. Conversely a 5% increase in price would lead to a fall in sales of only 5%.

b. Should he hold, decrease or increase his prices?

Exercise 4

A major problem in practice is *cut-off*. This is ensuring that a proper match is made between sales and the cost of the actual goods sold.

June has a a business retailing giftware. At 31 December 19x2, her year end, she took stock and included everything on the premises. On 5 January she received a consignment of goods which had been despatched and invoiced at £300 on 29 December. The goods had been in transit by rail. What could go wrong with the calculation of gross profit for 19x2?

Exercise 5

Claude gave his assistant Cecil the task of taking stock at his antique shop on 31 December. Each item has a coded ticket which can be used to calculate the input price. The stock was duly evaluated at cost and the gross profit calculated as £79,304. Claude later discovered that the following matters may have a bearing on the stock:

i. A settee sold to Cyril (cost £500) for £890 on 30 December was not collected by Cyril until 4 January.

ii. A table (cost £200) sold to Daniel in November for £700 was in the shop for repair.

iii. A clock purchased from Odile for £500 on 27 December was not paid for until 25 January.

iv. A barometer which had cost £950 in November was at the home of Ben, a customer. Ben was trying it out but eventually decided not to buy it.

What should have been the gross profit?

Expenses

The accruals convention is applied to all expenses and the following exercises should increase your familiarity with this idea.

Exercise 6

Rent: Dew paid rent as follows:

12 November 19x1	£3,000 for the half year to 31.3.19x2
4 April	19x2	£3,500 for the half year to 30.9.19x2
3 January	19x3	£3,500 for the half year to 31.3.19x3

What is the correct charge for the Profit and Loss Account for 19x2?

Exercise *7

Sven pays his manager Brenda a salary of £15,000 a year. Employer's national insurance is 10.4%. Payment is made monthly and the payment for December was £925 being £1,250 less tax and insurance. The PAYE and national insurance on the December salary was paid on 18 January 19x3. On 12 February, a bonus was paid to Brenda for her excellent work in 19x2. The gross amount of the bonus was £1,200.

What is the correct charge in the Profit and Loss Account for 19x2 in respect of Manager's Remuneration?

Completing a Trading and Profit and Loss Account

Exercise *8

Given a set of data, it is only a matter of slotting these into a pro forma Profit and Loss Account. Below are two sets of data. Prepare Profit and Loss Accounts from them.

Year ending 31 December 19x2

	Alpha	*Beta*
Sales on Credit	800,000	1,490,000
Cash Sales	630,000	
Opening stock	61,000	231,000
Closing stock	49,000	245,000
Purchases	840,000	780,000
Carriage inwards	17,000	12,000
Carriage outwards	23,000	35,000
Wages	187,000	202,000
Rent		30,000
Insurance	6,700	31,000
Rates	16,800	58,000
Depreciation	32,000	62,000
New Car		15,000
Sundry expenses	17,200	19,540
Advertising	67,900	102,000

	Alpha	Beta
Motor running expenses	12,450	35,000
Accountant's fee	3,000	5,600
Security costs	4,100	6,900
Stationery	2,600	9,100
Drawings	30,000	46,000
Loan Repayment	25,000	50,000
Loan Interest	13,500	21,000
Bank Charges	2,600	7,200
Settlement discount	4,700	
Rent Received		6,000

Notes:

For Alpha:

i.   Carriage inwards is regarded as part of the cost of purchases

ii. Wages do not include a bonus to the staff of £20,000 paid after the year end

iii. Rates include £7,200 for the half year to 31 March 19x3

iv. Settlement discount is the amount allowed to customers for quick payment. It goes in the Profit and Loss Account section.

For Beta:

i.   Carriage inwards is regarded as part of the cost of the purchases

ii. Insurance includes the fire insurance premium £2,400 for the year ending 31 May 19x3

iii. Stationery includes a consignment of posters £1,200 which were received on the last day of the year and were not opened until 4 January 19x3

iv. Rent received is for a part of the premises let to another firm.

Interpreting a Trading and Profit and Loss Account

Exercise 9

Below are the Trading and Profit and Loss Accounts for the two years 19x1 and 19x2 of Grace, a sportswear retailer:

Trading and Profit and Loss Account

For the Year Ending		19x1		19x2
Sales		215,000		262,000
Less Cost of Goods Sold:				
Opening Stock	36,000		52,100	
Purchases	162,100		178,600	
	198,100		230,700	
Less Closing Stock	52,100		46,000	
		146,000		184,700
Gross Profit		69,000		77,300

For the Year Ending		19x1		19x2
Less Expenses:				
Rent	10,000		10,000	
Rates	11,300		13,400	
Insurances	2,600		3,700	
Wages and Salaries	14,000		14,800	
Advertising	4,400		8,600	
Sundry Expenses	5,200		6,000	
Depreciation	4,300		4,300	
		51,800		60,800
Net Profit		17,200		16,500

Appraise the performance of the business over the two years considering especially:

❐ Turnover

❐ Stock levels

❐ Gross Profit to Sales ratio

❐ Each expense item

❐ the relationship between 19x1 and 19x2

❐ the relationship between each item in the accounts and all the others

❐ how much cash may have been generated by the profits.

Note that Grace works full time in the business and that inflation was about 4% between 19x1 and 19x2.

Exercise 10

Ruth is an optician. Her figures for 19x2 were:

Sales	41,700	Stock at 31.12.x1	1,320
Equipment at cost	7,150	Stock at 31.12.x2	1,532
Purchases	18,420	Rent, Rates & Insurance	5,120
Wages	6,700	Telephone	890
Advertising	2,100	Drawings	7,200

Note:

❐ depreciate the equipment at 20%

❐ accrued telephone charges are £129

❐ rates paid in advance amount £460

Required:

a. How much profit did Ruth make in 19x2?

b. What would be included in purchases and stocks? How would the figures for stocks be derived?

c. What are drawings ? Explain your treatment of drawings.

Exercise 11

Virtreal set up on 1 January 19x2 as an independent writer of software working from his home. He commissioned a series of programmes suitable for local authority use from a friend. In 19x2 he sold 5 copies of the programme for £3,000 each and four of these were paid for in 19x2 and one in 19x3. He has obtained orders for 6 copies for delivery in 19x3 and is hopeful of several more orders.

Some other data about the business in 19x2 are:

i.   He purchased computer equipment for £6,000 which he reckons will have a three year life.

ii. He paid his friend £5,000 for writing the programs and his friend did some revision work in December 19x2 which Virtreal paid for in January 19x3 at £1,200

iii. His other overheads cost him £1,400 in 19x2.

Discussion:

i.   How much profit did Virtreal make in 19x2?

ii. Do you think Virtreal could regard some of his household expenses as an expense of the business?

Exercise 12

Giles is a farmer who set up on 1 January 19x2. He wonders how he should treat some of his activities in measuring his profit for the first year. These include:

i.   He expended significant sums on seed and fertilizer in the year to produce a crop of wheat and potatoes. He kept the harvested crop in store until March 19x3 when he sold them.

ii. He bought some goats and expended material amounts of money feeding and caring for them. By the year end the goats had produced offspring. A few of these had been sold but most were still on the farm.

Discuss these problems in terms of annual profit measurement.

Exercise 13

Sheinton are a pop group. The five members normally play gigs locally and charge modest fees for their work. In 19x2 they spent £2,000 on recording fees for an album and had 3,000 copies made at a cost of £4 each. They sold 300 albums in 19x2 and are hopeful of selling the rest in the next few years.

Discuss the annual profit measurement problems here.

Exercise 14

Icicle started a business on 1 January 19x2, servicing some specialised equipment. He signed a number of contracts including:

Contract A. He received a lump sum of £3,000 to service some equipment over the ensuing four years. He should make a profit on the contract. *Contract B*. He will receive an annual sum of £1,200 for the next four years and will be able to do the work for only £300 a year.

Discuss these from an annual profit measurement point of view.

3 The end of the first year: the Balance Sheet

1. Objectives

The objective of this Unit is to introduce the second of the two principal **financial statements** — the Balance Sheet. We will see that this document presents a list of the **assets** employed in the business at the period end and a list also of what is owed (**liabilities**) by the business. Each of the assets and liabilities is assigned a (sometimes surprising) monetary value and the total of assets less liabilities is shown as the **net assets**. The sources of the funds which were required to acquire the net assets are shown as the **capital and reserves**.

SCENARIO 1 — Martin looks at his Balance Sheet

Anne produces what she calls a draft Balance Sheet as at 31 December 19x1. This is it:

Martin Padlocks Ltd
Balance Sheet as at 31 December 19x1

Fixed Assets	£	£	£
	Cost	Depreciation	Net Book Value
Computer	1,000	500	500
Stacking Equipment	3,000	600	2,400
	4,000	1,100	2,900
Current Assets			
Stock		14,730	
Debtors		51,200	
Prepayments		1,230	
		67,160	
Creditors: amounts falling due within one year			
Creditors		25,900	
Bank Overdraft		7,248	
		33,148	
Net Current Assets			34,012
Total assets less current liabilities			36,912
Creditors: amounts falling due after more than one year			
Loan at 10%			5,000
			31,912

Capital and Reserves

Share Capital	15,000
Profit and Loss Account	16,912
	31,912

Martin thinks he can make some sense of the Balance Sheet but has a number of questions.

Quick Answer Questions 3.1

1. At what date is this list of assets and liabilities made up?
2. Which items do you recognise from the cash flow forecast?
3. Comment on the Net Profit shown in the Profit and Loss Account, page 20 and the Profit and Loss Account shown in the Balance Sheet.
4. Which items are assets and which are liabilities?
5. What do you see as the essential differences between the Profit and Loss Account and the Balance Sheet?

SCENARIO 2 — Martin gets down to detail in his Balance Sheet

Martin feels that he has got the basic idea of the Balance Sheet in that he knows the assets from the liabilities but is still mystified by a great deal of it and he sits down with Anne to try and sort out the detail.

Tasks 1

1. What are the distinguishing features of the two sorts of assets – *fixed* and *current*?
2. Does the net book value of the fixed assets mean that I could get back these amounts if I sold them?
3. Who or what are *debtors*?
4. What are *prepayments*?
5. Who or what are *creditors*?
6. Explain the phrase *net current assets*?
7. Why is the bank overdraft in amongst the creditors which fall due in less than one year?
8. What are current liabilities?
9. What is the meaning of 'at 10%'?

2. Introduction

Every business produces a Profit and Loss Account measuring and demonstrating the profit or loss achieved in the year. All but the smallest also produce an additional financial statement — the *Balance Sheet*.

The Balance Sheet is simply a list of the *assets* and *liabilities* of the business at a specified *date*. The date will normally be the year end. Thus the Profit and Loss Account shows the profit (loss) earned over the period and the Balance Sheet shows the position at the end of that period.

In addition to the summarised list of assets and liabilities the Balance Sheet also gives values. The methods of valuation, particularly of assets, may seem odd to non-accountants. There is however a logic to them. They are based on historical input cost to the business. If a business bought an asset (say a motor van) for £3,000 six years ago. Then the *historical input* cost is £3,000 and the value placed upon it will be *derived* from that figure.

A Balance Sheet is a formal document and the format is important. Several formats are possible but a common one today is:

a)		*Evelyn Babel — builders' merchant*		
b)		*Balance Sheet as at 31 January 19x2*		
c)	**Fixed assets**			
d)		Cost	Depreciation	Net book value
e)	Plant and equipment	98,000	56,000	42,000
	Vehicles	41,000	17,000	24,000
f)		139,000	73,000	66,000
g)	**Current assets**			
h)	Stock		63,900	
i)	Debtors		164,200	
j)	Prepayments		1,800	
k)			229,900	
l)	**Less creditors: amounts falling due within one year:**			
m)	Creditors		95,400	
n)	Bank overdraft		102,700	
o)			198,100	
p)	**Net current assets**			31,800
q)	**Total assets less current liabilities**			97,800
r)	**Creditors: amount falling due after more than one year**			
	Loan at 12% from Tom			2,000
s)				95,800
t)	**Capital**			
u)	as at 31 January 19x1			86,100
v)	Net profit for the year			46,800

w)	132,900
x) Less drawings	37,100
y) As at 31 January 19x2	95,800

You will notice that the Balance Sheet comes in several sections:

i) *Fixed assets* are assets which have a long life (more than one year) and have more than a trivial value. Examples are land and buildings (none here as Babel rents her premises), plant, machinery, equipment, vehicles.

ii) *Current assets* are those which change frequently. The normal *categories* are those included in this Balance Sheet.

iii) 'Creditors: falling due within one year' are liabilities which need to be paid before 31 January 19x3.

Some Balance Sheets, including this one, have in addition 'Creditors: amounts falling due after more than one year' which are longer term liabilities like mortgages.

iv) Having calculated the assets less the liabilities to external persons (£95,800) there is an additional section which causes more difficulty in understanding. Lines (c) to (s) list the assets and liabilities in detail. Lines (t) to (y) consider the assets less liabilities as a single sum and how that single sum has changed from the end of the previous year to the end of this. The explanation is that the total assets less liabilities were *increased* by a *profit* and *reduced* by the *drawings* of cash and goods taken from the business by the owner in the year. The total assets less liabilities is a useful statistic in that it tells the proprietor how much *resources* she has tied up in the business. Another way of looking at it is to regard the capital as a liability of the business (seen as a separate entity) to the owner so that the assets in total equal the liabilities in total:

$$\text{Assets} = \text{Liabilities} + \text{Capital}$$

Considering the Balance Sheet line by line:

a) The name of the business should be made clear.

b) The title of the financial statement should be given and the date make explicit.

c) Fixed assets are considered in more detail in the next Unit.

d) It is usual to show three figures for each category of fixed asset:
  - ❏ the *original* cost to the business
  - ❏ the total amount by which the asset has *depreciated* since its acquisition
  - ❏ the difference which is called the *net book value* or *written down value*. This value is cost derived and will probably bear no resemblance at all to the possible amount for which the assets might be sold. This usually surprises people new to accounting!

e) Two categories of fixed assets are included here. Sometimes there are more such as land and buildings.

f) Totals are given. We can see the total 'value' of the fixed assets.

g) Current assets are more ephemeral and the categories are the usual ones. This business, like many, has a bank overdraft but some have cash at the bank and this would then be included as a current asset.

h) Stock is as counted at 31 January 19x2 and valued at input cost not selling price. Some items may be valued at less than cost. You will note that this item also appears in the Profit and Loss Account. Calculation of stock quantity and value is time consuming and the problem of stock determination is the main reason why financial statements are not produced more frequently than annually (although many businesses do produce monthly or quarterly or half yearly accounts).

i) Some businesses sell goods and receive payment at the same time. When I buy groceries at the supermarket I pay cash at the check out. However many businesses sell goods on *credit*. This means that on a sale, the sale is evidenced by the sending of an invoice to the customer setting out the goods sold and the amount due. Most invoices also state that payment is due at some specified time. Often this is 30 days after the sale. In practice customers often ignore this and pay anything up to several months after the date of supply of the goods. This whole business of credit is a major problem to many companies. Since Evelyn sells on credit there will always be some customers who have had goods and not yet paid for them. These customers are called *debtors* and at each year end the total amount of sales invoiced for which payment has not been received will be assessed and included in the assets as debtors.

j) This item is rarely significant and is often included with the debtors in a global sum. When expenses such as fire insurance or rent are paid the payment is often for a period in advance. For example fire insurance for the calendar year 19x3 £600 may be paid on 1st January that year. This means that on the year end date 31st January, 11 months fire insurance cover has been paid for and is still to be enjoyed. This is $\frac{11}{12} \times £600 = £550$ and would be included in the assets as a prepayment.

k) The total of the three kinds of current assets is demonstrated. There can be other categories of current assets. A great number of businesses have cash in the bank. Manufacturing businesses will have work in progress. Some will have various kinds of short term investments such as bank deposits.

l) Liabilities are usually shown in two separate sections. Short term liabilities which are those for which payment is due soon after the year end (in fact up to one year after the year end) and long term liabilities which are those such as loans which will be settled more than one year after the year end. Not all businesses have long term liabilities.

m) Just as Evelyn offers credit to her customers so she takes credit from her suppliers. At Balance Sheet date it is necessary to count up the amount she owes for goods and services which she has received but for which payment had not been made.

n) Many businesses borrow money from their bankers on overdraft. In fact the principal source of income to the high street banks is interest charged to business customers and the principal source of money to business is the bank loan or overdraft. Overdrafts are forms of borrowing in which the amount borrowed changes continually as money is paid in and cheques are drawn. For most businesses an overdraft once taken out is constantly renewed and is a form of long term liability. However as it is technically repayable on demand, an overdraft is normally included among the short term liabilities.

o) The total of the short term liabilities is shown. Note that in the past short term liabilities were always called *current liabilities* but that the modern term in Balance Sheets is 'creditors: amounts falling due within one year'.

p) A single figure for current assets less the short term liabilities is normally shown, This total is sometimes called the working capital which is the subject of Unit 8.

r) Liabilities such as mortgages and loans which have a repayment requirement more than one year away are included here. Evelyn has only one which is a loan from Tom. The actual repayment date is the end of 19x9 but this is not shown. Usually the *interest rate* is shown. The 12% means that Evelyn must pay Tom 12% of the sum outstanding (ie 12% × £1,000 = £120) every year as long as the £1,000 remains outstanding.

s) The total assets less liabilities is then shown as a single figure. Most people can understand a Balance Sheet up to this point. However the capital part always follows.

t) Capital is the assets less liabilities of the business expressed as a total sum. Some writers describe it as the *net worth*. Just as a person might add up his fortune by valuing his assets (house, car, money in building societies etc less his liabilities — mortgage, HP commitment, unpaid gas bill etc) and thus find out how rich he is so a business prepares a Balance Sheet. It must be emphasised that the Balance Sheet shows only business assets and liabilities.

u) This figure is the Balance Sheet value of the assets less liabilities in total at the beginning of the year.

v) The net profit for the year adds to the net total of assets less liabilities.

w) This sum is always put in but does not have any real significance.

x) The proprietor usually withdraws cash and goods from the business at various times during the year and the total is shown here.

y) If all accounting has been done accurately and correctly, this figure of the capital at the end of the year will be the same figure as the assets less liabilities.

3. Capital or capital and reserves

The Balance Sheet of a sole trader will have a capital section like that of Babel. However a limited company will have a capital and reserves section like that of Martin Padlocks Ltd. Fundamentally they give similar information. Let us compare them:

Sole trader		Limited Company	
Capital at beginning of *year*	x	Capital at *formation*	x
Profit earned in the *year*	x	Profit earned since formation*	x
	x		
Less Drawings in *year*	x		
Capital at *end* of year	x	Capital and reserves at end of year	x

* Profit earned since formation is after deducting dividends which are to companies what drawings are to sole traders.

Not-for-profit enterprises have similar capital sections. An example for a club:

Accumulated fund at beginning of *year*	x
Surplus earned in *year*	x
Accumulated fund at end of *year*	x

Essentially, capital in a sole trader, capital and reserves in a limited company and accumulated fund in a not-for-profit enterprise serve the same purpose. In the real world, other words are often used and much extra information is included. However, by cutting through the verbiage, you will usually be able to see the basic ideas presented here.

4. What a Balance Sheet is and is not

A Balance Sheet is a classified summary of the assets and liabilities of a business valuing the assets at cost or at a figure derived from cost. I should point out that the use of cost derived figures can be modified in certain circumstances. Assets which had no cost are normally omitted. The most notable asset under this heading is *goodwill* which is only included if it had an actual cost i.e. it was bought.

A Balance Sheet does not show the value of the assets if they were sold. The reasons for this include:

a) The long established convention is to use cost based values.

b) The possible selling value of an asset is very subjective and accountants like to be *objective*.

c) The possible selling value of an asset cannot always be easily estimated. For example what is the second hand value of an oil refinery?

The Balance Sheet does not show what the business *as a whole is worth*. That could only be reliably determined by actually selling the business and any estimate is unlikely to be more than approximate.

5. Accounting conventions and the Balance Sheet

Like the Profit and Loss Account, the Balance Sheet is also subject to the accounting conventions. We can now consider the Cost, Prudence and Substance over Form conventions:

Historical cost convention

Assets and expenses are included at their actual cost to the business.

The justification for this critical convention is that historical cost is objective and verifiable. Any alternative convention (e.g. showing assets at realisable value) would be highly subjective and lead to a wide variation in measurement.

The consequences of the convention include:

❏ assets are valued at cost or cost derived figures (e.g. fixed assets are shown at cost less depreciation)

❏ items which had no cost are ignored

❏ unrealised gains are ignored.

The drawbacks of the convention are:

❏ the actual information required by managers, investors and others may be the current values of assets and values based on historical costs may be irrelevant for their purposes

❏ in inflationary times profit is measured as sales at current prices matched against expenses which will include depreciation based on the original costs of the fixed assets.

Some fixed assets, particularly land and buildings, are sometimes revalued to market or resale values. So the fixed assets of a company may include some assets valued at recent prices and some by reference to historical cost. If buildings are valued upwards, depreciation continues to be applied but based on the revalued figures.

Conservatism or prudence

This can be seen as having two aspects — income and costs:

i) revenue and profits are not anticipated but are recognised in the profit and loss only when realised in the form of cash or other assets (e.g. a debt).

ii) Provision is made for all known liabilities (expenses and losses) whether an amount is known with certainty or is a best estimate in the light of information available. Provision means including in the Profit and Loss Account.

Two examples

a) Gribble who tarmacs drives is preparing his accounts for the year ending 31 December 19x2. He is reviewing two contracts for resurfacing of drives for which he has signed contracts and which he will carry out in January 19x3. Contract A is expected to make a profit and in consequence of (i) above he ignores it for the purposes of 31 December 19x2 profits. The profit will fall in to the 19x3 accounts. Contract B was a mistake and he expects to lose approximately £500 on it. In consequence of (ii) above he will provide for the £500 in the 19x2 accounts. This means that there will be an expense in the 19x2 Profit and Loss Account — *provision* for loss on Contract B.

b) Howe has two widgets in his stock at 31 December 19x2, his year end. Widget A cost him £100 and it is expected to sell in 19x3 for £150. In consequence of (i) above it will be valued in his accounts at cost £100 and any profit on its sale will fall in the year of sale — 19x3. Widget B cost him £100 also but it is obsolete and will probably be sold in 19x3 for £80 less 10% sales commission. As a consequence of (ii) widget B will be valued at its net realisable value of £72 and the expected loss of £28 will fall into the 19x2 accounts.

This convention is often seen as unnecessarily cautious.

Substance over form

Some transactions have a legal form which is different from their underlying commercial reality or substance.

The convention is to account for the substance rather than the legal form.

Two examples

a) Hire purchase transactions. The legal form is that the subject matter (e.g. a car) is on hire from the finance company and ownership only passes on the final instalment being paid. The substance is that the buyer acquires the car with the aid of a loan and this is how it is accounted for.

b) Some equipment or vehicles are leased from finance companies. Some leases are genuine rentals but some leases are arranged so that in effect the lessee buys the property with the aid of a 100% loan and the lease payments are in the nature of repayments with interest of that loan. Such leases are termed finance leases and are accounted for as purchase with loan. These areas are the subject of Statement of Standard Accounting Practice SSAP 21 — Accounting for leases and Hire Purchase contracts.

We will also revisit some of the conventions we met in the last Unit:

Business entity the Balance Sheet like the Profit and Loss Account puts the emphasis on the business. Business assets and liabilities only are included.

Money measurement the Balance Sheet gives money values to all the assets and liabilities. Measurement is in a common unit — money. This means that assets and liabilities must be capable of being measured in money terms. Assets like the quality of the employees or the excellence of the firms' reputation are not included.

Realisation the effect of the realisation convention on the Balance Sheet is the inclusion of a figure for debtors.

Accruals in a similar way the effect of the accruals convention is the inclusion of accruals and prepayments in the Balance Sheet.

Periodicity the Balance Sheet is prepared at intervals, usually annually but more frequently if desired.

Matching if expenditure in a year cannot be matched with revenue in that year, then it may be possible to match it with revenue in a following year. Consider, the business of Newitt who has a cold store. His main fixed asset is the refrigeration plant. He has negotiated a service contract for the care of the plant with Fixit and has paid in advance a sum of £3,000 in 19x1 for service in 19x1, 19x2 and 19x3. Essentially £1,000 of this is an expense of 19x1 to be matched with revenue earned from customers in 19x1 — it is part of the cost of providing the services charged to customers. The remaining £2,000 will be matched with revenues in the Profit and Loss Accounts of 19x2 and 19x3. At the end of the 19x1, the £2,000 will appear in the Balance Sheet under prepayments. A more complex example of the use of the matching convention is research and development.

Strikneen Ltd are manufacturers of pharmaceuticals. In 19x2 they spent £1 million on research and development of Koorall which is a cure for the common cold. Testing and licensing will take until 19x6 when the drug will be begin to be sold with enormous profits. Is the £1 million an expense of 19x2 or should it be regarded as an asset and carried forward on successive Balance Sheets until 19x6 when it can be matched against the revenues earned in that and subsequent years? The answer accountants would give is that the answer depends on a reading of SSAP 13 (Research and development) and the certainty or otherwise of successful sales of Koorall.

You may regard the realisation, accruals and matching conventions as really all the same. Some authorities certainly do so under the accruals label. I prefer to see them as separate but closely related.

SCENARIO 3 — Martin amends his Profit and Loss Account and his Balance Sheet

Anne explains that the Balance Sheet in paragraph 3 is at a draft stage which means that she will make some alterations to it before it can be finalised and typed up as the audited Balance Sheet. When it is finalised it will be sent to the company's *shareholders* (in fact only Martin and his wife are shareholders) and to the *Registrar of Companies* where it will be filed and can be seen by members of the public.

Before finalising the Balance Sheet Anne asks Martin a series of questions:

a. The stock is valued at cost but are there any items which are slow moving, damaged, obsolete etc which can only be sold for an amount below cost? Martin remembers that there is a case of RT padlocks imported from Italy which he is having much difficulty in selling. They cost him £1,200 and he thinks he will get only about £800 for them.

b. Are all the debtors collectable? Martin replies that yes they are except perhaps one. Dodgy Ltd owed £880 at the year end and have not paid. He understands that the company have appointed a receiver and the creditors will receive nothing.

c. Have I included all the prepayments? Martin looks through the list and then points out that there is nothing for advertising. He paid £600 for advertising in the Padlock Users' Monthly in October 19x1 and this was for six monthly insertions beginning with the November issue.

d. Are all the creditors included? Martin could only think of one that had been omitted. A consignment of padlocks had been received from a supplier in Tipton on 29 December 19x1 and taken into stock and counted in the stocktake at 31 December. Martin had queried the invoice and it had only been entered in the books when the dispute had been resolved last week. The agreed amount is £520.

e. The loan of £5,000 was received from Martin's father on 31 July 19x1 and I have not included any interest in the profit and loss account as I understand that interest does not start straightaway. That is true. The loan is repayable in five years time and interest starts to accrue only from 1 October 19x1.

Quick Answer Question 3.2

Would you expect the adjustments to the Balance Sheet needed would also affect the Profit and Loss Account?

Task 2

Prepare the finalised Profit and Loss Account and Balance Sheet for Martin Padlocks Ltd taking into account the adjustments required in the scenario. Remember that the Profit and Loss Account balance in the capital and reserves will be affected by the adjustments.

SCENARIO 4 — Martin reviews his financial statements

The revised Profit and Loss Account and the revised Balance Sheet will look like this:

Martin Padlocks Ltd

Trading and Profit and Loss Account for the year ending 31 December 19x1

		£	£
Sales			212,400
Less:	Cost of Goods Sold:		
	Opening Stock		
	Purchases	161,250	
	Less Closing Stock	14,330	146,920
Gross Profit			65,480
Less: Expenses			
Rent		4,000	
Rates		1,120	
Electricity		900	
Printing and Stationery		630	
Advertising		780	
Van Expenses		2,712	
Wages		18,000	
Director's Remuneration		9,600	
Employers' National Insurance		2,542	
Company Formation		250	
Audit and Accountancy		1,300	
Sundries		764	
Lease of van		2,400	
Bad Debt		880	
Bank Interest and Charges		2,990	
Loan Interest		125	
Depreciation		1,100	50,093
Net Profit			15,387

Balance Sheet as at 31 December 19x1

Fixed Assets	Cost	Depreciation	Net Book Value £
Computer	1,000	500	500
Stacking Equipment	3,000	600	2,400
	4,000	1,100	2,900

	Cost	Depreciation	£ Net Book Value
Current Assets			
Stock		14,330	
Debtors		50,320	
Prepayments		1,630	
		66,280	
Creditors: amounts falling due within one year			
Creditors		26,420	
Accruals		125	
Bank Overdraft		7,248	
		33,793	
Net Current Assets			32,487
Total assets less current liabilities			35,387
Creditors: amounts falling due after more than one year			
Loan at 10%			5,000
			30,387
Capital and Reserves			
Share Capital			15,000
Profit and Loss Account			15,387
			30,387

a. The conservatism convention requires that the stock be valued at the lower of cost and net realisable value and as the realisable value of the RT padlocks at £800 is lower than the cost, £800 will be their value in the accounts. This means lowering the stock in the Profit and Loss Account by £400 thus lowering the gross and net profit and lowering the stock in the Balance Sheet.

b. Common sense (as well as the conservatism convention) tells us that it is no good including a debt on the Balance Sheet when it will not be paid. The bad debt is a loss to the firm so it also has to be included in the expenses in the Profit and Loss Account.

c. The advertising was paid for in 19x1. But it is for adverts in six issues of the magazine — two in 19x1 and four in 19x2. This means that it is £200 as an expense of 19x1 and £400 as an expense of 19x2. £400 is a prepayment in the Balance Sheet.

d. Purchases must include all the purchases in the year and so the £520 must be included in purchases in 19x1 in the Profit and Loss Account and in creditors in the Balance Sheet. In practice getting all the creditors in the accounts presents many possibilities for error and accountants spend much time getting the cut-off right.

e.   The Balance Sheet balanced before these adjustments (balanced means the total of the net assets equals the total of capital and reserves) and as each adjustment changed figures in both financial statements, the Balance Sheet balances after the adjustments.

f.   Interest has accrued on the loan — 10% of £5,000 for three months.

Task 3

Martin remembered some other things which he thought might affect the accounts.

1.   Consider the following items. State whether each would be included in or excluded from the Balance Sheet giving reasons:

   a.   An invoice for £300 for padlocks sold to Rich a customer on 31 December 19x1. Rich paid on 12 February 19x2.

   b.   Martin considers that the *goodwill* of the business must have been worth at least £10,000 at 31 December 19x1.

   c.   Martin bought £200 worth of Padlocks in November from Brown, a supplier, on a *sale or return* basis. In fact Martin could not sell them and they were returned to Brown in January 19x2.

   d.   Martin's van knocked over the gatepost of Lowe, a customer in December 19x1 and after much argument he has agreed to pay £600 of damages to Lowe. The company are insured but have to pay the first £250 of any claim.

SCENARIO 5 — Martin finds out what a Balance Sheet is and what it is not

Martin shows his Balance Sheet to his father who is not an accountant and they discuss what it all means. His father says that the Balance Sheet shows *net assets* of £30,387 and the company is divided into 15,000 shares and therefore the *value* of each share is £2.026. Martin agrees that that is how he understands it. His father then says that must mean that Martin would be able to sell each share for £2.026. And that if the assets were sold they would fetch £69,180 and after paying off the liabilities of £38,793 there would be a surplus of £30,387 which could be paid out to the shareholders so that the holder of one share would receive £2.026.

Tasks 4

1.   Write a report on these ideas, concluding with a concise comment on the informational content of a company Balance Sheet.

2.   A way to become familiar with the ideas in Balance Sheets and Profit and Loss Accounts is to use a spreadsheet, so:

   1.   Update the Profit and Loss Account which you put onto a spreadsheet in Unit 2.

   2.   Add the Balance Sheet to the Profit and Loss Account on the spreadsheet in Unit 2.

   3.   Explore the relationships between the two financial statements by adding some transactions, for example:

a. Sell on credit a padlock in stock which had cost £20 for £30. This will change:

Stock	− 20
Sales	+ 30
Debtors	+ 30

b. Pay £70 for some advertising so that £30 is an expense and £40 is a prepayment. This will change:

Advertising	+ 30
Prepayment	+ 40
Overdraft	+ 70

c. Incurring a bad debt of £500.

Note that the utility of spreadsheets of Profit and Loss Accounts and Balance Sheet can be greatly improved if the spreadsheet can automatically do the additions. For example the cell showing gross profit can use a formula subtracting the cost of goods sold cell from the sales cell and the cell showing the net current assets can be a formula deducting creditors falling due within one year from the current assets. Also the Profit and Loss Account can be related to the Balance Sheet by having the cell for stock in the Balance Sheet being the same as the cell for stock in the Profit and Loss Account.

SCENARIO 6 — Martin extends his studies to his household accounts

Martin thinks that preparation of a cash flow forecast and the annual preparation of financial statements showing the results of the year's activities and the assets and liabilities at the end is a good idea. He wonders that it is not widespread domestically. He reads in a Victorian novel that household accounts were certainly produced in earlier times.

Tasks 5

1. Design a cash flow forecast, a Profit and Loss Account and a Balance Sheet for your household. Give suitable headings.
2. What incomes, overheads, assets, liabilities and capital expenditures have you identified?
3. What is the meaning of any figure which is the difference between assets and liabilities?

6. Personal accounting

Domestically, we all spend money on household goods and services. Some of these things are consumed over a short period like food, telephone bills, electricity, window cleaning. We can classify these as revenue expenditure. Some expenditure is on more long lasting goods and services such as double glazing, a new refrigerator or a new bookcase. Such expenditure brings into existence fixed assets and can be termed capital expenditure. It is possible to prepare each year a domestic Profit and Loss Account which would include revenue expenditures and a Balance Sheet which would show the fixed assets. Most of us do not do this but a sort of Balance Sheet is drawn up when we die. This is to determine if we must pay any Inheritance Tax but also so that the beneficiaries of the will can know how much they are to receive.

Entity → *Nasturtium Ltd*
Trading and Profit and Loss Account for the year ending 31 December 19x2

Periodicity

Realisation

Matching

Accruals

	£ ← Money
Sales	400,000
Less: Cost of goods sold	250,000
Gross profit	150,000

Wages	61,000	
Rent and rates	13,500	
Sundry overheads	31,900	
Provision for loss on future contracts	4,700 ← Prudence	
Uninsured loss of stock by fire	6,800	
Depreciation	6,910	124,810
Net profit		25,190

Cost

Balance Sheet as at 31 December 19x2

Cost →

Fixed assets at cost		52,500
less depreciation		21,000
		31,500

Current assets		
Stock	28,000	
Debtors	61,000	
Prepayments	1,900	
	90,900	

Prudence →

Accruals →

		£
Creditors: amounts falling due within one year		
Creditors	38,000	
Overdraft	20,480	
HP commitments	6,000	
	64,480	

Substance over form →

Net current assets	26,420
Total assets less current liabilities	57,920
Creditors: amounts falling due after more than one year	10,000
	47,920

Capital and reserves	
Called up share capital	2,000
Share premium account	6,000
Profit and Loss Account	39,920
	47,920

The two parts of a Balance Sheet

Capital	=	Cash	The beginning of a company — shareholders invest cash
Capital	=	Net Assets	The investors cash is turned into a set of assets less liabilities
Capital and Reserves*	=	Net Assets	A Profit is made so net assets are more

* = Profit and Loss Account

Note:

1. The two parts of the Balance Sheet must always be the same monetary amount.
2. Any increase or decrease in net assets must be reflected in a similar increase or decrease in Capital and Reserves.
3. The Net Assets show what assets the business has and what liabilities it has to others.
4. The Capital and Reserves explain how the Net Assets were financed.

7. Summary of Unit 3

❐ Enterprises produce Balance Sheets at intervals of not more than one year.

❐ A Balance Sheet is a classified summary of the assets and liabilities of the business at the Balance Sheet date.

❐ The Balance Sheet is a formal financial statement and should be in an appropriate neat and tidy format.

❐ The sections of a Balance Sheet include:

> fixed assets;
>
> current assets;
>
> current liabilities (or creditors: amounts falling due within one year);
>
> long term liabilities (or liabilities: amounts falling due after more than one year);
>
> and capital.

❐ Fixed assets are assets such as land and buildings, plant and machinery and vehicles.

❐ Current assets include stocks, work in progress, debtors, prepayments and cash at bank and in hand.

❐ Current liabilities include creditors and bank overdrafts.

❐ Long term liabilities include loans and mortgages.

❐ The capital is the assets less liabilities expressed as a single sum. In sole trader businesses it is usual to show

$$\text{the capital at the date of the previous balance sheet} + \text{the profit in the period} - \text{the drawings} = \text{the capital at the date of the balance sheet date *}$$

* which should also equal the assets less liabilities.

In limited companies, it is usual to show:

Capital and Reserves:

Share Capital

Profit and Loss Account

❏ The Balance Sheet shows the assets at cost derived figures. It does not pretend or purport to give the saleable values of the assets or of the business as a whole.

❏ The rules or conventions which accountants use in drawing up a Balance Sheet have been identified in a body of theory. The conventions used include the cost convention, the accruals convention, the business entity convention, the prudence convention, the substance over form convention, the money measurement convention, the periodicity convention, and the matching convention.

Formation of Balance Sheets

First, an exercise to enable you to practise the formation of Balance Sheets.

Exercise *1

The following data relate to three businesses at 31 December 19x2:

all in £'000	A	B	C
Stocks	28	102	74
Trade creditors	21	140	68
Plant and Machinery at cost	46		
Equipment at cost		62	42
Equipment depreciation to date		51	12
Premises at cost	100		280
Debtors	53	203	
Loan to Philip repayable on 29 June 19x3	10		
Capital at 31 December 19x1	132	?	108
Vehicles at cost	54	180	74
Prepayments	2	6	9
Vehicle Depreciation to date	18	43	39
Premises depreciation to date	20		14
Drawings in 19x2	38	30	51
Net Profit in 19x2	41	51	73
Cash at Bank	17		
Bank Overdraft		62	?
Loan from Immutable Assurance at 18% repayable 19x8	80		170
Accrued rent and rates	5	12	4
Plant and Machinery depreciation to date	31		
Hire purchase commitment		36	

Required:

a. Prepare a Balance Sheet for each business.

b. The businesses are a retailer, a manufacturer and a wholesaler. Which is which?

Profit and Loss Accounts and Balance Sheets

It is not too difficult to slot the necessary data into a pro forma Profit and Loss Account or Balance Sheet. It can be more difficult to sort out data which might go into either or both. Here is an exercise to give you more familiarity with these financial statements:

Exercise *2

The following data relate to the businesses of Alan, Brian and Kate for the year ending 31 December 19x2:

	Alan	Brian	Kate
All in £'000			
Sales	750	310	510
Creditors	35	31	80
Debtors	150	12	130
Stock at 31 December 19x1	52	18	71
Stock at 31 December 19x2	56	23	65
Premises at cost	200		130
Premises Depreciation to 31 December 19x1	20		52
Equipment at Cost	65	78	90
Equipment depreciation to 31 December 19x1	21	16	59
Purchases	520	153	340
Rent, Rates and Insurances	32	45	32
Wages	128	43	154
Other Overheads	21	24	46
Bank Interest and Charges	12	2	31
Cash at Bank	49	12	
Bank Overdraft			76
Capital at 31 December 19x1	438	48	241
Drawings	35	18	34
Loan from David at 10% repayable in 19x5			40

Note:

Alan:

❐ Depreciation for 19x2 will be: on the premises £5,000 and on the equipment £13,000

❐ Rent rates and insurances include a fire insurance premium of £6,000 for the year ending 31 August 19x3 but do not include the rates for the quarter ending 31 December 19x2 £7,000.

Brian:

❐ Depreciation for 19x2 should be £6,000

❐ Wages does not include a bonus to the staff of 10% of the profit after charging the bonus.

❐ Other overheads includes a payment for a maintenance agreement £3,000 for 19x3

Kate:

☐ Depreciation for 19x2 should be £4,000 on the premises and £9,000 on the equipment

☐ No interest was paid on the loan in 19x2 and the 19x2 interest was paid in January 19x3

☐ Wages includes an advance of £3,000 to an employee which will be repaid by deduction from her salary in 19x3

Required:

a. Prepare a Trading and Profit and Loss Account for the year ending 31 December 19x2 and a Balance Sheet as at 31 December 19x2 for each business.

b. Write short notes on the situations shown by these accounts.

Case Study/Assignment 1

Roy started in business on 1 January 19x2 as a dealer in widgets. (Note that all widgets are identical.)

His transactions in the first month were:

January:

1. Opened a business bank account with £1,200, his personal savings
2. Put his car valued at £2,400 into the business
3. Purchased 40 widgets on credit from Apple at £30 each
14. Purchased 60 widgets from Bramble on credit for £36 each
16. Paid the insurance premium on his car for the year to 31 December 19x2 £720
18. Sold 10 widgets to Cherry for £60 each on credit
20. Sold 20 widgets for cash to Greengage for £50 each
21. Purchased 25 widgets on credit from Framboise at £40 each
25. Sold 11 widgets on credit to Lemon for £70 each
27. Received £500 from Cherry
29. Sold 50 widgets on credit to Logan at £70 each
30. Paid Apple the amount due to him
31. Discovered that Cherry had decamped and would be unable to pay him the balance due
31. Took stock and found he had 31 widgets in stock
31. Drew £50 from the bank for private purposes

Note:

☐ the car depreciation is £600 a year.

☐ assume there are no other expenses.

Required:

a. Prepare a Trading and Profit and Loss Account for the month of January 19x2 and a Balance Sheet as at 31 January 19x2.

b. Comment on the problems you have met in dealing with this problem and how you have solved them.

Case Study / Assignment 2

Scoff rents a small unit on a trading estate and prepares dinners and buffets for commercial and other customers. His accounts for the two years 19x1 and 19x2 show:

Profit and Loss Account

	£	19x1	£	19x2
Sales		165,000		178,000
Cost of Materials	40,000		46,000	
Wages	52,000		56,000	
Rent, Rates and Insurance	18,200		19,900	
Electricity	6,900		7,800	
Van Expenses	13,700		15,400	
Sundry Expenses	5,600		6,200	
Depreciation:				
Vans	4,000		4,000	
Equipment	6,000	146,400	5,400	160,700
Net Profit		18,600		17,300

Balance Sheet

Fixed Assets				
at cost less depreciation		37,000		35,000
Stocks of Materials	4,200		5,900	
Debtors	35,400		40,200	
	39,600		46,100	
Creditors	12,700		16,300	
Bank Overdraft	30,600		33,200	
	43,300		49,500	
		(3,700)		(3,400)
		33,300		31,600
Capital at beginning of year		33,900		33,300
Profit for year		18,600		17,300
		52,500		50,600
Drawings		19,200		19,000
at end of year		33,300		31,600

Note:

❑ Inflation was 4% between the two years

❑ The bank have written to Scoff requesting a reduction of the overdraft

❑ The vans desperately need replacing

❑ Scoff has a wife who helps in the business (her wages are in wages in the Profit and Loss Account), two children, a nice house with a large mortgage.

❑ Scoff is very much in demand and at peak times, his services have to be booked a year in advance.

Discuss the performance of the business over the two years and indicate his problems. Suggest some ways he might improve things.

Exercise 3

Mr and Mrs James and their two children live in a detached house in Birmingham. Mrs James is expecting their third child and will have to reduce her working hours as a free-lance computer programmer from 1 January 19x7. They feel they need to budget carefully for 19x7 and as an aid produce a set of financial statements for 19x6 as follows:

Income and Expenditures

Expenditures	£	Incomes	£
Rates	980	Salary of Mr J less tax etc	16,280
Insurances	420	Earnings of Mrs J less tax etc	12,100
Mortgage Interest	3,600		
Motoring (2 cars)	2,800		
Food	5,100		
Other household	3,190		
Holidays	2,400		
Life Assurance	2,000		
Entertainment	1,650		
Private medicine	800		
Covenants to charities	800		
Depreciation of cars	3,200		
Christmas presents	650		
	27,590		
Surplus	790		
	28,380		28,380

Balance Sheet

House at cost (purchased in 19x2)		95,000
Cars at cost less depreciation		9,400
		104,400
Debtors re Mrs J's business	2,200	
Bonus for 19x6 due to Mr J	2,600	
Cash at bank	500	5,300
		109,700
Creditors for household bills and other expenses		3,120
		106,580
Mortgage		51,000
		55,580
Capital		55,580

Cash flows for the year

Inflows

Salary	14,500
Earnings of Mrs J	11,500
	26,000

Outflows

Rates	1,020
Insurances	400
Mortgage	5,200
Motoring	2,820
Food	5,050
Other household	2,900
Holidays	2,400
Life Assurance	2,000
Entertainment	1,600
Private medicine	1,000
Covenants to charities	800
Christmas presents	650
	25,840
Balance at beginning of the year	340
Balance at end of year	500

Required:

a. Comment on the accounting treatment of the following items and their appearance in the three statements: rates, mortgage and mortgage interest, motoring and the motor cars, salary and bonus, earnings of Mrs James, surplus, capital.

b. Mrs James expects her income for 19x7 to be 2/3 that of 19x6. Expenditure on the mortgage, life assurance and covenants is expected to be the same as 19x6. Depreciation is at 20% straight line. All other items are likely to grow at 4%. Mr J would like to trade in his car (at book value £5,000) against a new car costing £12,000.

Prepare a set of forecast statements for 19x7 based on these figures making any reasonable assumptions you like about accruals and prepayments. Mr and Mrs James realise that this shows impossible financial difficulties. Make some suggestions how they may change things to be possible and comment on the utility of historical and forecast financial statements using this example.

Assignment 3

Obtain a copy of the annual accounts of a public body (e.g. an NHS Trust or a local authority) or a major charity. Write a comment on the headings and sub-headings used in the Balance Sheet and Income and Expenditure Account.

4 Depreciation

1. Objectives

The objective of this Unit is to introduce the idea of depreciation of fixed assets. We will find out how depreciation is calculated and how it affects the annual profit and the values of fixed assets on the Balance Sheet.

SCENARIO 1 — Martin considers depreciation

When the final typed accounts arrive from Anne's office, Martin spends some time going through them. One of the areas he is not at all sure about is fixed assets and the depreciation.

The accounts show:

On the Balance Sheet:

Fixed Assets

	Cost	Depreciation	Value
	£	£	£
Computer	1,000	500	500
Stacking Equipment	3,000	600	2,400
	4,000	1,100	2,900

and in the Profit and Loss Account among the expenses:
Depreciation   £1,100

Quick Answer Questions 4.1

1. What are fixed assets?
2. What does 'cost' mean?
3. What is the amount of the depreciation?
4. Would it have been different if three years instead of five had been chosen as the life of the stacking equipment?
5. Would the profit then have been different?
6. Does the depreciation in the Balance Sheet agree with the amount of depreciation which is an expense in the Profit and Loss Account?
7. What is the total value of the fixed assets according to the Balance Sheet?
8. Do you think that this means that the company could sell the fixed assets for £2,900?

SCENARIO 2 — Martin finds out how to calculate depreciation

Martin thinks he understands what depreciation means and how it has affected his profit and the figures on the Balance Sheet. However he now wonders if he was not too quick in answering Anne's questions about the fixed assets. He rings her up and asks her what assumptions have been made in calculating the depreciation.

She tells him:

Asset:	Computer	Stacking
Estimated useful life	2 years	5 years
Salvage value	nil	nil
Depreciation policy	Straight Line	Straight Line

She also tells him that she had thought of using *reducing balance* depreciation.

Martin thinks about these assumptions and says to Anne:

'Suppose the assumptions were different, would that make the profit and Balance Sheet values different?'.

'Yes'. Says Anne.

Firstly, he makes sure that he understands the terms *Salvage Value, Depreciation Policy,* and *Straight Line,* then he suggests that it would be more accurate to change the assumptions to:

Asset:	Computer	Stacking
Estimated useful life	3 years	3 years
Salvage value	£125	£300
Depreciation policy	Reducing Balance	Straight Line

Task 1

What did Anne mean by the terms: salvage value, depreciation policy, straight line and reducing balance?

Quick Answer Question 4.2

Calculate the depreciation to go in the Profit and Loss Account and the figures for the Fixed Assets in the Balance Sheet based on the new assumptions. Reducing instalment rates for the computer are 50%.

Tasks 2

1. He has a choice of depreciation policy of straight line or reducing balance. What thinking lies behind his choice of reducing balance for the computer?
2. Which method should he choose if:
    i.   He wants to report as high a profit as possible to the bank.
    ii. He wants to be absolutely *objective* about the measurement of his profit?

SCENARIO 3 — Martin puts his fixed assets in the Balance Sheet

In the second year Martin intends to continue to lease the van but to buy an additional van for £7,000. He also intends to buy a skin-packing machine for £3,000. He reckons appropriate estimates for these are:

	Van	*Machine*
Cost	£7,000	£3,000
Salvage value	£2,400	£1,000
Life	3 years	5 years
Depreciation Policy	Reducing Balance	Straight Line

Tasks 3

1. Show the Depreciation total in the Profit and Loss Account for all four Fixed Assets for the second year assuming that the new assets receive a full year's depreciation in their first year.

2. Show the Fixed Assets section in the second year's Balance Sheet in the form:
Fixed Assets

	Cost	Accumulated Depreciation	Net Book Value
Computer	x	x	x
Stacking Equipment	x	x	x
Van	x	x	x
Skin-Packing Machine	x	x	x
	x	x	x

3. Explain why the Company will have spent £10,000 on new Fixed Assets in year 2 but the Profit of that year will be reduced by only £2,500 as a consequence.

2. Introduction

A business can have at least two types of expenditure:

Revenue expenditure

Capital expenditure

Revenue expenditure is on goods and services that are consumed in the short term. It includes the input cost of the business's products. These costs can be simply the cost of goods purchased for resale or the costs (materials, labour etc) of goods manufactured for sale. Revenue expenditure also includes overhead costs such as rent, rates, insurance, salaries, electricity, repairs, motor running expenses and many others.

Capital expenditure is the cost of acquiring fixed assets.

The Exposure Draft of the Statement of Principles for financial reporting issued by the Accounting Standards Board in 1995 defines assets as *rights or other access to future economic benefits controlled by an entity as a result of past transactions or events.*

This clear, but perhaps not entirely understandable, definition includes for example:

- debtors: rights to receive cash from the persons who owe the entity money
- machinery: access to future economic benefits (use of the machine to make things to sell)
- prepaid rates: rights (no need to pay rates until the next period starts) as a result of past transactions (payment of the rates).

You might think about any asset you see on a Balance Sheet in these terms!

Assets are things possessed by a person or business and include real things like stocks, motor cars, cash in the bank and also debts due from other people or firms.

Fixed assets are assets which cost a significant amount and give economic benefits for more than one accounting year. Examples are land and buildings, plant and machinery, motor vehicles and office equipment. Items of very small value (for example a ruler or stapler in the office) may well last for several years but are not regarded as fixed assets.

3. Depreciation

If a fixed asset is acquired in a particular accounting year then it will give economic benefit to the enterprise not just in that year but for one or more years after that.

For example Martin's business might buy a new machine in 1994 for £2,000. This machine may well last for say five years and cease to be effective only in 1998.

In measuring the profit for 1994 it would be unfair to include the whole £2,000 as an expense reducing the profit for that year. This is because the machine will give economic benefit for each of the years 1994 to 1998. It is necessary to spread the £2,000 over these years on some rational basis.

Allocating an appropriate share of the £2,000 over these years is called the depreciation process.

Before considering how this is done, it is necessary to gather together some data: the cost (which we know to be £2,000) and some estimates. We need to estimate the useful economic life of the machine. We will suppose this to be 5 years. We also need to estimate the salvage value at the end of the asset's life. This is clearly more difficult but we will suppose this to be £200.

Using this data and these estimates we can quickly see that the ultimate cost of the machine will be £2,000 less £200 = £1,800. As the machine will give benefit over 5 years, the most logical way of spreading the cost will be £1,800/5 = £360 a year.

This approach is called the straight line method and is the most frequently found in practice.

The consequences for profit measurement are that the profits of each of the years 1994 to 1998 are reduced by £360 each year. Note that cost in 1994 does not reduce the profit of 1994 by £2,000 but by £360.

Many accountants consider that the *straight line* method does not reflect reality in that the machine gives up its value more quickly in its early years than it does in its later years. They consider that the £1,800 should be allocated between the years 1994 to 1998 so that there is more depreciation in the earlier years. A way of doing this is to use the *reducing instalment* method of depreciation.

This is best explained by an example.

Example

	£
1994 Cost of machine	2,000
1994 Depreciation 37% of £2,000	740
	1,260
1995 Depreciation 37% of £1,260	466
	794
1996 Depreciation 37% of £794	294
	500
1997 Depreciation 37% of £500	185
	315
1998 Depreciation 37% of £315	116
	199

You will notice:

a) The depreciation and, hence the profit measurement, is unevenly distributed over the years. The reduction of profit in 1994 is £740 and in 1998 only £116.

b) The adoption of 37% as the rate does not exactly reduce the final value to the estimated salvage value of £200. This is because the rate chosen should be 36.9% and you may be wondering where the 37% came from. It comes from a formula linking cost, salvage value and expected life. Most accountants do not know this formula and fewer still actually use it. So I will not give it.

In practice the reducing instalment method is much used but accountants tend to ignore the salvage value and the expected life and simply take a fixed percentage. A very common percentage is 25%.

Note that the total depreciation over the 5 years is the same for both methods. Only the distribution over the years is different.

Depreciation will normally appear in the Profit and Loss Account as:

Depreciation   £x

This will be the whole depreciation for the year for all fixed assets.

4. Balance Sheet values

So far we have considered the effect on profit measurement of the depreciation process. The depreciation process also affects the valuation put on assets in the Balance Sheet.

Using our example we can draw up a table showing the valuations which would appear in the Balance Sheet at the end of each year:

	1994	1995	1996	1997	1998
	£	£	£	£	£
Straight line	1,640	1,280	920	560	200
Reducing instalment	1,260	794	500	315	199

You will notice that the valuations are different for the two methods.

It is necessary to appreciate what is meant by value. If a person is asked 'What is the value of your car?'. She will assume the value requested is the estimated price for which the car can be sold based on advertised prices, guides to car prices etc. Balance Sheet values are *not* intended to indicate the prices for which assets can be sold. Consider a machine which is purchased for a special use unique to the buying company. It may have five years of economic use but at no time will it have any saleable value except as scrap.

A way of considering Balance Sheet values of fixed assets is to assume that when purchased the cost price represents the *utility* of the asset *to the firm*. As time progresses and the machine becomes worn out it gradually gives up its utility. The amount of utility given up in the year is the depreciation and the Balance Sheet value is the utility remaining.

The Balance Sheet value is called the *net book value* or *the written down value* or sometimes as the *carrying value*. You will now appreciate that this value may be below or above the second hand or resale value of the asset. Bear in mind that some assets have little or no second hand value — an example is special purpose machinery.

Fixed assets are usually shown in Balance Sheets like this:

	£		
	Cost	Depreciation	Net book value
Land	10,000	–	10,000
Buildings	80,000	12,000	68,000
Plant	32,000	11,306	20,694
	122,000	23,306	98,694

Note that the *original* cost of the fixed assets (which were bought at various times in the past) is always shown. This information is not of great value but it is always given. The depreciation is all the depreciation on the fixed assets for *all* years up to the present. It is *not* just the depreciation for the year.

5. Types of fixed asset

There are several categories of fixed asset:

land, buildings, plant, vehicles, office equipment etc.

The theory is that they all have limited lives except land. Consequently they all need to be depreciated except for land. The causes of having limited lives include wear and tear, effluxion of time (this strange phrase is always used and it means assets depreciate because of the passage of time) and obsolescence.

Land does not depreciate in normal circumstances.

Buildings have limited useful lives and therefore are depreciated. Commonly the useful life is estimated at 40 or 50 years and the straight line method is normally used.

Plant and vehicles have shorter lives (5 to 10 years?) and may be depreciated by either method.

6. Depreciation policies

Estimates are required of useful lives and salvage values and as these are subjective the depreciation and hence the measurement of profit will depend on who makes the estimates. In addition the firm has to have a policy on which depreciation method to use. But note that the method once chosen should be applied consistently.

Published accounts should give the useful lives and the depreciation policies in a statement included with the accounts called *the statement of accounting policies*.

7. Disposals

Anton's business started on 1 January 19x2 and he bought on that date a Rover car for £12,500. He depreciated it on the basis of a life of 5 years with a salvage value of £2,000. Thus the depreciation was £2,100 a year.

In his Balance Sheet at 31 December 19x4 the car stood at:

	£
Cost	12,500
Accumulated depreciation	6,300
Written down value	6,200

On March 19x5, he sold the car for £4,500 and bought another. What should be the depreciation charge for the car in the Profit and Loss Account of 19x5?

The answer is simply £6,200 – £4,500 = £1,700. This will appear in the Profit and Loss Account simply as depreciation £1,700 (it will probably be included in a global figure of depreciation and not be shown separately) or possibly as '*Loss on sale of vehicle £1,700*'.

SCENARIO 4 — Martin finds out about depreciation in different kinds of asset

Martin is talking at the Golf Club to his friend Carlo who has had a haulage business for several years. Carlo confides that he does not really understand the accounts his accountant produces for him and confesses that the fixed assets and depreciation mystify him especially.

Martin is full of his new found understanding of this subject and offers to explain Carlo's accounts to him. Carlo produces these and Martin sees:

Balance Sheet

Fixed Assets	Cost	Accumulated Depreciation	Net Book Value
	£	£	£
Land	30,000	–	30,000
Buildings	185,000	68,200	116,800
Lorries	243,000	102,000	141,000
Plant and Equipment	84,000	53,400	30,600
	542,000	223,600	318,400

Profit and Loss Account:

Depreciation:

Buildings	4,625	
Lorries	43,600	
Plant and Equipment	7,600	
Loss on Sale of Lorry	2,180	58,005

They manage to find a section in the accounts called 'accounting policies' and in it find:

Depreciation:

'Depreciation is calculated so as to write off the cost of an asset by the straight line method over the period of its useful life as follows:

Freehold Buildings	40 years
Lorries	5 years
Plant and Equipment	10 years

Martin recognises many of the words but is unclear about some of the others. He resolves to ask Anne for further enlightenment.

Task 4

Write a memo as from Anne explaining:

a. *Accumulated Depreciation* and why this is different from the depreciation in the Profit and Loss Account.

b. Why land is not depreciated?

c. Martin works out that the cost of the buildings (£185,000) divided by 40 gives £4,625 which he can see in the Profit and Loss Account. However he is not clear why the accumulated depreciation on the buildings is not an exact multiple of £4,625.

d. Explain what is meant by *'loss on sale of lorry'* and how it was calculated.

e. Carlo reckons that the premises are worth about £500,000 and wonders why the property is valued at only £146,800.

f. Carlo also reckons that the plant and equipment is old and would only fetch about £5,000 at auction.

SCENARIO 5 — Martin takes his studies to the Golf Club

Martin is a member of an old established and exclusive Golf Club with 1,000 members and has just received the annual accounts. The Club is a company limited by guarantee. He does not normally read these but decides to do so in order to see what happens about Fixed Assets and Depreciation. He sees:

Fixed Assets

	Cost	Accumulated Depreciation	Book Value
	£	£	£
Freehold Golf Course	240,000	nil	240,000
Club House	90,000	54,000	36,000

The accounting *policies* state:

❒ the Freehold Golf Course is not depreciated

❒ the Club House is depreciated over 50 years.

The directors' report contains a paragraph to the effect that the Freehold Golf Course may be worth significantly more than its *historical cost* but that the directors decline to put a value upon it as there is no intention to sell it.

Quick Answer Questions 4.3

1. How can Martin calculate the age of the Club House?

2. Why do you think the Freehold Golf Course is not depreciated?

SCENARIO 6 — Martin discovers that financial statements do not reveal all

Martin knows that planning permission might be obtained to build houses on the Golf Course as it is in the middle of a residential area. Planning permission may also be obtainable to build a new Golf Course in the nearby countryside on what is now farming land.

Martin thinks that he would give more relevant information than the *limited* and *historical* nature of the *information* given in the Annual Accounts.

Tasks 5

1. Write a criticism of the Golf Club's depreciation policies and suggest alternatives that might be more informative.

2. Set up Martin's two fixed assets and the depreciation on them on a spreadsheet and explore different depreciation policies and assumptions on the Balance Sheet and Profit and Loss Account.

8. Revaluation

Generally accounting recognizes depreciation and ignores appreciation. This has led to some distortion in the view given by financial statements. For example Stubby Breweries plc a small independent brewer bought its brewery premises in 1960 for £63,000 (land £7,000 + buildings £56,000). Depreciation policy was to write off the buildings over 50 years.

Thus by 1990 the brewery stood at £63,000 − [31 × $\frac{£56,000}{50}$] = £28,280.

In fact the buildings were well maintained and an independent valuation gave the brewery a value of £480,000 (land £120,000 and building £360,000).

It is possible to take this valuation into the accounts. The effect would be:

❑ the land will be shown at valuation £120,000

❑ the buildings will be shown at valuation £360,000

❑ the buildings will be depreciated over the remaining useful economic life of the buildings. This was estimated at 30 years. Thus for 1990 and later years the depreciation will change from £1,120 a year to £12,000.

❑ the increase in value is £480,000 − £28,280 = £451,720. This is not regarded as an item in the Profit and Loss Account of 1990 but is added directly to the figure of capital (capital and reserves in a company).

9. Other methods of depreciation

Several other methods of depreciation are found in practice as well as the straight line and reducing balance methods.

These include production unit and sum of digits.

Production unit method is illustrated by Camrat Ltd which purchased a hedonite mine on 1 January 19x1 for £6 million.

The land itself has no real value (in fact it might cost money to restore it). The £6 million is really spent on the mineral Hedonite. Output is estimated at 4000 kilograms over its life. In 19x1 280 Kg were extracted. Depreciation is regarded in 19x1 as £6 million × 280/4,000 = £420,000. In the case of mines and quarries, the production unit method is called the depletion method.

Sum of digits:

Suppose Dulcie starts a business on 1 January 19x2 with a machine which cost £10,000. She estimates its life at 4 years and its salvage value at £1,000. Total depreciation for the four years is thus £9,000.

Under the sum of digits method, the depreciation is calculated by:

4	$\frac{4}{10} \times 9,000$	3,600
3	$\frac{3}{10} \times 9,000$	2,700
2	$\frac{2}{10} \times 9,000$	1,800
1	$\frac{1}{10} \times 9,000$	900
10		9,000

The sum of digits has the same effect as reducing the balance by putting more depreciation into the earlier years. However the effect is not quite so marked. Sum of digits is not often found in practice.

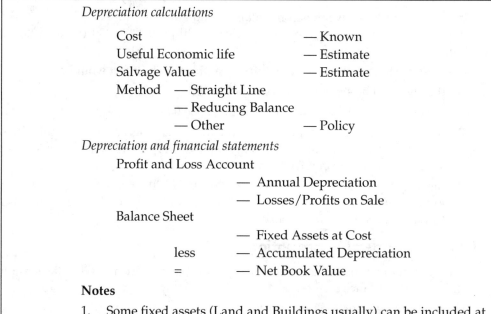

Depreciation calculations

Cost	— Known
Useful Economic life	— Estimate
Salvage Value	— Estimate
Method — Straight Line	
— Reducing Balance	
— Other	— Policy

Depreciation and financial statements

Profit and Loss Account
— Annual Depreciation
— Losses/Profits on Sale

Balance Sheet
— Fixed Assets at Cost
less — Accumulated Depreciation
= — Net Book Value

Notes

1. Some fixed assets (Land and Buildings usually) can be included at a valuation. But then depreciation is applied to the valuation.

2. Land is not usually depreciated.

3. When assets are revalued upwards, the net assets are of course increased. The Capital and Reserves have therefore also to be increased and this is done by including an amount headed Revaluation reserve.

10. Summary of Unit 4

- ❐ Fixed Assets appear in the Balance Sheet under a small number of convenient headings such as land, buildings, plant, equipment, vehicles etc. A value is also shown which has three components: cost, accumulated depreciation and net book value.

- ❐ Annual Depreciation is calculated by reference to the cost, the salvage value and the estimated useful life of the asset.

- ❐ There are two common (and many less common) methods of calculating depreciation: straight line and reducing balance.

- ❐ Each firm has to select one of the methods for depreciation. That is then its depreciation policy and it is then usually adhered to for all years.

- ❐ Salvage value is the amount expected to be recovered from the sale of the asset at the end of its life. This is often regarded as nil.

- ❐ Net book value is also known as written down value or *carrying value*. It is simply cost less accumulated depreciation. It has no economic meaning except that it might be considered the value of the asset to the business or the value in use. There is always an assumption that the net book value (which is the undepreciated portion of the original cost) can be recovered by charging it as an expense in the Profit and Loss Account over the remaining life of the asset.

- ❐ Each fixed asset owned is depreciated each year and the total depreciation suffered over the years is called the accumulated depreciation. It is this which appears in the Balance Sheet.

- ❐ When a fixed asset is sold, or otherwise disposed of, the difference between the book value and the disposal proceeds is either a *loss or a profit on sale*. This loss or profit appears in the Profit and Loss Account.

- ❐ The depreciation undergone each year by the fixed assets is an expense which appears in the Profit and Loss Account.

- ❐ This expense depends on the assumptions made (estimated life and estimated salvage value) and the depreciation policy selected. Consequently the measurement of profit is much affected by depreciation.

- ❐ Land is not depreciated but buildings are. The value of premises in the sense of what the premises can be sold for can be estimated. It is usually very different from the book value.

- ❐ Depreciation represents a fairly subjective area of accounting but has a significant effect on the Profit and Loss Account and the Balance Sheet.

- ❐ Depreciation shows the limitations on the informational value of Annual Accounts. The amount of information given is strictly limited by the accounting conventions and is historical in nature.

- ❐ Other methods of depreciation include sum of digits and the unit of production or depletion methods.

Exercises in basic depreciation

Exercise *1

Judith started her computer programming business on 1 January 1992 and immediately bought some computer equipment at a cost of £6,000.

a. What estimates will Judith need to make in order to decide on the depreciation of the equipment?

b. What factors will cause the equipment to have limited life?

   If she decided that the equipment would have a useful economic life of 3 years and have a salvage value at the end of 3 years of £2,500.

c. Calculate:

   i.   Depreciation for 1992, 1993 and 1994.

   ii. The Balance Sheet values of the equipment at the end of each year.

       using (i) the straight line method and (ii) the reducing instalment method using a rate of 25%.

d. Comment on the effect on profit and Balance Sheet values of the two methods.

   In 1993, she realised that her equipment was becoming obsolete and she sold it for £1,500 and bought some replacement equipment for £9,000. The sale and purchase took place in August 1993.

e. Assuming that she uses the straight line method, calculate:

   i.   The depreciation for 1993 for the original equipment and the Balance Sheet value for it at the end of 1993.

   ii. The depreciation on the new equipment assuming that its estimated life is 4 years and its salvage value £1,000.

   iii. The Balance Sheet value at the end of 1993 for the new equipment.

   In January 1994 she is in conversation with a computer equipment dealer who tells her that the second hand value of her new equipment is only £5,000.

f. Comment on the dealer's remarks in the context of Judith's Profit and Loss Account and Balance Sheet.

   It turns out that the new equipment is excellent and at the end of 1996 she is still using it and expects to continue to do so for at least two more years.

g. What will be the effect on profit and Balance Sheet values for the years after 1993?

Exercise 2

Davinder has a parcels delivery service and has four vans. He bought these at various dates in the past and the position at the end of 1995 is:

	Ford	Rover	Renault	Seat
year of purchase	1991	1992	1993	1994
Estimated life (years)	5	5	6	4
Estimated Salvage value (£)	500	1,000	200	600
Cost (£)	8,500	7,000	7,400	3,800

Complete the entry in Davinder's Balance Sheet as at 31 December 1995:

Fixed Assets

	Cost	Accumulated Depreciation	Net Book Value
Vans			
Office Equipment	£3,500	£1,960	£1,540

Exercise *3

North started in business on 1 January 19x2.

He acquired the following fixed assets:

1 January 19x2	Lorry	£35,000
5 March 19x2	Computer system	£16,000
9 June 19x2	Delivery Van	£10,200
19 November 19x2	Copier	£4,000
13 December 19x2	Warehouse	£105,000
8 March 19x3	Ford Car	£16,000
24 July 19x3	Fax machine	£800

Required:

i. Calculate the charge for depreciation in the accounts of North for the years ending 31 December 19x2, 19x3, 19x4 and 19x5.

ii. Show the Balance Sheet figures for each year end using the format:

	Cost	Accumulated Depreciation	Net Book Value
Land			
Buildings			
Vehicles			
Office Equipment			

You should use the following discrete set of assumptions and policies:

a. ❐ Vehicles last 4 years and have a salvage value of 20% of original cost

   ❐ Office Equipment has a life of three years with no salvage value

   ❐ Land is not depreciated

   ❐ Buildings are depreciated over 40 years

   ❐ the Warehouse includes land at £25,000

   ❐ straight line is used throughout

   ❐ items bought before 30 June in a year have a full year's depreciation but items bought later have only a half year's depreciation in the first year.

b. ❐ Vehicles and office equipment are depreciated at 25% per annum on the reducing balance basis

   ❐ Land is not depreciated

   ❐ Buildings are depreciated over 25 years on the straight line basis

   ❐ the land part of the buildings is estimated at £35,000

❐ all items bought in a year are given a full year's charge for depreciation in that year.

Exercise 4

Dwight has a year end of 31 December and depreciates his vehicles on the basis of 25% per annum reducing balance. He sold a vehicle that he bought in 19x2 for £13,000, for £3,000 in 19x7.

a. Calculate the depreciation charge for the vehicle in 19x7.

b. Recalculate a. on the basis that the vehicle was sold for £5,000.

Exercise *5

Durham Widgets Ltd operate from a warehouse they bought in 19x0 (land £10,000 + building £50,000). Depreciation of the buildings is over 40 years.

In 19x9 the warehouse was sold for £100,000 and another bought (land £30,000 + building £120,000).

Profit before including building depreciation in 19x9 was £34,000. Assuming the new building is depreciated over 40 years also, calculate the depreciation on the warehouses for 19x9 and recommend a way of showing this in the Profit and Loss Account of the company.

Exercise 6

Whizzbang PLC is a manufacturing company with net assets of £6.4 million. Its profits before tax have hovered around £1 million which gives a return on capital employed of 15.6% which is considered good in the industry. A takeover is rumoured for Megabang PLC and as a part of its defence, Whizzbang PLC decide to have their property revalued. The property stands at:

Land at cost £600,000

Buildings at cost £4 million less 5 years of depreciation at £100,000 a year

The valuers give a value of Land £1.4 million

Buildings £6.4 million

Before incorporating the revaluation in the accounts the directors wish to see the effect it would have on profits and capital employed.

Calculate:

a. The surplus revealed by the revaluation. How would it be treated in the Profit and Loss Account and the Balance Sheet?

b. The annual profit if the estimated life of the building remained as before.

c. The capital employed.

d. The return on capital employed.

Note that return on capital employed (as a percentage) is calculated as:

$$\frac{\text{Profits}}{\text{Capital}} \times 100$$

We will discuss it in more detail in a later Unit.

Exercise 7

What will be the depreciation in 19x2 when 700 Kg were extracted? In 19x3, extraction was 800 Kg and at the year end a reappraisal of the mine indicated remaining reserves of 6,000 Kg.

Exercise 8

Contrast the depreciation of a machine costing £8,000 with a life of 4 years and a residual value of £2,500 on the straight line, the reducing balance and the sum of digits method.

Exercise 9

The impact of depreciation on profit

The choice of depreciation policy (straight line, reducing balance etc) does not usually make a large difference to profit. Similarly varying estimates of salvage value and life do not often affect profit greatly. However in some industries, depreciation is of paramount importance.

Consider a company which operates in the shipping industry.

It has one asset — a ship which cost £6 million in year 1.

Expected revenues and costs for the first three years are: (all figures in £'000)

Year	1	2	3
Revenues	1,200	1,600	1,600
Expenses (excluding depreciation)	500	800	800

The ship will last at least 20 years but the directors note that comparable companies write off their ships in anything from 8 to 20 years.

Salvage value is likely to be about £0.5 million at any time except the first few years.

Discuss the attitudes of the directors in reporting profits to the suppliers of capital for the company. You may ignore taxation as tax calculations are unaffected by depreciation policy.

Exercise 10

Meticulos prepares annual accounts for his household. Suggest suitable depreciation policies and estimates for his fixed assets. You should consider which household items may be considered to be fixed assets. They may include double glazing, the construction of a garden pond, a replacement boiler and new lounge curtains.

Assignment 1

This assignment summarises the problem of depreciation and illustrates its effect on profit and the carrying values of assets in the Balance Sheet.

On 1 January 1997, Dodgy PLC acquired a quarry from Boggs Ltd. The precise terms for the acquisition were:

❐ Dodgy acquired the rights to extract the mineral stonite from the quarry until 31 December 2001. Dodgy estimated that all the mineral would be extracted by that date and the total quantity would be 800,000 tons.

- The freehold of the site would remain with Boggs and Dodgy would return the site at the end of 2001.

- Dodgy would landscape the site before quitting it.

- The consideration payable to Boggs was £4 million.

Dodgy estimated that the cost of landscaping and other restoration work in 2001 would be about £1 million.

In addition to the acquisition of the quarry, Dodgy also purchased the following fixed assets in connection with the site:

- Ten lorries, each costing £80,000. They would have to be sold at the end of 2001 and would probably fetch about £5,000 each.

- Extraction and processing equipment costing £900,000. This should last the five years and would then either be scrapped and sold for about £50,000 or transferred to other sites yet to be acquired.

At the same time as the quarry was acquired, Dodgy also acquired the following assets for other uses:

- A 99-year lease on an office building for £120,000. The lease required Dodgy to pay an annual rent of £3,000.

- A ten-year lease on a showroom for £30,000. The annual rent is £4,500.

- A freehold factory for £600,000 + legal and professional charges of £48,000. A valuation suggests that the land element is £260,000. The estimated useful life of the building is 30 years.

- A computer system for £220,000. The estimated life is 4 years with a salvage value of £13,750. The company feel that reducing balance is the appropriate method for this fixed asset as early obsolescence is possible . The formula is $100 (1 - (S/C)^{1/4})$ as a percentage where S = the salvage value and C = the cost. It evaluates to 50%.

- An aluminium ladder for £45. Its estimated life is at least 20 years.

Required:

a. Discuss the appropriate depreciation policies for each of the fixed assets.

b. Calculate the depreciation for 1997 and 1998 under the policies you favour and show the Balance Sheet values for each asset as at the end of 1997 and 1998. Extraction in 1997 was 170,000 tons and in 1998 230,000 tons.

c. Discuss possible accounting treatments for the landscaping costs.

d. In 1999, one of the lorries was found to be surplus to requirements and was sold for £40,000. In 2000, another lorry received uninsured damage and had to be sold for scrap for £2,000. Calculate and explain the effect on the profit for these two years and on the Balance Sheet values.

e. At the end of 2001 it was found possible to transfer the extraction and processing equipment to a newly acquired site. It is estimated that this made it possible to develop the new site without spending £250,000 on new extraction and processing equipment which would otherwise be required. The old equipment should last at least another 4 years. Discuss the effect of this on annual profits.

f. Explain why Dodgy agreed to pay a capital sum for the ten-year lease even though an annual rent is payable.

g. In 1998 Dodgy PLC reported an annual operating profit on all its activities of £16, 248,543. Discuss apparent precision of this figure using the data and ideas in this assignment.

5 Costing and pricing a product

1. Objectives

The objectives of this Unit are to introduce some costing terminology (costing terminology can be rather confusing) and to see how the costs of manufacture of a product can be measured and the information used in fixing a selling price for the product. Finally we shall see how costing information can be used in some simple **decision making** situations and we shall also look at a **breakeven chart**.

SCENARIO 1 — Martin explores costs and how to set selling prices

Martin finds that his business of buying in complete padlock sets and selling them to his customers has worked well in the first two years. However in the third year he has difficulty in finding a sufficiently low priced padlock called the SP. He feels that he could manufacture the product himself from bought in parts and at the same time add some features which would help its saleability. He decides to set up a small assembly plant in a small factory unit near his warehouse.

Before he does so he contacts his accountant who advises him to carefully forecast all his costs. This he does and the following is the result:

Capital expenditure – machinery	£15,000
(life 5 years, salvage value £3,000, straight line depreciation)	
Rent, rates, insurance, repairs etc	£10,000
Other overheads	£1,500
Electricity	£3,000
Foreman/Supervisor	£10,500

The above revenue costs are for one year.

Labour costs – Piecework rates (adjusted for national insurance, holiday and sick pay) 30p a padlock

Material costs 50p a padlock

Martin estimates that the factory will be able to produce about 60,000 padlocks a year.

Quick Answer Questions 5.1

1. What is the annual depreciation on the machine?
2. What will be the *total cost* of manufacturing the 60,000 items?
3. What will be the *cost per unit*?

SCENARIO 2 — Martin learns some costing words

Martin takes the cost list to his accountant and they discuss the costs and how Martin might fix a selling price for the product.

Tasks 1

1. Calculate and produce a formal statement showing the manufacturing cost for each padlock SP, showing the *direct costs,* the *prime cost,* the *manufacturing overheads* and the total manufacturing cost.

2. Calculate a selling price based on the idea that the selling price should be manufacturing cost + 30%. The 30% is necessary to cover *non-manufacturing overheads* as well as giving a profit. Martin thinks that 30% should be enough.

2. Total absorption costing

Total absorption costing involves the terms *direct cost* and *indirect cost.* A direct cost may be *materials* (e.g. wood in a piece of furniture), *labour* (e.g. the wages of a lathe operator turning a table leg) or *expenses* (e.g. a royalty payable on the production of a specific product.) The characteristic of a direct cost is that it can be *traced* to or associated with a particular product. Note that a product can be a good (e.g. a table) or a job (e.g. a particular estate of a housing developer) or a service (e.g. an operation on Fred Smith in a private hospital or the 9.25 train service from Wolverhampton to London).

Traceability is the key. Some costs are actually direct but are treated as indirect as they cannot be traced without excessive expense. An example might be power. The specific electricity used in powering the lathe that is turning the legs of a particular table can in theory be measured but in practice such electricity is treated as an indirect cost.

Indirect costs are all costs including materials (e.g. lubricating oil), labour (e.g. the managing director's salary) and expenses (e.g. rent or rates) that cannot be traced to specific products. Indirect costs are often called *overheads.* They are *shared* by all of the products.

Indirect costs can be further categorised into:

> *Production costs*
>
> *Administrative costs*
>
> *Selling and Distribution costs.*

The *total absorption cost* of a product (which may be a job, a product or a service depending on the nature of the business) is the total of:

> Direct costs + an appropriate share of the indirect costs.

In theory all indirect costs can be included in a total absorption cost but usually only *production costs* are so included.

The total direct costs of a product are termed the *prime cost.* They are conceptually not difficult to determine but complex systems are required in practice to collect and allocate costs. For example the operator of lathe may make many different items in the course of a day and the time spent on each has to be recorded accurately.

The appropriate portion of indirect costs is usually not clear cut and complex methods have been developed to establish these in *multiproduct* firms. We shall explore these later.

In single product firms the appropriate share of production overheads per product is more easily conceived. Suppose a firm make a single identical product — a widget and that they make 20,000 of these a year. The total indirect costs add up to £126,000 a year.

Then the appropriate share of the £126,000 to be allocated to each widget is £126,000/20,000 = £6.30.

If the company is operating in a recession then output may be restricted because sales are reduced. Suppose that the output was only 18,000 but that overheads remained at £126,000 then the appropriate indirect cost of each product is £126,000/18,000 = £7. In practice, firms attempt to maintain unit cost by reducing overheads by for example making staff redundant or cutting back on training.

In practice the cost of a single product is not always measured but instead the cost of a set of products is found. The set of products is called the *batch*. For example in baking, individual loaves are produced in sets or batches and the unit cost measured is the cost of each batch.

Accountants tend to formalise their procedures by producing *formal statements* as for example the Profit and Loss Account or Balance Sheet. In costing procedures formal statements are also produced. An example is the *job cost statement*.

Suppose that the cost of a widget is:

			£
Direct costs	—	materials	3.89
	—	direct labour 2 hours at £4 an hour	8.00
	—	painting done by outworkers	2.10
Indirect costs	—	as paragraph 8 above.	

then the accountant could produce a statement as:

Widget — Job Cost statement

	£
Direct costs:	
Materials	3.89
Labour	8.00
Outwork costs	2.10
Prime cost	13.99
Indirect production cost	6.30
Total production cost	20.29

The total production cost can also be called the *total absorption cost* as all production costs (both direct and indirect) have been or can be assigned to products. As a cost is assigned to a product it is said to be *absorbed* by that product.

The production cost of a product, job or service can be used in several ways:

a) In measuring profit, it is necessary to establish the cost of stocks of finished and part-finished items at the period end. The total absorption cost is taken as the cost for this purpose.

b) The TAC can be used in *pricing*. An enquiry may be received for the production of a made-to-measure widget from a prospective customer. The estimating department calculate the expected production cost and then add a percentage (say 20%) to it to produce a possible selling price to quote to the customer. The percentage added should be enough to cover non-production overheads and to give a profit. In the above case the selling price arrived at will be:

Estimate of selling price re enquiry No 299

	£
Total production cost	20.29
Margin added	4.06
Selling price	24.35

In practice the cost plus approach to selling prices has to be modified to reflect market conditions. But knowing this figure is very useful in pricing decisions.

SCENARIO 3 — Martin explores the relationship between volume and selling prices

Martin is in regular contact with all his customers and he considers that the price asked will affect the number of units of SP that he can sell.

He feels he can draw up a table of probable sales in units against selling price:

Selling price	£1.80	£1.75	£1.69	£1.65	£1.55
Sales in 1,000 units	40	50	60	70	90

Quick Answer Questions 5.2

1. Explain why more than twice as many of the product can be sold if the price is reduced from £1.80 to £1.55.

2. How certain do you think Martin is that the sales will be achieved at the suggested prices?

3. What is the constraint on output mentioned in the first scenario?

4. How do you think that the level of output will affect each of the costs listed in scenario 1?

SCENARIO 4 — Martin makes some decisions

Martin has to decide the level of output and sales which will bring him in the greatest profit. To make the decision on price and hence on output he has gathered together some more data:

❑ He cannot get a smaller factory unit but he can get a larger one. The larger one would enable output to rise to 90,000 units but would cost annually £15,000 in rent rates etc.

❑ more machinery would be needed and as he would lease these the annual leasing charge would be £12,000.

❑ Electricity would cost £900 at either factory + a cost would which would *vary linearly with output* of 3.5p a padlock.

❑ the Foreman/Supervisor would need to have better qualifications at the larger factory and would cost £13,500 a year.

Task 2

Which selling price should Martin choose to maximise his profit?

You might find that a solution to the problem will be found by making a Profit and Loss Account at each level of sales e.g.:

Sales quantity × price	x
less costs:	
Variable costs: quantity × cost per unit	x
Total *Contribution*	x
Fixed costs	x
Net Profit	x

Quick Answer Question 5.3

What considerations, other than the maximisation of profit, might Martin take into account in making his decision?

Task 3

How might the third year cash flow forecast be changed as a result of Martin's decision to go ahead with manufacturing?

3. Cost behaviour, marginal costing and breakeven charts — general

Costs can be categorised in many ways. We have already met the idea of categorising costs into *direct* and *indirect*. Another categorisation is to divide all costs into either *fixed* costs or *variable* costs.

Fixed costs are those costs which remain constant over wide ranges of *activity* for a specified time period.

Variable costs are those which vary in direct proportion to the *level of activity*.

Examples of fixed costs include rent, rates, many salaries, leasing charges for cars etc. The rent of a factory is constant for at least the near future. It will be unaffected by the level of output. However if the output was to rise very significantly, it may be necessary to rent further space and then the rent would of course be greater.

Examples of *variable* costs include direct materials, direct labour (especially if paid on piecework) and probably power. Most variable costs are assumed to change in direct proportion *(linearly)* to output but variations may occur. For example doubling output may double the purchase of materials but quantity discounts may then be available so that the cost increase is slightly less than the increase in output.

Several other terms are also used. These include:

❏ *semi-variable costs*. These are costs which have both a fixed and variable component. Examples are telephone charges where there is a rental charge which is fixed and a charge for calls which is variable. Motor car costs include tax and insurance which are fixed and petrol which is variable with usage.

❏ *stepped fixed costs*. These are fixed costs which are constant over specific levels of output but which may jump when output rises to a critical level. The example of rent has already been mentioned. A further example might be supervision. One supervisor is required for all output up to say 10,000 units. At higher levels she cannot handle the production and an additional supervisor has to be engaged.

You should note the effect of fixed and variable costs on the costs of each unit of output at different levels of output. The following example illustrates this:

Dave is a manufacturer of gold rings. If he doubles his output he will have to buy twice as much gold but each ring will still use 1.5 grams of gold and the cost of gold per ring will be the same. Gold is a variable cost. He can double his output from 5,000 rings a month to 10,000 rings a month without changing his rent of £300 a month. The rent is fixed and unaffected by levels of output but the cost per unit of output changes.

The cost per unit will be $\dfrac{£300}{5,000}$ = 6p at 5,000 units a month but will be only 3p at an output of 10,000 a month.

4. Behaviour of costs

In theory it is easy to divide all costs into fixed and variable but in practice it turns out to be considerably harder. Some difficult items include:

❐ Direct labour. Piecework remuneration is clearly variable but labour paid per hour is less certain. Consider a small factory manufacturing aluminium castings. There are three direct labour employees who are paid a standard sum each for a 38 hour week. Observation shows that at an output of 20,000 castings a week they appear to be fully employed. However in a period of extra demand they succeed in pushing output to 25,000 units a week. They were unable to increase output beyond this level in a standard week and when demand increased to 30,000 units overtime had to be worked. Overtime is paid at time and one half. This means that if standard time is paid at £4 an hour, overtime is paid at £6 an hour.

❐ Telephone. Rentals are clearly a fixed cost. But it is questionable if call costs are related at all to output. If output is doubled do telephone calls double? The only way to discover the relationship between output and telephone call costs for a particular firm is to measure costs against output for several successive periods.

5. Contribution

Cost accountants have coined the word *'contribution'* for an important concept in decision making. The contribution made by a product is its sales price less the variable costs associated with it.

An example

❐ In the gold ring factory. Sales price of each ring is £25 and the variable costs of production are £17 for the gold and £2 piecework labour in pressing, making and polishing. The contribution is thus £25 – £19 = £6. Two things can be said about this. Firstly every time one more ring is made extra income is £25 and extra outgoings are £19. For 'extra' accountants tend to use the word *'marginal'*. Approximately all other costs in the factory stay the same whatever the level of output. Secondly the total of all the individual contributions from each ring made and sold has to be sufficient to cover all the fixed costs and make a profit.

The concept of the extra cost of one more unit of output beyond the edge or margin of production has led to the whole concept of dividing costs into fixed and variable being called *marginal costing*.

It is possible to value stocks at marginal cost instead of total absorption cost. Valuation at total absorption cost is now mandatory for legal reasons for published accounts and consequently marginal costing is not normally used for stock valuation.

Marginal costing is however much used for *decision making*.

6. Breakeven

Suppose I am organising a barn dance. I have booked the hall and the band at a total cost of £162. These are the fixed costs. Each ticket sold will bring in £3 and will involve the purchase of a fish and chip supper for delivery from the local shop at £1.20. The variable costs are thus £1.20 a ticket and the contribution from each ticket is £3 – £1.20 = £1.80. How many tickets do I need to sell to break even, that is to make no profit or loss?

The answer is that I need to sell 90 tickets. This is calculated by dividing the amount required (the fixed costs) by the contribution from each ticket £1.80. If I sell 90 tickets I have 90 × £1.80 =£162 which is just sufficient to cover costs. If I sell 91 tickets I shall make a profit of £1.80 but if I sell 89 tickets I shall make a loss of £1.80.

It is possible to represent this break even concept in a break even chart. This is constructed on graph paper (or these days on a computer screen) as follows:

> Vertical (y) axis — £ sterling
> Horizontal (x) axis — output in units

Example

A garden fork factory

Fixed costs	£50,000 a month
Selling Price	£6 each
Variable costs	£2 each

See diagram on following page.

Note that the fixed cost (FC) line is usually drawn first. The total cost (TC) (fixed + variable costs) line is then drawn from the fixed cost level at the junction with the y axis.

The total sales revenue (SR) is then drawn from the origin.

The point were the total sales revenue crosses the total cost line is the breakeven point. Left of this point total costs are greater than sales revenue and the business is in loss. Right of the line the business is in profit.

Break even can also be calculated from the contribution approach.

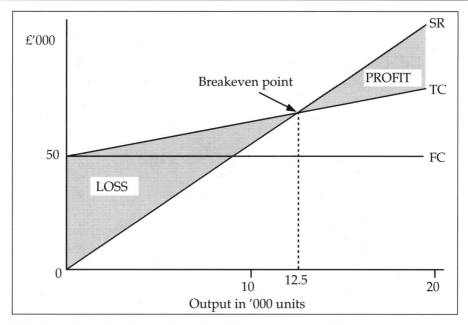

Special points about breakeven charts include:

❒ *relevant range.* There is little point in drawing the output from 0 to infinity. Output is likely to fall between certain levels. For example Jan has a boutique. Sales may in theory be anything but in practice they are exceedingly unlikely to fall below say £300 a week and equally unlikely to rise above £600 a week. The relevant range is thus between £300 to £600.

❒ *margin of safety.* Suppose that Fred's business makes gateaux for restaurants. He finds that his breakeven point is 2,000 gateaux a week. However he finds that his sales in a normal week average 2,500. He sees that his current sales give him a margin of safety of 500 gateaux a week before he would start to make a loss. The margin of safety can also be expressed as a percentage:

$$\text{Margin of safety} = \frac{\text{Margin of safety in unit sales}}{\text{Expected sales in units}} \times 100$$

❒ *output* (the x axis dimension) can be expressed in units as used in the barn dance example where the unit is one ticket sold. Output can also be expressed in sales in £s. In a shop many different articles are sold so unit sales are not usable but if the profit margin is fairly constant when averaged then a chart like that on the following page can be constructed.

As before the y axis is in £ but this time the x axis is turnover per week. The fixed cost (rent, rates, wages etc) is labelled FC. The contribution line is labelled C. The contribution is calculated as 40% of turnover on the assumption that on each £1 of sales, a contribution of 40p is made as the average input cost per article sold is equal to 60p per £1 of sale price.

The break even sales can be seen as £1,600 a week. This is very useful for a shop owner for whom bookkeeping is a chore. He must keep a record of his daily sales and he knows that if his weekly sales exceed £1,600 he is at least not making a loss.

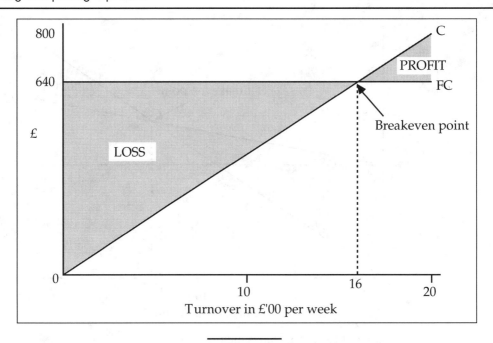

SCENARIO 5 — Martin draws a breakeven chart

Martin decides to go ahead with the original (maximum output 60,000 units) small factory plan and price his product at £1.70. He is not at all certain that 60,000 units can be sold and worries that a loss will be incurred if he fails to sell enough. He organizes a sales conference with the two agents who sell his padlocks and confides his need to sell enough of the SP to avoid making a loss. He is technologically minded and shows them an overhead projector slide illustrating the need to sell sufficient SP.

Task 4

Prepare a breakeven chart based on data as:

Sales price	£1.70
Variable costs	£0.835
Fixed costs	£25,300.00

SCENARIO 6 — Martin considers the behaviour of costs

Martin has categorised his costs as fixed and variable:

Variable:	Materials
	Labour
Fixed:	Rent
	Rates
	Insurance
	Repairs
	Electricity
	Foreman

He is not sure if all of these costs are truly fixed or truly variable even in the relevant range of up to 60,000 padlocks produced.

Task 5

Discuss each cost and decide how it would behave at different levels of output comparing say 40,000 units with 60,000 units.

7. Effects of sales mix on breakeven

Jacob sells two types of garden shed: the standard and the special.

Variable costs are £100 for the standard and £180 for the special. Selling prices are £200 for the standard and £430 for the special. His fixed costs for the year are expected to be £60,000. His budget for 19x2 shows:

	Standard	Special	Total
Sales volume (units)	600	80	
Sales	£120,000	£34,400	£154,400
Variable costs	£60,000	£14,400	£74,400
Contribution	£60,000	£20,000	£80,000
Fixed costs			£60,000
Net Profit			£20,000

Is it possible to calculate a breakeven volume? If we assume that the sales mix remains constant then we can using the following reasoning:

At breakeven contribution = fixed costs = £60,000.

Turnover/Contribution ratio is $\dfrac{£154,400}{£80,000} = 1.93$

At breakeven, sales in £'s will therefore be $1.93 \times 60,000 = £115,800$.

If sales mix remains the same then breakeven sales will be: Standard £90,000 and Special £25,800.

In quantity terms that is 450 standard and 60 special.

Suppose however that sales of standard are likely only to be 360 units due to competition but the sales of specials are likely to soar as up market sheds have become more in demand. What would be the breakeven sales of Specials in these circumstances?

This chain of reasoning may be useful:

Breakeven total contribution must be £60,000

Contribution from standards is $360 * £100 = £36,000$

Therefore contribution from Specials must be £24,000.

At £250 contribution per special the sales must be 96 units or £41,280 in money terms.

Cost categorisations

1. Direct — traceable to individual products

   Indirect — overheads — shared by products

   Use: In Total Absorption Costing to find:

   - ❏ cost for fixing selling prices
   - ❏ valuing stock for Accounts purposes

2. Fixed — remains the same at different activity levels

   Variable — changes as activity changes

   Use: In marginal costing in making decisions e.g:

   - ❏ making or buying in a product
   - ❏ output levels
   - ❏ choosing between production methods
   - ❏ what to make when resources are limited

   There are other categorisations e.g:

   a. Materials: Labour: Services

   b. Manufacturing: Administration: Selling and Distribution

   c. Controllable: Non-controllable

Use: we shall see uses for these in later Units.

---

8. Summary of Unit 5

- ❏ A product cost under total absorption costing principles is the sum of direct costs and an appropriate proportion of indirect costs.
- ❏ Direct costs form the prime cost of a product.
- ❏ The overheads to be included will be production costs only, when a cost is to be found for stock valuation purposes.
- ❏ For other purposes, including selling price determination, administration and selling and distribution costs may be added.
- ❏ Fixed costs remain the same (within certain limits of output and time) whatever the output.
- ❏ Variable costs tend to vary with the level of activity.
- ❏ Fixed costs per unit vary with output.
- ❏ Variable costs per unit tend to stay the same at all levels of output.
- ❏ Semi-variable costs contain both fixed and variable elements.
- ❏ Stepped fixed costs increase/decrease by discrete amounts at critical levels of output.
- ❏ The behaviour of costs in relation to changes in output is not easy to predict.
- ❏ Contribution is the sales price less the variable costs. It can be expressed as a total, per unit or as a percentage of sales.

❐ Marginal costing is that system of costing where only variable costs are related to products.

❐ Marginal costing can be used to value stocks but total absorption costs are preferred for this purpose.

❐ Marginal costing is often used for decision making purposes.

❐ The breakeven point is the level of activity where there is no profit or loss.

❐ A breakeven chart is a chart which indicates approximate profit or loss at different levels of sales volume or output within a relevant range.

❐ The margin of safety indicates the extent to which the forecast turnover exceeds breakeven.

❐ Relating breakeven point to some easily measurable statistic like weekly sales is of great use to management.

Exercise 1

Codd makes filing cabinets. Divide the following costs, firstly, into materials, labour and services and secondly into direct costs and indirect costs:

Steel sheet	Maintenance wages
Paint	Window cleaning
Letterheads	Depreciation of a fax machine
Drawer handles	Van spares
Advertising	Cost accountant's salary
Bank Interest	Cleaning contract
Debt collection fees	Sheet metal workers' wages
Packers' wages	Heating Oil

Finally attempt to divide the overheads between production and non-production.

Exercise 2

Haddock Brothers have an architectural practice. Divide the following costs, firstly into materials, labour and services and then into direct costs and indirect costs:

Drawing paper	Technicians' salaries
Advertising	Accountants' fee
Textbooks	Travelling expenses
Repairs to partner's car	Telephone
Subcontract work	Computer software
Repairs to office building	Professional Indemnity Insurance
Pension scheme re employees	Typist's salary
Donation to Client's favourite charity	

Exercise *3

Munday has a business making a single product – a widget. His costs are forecast for 19x3 as:

	£
Materials	134,000
Direct labour	160,000
Production Overheads	100,000
Administration Costs	60,000
Selling and distribution	90,000

Output from these costs is forecast at 20,000 units.

Required:

a. What is the forecast total prime cost?

b. What is the prime cost per unit?

c. What are the total manufacturing costs?

d. What are the manufacturing cost per unit?

e. If selling price is £30 what should be the profit?

Exercise 4

Same figures as in question 3 but Munday makes a range of widgets. He recognises that the cost of production is prime cost + manufacturing overheads.

Required:

a. Munday reckons that the overheads to be added for any given widget will be a percentage on prime cost. Calculate a suitable percentage and calculate a manufacturing cost for a widget whose prime costs are materials £30 and Direct Labour £15.

b. Munday requires a rule of thumb approach to pricing his widgets and to that end would like to have a price which was calculated as:

> Prime cost
> +   manufacturing overheads
> =   *manufacturing cost*
> +   a percentage on manufacturing cost to give him a profit equal to 10% of total cost.

Give him a formula to find the selling price for his products.

Note that selling prices arrived at in this way are usually regarded as a first guess. The company then have to assess the customer to determine if more or less can be obtained from the customer.

c. Same facts as in b. but Munday wants his profit to be 10% of his selling price. Now find a formula.

Exercise 5

Tuesday has a has a business making bespoke chemicals for the cleaning industry. Her costs for 19x3 are forecast as:

	£
Materials	230,000
Direct labour	345,000
Production Overheads	260,000
Other Overheads	180,000

She prices her chemicals on the basis of:

Prime cost
+ a percentage for production overheads
= *production cost*
+ a percentage on production cost for other overheads
= *total absorption cost*
+ 20% for profit
= *selling price*

Required:

a. Calculate the selling price for chemical XY which cost: materials £80 and Direct labour £45.

b. She meets a competitor at a conference who tells her that he prices his products on the basis of material cost + various percentages for the other costs. Calculate the selling price of XY on this alternative basis.

c. Explore the effect of Tuesday determining her selling prices differently from her competitors in terms of getting sales and making profits.

Cost behaviour, marginal costing and breakeven charts

Exercise 6

Describe the behaviour of the following costs at different levels of output in a foundry which melts iron in an electric furnace and makes a variety of iron castings to meet customers' individual wants:

Iron	Telephone
Sales representatives	Foundry workers (piecework)
Sand	Rates
Product Liability Insurance	Tools
Protective clothing	Stationery
Electricity	Refractory materials
Building repairs	Dust extraction equipment
First Aid Materials	Wooden Pallets
Wages Office Salaries	Wood patterns

State any assumptions you make.

Exercise 7

The Cut Railway Co PLC run a steam railway both as a service to the local population and as a tourist attraction. All staff are paid professionals.

a. Describe the behaviour of the following costs at different levels of output:

Coal	Depreciation of rolling stock
Track repair materials	Wages of Drivers
Wages of booking office staff	Advertising
Electricity	Public Liability Insurance
Weedkiller	Paint
Sponsorship of local arts festival	Oil and Grease
Interest on Loans	Bank Charges

State any assumptions you make.

b. What is meant by output in this case? How might output be measured?

c. How might the knowledge of cost behaviour assist management in this case? What decisions might be assisted?

Exercise *8

Willa has discovered that the cost of raw cloth in her textile factory is a function of quantity bought which in turn is very closely correlated with usage as little stock is carried. Usage is measured in square metres. She finds that the average cost per square metre is not linear with usage but is given by the formula:

Cost per metre = $(0.6 * U - (0.01 * U)^2)/U$

where U = number of batch purchases. Each batch is 1,000 square metres.

This is over the relevant range of 400 to 1,200 batches.

She also discovers that the cost of preparing the cloth for processing is 10p a square metre as all the cost is outwork which is paid on a piecework basis.

The annual cost of buying and storing the cloth is £200,000 which consists of rent, rates, heating etc and the salaries of staff.

Required:

a. Calculate the total cost and the cost per square metre of

   i. 600,000 square metres and

   ii. 1,200,000 square metres.

b. Comment on these figures.

Exercise 9

Edwige operates an introductions bureau. Her modus operandi is to invite enquirers to a dinner party at a hotel.

Her costs are estimated to be:

Hire of dining suite	£200
Flowers, print costs etc	£50
Meal and wines	£20 a head

Maximum numbers are 30 per party and minimum 20.

Required:

a. Calculate total cost of a party and cost per person if
   i. 20 people attend and
   ii. if 30 people attend.

b. How might Edwige use these figures in her decision making?

Exercise 10

Calculate the contribution in the following cases:

a. Joe's wine bar: cost of a case of six bottles of Chateau Bilston £12.40, selling price per bottle £5.80.

b. Krishan's restaurant: Materials for set meal A £2.10, selling price £8.00

c. Ram's sari factory: cost of sari type B, materials £5.60, direct piecework labour £4, selling price £15.20.

d. Lewis's curtain contracting: cost of Job C Materials £194, Direct Labour 16 hours at £7 an hour, sales commission 10% on selling price, selling price £400.

Exercise *11

The following sets of figures relate to a a number of businesses:

Fred's snooker club:

Fixed Overheads	£26,000 a year
Selling Price	60p per person per game

Based on previous years, Fred expects a minimum of 400 persons a week with each playing an average of 2 games and a maximum of 600 persons a week. Most likely average is 500 persons per week.

Ken's lollipop factory:

Fixed Overheads	£40,000
Variable overheads	£30 a batch
Selling price	£50 a batch
Maximum output	4,000 batches
Sales budget	2,500 batches

Lila's delicatessen:

Fixed Overheads £18,000 but she will have to take on an additional assistant at a cost of £6,000 a year if turnover exceeds £38,000

Gross Profit to sales ratio averages 60%

Turnover last year was £39,000 but she expects an increase of 10%.

Rufus's one man driving school:

Fixed Overheads	£6,000
Variable overheads	£1.50 a lesson
Selling Price	£9.00 a lesson

Rufus has been offered a job as an instructor for a large firm at a salary of £10,000 a year.

He reckons to do 2,200 lessons a year.

Todd's wholesale stationery business:

Fixed overheads increase at various turnover points because of the need for extra accommodation and staff. Probable figures are:

Turnover (in £'000)	Up to 600	601 to 1,000	1,001 to 1,400	1,400 to 1,600
Fixed Costs (£'000)	180	200	320	450

Maximum sales are £1,600,000 and sales are exceedingly unlikely to fall below £400,000.

Gross profit to turnover rate is 30%.

Required:

a. In each case calculate where possible:

- ❐ breakeven point(s)
- ❐ relevant range
- ❐ margin of safety
- ❐ some easily measurable statistic to assist the proprietor in knowing how the business is faring.

b. Draw a breakeven chart for each business.

Exercise 12

Liz intends to start a gift shop. She estimates her annual fixed costs at £10,000. Her gross profit margin is 40%. Calculate her break even sales and draw a break even chart.

Exercise 13

Hugh makes widgets. His annual fixed costs are £50,000 up to 10,000 units and £70,000 up to a maximum of 15,000 units. The sale price of a widget is £12.50 and the variable costs are £6.50. Expected sales are 11,000 units but he guesses that they will fall between 8,000 and 14,000 units.

Calculate and show on a breakeven chart the breakeven points, the relevant range and the margin of safety.

Exercise 14

Lily manufacture two types of bicycle – the de Luxe and the super. Costs and selling prices are:

	Fixed Costs	£70,000	

	de Luxe	Super
Variable costs (per unit)	£123	£185
Selling Price (per unit)	£220	£400

The company has budgeted to sell 500 de Luxe in 19x2 and 200 super.

Required:

a. Prepare a budgeted Profit and Loss Account in marginal costing form.

b. Assuming that sales mix remains the same, calculate the breakeven point and the margin of safety.

c. Draw a breakeven chart of (b).

d. Sales of Super may prove difficult and the sales director fears that only 100 will be sold. How many de Luxe need to be sold to achieve the same profit as that forecast in the budget?

Case Study / Assignment 1

Tangerine Ltd is a wholesaler and importer of a wide range of computer hardware, peripherals and software packages. The Chief Executive has produced a breakeven chart and intends to present it to the sales force at a sales conference.

a. Design a suitable chart and prepare a speech for the Chief explaining the chart and its significance.

b. Summarise the assumptions underlying the chart.

c. Two of the company's best sellers are the Quick X Printer which sells for £150 and the Rapid Y Printer which sells for £200. These prices enable the company to just undercut rival products from other suppliers. The company buys these printers in Taiwan for £100 and £150 respectively.

The company pays a commission to its salespersons of 10% of the sales price. Discuss whether the company might do better to have commission rates which vary from product to product.

Case Study / Assignment 2

Sheila manufactures a single product: a wadget. Her budget for 19x8 showed:

❐ Selling price £120 per unit. Turnover 2,400 units. Variable costs per unit: Labour (piecework) £20, Materials £30. Sales commission 10%.

❐ Manufacturing overheads £55,000. Administrative overheads £22,000. Marketing and Distribution costs £42,000.

Requirement (a):

i. Prepare a budgeted Profit and Loss Account for 19x8.

ii. Prepare a break-even chart and calculate the break-even point.

iii. Sheila is in an interfirm comparison scheme whereby statistics about member firms are collated by the organisers of the scheme. All she is told is the averages which are:

	%
Turnover	100
Direct costs	36
Manufacturing overheads	20
Administrative overheads	5
Marketing and distribution	14
Selling costs	6
Profit	19

Comment on her budget in comparison with these figures. What actions might she take as a result of her review of the figures.

Sheila feels that an increase in turnover of 40% might be achieved if she reduced her prices by 10%.

Requirement (b):

i. Recast the budgeted Profit and Loss Account assuming no change in the amounts of overheads.

ii. She feels that in practice both the direct and indirect costs would change with a 40% increase in turnover. Select some examples from both direct and indirect costs and consider how they might change with turnover.

Sheila is considering adding another product: a super wadget. The costs associated with such a product are:

Development and launch costs	£50,000
Direct costs per unit: materials	£40
Direct costs per unit: labour	£35
Manufacturing overheads (per year)	£32,000
Administrative costs (per year)	£6,000
Marketing and distribution costs (per year)	£18,000
Sales Commission	10%

These overheads are in addition to those budgeted for in the first part of the assignment and would occur only if she went ahead with the super wadget.

She is unsure of the price to be charged to customers but has forecast the relationship between sales and price as:

Unit price £	200	220	240	260	280
Sales in Units	800	700	600	550	450

Requirement (c):

i. Prepare a budgeted Profit and Loss Account at each level of price/turnover.

ii. Recommend the price she should charge and comment on the relative risks attached to each possible price.

6 Budgeting

1. Objectives

This Unit introduces the need to **budget**.

SCENARIO 1 — Martin contemplates alternative strategies

Towards the end of his third year, Martin is reviewing his progress so far and considering what to do in the fourth year. He has achieved a turnover of £600,000 in his wholesaling business and £100,000 in the SP product which he is making in his small factory unit. He is confident that the company is now well established in the market and he can double his wholesale turnover and more than double his sales of the SP product in the coming year. There are also several other products that he could manufacture profitably. He decides that he must contemplate several alternative strategies:

a. Stay in his present premises.

b. Retain the wholesaling in his original unit and move the manufacturing to larger premises.

c. Retain the original manufacturing unit and move the wholesaling into larger premises.

d. Move both activities into separate larger premises.

e. Move into larger premises and operate both activities under one roof.

If he decides to move either or both premises he can either buy or rent.

Quick Answer Questions 6.1

1. From your reading so far, what essential actions must Martin take in order to make a choice?

2. What might be the consequences of a wrong choice? You should consider each choice?

SCENARIO 2 — Martin starts to budget

Martin decides to keep the two activities apart but to move both activities into separate new premises which will be large enough to accommodate expansion for several years. He decides to rent both sets of premises. He sets about producing a set of budgets for each activity. We will concentrate on the manufacture of the SP padlock. He has decided to concentrate his own time on the wholesaling and appoint a manager to run the manufacturing. Information he has collected includes: (all data are for one year)

The SP Padlock:

Sales 150,000 units at £2.00 each

Material costs 60p a unit

Labour cost 40p a unit

Manager's salary £20,000

Rent £12,000

Rates £7,000

Other factory overheads £40,000

Capital expenditure £60,000 (he will buy the equipment).

Quick Answer Questions 6.2

1. Which of these costs are fixed and which are variable?
2. What is the prime cost of one SP padlock?

SCENARIO 3 — Martin gets into the detail of budgeting

He will carry no stock of finished goods as finished goods will be shipped on completion to the customers.

The equipment will last about five years and have a salvage value of about £5,000.

Ignore interest.

Tasks 1

1. What is the *principal budget* factor here?
2. Prepare a budgeted Profit and Loss Account for the SP Padlock for the fourth year for the SP padlock.
3. Prepare a budgeted balance sheet as at the end of the year. You can assume:

   Opening capital is £28,500

   Creditors will be equal to two month's purchases

   Debtors will be equal to two month's sales

   The balance sheet will be balanced by including a figure for bank balance.
4. The newly appointed manager has been asked to prepare *subsidiary budgets*. List the budgets that will be required and explain the contents of each. What action will be necessary as a result of each budget.
5. Explain how the budgets will be useful to Martin under the headings:

   Coordination, Communication, Motivation, Control, Evaluation and Delegation.

---

2. Introduction

It is possible to manage a business by continuing as before and responding to events as they occur. Many small and some large businesses behave in this way and survive. However even in these businesses the management have some implicit plans which might be simple such as 'to increase sales' or 'reduce costs' or to explore the possibilities of additional products.

Most businesses prefer to make their plans explicit and may do so in qualitative or in quantitative terms. One of the best ways of approaching the *future* is by *budgeting*. Budgeting is making a *plan* expressed in *money* terms.

The objectives of budgeting are multifold and seven are usually identified specifically.

These are:

a) *Planning*. A budget is a plan expressed in money terms. The budget is normally for one year ahead and should take into account:

 ❐ any longer term planning processes

 ❐ expectations of economic conditions and events in the ensuing year

 ❐ anticipate problems and difficulties as they may arise.

b) *Coordination*. A budget in a firm is made up of *subsidiary* or *sectional* budgets. It is important that each budget coordinates with all the others. For example the sales budget may be for a specific quantity of specified products. Production must be budgeted to meet the needs of sales. Similarly, capital expenditure may need to be planned to enable the planned output to be achieved and new labour may need to be hired and trained (or labour may need to be shed). All this has implications for cash levels and borrowing may need to be planned. Overall the budget must indicate a satisfactory level of profit or must be reprogrammed until it does. All this coordination is not usually achieved at the first draft and much negotiation amongst managers is often required before the budget can be adopted. A side effect of all this is that a manager becomes more aware of the activities of other departments and how his/her department fits into the whole.

c) *Communication*. Once the master and subsidiary budgets have been adopted they need to be communicated to all appropriate personnel in the company. The management have expectations in the budget and the budget also implies the means to fulfil them. By communicating the budget to relevant personnel the management are able to inform staff of the management's hopes and aspirations. In addition the formation of the budget requires that much learning of company objectives and inter-relationships is acquired by staff.

d) *Motivation*. The budget can be seen as a device for motivating staff to fulfil the plans of the management expressed in the budget. There is a large literature on the *behavioural* effects of budgeting and especially on its dysfunctional effects.

e) *Control*. Control means finding means of ensuring that the plans are *achieved*. Essentially this means that where the outcome of activities varies from the budget these variations can be identified and management can correct them. A technique which has grown up with budgeting is *management by exception*. The great mass of activities that go according to plan require little management attention and all their concern can be put into matters that diverge from the budget.

f) *Evaluation*. Budgets form an objective standard of attainment that actual performance can be measured against and managers are motivated to achieve budgets. Senior management can evaluate the performance of line managers and other staff by reference to the budgets.

g) *Delegation*. Budgets can be broken down into sub-budgets by function (eg capital expenditure, personnel, purchasing, sales, manufacturing, marketing, accounting etc) and each of these can be further subdivided if required (eg sales into regions, manufacturing into departments or sections). Each sub-budget can be given to a specific person who is then *responsible* for that budget. Once the budget has been agreed and approved then each budget holder has a plan to work with and higher management can leave her to it. Adherence to the budget will be monitored and only *variances* need to take up management time. The alternative is either for higher management to supervise the line management continuously or to allow the line managers to act independently with the risk of uncoordinated activity and actions which run counter to management policy.

The above are usually seen as the functions of budgeting. Successful budgeting is realised when the budget is the result of a process of *consultation* and *negotiation* when all relevant personnel are involved and can bring their special knowledge to the issue. Budgets imposed from above are rarely effective as dysfunctional behaviour often follows.

Budgeting can be effective in all types of enterprise including non-profit ones. It is important to realise all the objectives and not the simple approach of many line managers who may see the budget simply in terms of *authorisation*. Ellen, the head of department X, has a budget of £y which is agreed under a series of expenditure headings. Her attitude might be that she has to spend all the amount allowed by the budget or she will lose the benefit of any unspent sums both this year and probably next year as well, as next years budget will be less to follow reduced actual expenditure this year. This is clearly against the best interests of the organisation as a whole which could benefit from more economical spending. Many organisations now apply *virement* which means that sums unspent under one heading can be transferred to overspent headings.

3. Preparation of a budget

This is normally a process requiring much expenditure of time on the spreadsheet and acres of printout but we will try to simplify the process to give you the bones of the process.

Gubbins Marketing Ltd have a Balance Sheet at 31 December 19x2 as

Balance Sheet as 31 December 19x2

(all figures in £'000)

Fixed assets		
Cost		340
Less Depreciation		162
		178
Current assets		
Stocks	90	
Debtors	87	
	177	
Creditors — amounts falling due within one year		
Creditors	67	
Overdraft	44	
	111	

Net current assets	66
Total assets less current liabilities	244
Capital and reserves	
Share capital (£1 shares)	100
Profit and Loss Account	144
	244

The first action is to determine the *principal budget factor* which is the item which restricts activity. We shall assume that it is sales (it usually is).

The second action is to determine the sales budget — itemised by product with quantity and price. We will make this £600,000 in total.

The third phase is to identify any management policies which need to be incorporated in the budgets. These are:

❐ stock must be held down to no more than £95,000

❐ creditors must be paid on average no more than two months after the goods are invoiced.

The fourth phase is to construct the subsidiary budgets:

a) The purchases budget. On average the mark up on cost is 50%. Therefore given the sales, cost of goods sold will be £400,000. As opening stock is £90,000 and closing stock can be no more than £95,000, purchases will be £405,000. I assume that stocks in the past have been a lower portion of cost of sales than that planned in 19x2.

b) The labour budget. The expected throughput requires a staff of 8 and at an average cost of £8,500 each, labour will cost £68,000. Currently only 6 are employed so two more will have to be recruited.

c) The Overheads budget. Knowing the expected levels of rent, rates etc a total budget of £58,000 is envisaged.

d) The capital expenditure budget. The expected level of sales implies additional handling equipment and an additional van so that £40,000 needs to be spent.

The fifth phase is the construction of the master budget. This will be in the form of a trading and Profit and Loss Account:

Budgeted trading and Profit and Loss Account for 19x3

Sales		600
Cost of sales		400
Gross profit		200
Labour	68	
Overheads	58	
Depreciation	38	164
Net profit		36

I have assumed a depreciation rate of 10% straight line.

And a Balance Sheet:

Budgeted Balance Sheet as 31 December 19x3

(all figures in £'000)

Fixed assets

Cost		380
Less depreciation		200
		180

Current assets

Stocks	95	
Debtors	150	
	245	

Creditors — amounts falling due within one year

Creditors	67	
Overdraft	78	
	145	

Net current assets	100
Total assets less current liabilities	280

Capital and reserves

Share capital (£1 shares)	100
Profit and Loss Account	180
	280

I have assumed that debtors will be equal to three month's sales. All the other figures but one can be calculated from the figures so that the only figure to put in is the overdraft. In practice this would be calculated on a month by month basis. However it can be seen that an increase has to be negotiated with the bank manager.

4. Budget review

The above budget setting exercise is simple and is for a trading company of a small size. Larger companies who manufacture and have large numbers of products, complex production systems and numerous departments find the budgeting process very expensive. However the principles are the same in all budget setting routines. At the end of the process, a review can be made and questions asked such as:

Is the profit satisfactory?

Is return on capital employed sufficient?

Is cash flow acceptable?

If the answer to any of these questions is no, then it is possible to review the budget in detail and make changes as desired. In effect the budget is a proposed plan. Alternative plans are possible. However the proposed budget is coordinated and any alternative would require the detailed working that would make it also a coordinated plan.

SCENARIO 4 — Martin budgets in a club

Martin is a member of the committee of his local social club. At a meeting, the committee are discussing the coming year's activities. The club is proposing to build an extension, generally overhaul the premises, introduce larger bar facilities with longer hours and a paid part time barman, organise a range of social/fund raising activities, recruit new members and induce current members to be more active. The committee agree to be sub-divided into a number of sub-committees to arrange these matters. Martin feels that the club is an ideal subject for some budgeting.

Tasks 2

1. Suggest the titles of the various sub-committees the committee should set up.
2. Outline the way budgeting may assist the club in meeting its objectives.
3. What master and subsidiary budgets should be prepared?
4. How will the budgeting process be helpful under the headings: Co-ordination, Communication, Motivation, Control, Evaluation and Delegation.

5. Budgeting and not-for-profit enterprise

Budgeting is almost essential for commercial and industrial businesses today. It is also practised by Central Government (the word Budget comes from the Old French for leather pouch or wallet and the Chancellor of the Exchequer carries the Government Budget to parliament in one) and local government. Increasingly all enterprises — profit seeking and not-for-profit — prepare budgets. Once each section of the enterprise has prepared a budget then each budget can be reviewed and consistency with each other obtained by negotiation or dictat until the final budget is feasible and within resources.

6. Zero-based budgeting

Much budgeting works on the basis of taking last year's expenditure and adding on a few percent for inflation and making any necessary changes for changed circumstances. This applies very much in local authorities and public bodies such as the Health Service but it also applies in the private sector. In a manufacturing firm, the running of a department may involve expenditure on staff, energy, maintenance, dust extraction etc. Here the manager might simply start with last year's expenditure and add on 6% for pay rises and other inflation caused extra costs and then add £X,000 for an additional person to assist in monitoring pollution control within the department.

The point is that last year's expenditure is considered satisfactory and argument and negotiation centres around changes.

An alternative is to adopt zero based budgeting. This approach starts with a base of nil expenditure, a clean slate. It requires the manager to justify everything he puts in his budget. This has the effect of enlarging and prolonging the budgetary process as arguments and negotiations apply to the whole budget and not just to changes.

Many organisations apply normal budgetary processes but select particular activities or departments for zero based budgeting.

An example of zero based budgeting in a local authority may be in a day centre for the elderly and handicapped. The manager might be asked in a normal budgeting process to start with last year and add so much for inflation and proposed changes. In a zero based budget, he might be asked to produce a yearly package:

- ❑ setting out the objectives and justification for the centre
- ❑ setting out and justifying the proposed means of meeting the objectives
- ❑ costing the means.

Alternative packages with different approaches and costs may also be produced.

It is then up to the local authority to approve, select or reject or negotiate on the package.

7. Flexible budgeting

Most budgets are produced on an assumption of a particular level of output or activity. For example, the lathe turning department of Rake's metal parts factory has a budget for period 21 as:

Output	3,000 standard hours
	£
Direct Labour	3,600
Supervision	1,100
Consumable stores	1,000
Energy	600
	6,300

The department processes a wide range of products and output is expressed in terms of standard output from an hour of lathe turning.

In practice the output is not likely to be exactly 3,000 standard hours for any number of reasons — work availability, machine breakdown, labour sicknesses etc. For *control* purposes it is important to know the budgeted costs at any level of output within the relevant range. The actual costs can then be compared with the budgeted costs at that level.

To do this a flexible budget is required. Suppose that costs would vary as: (x is the level of output in standard hours)

Direct Labour $£2,600 + \dfrac{x}{3}$

Supervision $£1,100 + \dfrac{x - 3,000}{10}$ [if x is greater than 3,500]

Consumable stores $\dfrac{x}{3}$

Energy $£100 + \dfrac{x}{6}$

Then it is possible to calculate the budgeted expenditure at this level.

At an output of 3,600 hours expenditure is budgeted at:

		£
	Direct Labour	3,800
	Supervision	1,160
	Consumable stores	1,200
	Energy	700
		6,860

8. The actual results for periods 21 and 22 were:

Period	21	22
Standard hours	2,800	3,800
Direct Labour	£3,600	£3,780
Supervision	£1,150	£1,150
Consumable stores	£947	£1,240
Energy	£602	£786

Flex the budget, contrast it with *actual* and comment on the *variances* found, suggesting possible reasons for them.

8. Budgeting and behaviour

Much has been written about the behavioural effects of the budgeting process and this introductory book is not the place for an exhaustive treatise on the subject. However it is possible to summarise some of the benefits, which are largely behavioural, of involving managers and other staff in the budget setting process. These include:

a. Managers and staff have detailed knowledge which the budget makers ought to draw on. Solutions to problems are often produced by management or consultants without reference to the immense body of knowledge held by people on the ground. It is to the organisation's benefit to draw on the ideas and creativity of the employees.

b. Budgets produced in collaboration with staff are usually felt to be owned by the staff who then feel responsible for them. This ensures a greater level of commitment to the budgets by the staff.

c. In most firms there is a tendency to a lack of goal congruence by staff. Budgets drawn up in collaboration with staff enable the different goals to be verbalised and common goals agreed.

d. The exercise of collaborative budgeting makes staff more aware of corporate aims and also of the difficulties and problems of colleagues in other departments of the organisation. This tends to build corporate morale and identification with the employer.

e. Conflicts of interest between departments (eg on allocation of resources or responsibilies) are brought into the open and resolved by agreement.

f. A thorough understanding of the budget is gained by more members of staff and this enables greater delegation.

g. Staff are much more motivated.

h. Corrective behaviour required as a response to variances is easier to orchestrate when the staff own the budget.

i. Staff are more willing to be judged, evaluated or assessed in relation to a budget which they had a hand in producing.

k. Necessary changes to plans required by changed circumstances are recognised by staff more quickly when they fully understand the budget.

l. When staff more fully recognise the purposes of budgeting they are less likely to engage in practices like building in budgetary slack and overspending just because a budget allows it.

Budgeting

Negotiation   Participation

Master Budget   Communication

Subsidiary Budgets   Motivation

Zero-based   **Budgets**   Behavioural aspects

Coordination   Control

Anticipation   Evaluation

Delegation   Flexible Behaviour

Rigidity

---

9. Summary of Unit 6

☐ Most enterprises tend to plan the future rather than simply let it happen.

☐ The ideal way of planning the future of any enterprise is budgeting. A budget is defined as a plan expressed in money.

☐ The objectives of budgeting can be summed up in the words: planning, co-ordination, communication, motivation, control, evaluation, and delegation.

☐ It is highly desirable that a budget should be constructed by negotiation and agreed by consensus after consultation.

☐ The master budget is a set of financial statements including budgeted Profit and Loss Account, Balance Sheet and cash flow forecast. Subsidiary budgets need to be established for areas like sales, purchases, labour, overheads, stocks, capital expenditure, training and recruitment and cash flows.

☐ Budgeting is an iterative process and after establishing budgets, they should be reviewed and if necessary modified, reviewed again and so on until the optimum plan is achieved.

☐ Feedback by measuring actual performance and variances therefrom is essential.

❑ Budgeting is now practised by enterprises of all types — manufacturing, trading, service, not-for-profit and many private individuals.

❑ Zero based budgeting requires budgeting with the assumption of a clean sheet and a new start.

❑ Flexible budgeting produces budgets which adjust for different levels of output.

❑ Budgeting has behavioural effects which are often not understood.

Exercise 1

Stubby Air Systems PLC are manufacturers of highly sophisticated components for the aircraft industry and they are currently preparing their 19x4 budget. They have about 1,000 employees in total. The following facts have been identified as being relevant to the budget:

❑ demand will be 10% less than in 19x3 due to a recession in the aircraft industry

❑ updating of plant and manufacturing systems must continue during the year

❑ systems of 'just in time' supply of parts will be extended in 19x4

❑ elimination of the last remaining old Spanish customs among the skilled workers is a top priority

❑ constant change in recent years has caused a loss of morale among some managers and other staff, particularly as hierarchical systems have become more democratic. Good morale is seen as essential to the company

❑ the company faces a difficult year and a fear of takeover, if results are poor, worries top management

❑ the work force needs to be reduced to about 800.

Required:

a. Discuss the relevance of each of these thoughts to the budgeting process and how the budgeting process can be useful in achieving the aims of the company.

b. Consider what budgets and sub-budgets might be required and who might be responsible for their production.

Exercise *2

Ape Ltd supply copying machines to businesses. All machines are subject to a service agreement and the servicing of the copiers is the responsibility of Margaret. The sales budget has specified the expectations of the company in terms of the number of copier service agreements extant in 19x3. Margaret has constructed a budget of the costs to maintain the level of service required:

	£
Salaries and National insurance of 8 staff to provide:	104,000
1,800 hours each of service work	
100 hours of sick leave	
100 hours of training	
Clerk to control activities	8,500

		£
Margaret's own salary to provide:		18,000
	1,000 hours of service work	
	900 hours of management	
	100 hours of training	
Courses and other training costs		5,000
Vehicle running costs		18,000
Changing 3 vans (now 4 years old)		24,000
Stationery		3,000
Tools etc		2,000

The budget officer (who is the company chief accountant) has told her that the company must be leaner and fitter to make a profit in 19x3 and that she must take 10% of her total budget claim.

Required:

a. Discuss how she might prune her budget.

b. Discuss the firm's approach to budgeting revealed in this scenario.

Exercise 3

Here are some data re expectations of VG Ltd for January 19x6:

	Product	Quantity	Price
Sales:			
	Size 1	5,000	£230
	Size 2	3,000	£370

Materials used in producing one unit of these products are:

	Metal	Component A	Packaging
Size 1	10 Kg	4	1 set
Size 2	14 Kg	6	2 sets

Metal is £3 a Kg, Component A can be bought for £10 in January, and one set of packaging cost £15.

Stocks at 1 January are:

Size 1	Size 2	Metal	Comp A	Packaging Sets
2,000	400	2,000 Kg	18,000	2,500

Stocks projected for 31 January:

1,500	1,200	6,000 Kg	10,000	2,000

Required:

a. Prepare: a sales budget in quantity and value

   a production budget showing quantities to be produced

   a material usage budget

   a purchases budget in quantity and value.

b. State what is the principal budget factor here.

c. Explain the wide fluctuations in stock levels and expectations.

d. Rework the problem on the basis that 10% of all production will be rejected and that all the metal in the rejected production will be scrapped along with 50% of component As. No packaging sets are used on rejected production.

Exercise 4

The hands on staff of Chicory Ltd comprise:

12 skilled staff

8 semi – skilled staff

8 unskilled staff

In period 8 a skilled person can work 480 hours, a semi-skilled person 440 hours and an unskilled person 500 hours. These hours can be boosted by 10% by working overtime at time and one half.

Production requirements for period 8 are budgeted at 1,600 units. Each unit will require:

5 skilled man hours

3 semi-skilled man hours

2 unskilled man hours

Required:

a. Calculate the availability of labour in the period.

b. Calculate the demand for labour in the period.

c. Suggest and discuss various solutions to the mismatch.

d. Discuss how the mismatch might have come about.

Exercise 5

The Income Statement for 19x2 for St Chad's Hall is:

	£	£
Lettings 1,400 hours at £14 an hour		19,600
Administrative staff 400 hours at £3 an hour	1,200	
Electricity	6,800	
Planned Maintenance	2,000	
Repairs	2,600	
Caretaker – salary	2,000	
Cleaning Staff 2,000 hours at £2.50	5,000	
Sundry expenses	900	20,500
Loss		900

The honorary treasurer is preparing his budget for 19x3 and will take into account:

❐ the administrator needs a pay rise of 10%

❐ electricity is to rise in price by 8%

❐ planned maintenance is not sufficient and the committee wish to raise the provision to £2,500

❏ repairs will cost about the same

❏ the caretaker will accept the same salary but needs a deputy at a cost of £400 a year

❏ complaints about cleaning have led the committee to up the cleaning hours to 2,400

❏ sundries will rise by about 5%

❏ a necessary structural alteration to meet environmental requirements has led to the borrowing of £5,000. The interest on this is at 12% and repayments will be by equal annual instalments over 5 years beginning at the end of 19x3.

Required:

a. Prepare a budget for 19x3 such that lettings of 1,400 hours will just cover all outgoings.

b. The required letting fee rise is unacceptable to many users and the committee have decided to have a differential fee policy:

day time use 800 hours at 5% above 19x2 rates

evening use 600 hours at a rate to provide the rest of the required revenue.

What should the evening rate be?

c. A keep fit group have asked to use the hall in the early mornings when the hall is not in use. They are prepared to pay only £8 an hour for about 200 hours use a year. The associated outgoings are only caretaking at £1 an hour. Should the committee accept the booking?

Case Study / Assignment 1

Kale manufactures tents. He has two types: the Orange and the Green. His budgeted sales for 19x5 are; Orange 5,000 at £160 and Green 3,000 at £130.

His stocks at the beginning of the year are 1,500 Orange and 100 Green. By the year end he hopes to change that to 500 Orange and 300 Green. His stocks of finished tents were valued at 31 December 19x4 at £158,000 at prime cost.

He has in stock 30,000 metres of canvas and hopes to get the stock down to 20,000 metres by the year end. Each Orange uses 30 square metres and each Green 22 metres. He has a long term contract with his canvas supplier for supply at £1 a metre.

He has in stock £20,000 of other direct materials and components. He intends to increase the stock to £25,000 by the year end. Each Orange uses £25 worth and each Green £19 worth.

Direct labour is all piecework and costs £50 an Orange and £40 a Green.

Overheads can be assumed to be all fixed and amount to in 19x5:

	£
Factory	200,000
Administrative	100,000
Selling and Distribution	100,000

Required:

a. Prepare:
- ❐ a sales budget in quantity and money terms
- ❐ a production budget in quantity terms
- ❐ a materials budget in quantity and money terms
- ❐ a direct wages budget.

b. Kale produces his master budget using a template as:

**Budgeted Manufacturing, Trading and Profit and Loss Account
for the year ending 31 December 19x5**

Materials: £

	Canvas	Other

Opening Stock
Purchases
Closing Stock
Consumed
Direct labour
Prime cost
Opening Stock of Finished Goods
Closing Stock of Finished Goods
Cost of Goods Sold
Sales
Contribution
Production Overheads
Gross Profit
Administration Costs
Selling and Distribution Costs
Net Profit

Complete the template for 19x5. Note that closing stock of finished goods should be valued at prime cost.

c. Would the results be different if stocks were valued at total absorption cost instead of prime cost in 19x5?

d. Explain how the reduction in stocks of Orange will ease Kale's cash position.

e. Kale is dissatisfied with the budgeted profit. Suggest some possible changes he could make to increase profit. State any assumptions you make.

f. Might the budget be different if Kale paid strict attention to all the objectives of budgeting outlined in of this book?

Exercise *6

Contrast the responses of a public relations department of a manufacturing firm under conventional budgeting approach and a zero based budgeting approach.

Exercise 7

Outline a zero based budgeting approach to the pathology department of a private hospital.

Case Study / Assignment 2

The maintenance department of Stubby Metal Bashing PLC provide a service to the company's large factory which includes maintenance and repair of machinery and buildings including office equipment. The service is on a planned and preventative maintenance and an emergency repair and breakdown basis. The department currently has twelve employees who work shifts.

The company's cost accounting staff have produced the 19x2 budget for the department on the basis of the 19x1 expenditure on personnel, tools, training and office support + 5% when inflation would require 10%. The factory has also increased about 8% in activity. The staff of the department are furious and the department head is trying to find ways of making the necessary economies.

Discuss an approach to the departmental budget which might have benefited the company more than the top down axe approach currently employed.

Assignment 3

Anita runs the Wellington branch of Widget Distributors PLC. She is known for sticking rigidly to her budgets on costs and usually exceeds her budgeted turnover. As a consequence she is highly regarded by Head Office. Unknown to them, her staff are often not fully occupied and she has consistently overbudgeted on expenditure headings and underbudgeted her expected sales. She keeps an eye on each heading and spends unnecessarily on items like courses, computer equipment etc in order to ensure budgeted expense headings are all spent. She also delays sales around the year end in order not to show too high a sales figure and to give her a good start into the new year.

Discuss this scenario and consider how Head Office have gone wrong in their budgeting procedures. Suggest alternative procedures.

Assignment 4

Many managers do not come in contact with Profit and Loss Accounts or Balance Sheets or Cash Flow Statements. However most do come in contact with the budgeting process either as budget holders or as one of the resources administered by a budget holder.

Record your own connections with the budgeting process and explain how it works in your organisation and the uses and benefits it apparently gives your organisation. Consider also its shortcomings and how it may be improved.

Assignment 5

Camoes Tours Ltd are tour operators running coach holidays to France and further afield. The company are considering running a tour in 19x8 to a new destination and have collected probable costs as:

Hire of coach	1,400	Ferries and tolls	930
Courier and drivers	1,240	Hotels	6,950
Diesel fuel	1,100		

The company have a general budget for 19x8 as:

Direct costs	3,420,000
Overheads	860,000
Profit	470,800

Required:

a. Calculate a selling price for the tour. Costs should include 10% commission payable to travel agents who sell the tour for Camoes and also a proportion of the overheads of the company. The price should give a margin for profit. The coach will carry a maximum of 40 customers.

b. All the costs are negotiated and cannot be reduced even if the coach is less than full. Calculate the break even number of customers.

c. What costs might be included in the overheads of this company?

d. How much profit would the company make if all its tours exactly broke even? Explain.

7 Marginal costing

1. Objectives

This Unit introduces the uses of **marginal costing** in decision making.

SCENARIO 1 — Martin decides between manufacturing and importing

In the factory the fourth year gets under way as budgeted. In March, Martin finds a customer who wants to buy a product with a particular use. Martin designs a suitable padlock and asks the Manager (Janet) to determine costs etc.

Janet finds that it is possible to *have the product made* in China for £2.50 each but Martin would have to pay for some special tools which would cost £6,000. Transport of the products to the UK would cost £100 for each batch of 500. Martin's factory would need to box the products at a cost of £1,000 for a machine and 30p each for labour and parts. The special tools would have no salvage value and would last for 5 years. The machine in the factory would last four years and have a salvage value of £200.

Alternatively Janet could *make the product in the factory*. This would necessitate the purchase of machinery costing £20,000 which would last five years and have a salvage value of £2,000. Materials would cost £1.00 a padlock and labour would cost 70p a unit. It would be necessary to hire a supervisor to oversee the production at a cost of £12,000 a year. Extra overheads including insurance, power and stationery would come to about £3,000 a year.

Martin reckons that the selling price will be £4.

Tasks 1

1. What is the *breakeven* sales volume (numbers of padlocks to be sold) if:
   i. The padlock is purchased in China
   ii. The padlock is made in the company's own factory?
2. Sales are forecast at 20,000 units a year. Should the company make the padlocks themselves or buy it in China?
3. At what turnover would buying and making be equally profitable?
4. Discuss the merits and demerits of the two choices in addition to purely financial considerations.

---

2. Introduction

Marginal costing is not normally used in profit measurement but is extensively used in *decision making*. We will review a number of decisions which can be made with the assistance of *marginal costing*.

Note that accountants produce costs which are produced for management use. Many costs so produced are estimates and may turn out differently from the forecast. Accountants produce figures in terms of money and can also supply management with techniques to employ in using the figures in making decisions. Decision making *is a management* task and managers have other criteria to take into account in making decisions. The financial effect of a decision is always very important and financial survival is a necessity for most organisations. However other factors may be relevant:

a) Decisions may have effects not perceived by the management accountant in supplying his figures. For example, the dropping of a product on financial grounds may have effects on the sales of other products or on personnel morale.

b) Aspects of business such as quality control, health and safety, energy conservation and pollution control must be taken into account and altruism is not entirely lacking in business. The effect of a decision which involves redundancy or relocation should be taken only after due consideration of these consequences.

c) Management often have priorities and goals not known to the management accountant. Examples may be a desire to take a larger market share whatever the cost or to expand to feed a manager's ego.

d) Some alternatives may have similar financial effects but may have dissimilar risks. Risk is implicit in all business decisions and it is not easy for an accountant to incorporate quantitative measures of risk. There are some complex statistical ideas available for such assessments but accountants do not normally use them. It is for management to assess risks and act according to the perceived risks and their risk preferences.

3. Breakeven

The simple technique of determining the breakeven point can be useful in decision making. Here are two examples:

1. Danielle is considering using her redundancy money in starting a new boutique in a suburban precinct. She estimates that she should be able to sell about £1,000 worth of clothes a week. She has worked out all the overheads including rent, rates, depreciation, interest, and wages. These will total £21,000 a year. She estimates that on average her clothes will be sold at cost + 60%.

    Calculate her breakeven sales. Fixed costs are £21,000 so she must have a *contribution* or gross profit which at breakeven is £21,000. To calculate breakeven sales:

Sales	?	160
Cost of sales	?	100
Gross profit	£21,000	60

    Note that if cost of sales is seen as 100, then gross profit will be 60 and sales 160.

    Breakeven sales are 160/60 × £21,000 = £56,000 a year or £1,077 a week. This is slightly more than her estimated sales so the project may not quite be viable.

2. Daniel intends to start a part time business as a photocopying shop. He can either hire his equipment or buy it outright. Costs for a period are likely to be:

	Hire	Buy
Variable costs	3p a copy	1.5p a copy
Fixed machine costs		£2,000
General fixed costs	£2,000	£2,000

He estimates that he will sell 150,000 copies at an average of 7p a copy.

The profits at 150,000 copies would be:

	Hire	Buy
Sales (at 7p)	10,500	10,500
Variable costs	4,500	2,250
Contribution	6,000	8,250
Fixed costs	2,000	4,000
Net profit	4,000	4,250

He concludes that at his expected sales, he will make more profit by buying. He also calculates that every copy sold over 150,000 will bring him extra profit of 4p if he hires and 5.5p if he buys.

However his accountant, who is ever cautious, advises him to calculate his breakeven point on each mode of operation:

	Hire	Buy
Fixed costs	£2,000	£4,000
Contribution per copy	4p	5.5p
Breakeven	$\dfrac{£2,000}{4p} = 50,000$	$\dfrac{£4,000}{5.5p} = 72,727$

Daniel is worried that he will not achieve the expected sales and can gain comfort from hiring his machines and having a lower breakeven point. He takes a smaller risk by hiring. However, he expects a smaller profit. In general, the higher the risk, the greater the profit (or return as academics call profit in the context of investment).

4. Make or buy

A common problem in industry is whether to make a product in-house or to buy it in from a supplier.

Sheinton Ltd make cast iron door furniture. A new product has been developed and the management are considering whether to make it in the factory or to have it made in Hungary. Cost data for a year are:

	Make	Buy
Fixed costs	£70,000	£2,000
Variable costs (per 100 items)	£10	£50

Sales price is 70p and expected sales are 200,000 items.

Profits expected are

	Make	Buy
Sales	140,000	140,000
Variable costs	20,000	100,000
Fixed costs	70,000	2,000
Net profit	50,000	38,000

At the turnover predicted, it would be cheaper to make the product. However various other scenarios are possible:

❐ Turnover may be less and below 170,000 items it is more profitable to buy in.

❐ Once the figures are known it may be possible to obtain an even lower price from the Hungarians.

❐ Other matters may be important — continuity of supply, control over quality, staff morale etc.

SCENARIO 2 — Martin considers marginal cost pricing

Martin sells the type ER2 padlock to wholesalers in the UK. He imports these for £2.00 each and sells them at £4.20. He has received an enquiry from a French company who want the ER2 but with a modification. The modification will involve design expenditure of £3,000. In addition modifying the padlocks will cost £0.50 in labour and materials and transporting them to the customer will cost £100 a case. A case contains 500 padlocks.

The French firm are willing to give a firm order for 5,000 a year for two years and they may require more in future years. They are looking at a price of £2.50 but Martin knows that that is negotiable.

Tasks 2

1. What is the *minimum price* that Martin can accept from the French company that will just allow him to break even on the deal?

2. What would be the minimum price if the acceptance of the order enabled Martin to negotiate a reduction in price from his supplier to £1.80 each? Currently he buys 60,000 padlocks a year.

3. What might be the advantages and disadvantages of accepting the order at a price which was *less than the normal* price of £4.20 but which was profitable to Martin.

5. Special order pricing

Burn Ltd manufacture cookers for the home camping market. These sell at £65 each and the costs of manufacture are:

Variable manufacturing costs	20
Fixed manufacturing costs	* 18
Administration costs (all fixed)	8
Fixed selling/distribution costs	† 6
Variable selling /distribution cost	3
	55

* based on total costs of £180,000 and output of 10,000 units.

† based on total costs of £60,000.

The company have received an enquiry from a Dutch company for the supply of 3,000 cookers. The price they are prepared to pay is £40 a unit.

Burn Ltd reckon that the additional output is possible with the use of overtime such that the variable manufacturing cost will be £22 a unit. There will be an increase of £6,000 in fixed manufacturing costs and £9,000 in administration costs. The variable selling/distribution costs will not apply but a carriage cost of £4 a cooker will have to be paid.

Should the order be accepted?

The marginal costs of making and supplying the 3,000 cookers will be:

	£
Variable manufacturing costs	66,000
Fixed manufacturing cost	6,000
Fixed administration costs	9,000
Carriage	12,000
	93,000 or £31 a unit

Thus the marginal revenue £40 is greater than the marginal cost so the order should be accepted.

Note that:

❑ Original fixed costs remain the same whether or not the order is accepted and therefore they can be disregarded in the decision.

❑ Additional fixed costs will be incurred and they must be part of the decision.

❑ All the relevant variable costs must be taken into account.

❑ The order is at a price much below the UK selling price. If this price becomes known then UK customers may demand a price reduction. Also the items sold to the Dutch may find their way back to the UK and undercut normal UK sales.

❑ It is clearly of advantage to sell goods at above marginal cost in new markets as long as current markets are not disturbed. This is a matter of management judgement.

6. Marginal cost pricing

Special order pricing is really a special case of marginal cost pricing. Marginal cost pricing means setting low prices that are above marginal cost so that some benefit is earned by the enterprise. This phenomenon has become very widespread. Examples include:

❑ Public houses with 'happy hours' and two for the price of one meals in mid-week.

❑ Airlines and tour operators with unsold seats.

❑ Hotels with cheap weekend breaks.

❑ Market traders selling unsold perishables at the end of the day.

It is generally profitable to sell any goods or services that would otherwise not be sold at a price so that marginal revenue exceeds marginal cost. An airline that has sold 200 seats on a 300 seater scheduled flight will usually try to do so. It costs almost as much to fly 200 passengers as 300 (there may be extra cost in terms of a small amount of extra fuel and 100 meals made up by extra sales of duty free goods!) so any extra money is almost all profit.

The problem of this approach is the possibility of *self-competition*. Customers who would normally pay the full price may opt to pay the lower prices. I may decide to drink in the happy hour instead of later in the evening because it is cheaper.

Selling goods in international markets on marginal cost pricing principles is known as *dumping*.

SCENARIO 3 — *Martin meets resource limitations*

During the year the factory added two new products – the AM and the PM. These require machining by a neighbouring firm and this firm is the only one that the company can find to do the machining at a reasonable price. The costs of manufacture of the new products are:

	AM	PM
	£	£
Labour	2.40	3.10
Materials	3.10	3.90
Machining	2.00	4.00
Sales Price is	11.00	15.00

Martin expects sales of the two products to be 6,000 AMs and 9,000 PMs in the next six months.

The machining firm charges £12 an hour for machining and can supply an absolute maximum of 3,400 hours in the next six months.

Martin eventually finds another firm that will do the machining but they want to charge £30 an hour. He knows this is negotiable.

Tasks 3

1. Assuming that output should not exceed expected sales and that the company wish to maximise profit, how many AMs and how many PMs should be made?
2. What is the maximum price that Martin can pay per hour for machining to make up the shortfall at a profit?

---

7. Scarce resources

In some situations there is a shortage of a some resource and output has to be restricted. The shortage may be of a material, of skilled labour, of machine time or even of money to fund output. The resource in short supply may be called the *limiting factor* or the *key factor*.

An example

Penny Widgets Ltd manufacture three products whose per unit sale prices, variable costs and potential sales are:

	Alpha	Beta	Gamma
Sale price	£28	£44	£56
Variable costs	£16	£24	£38
Potential sales	6,000	8,100	1,500

The limiting factor is the supply of skilled labour. The quantity of skilled labour to make each product is 30 minutes for an Alpha, 20 minutes for a Beta and 12 minutes for a Gamma. The total supply of skilled labour is limited to 4,600 hours in period X. The problem is to decide which items to manufacture to maximise profit.

The answer can be found by a table as:

	Alpha	Beta	Gamma
Sales price (£)	28	44	56
Variable costs	16	24	38
Contribution	12	20	18
Skilled labour (minutes)	30	20	12
Contribution per minute of skilled labour	40p	100p	150p
Ranking	3	2	1
Manufacture Gamma			4,500
Skilled labour used(hrs)			900
Manufacture Beta		8,100	
Skilled labour used(hrs)		2,700	
Total skilled labour (hrs)		3,600	
Manufacture Alpha	2,000 (b)		
Skilled labour use (hrs)	1,000 (a)		
Total skilled labour used (hrs)	4,600		

(a) Only 1,000 hours remain and all of these can be used in making Alphas.

(b) The 1,000 hours will enable 2,000 Alphas to be made.

The secret of this type of exercise is in the line in italics. The greatest profit comes from using the scarce resource to the greatest advantage and the products which give the *greatest contribution per unit of scarce resource* are to be preferred. Beta may give the highest contribution per unit but only 3 of these an hour can be made. Whereas 5 gammas can be made in an hour of scarce labour.

SCENARIO 4 — Martin gets into school finances

Martin is a governor of his local primary school and is attending a meeting. The main item on the agenda is the school budget for the coming year. The money allocated to the school is substantially less than proposed expenditure and the governors are desperately looking at possible economies to avoid making a part time remedial teacher redundant. Martin thinks he may have an idea which would need his new found knowledge of marginal costing to evaluate. Currently the school is hired out in the evenings for community activities and Martin wonders whether this pays, as the school has to be heated and the caretaker has to work late hours. At this point also the full time caretaker concerned is taking early retirement and a decision has to be made on her replacement.

The head manages to produce the following budgeted figures:

❒ letting fees for a year £5,600

❒ direct costs of evening use : water, electricity, gas, repairs, cleaning £2,560

❒ probable cost of full time caretaker to include evening and week end work £12,300

❒ probable cost of part time caretaker for school hours only £8,900

❒ the school's administrative officer spends about 20% of her time on evening bookings and arrangements. She is full time and costs £9,100 a year.

Task 4

Prepare a report setting out the pros and cons of ceasing evening lettings. You may wish to use your imagination and the ideas of some of the governors:

☐ community use of the school is vital for community relations and recruitment of local children

☐ the ending of community use would enable the school to hold school and parents association meetings in the evenings

☐ lettings are far too low: a vigorous campaign could get far more bookings

☐ the head could make better use of the administrative officer's time

☐ evening use causes the school to look scruffy in the mornings

☐ security would suffer if the building was empty in the evenings.

---

8. Deletion of a segment

Management expect all segments of a business to make a profit. Any segment which fails to make a profit is normally discontinued. Here is an example.

Poshshop plc is a department store in Walsall. The Pottery department is on the second floor and the latest profit statement for the department shows:

	£
Sales	80,000
Cost of goods sold	50,000
Wages	16,000
Share of fixed overheads	18,000
Net loss	(4,000)

Note:

☐ the cost of goods sold and wages are variable costs, changing more or less in line with sales

☐ the fixed costs (rent, rates, insurance, heat and light, administration etc) would remain unchanged if the department were closed.

Should the department be closed?

We can answer this question by considering what would *change* if it was closed. The contribution made by the department is (£80,000 – £50,000 – £16,000) £14,000 and this would be lost if the department closed but fixed overheads would remain the same. Consequently the company would be £14,000 worse off if the department closed.

Another point to consider is that the space occupied by the department might be more profitably used. Suppose that the space could be let on concession to Fred's China Figures at a rent of £17,000. Then the rent would be greater than the contribution from the department and the letting would be more profitable. It is possible to say that the *opportunity cost* (the value of a benefit sacrificed in favour of an alternative course of action) of continuing the department would be the rent foregone.

9. Opportunity cost and relevant cost

Two important concepts in costing that are very significant in decision making are opportunity cost and relevant costs.

Opportunity cost can be defined as the value of a benefit sacrificed in favour of an alternative course of action.

An example: Onions has 20 square metres of his warehouse unused at present. He considers that it is costing him nothing so that using it for skin packing some of his products, instead of subcontracting the skin packing to another firm, will be worth while as he will save £30 a week by so doing. In fact he could let the spare space for £100 a week to another firm. In considering the implementation of skin packing he needs to see the opportunity cost (£100 a week) as a real cost.

Relevant cost can be defined as any costs appropriate to a specific management decision.

An example: Horace is considering repairing and then selling a redundant machine. Business is slack and his fixed salary foreman is not fully busy. Horace reckons he could use one day of the foreman's time (cost £60 + a proportion of fixed overheads) to install the spare sprogget which he has in stock and which cost £80, five years ago. The machine can then be sold for £200. Alternatively he can sell the spare sprogget for £100 and sell the unrepaired machine for scrap for £5. What should he do?

He has two alternatives: repair the machine, do not repair the machine. Relevant cost data are:

	Repair:	*Do not repair*
Revenue	£200	£105

The cost of the foreman's time is irrelevant since his salary and overheads will be spent anyway. The cost of the sprogget is irrelevant since it is a past or sunk cost which cannot be changed.

10. Differential/incremental costs and revenues

In essence this whole chapter is about these concepts but we will look at a few special situations where the words have special relevance. Firstly we can define the words as the difference in revenues and costs if we do something as opposed to not doing it.

Suppose I am running a fund raising dinner for a charity. I have capacity for 100 guests and am charging £20 a head. I have sold only 90 tickets and Mr and Mrs Pore have asked to go but can only pay £12 a head each. The cost of supplying two more meals is calculated at only £4 each. Should I sell them the tickets at £12 each?

Marginal revenue is £24 and marginal cost is only £8 so it clearly makes sense to sell them the tickets. However nothing is simple and I might consider:

❐ revenue may be greater as they will buy drinks at a profit for the charity

❐ other guests may insist on having a cheaper price if they know the Pores have been sold cheap tickets

❐ there may be a last minute demand for 10 tickets at full price.

11. Summary of Unit 7

- ❐ Marginal costing is not usually employed in profit measurement but is an excellent tool for decision making.

- ❐ Accountants provide figures to management and also techniques for using them (eg Scarce Resource analysis) but decisions are made by management.

- ❐ Management often make decisions by considering non-financial as well as financial data.

- ❐ Breakeven analysis can be used as a measure of risk and in choosing between alternatives including whether or not to start a new business or business segment.

- ❐ Make or buy decisions are assisted by marginal costing.

- ❐ Special order pricing at any price above marginal costs may be beneficial but may have unfortunate consequences.

- ❐ In the presence of a scarce resource the most profitable course of action is to maximise contribution per unit of scarce resource.

- ❐ The deletion of a segment can be assessed by measuring the contribution foregone. The measurement of opportunity cost as contribution foregone has many applications.

- ❐ Marginal cost pricing is a way of selling off surplus goods. Make sure that marginal revenue is greater than marginal cost and that there is no self competition. International dumping is frowned upon.

- ❐ Opportunity cost is the value of a benefit sacrificed in favour of an alternative course of action.

- ❐ Relevant cost are any costs appropriate to a specific management decision.

- ❐ Differential or incremental cost is the difference in total cost between alternatives. Marginal cost is the cost of one unit of product or service which would be avoided if that unit were not produced.

Marginal Costing

Make or buy decisions	Opportunity cost
How to make decisions	Self competition
What to make if resources are limited	
Break even analysis	
Special order acceptance	Dumping
Contribution analysis	Incremental cost
Dropping a product	Relevant cost

Exercise 1

Legge makes Wotsits. His budget for 19x2 is:

Selling price	£20 each
Variable cost	£8 each
Fixed costs	£42,000

Required:

a. Calculate contribution per item

b. Calculate breakeven point in units and total sales revenue

c. If his expected sales are 4,000 calculate his margin of safety.

Exercise 2

Costas is considering opening a new fish and chip shop in a new shopping parade in the suburbs. He envisages that his costs would be:

Fixed costs £27,000

Variable costs (materials etc) 40% of sales

a. What costs might be included in the fixed costs?

b. Calculate the weekly takings that would enable the shop to break even.

Exercise 3

Ludwig is considering sinking his savings into a shop which would sell music/instruments/tapes and discs etc.

He has £70,000 in a building society earning 11% gross. The shop he wants is freehold and would cost £50,000. He would spend a further £10,000 on a shop front and general repairs to the shop. The remaining £10,000 would form his working capital (roughly = stock at cost less creditors).

He currently earns £12,000 a year as a clerk, a job he has held for two years.

He reckons the fixed costs of running the shop (rates, insurance, part time staff wages, telephone, electricity etc) are likely to be about £15,000 a year.

He knows that he will make an average gross profit to sales ratio of about 40%.

Required:

a. Calculate the weekly turnover that would make the project worthwhile.

b. Summarise the other factors that Ludwig should take into account in deciding on whether or not to take the plunge. Bear risk in mind as a major factor.

Exercise *4

Fiona is considering setting up as a self employed computer systems consultant. She would need to borrow about £10,000 from the bank at 20% interest to pay for equipment and for working capital. She would have to give up her part time job as an analyst with its salary of £8,000 a year.

Her mode of operation would be to obtain commissions from clients and analyse the systems required. Actual programs would be written by a friend who would be paid 20% of the sales price in advance.

She estimates that fixed costs (depreciation of equipment, motor expenses, advertising, etc) would cost no more than £6,000 a year.

Required:

a. Why would she need a sum for working capital?

b. Calculate the annual turnover she would need i. to simply break even and ii. to make the project viable.

c. Assess any other factors that may influence her decision to go it alone.

Exercise 5

Megan makes souvenirs. One of her products is a gift marked 'a present from Wolverhampton'. Currently each of these costs:

Variable costs	£5
Fixed costs	£4

She is considering sub-contracting the manufacture of this item to Dilys who has quoted £7 an item. Currently output of the product is 3,000 a year and if she ceases manufacture Megan would save £3,000 of fixed costs.

Should Megan make or buy? How would your answer differ if fixed costs saved were £8,000?

Exercise 6

Dill supplies quaggles to the leather trade. His budget for 19x2 is:

	£
Sales	50,000
Cost of goods sold	30,000
Contribution	20,000
Fixed Costs	7,000
Net Profit	13,000

He considers the profit very low for the effort he puts in and the needs of his family and is planning changes. He currently buys in all the quaggles from a variety of sources but reckons he can make them more cheaply in a rented corner of his brother's factory.

If he did this he reckons:

❑ rent and other fixed overheads would cost £3,000

❑ £4,000 of his budgeted fixed costs would still be spent

❑ materials would cost him £12,000

❑ part time machine operatives would cost him £7,000

❑ he would need to spend £15,000 on a machine that would last him 5 years and have a scrap value at the end of its life of £5,000

❒ he would borrow the money to buy the machine from the bank. Interest would be at 15%.

Required:

a. Produce a revised budget assuming he goes ahead with manufacture

b. Calculate the breakeven sales under both alternatives

c. Suggest some other factors that he might take into account in making his decision

d. Discuss the risk factors involved.

Exercise *7

Cressage Ltd has developed a new product – a household electrical appliance. The company can make the product in their factory or buy it in from a Czech manufacturer. They have collected some data to assist in deciding which course of action to take:

Selling price (units)	£300	£320
Sales	5,000	4,500

Costs:	*Fixed*	*Variable*
made in own factory	£600,000	£130 each
made abroad	£200,000	£200 each

Required:

a. Produce forecast Profit and Loss Accounts showing the net profit on each of the four alternatives.

b. Which alternative gives the highest profit? Suggest reasons why Cressage may not opt for the best alternative.

Exercise 8

Rosemary makes a component for its main product and the cost accountant has produced a cost statement of the cost of manufacture of this component as:

Costs of component CJ	£
Materials	15.00
Labour	17.00
Variable overheads	4.00
Fixed overheads	24.50
	60.50

A company in Turkey has offered to make the component for £48.00.

Currently the company makes 5,000 of the components a year.

If manufacture was discontinued then fixed costs would reduce by £40,000.

Required:

a. What are the total fixed overheads currently absorbed by the component?

b. Why would this sum only reduce by £40,000 if manufacture was discontinued?

c. Should Rosemary continue to make the component or buy it in Turkey?

d. What is the lowest Turkish price that would make it just favourable to buy the component from the Turkish supplier?

e. Discuss reasons why the Turkish supplier can make the component more cheaply than Rosemary.

Exercise 9

Olly makes a product which he sells using his sales force of 10 full time representatives. Each representative costs £20,000 a year in salary and expenses. Each representative is also paid a commission of 2% of the sales he makes. The budgeted sales of the product for 19x2 are £3,000,000. All of the representatives are relatively recent appointments and turnover of reps is high.

Olly is considering making his representatives into self employed agents and paying them a straight 8% commission.

Required:

a. On financial grounds should Olly employ reps or agents?

b. At what level of sales would employment of agents cost the same as employment of reps?

c. Discuss other factors that may be relevant to the decision.

Exercise 10

Michelle makes and sells jewellery exclusively for the American market. A French firm have offered to buy 100 units of her standard line at a maximum price of £20. Her usual price to the USA is £35. She can make the extra 100 units at a cost of:

Materials	£10 each
Labour	£2
Additional overheads	£600

Should she accept the order?

Exercise 11

Sage manufactures a range of products for export. One of these has an expected profitability as:

	£	£
Selling Price		50
Variable Manufacturing cost	26	
Fixed Manufacturing cost	8	
Variable selling cost	4	
Fixed selling cost	6	44
Net Profit		6

These figures are based on a turnover of 5,000 units.

Sage has been asked by a manufacturer on the same trading estate to supply him with 500 units at a price of £35 each. Sage has the capacity to do this.

Required:

a. Should Sage sell him the products at this price?

b. What is the lowest price that Sage could sell them at and still make a positive contribution?

c. What other factors may Sage consider?

Exercise 12

Thyme makes and sells car kits in the home (UK) market. She sells direct to consumers through specialist magazines Her budget for 19x2 shows:

	£	£
Sales (100 units)		200,000
Materials	50,000	
Direct Labour	30,000	
Variable Overheads	5,000	
Fixed Production costs	35,000	
Fixed Admin cost	23,000	
Fixed Selling costs	18,000	161,000
Net Profit		39,000

Thyme has been approached by a dealer in Belgium who reckons she can sell 20 units a year. However she is only willing to pay £1,200 a unit.

Thyme reckons that if she accepts the order from Belgium she will:

❑ Spend 5% less on all her materials as she can buy larger quantities.

❑ Increase fixed production cost by 10% and admin costs by £2,000.

Required:

a. Calculate the breakeven volume implied by the original budget.

b. Recast the budget on the assumption that she accepts the Belgian order.

c. Should she accept the Belgian order?

d. If you ran the company what initiatives would you take?

One year later:

Thyme accepted the order and in fact sold 40 units in the first year to the Belgian. The Belgian dealer sells them for £1,700 in Belgium and also in Holland.

Thyme has heard that several of the units were in fact sold by the Belgian dealer to British customers.

e. What should Thyme do about the sales from Belgium to the UK?

Exercise 13

Webb is a manufacturer of domestic kettles for sale in the UK and EC. He has spent a great deal on installing automatic plant which produces the kettles almost without human intervention.

His budget for 19x2 is:

(all figures in £'000)

	£	£
Sales		4,000
Variable costs:		
Production	1,200	
Selling	300	
Fixed Costs:		
Production	1,800	
Admin	400	
Selling	600	4,300
Net Loss		(300)

Output achievable from his plant without any increase in fixed costs is actually $2\frac{1}{2}$ times the output implied by his budget but his salesmen tell him that at his prices these are the maximum sales attainable. He is considering two strategies:

i. Reducing prices by 15% which should increase sales by 50% and reduce variable unit production costs by 5%.

ii. Selling his kettles in North America at a price 30% below his UK price. This should enable him to double his unit sales and reduce unit production cost by 5%.

Required:

a. Calculate the breakeven sales on his original budget.

b. Discuss his two additional strategies and make recommendations.

Exercise *14

Lily makes three types of model. Statistics are:

Type	A	B	C
Sales price	£8	£10	£12
Variable cost	£3	£4	£5
Maximum Sales in period 1	4,200	3,000	2,700
Usage of machine W time (minutes)	5	2	6

What should be made if production should not exceed sales and time on machine W in period 1 is restricted to 600 hours.

Exercise 15

Cohen makes three types of widget – statistics re these are:

	X	Y	Z
Selling Price	£50	£40	£23
Variable costs	£35	£23	£8
Maximum sales in period 1 (units)	1,000	2,100	2,500
Usage of Machine M (minutes)	12	20	15
Usage of Skilled Labour (minutes)	10	8	5

Required:

a. Assuming that usage of Machine M is restricted to 1,000 hours and that the company will not make more than can be sold, what and how many widgets should be made in period 1, to maximise profit? There is unlimited skilled labour available in this period.

b. How much profit would then be made? Assume fixed costs are £40,000.

c. How much more profit would be made if the restriction could be removed?

d. Assume that the figures are the same in period 2 except that maximum sales of Z will be only 2,400 and once again that the company do not wish to make widgets they cannot sell. In period two there is no restriction on the use of Machine M but skilled labour is limited to 500 hours. What types should be made and in what quantities to maximise profit?

e. How much profit will then be made?

Exercise 16

Kaur makes suits of three patterns:

	Check	Spotted	Striped
Details of these are:			
Selling price	£80	£85	£100
Variable costs	£30	£40	£52
Maximum Sales (Units)	500	300	270
Time on special machine (minutes)	30	40	40
Usage of special buttons	10	12	6

Required:

a. Assume that the maximum time available on the special machine in period 3 is 400 hours and that unlimited buttons are available and that output should not exceed sales, what should be produced in period 3 to maximise profit?

b. What profit will then be made? Assume fixed costs are £30,000.

c. Assume the same data in period 4 but that machine time is unlimited but supply of special buttons is limited to 7,000 in the period. What types and in what quantities should be made in period 4 to maximise profit? Again, output should not exceed sales.

d. What profit should be earned?

e. In period 4 a supply of buttons can be made available but from a source which charges £3 a button more than the usual supplier. Should these be purchased?

Exercise 17

Oldfash Ltd produces its budget on total absorption accounting principles as this one, for 19x2: (all figures in £'000)

Product	Big	Bigger	Biggest	Total
	£	£	£	£
Sales	240	180	70	490
Variable costs	120	100	35	255
Fixed Costs	85	60	45	190
Profit (Loss)	35	20	(10)	45

The Board consider this and decide to discontinue the manufacture of Biggest which they see as making a loss.

Before doing so they fortunately ask Len, a bright young manager, to look further into the matter. Len discovers that if manufacture of Biggest were discontinued, fixed costs would reduce from £190,000 to £170,000 only. What should the decision be on financial grounds.

Exercise 18

Swade operates bus routes. He runs 10 buses and 4 routes and revenues and costs are: (all figures in £'000)

Route	1	2	3	4
Revenues	30,000	36,000	23,000	18,000
Variable costs	12,000	14,000	10,500	11,000
Fixed costs	10,000	10,000	10,000	10,000

Swade thinks that he should drop route 4.

Required:

a. What costs might be included in variable costs?

b. What costs might be included in fixed costs?

c. How has his accountant distributed the fixed costs over the four routes?

d. Might this be justifiable?

e. If Route 4 is discontinued, fixed costs would be reduce by $\frac{1}{8}$ only. Would discontinuance increase profits?

f. What actions do you think Swade might take to increase profit on route 4?

Exercise 19

Anthea buys scrap from metal processes and reprocesses it to extract the valuable metals which she then sells. She has some scrap materials which she bought some time ago for £100. She can process it at a cost of:

Electricity	£30
Water	£5
Labour	£10
Overheads	£30

and then sell the metal for £40 or resell it unprocessed for £20 or deposit in the town dump at a cost of £5.

What should she do, assuming that the overheads are all fixed and that alternatively:

i.   The labour is overtime which would not otherwise be spent; or

ii.   The labour is of the full time workforce that are underemployed at present?

Exercise 20

Nat purchased a machine for use in his toymaking factory in 19x2 for £20,000 and determined his straight line depreciation policy on the assumption the machine would last 5 years and have a zero scrap value at the end of that time. In mid 19x3 he discovers that there is a new machine on the market that will do exactly the same things as the old machine but will save £10,000 a year in wages, materials and energy. The new machine will cost £18,000 and the suppliers will take the old machine in part exchange for £2,000. What should Nat do?

Exercise 21

Owain makes special order engineering products. He has received an enquiry from a customer for a Thingum and has costed it as follows:

Materials:	Material A 10 Kg. He has some 15 Kg of this in stock which cost £13 a Kg. Buying it was a mistake and he cannot now use it except on the order for the Thingum. He could however sell it as scrap for £40 the lot.
	Material B 5 Kg. This material is regularly used and he has 20 Kg in stock which cost £25 a Kg. The current price is now £35 a Kg.
	Material C 20 Kg. This material is also regularly used and there is a stock amounting to 30 Kg which cost £4 a Kg. The material can now be bought for £2.50 a Kg.
Labour:	David 12 hours at £5 an hour. David is paid by the hour.
	Frank 8 hours at £6 an hour. Frank is skilled and if he is used on this job he will have to be taken off the manufacture of Job 23 and Jeb brought in at a cost of £100 to finish Job 23.
	Lewis 4 hours. Lewis is also skilled and if he works on the Thingum he will need to be paid in overtime at time and one half as he is currently fully occupied. His normal rate is £9 an hour.
Overheads:	Royalty for use of patent process – 10% of selling price.
	Variable overheads (energy etc) – £120
	Fixed Overheads – usual recovery rate is 60% on prime cost.

What is the lowest price that Owain can quote to just make a profit on the Thingum?

Exercise 22

Fiona makes wedding cakes to order. She has made one for £25 but the groom has been killed in an accident and she is unable to collect the £25 but she still has the cake. Another bride, hearing this has offered £10 for the cake. Fiona will have to rework the words in icing sugar. This will cost £5 and she will also have to refuse an order for a small birthday cake on which she would make a profit of £3. Discuss the problem.

Exercise 23

Consider again Assignment 5 in Unit 6. The company went ahead with the tour and ran it for three months with weekly departures. The selling price was set at £375 per passenger.

Required:

a. Calculate the contribution to profit if all 12 of the planned tours went ahead with (i) every seat sold, (ii) 80% full, and (iii) 60% full.

b. The last tour was at the end of the season and only 20 seats have been sold. The company is considering what to do. The alternatives seem to be:
   ❏ Offer the remaining seats on the tour as a bargain offer at £200. The remaining seats should sell at that price.
   ❏ Cancel the tour. It is possible to do this without incurring any of the direct costs. However those who have bought seats will have to be offered their money back or seats on a tour offered by a rival company (this will cost Camoes £450 a seat) or offer £100 cash and seats on the tour in the following year.

Review these choices and make recommendations.

Exercise 24

Phyllis has the concession for the restaurant at the Haygate museum of dolls houses. The restaurant is only open at lunch time. She finds that there are three ways of preparing the meals — buying them in, preparing them during the morning, preparing them in advance and freezing them. Comparative costs are:
   ❏ Buying in meals: average cost is £3.40. Some 10% stay in stock until after their sell by date and have to be scrapped.
   ❏ Preparing in the morning: average cost of materials £1.20. Other costs are the chef at £200 a week and electricity etc costs of £50 a week. She finds that the average wastage rate is 20%: she does not freeze them because some are not suitable for freezing and she can advertise fresh food.
   ❏ Preparing in advance: average cost of materials £1.00. Other costs are the chef at £180 a week (cheaper than above as she can work at her choice of time) and electricity etc £50 a week. Wastage rate is 10%.

Required:

a. Calculate the cost of goods sold if sales are (i) 60 meals, (ii) 80 meals, (iii) 100 meals, (iv) 120 meals a week.

b. She is committed to only one mode for the whole season once she has made her decision. She does not really know how many meals will be sold but feels that it will be somewhere between 50 and 130. Advise her on the best strategy.

8 Working capital

1. Objectives

This unit introduces the idea of **working capital**, the problems it causes and how to manage it.

Working Capital can be defined as:

Stocks + Debtors — Creditors — Overdraft

Most firms find that stocks have a tendency to increase even without an increase in business and that customers have a tendency to take even longer to pay for the goods supplied to them. When customers do not pay on time, money becomes tight and the firm tends to want to take longer before paying suppliers. Not unnaturally suppliers do not take kindly to this. Paying suppliers on time when customers do not pay on time, may require an increase in overdraft and, unless this is agreed by the bank, trouble may ensue. In any case a large overdraft costs a great deal in interest. Slow payment is a major problem in the UK and the larger firms are especially slow and cause much anguish among the small firms that supply them.

SCENARIO 1 — Martin discovers working capital

At the end of the fourth year, Martin Padlocks Ltd shows the following figures in part of its Balance Sheet:

Current Assets

Stocks:

Goods for resale	£84,000
Raw Materials and components	£35,000
Debtors	£187,000

Creditors: amounts falling due within one year

Trade creditors	£80,000
Bank Overdraft	£109,000

Martin knows that the goods for resale are in stock in the wholesale warehouse and that the raw materials and components are in the factory.

The debtors and creditors are not distinguished between the two parts of the company.

Quick Answer Questions 8.1

1. How are the stocks valued?
2. What is the working capital?

SCENARIO 2 — Martin worries about debtors, creditors and stocks

Martin is worried about the size of the overdraft and the interest it is costing. The Bank have agreed an overdraft limit or facility of £120,000. Nonetheless Martin would like to reduce the overdraft. In order to find a way to reduce it he asks for an analysis of the figures from his bookkeeper who manages to produce the following data:

	September	October	November	December	Total
Sales	75,000	73,000	76,000	84,000	308,000
Paid before 31/12	62,000	42,000	15,000	2,000	121,000
Unpaid at 31/12	13,000	31,000	61,000	82,000	*187,000
Purchases	47,000	46,000	54,000	51,000	198,000
Paid before 31/12	47,000	44,000	27,000	nil	118,000
Unpaid at 31/12	nil	2,000	27,000	51,000	*80.000
Stocks at 31/12 – date of acquisition					
Raw materials	6,000	9,000	7,000	13,000	*35,000
Goods for resale	8,000	18,000	22,000	36,000	*84,000

* As per the Working capital figures in Scenario 1.

The bookkeeper warns Martin that the information on stocks is approximate and that some of the items labelled as being acquired in September were actually acquired before that date.

Note that the total sales and purchases figures are given to put the debtors, creditors and stocks into perspective.

Martin wants to make sense of all this information and tries to see what messages for him are contained in it.

Quick Answer Questions 8.2

1. What proportion of the customers pay:
   - ❐ in the month after the sale?
   - ❐ in the month after that?
   - ❐ in the third month or more after the sale?
2. When does Martin pay his suppliers?
3. What would happen to the overdraft if:
   - ❐ all customers paid in the month after the sale?
   - ❐ goods spent a shorter time in stock before being sold or used?
   - ❐ the suppliers were paid more slowly?

SCENARIO 3 — Martin has problems with his overdraft

Martin is distracted by other matters and does nothing about his working capital problem until July when his bookkeeper reports that he cannot pay any of the June accounts as the overdraft is on the limit. He presents a summary as at the end of June similar to the one produced for the end of December:

	Jan to Mar	April	May	June
Sales	320,000	102,000	96,000	94,000
Paid by 30/6	287,000	54,000	25,000	nil
Unpaid at 30/6	33,000	48,000	71,000	94,000

Purchases		72,000	59,000	67,000
Paid by 30/6		66,000	nil	nil
Unpaid at 30/6		6,000	59,000	59,000

Stocks at 30/6 – date of acquisition

	Jan to Mar	April	May	June
Raw Materials	9,000	7,000	9,000	17,000
Goods for resale	14,000	29,000	32,000	48,000

Martin remembers that he had agreed to increase the overdraft limit to £130,000 and that the working capital had increased because of the profitable trading in the first six months of the year. The overdraft now stands at £131,000.

Tasks 1

1. Analyse the data at 30 June in the same way as the data at 31 December and comment on the differences shown.
2. Analyse the differences in sales, purchases and stocks between the two half years and explain the difference this will make to working capital and the bank overdraft.
3. Make suggestions to Martin as to how he can reduce the average credit period taken by his customers.

SCENARIO 4 — Martin invents excuses for non-payment

Martin's bookkeeper reports that as a result of the working capital problem he cannot now take *settlement discounts* from some of the suppliers who offer them. For example Amalgamated Padlocks Ltd offer 5% for payment within 5 days of invoice date.

He suggests that if Martin offered similar discounts to his customers, the customers would pay more quickly and the company could then take advantage of the discounts offered by suppliers.

The bookkeeper also says that suppliers are ringing up and asking for their money. Should he say to them that the company is having temporary working capital or cash flow problems and will pay very soon or should he make some other excuses?

Tasks 2

1. Evaluate the suggestion of the bookkeeper that settlement discounts should be offered to customers.
2. What excuses could the bookkeeper make to suppliers for non-payment?
3. Martin's bookkeeper says that, in his previous firm, he used to manage the creditors by paying some quickly and some after a long interval. Explain how managing creditors may help to finance Martin's business and the problems that might be encountered.
4. Martin hopes to increase his turnover rapidly. What financial problems might this cause?

---

2. Introduction

Working capital can be defined simply as current assets less current liabilities or also as current assets less creditors and overdraft if any. Managers and accountants often speak of having a working capital problem. Essentially what they mean by this is an inability to pay creditors when they want to, as the overdraft has a ceiling which cannot be exceeded. The reason why working capital comes into this problem can be explained by regarding working capital as a *single entity* which can be *subdivided*.

Suppose Stubby Traders Ltd was formed to market pencils. Initially the company was formed with a share capital of £30,000. Of this £20,000 was required for fixed assets and the balance was available to be invested in working capital. After some 9 months trading, during which no profit was made, the working capital looked like this:

	£	£
Current assets		
Stock	28,000	
Debtors	40,000	
		68,000
Current liabilities		
Creditors	28,000	
Overdraft	30,000	58,000
Working capital		10,000

The amount of working capital (£10,000) can only be changed by either raising *new finance* from shareholders or long term loans, and we will presume this is not possible, or by making *profits* and this has not occurred yet.

Stock is the minimum necessary to continue trading. Anything less would lead to stock outs and loss of sales.

Debtors cannot be reduced without turning away customers and collection is as fast as can be achieved without alienating good customers.

The bank overdraft is as high as the bank will allow and any increase may lead to the bank dishonouring cheques.

The only flexible item is creditors. This represents unpaid accounts and represents 3 months supplies on average. Some suppliers are very tolerant but others are restive. Some have refused further supplies and some have threatened court action if payment is not made in a few days. Stubby Traders' bookkeeper is reduced to such excuses for non-payment as: the cheque is in the post (it is not); I cannot send a cheque today as the director is out of town (he is sitting on the desk); we have used the last cheque in the book and the bank is closed (just untrue); we will not pay your £3,000 bill going back 4 months because we are waiting for a credit note to correct the price of the four sprockets invoiced at £2.50 each instead of the agreed £2.40; we will send you a cheque today (we will, but it will not be signed and you will have to send it back for signature thus giving us another week).

The problem is that the company cannot pay its bills but the cause is that the total of working capital is too low. How can this be corrected? This chapter will pursue some solutions.

3. Increasing working capital

If working capital is too low then some way should be found to increase it by raising finance from other sources. These may include:

a) An issue of shares to existing shareholders if they have any cash available.

b) An issue of shares to an institution that will buy equity in small companies. There are now several *venture capital* suppliers in the market.

c) Raising a long term loan from the bank or other institution.

d) Financing the fixed assets by leasing or hire purchase.

e) Factoring the debts.

Unit 16 reviews these ideas and others.

4. Debtors

Some firms are fortunate in that they sell goods with cash paid at the time of sale or even earlier. Examples are supermarkets where cash is paid as sales are made and travel agents who collect the cash before the holidays are taken. Many firms however have to sell on credit. It is very easy to put 'nett cash 30 days' on the invoice but many customers ignore this and pay only after several reminders and threats, months after the invoice date. For many firms, collecting debts is a major headache. How can debtors as a total be kept as low as possible?

Possible procedures are:

a) Avoid selling to firms that are very slow in paying.

b) Raise selling prices to such customers to compensate for slow payment.

c) Invoice promptly and send monthly statements on time.

d) Chase slow payers by stickers on statements, letters, telephone calls, cutting off further supplies and finally legal action.

e) Offer discounts for prompt payment. This is a common device but often misfires and can be very costly. The cost can be expressed as a rate of interest using the formula:

$$\text{cost of discount} = \frac{12r}{m}$$

where: r = rate of discount as a percentage

m = the average credit, in months, taken by the customer.

Suppose C Ltd, a customer, takes 3 months on average and is offered 5% discount for immediate payment on receipt of the invoice then:

$$\text{cost of discount} = \frac{12 \times 5}{3} = 20\%$$

This is high and it would pay to borrow from the bank if the APR were lower than 20% rather than give the discount.

In practice the situation is usually *worse* as:

a) Slow paying customers do not take advantage of the discount.

b) Quick paying customers do take advantage. Suppose X ltd normally pay in the 30 days but, along with other customers, are offered 5% for immediate payment. If they accept (they are almost sure to do so) then the cost is:

$$\frac{12 \times 5}{1} = 60\%$$

c) Some customers will take the discount and still pay late. This leads to acrimonious relations with the customer and often the discount has to be conceded.

A point about slow payers is that if they fail then the amount lost is say four months sales rather than the say one month of a quick payer. It is worth noting that the actual loss in a bad debt is the cost of the goods sold not the selling price and also that the VAT is now recoverable.

The protection of selling goods on reservation of title contracts (so-called Romalpa contracts where the title to the goods remains with the seller until payment is made) is largely illusory in practice.

5. Creditors

Prompt payment of suppliers is good practice and wins supplier goodwill which can result in good service and preference in time of shortage. However to minimise working capital requirements many firms take excessive credit. This may have a number of effects:

a) Supplier badwill.

b) Some suppliers may increase prices to slow payers.

c) Some essential suppliers may refuse further credit and insist on cash with order.

d) A reputation for slow payment may lead to some desirable suppliers refusing credit.

e) A supplier may lose patience and issue a writ. This can have a snowball effect if other suppliers hear of it and do likewise. The effect may be receivership or liquidation.

f) Loss of potential settlement discounts. It is almost always advantageous to take settlement discounts.

6. Overtrading

Refer back to the working capital calculation in paragraph 1 and consider the effect of a 20% increase in sales.

If sales are increased by 20% then working capital will be:

Stock	33,600	
Debtors	48,000	
		81,600
Creditors	41,600	
Overdraft	30,000	
		71,600
		10,000

I have assumed that working capital remains at £10,000 and the overdraft at £30,000. The effect is that creditors have been increased by 48%. If we assume that creditors were at the limit of tolerance on an average of three months then an increase of 20% would keep the situation stable but an increase of 48% would push the creditors too far and lead to receivership.

The phenomenon of being unable to pay creditors because of an increase in business is called overtrading. It is quite common. The solution is to ensure that before increasing sales (which is obviously desirable) extra finance is available from long term or short term sources.

7. Taxes

At one time the response of many firms to difficulty in paying trade creditors was to delay payment of taxes including corporation tax, PAYE and National Insurance and VAT. The taxing authorities now have sanctions against late payment in the form of interest and penalties.

Delay in payment of taxes is no longer recommended.

8. Ratio analysis of working capital items

A fairly crude analysis of the sizes of debtors, stocks and creditors can be made by comparing period end figures with annual throughputs. Suppose Angela Ltd had figures as:

Balance Sheet	£	Profit and Loss Account	£
Stock	24,600	Sales on credit	160,740
Debtors	31,790	Purchases	79,300
Creditors	19,200	Cost of goods sold	74,600

Average payment time for debtors is $\dfrac{31,790}{160,740} \times 365 = 72$ days

Average payment time for creditors is $\dfrac{19,200}{79,300} \times 365 = 88$ days

Average time stock is in stock is $\dfrac{24,600}{74,600} \times 365 = 120$ days

This global form of measurement is crude for many reasons. The reasons include the fact that period end figures may be untypical, average figures may include extremes (some items of stock may be in stock just a day and others may stick for many months) and throughput figures are rarely uniform through the year. The analysis in this Unit and the Unit on stock is more useful.

SCENARIO 5 — Martin meets a busy fool

Martin has an old house and the central heating system is now very old and decrepit. He decides to have a brand new system installed and obtains tenders from a number of suppliers. One of these is from Ted whose tender is the lowest by 25% and as Ted has a good reputation locally. Martin commissions him to install the new system at a price of £5,100 to be paid when the system is complete and working satisfactorily.

On August 5th Ted appears with an apprentice in an ancient van and does three days work. He then disappears for a week and when he returns Martin irately asks him where he has been. Ted is apologetic and says that he has been completing another job. He then works for a further four days before not appearing again. During this work period, the boiler and all the radiators are delivered to Martin's house from a local plumbers merchant.

Ted and his apprentice work intermittently until early December when Martin finally insists on completion before Christmas. Ted then starts to work very hard during the day, in the evenings and at the weekend. On December 15th he asks Martin for an advance payment of part of the sum due as he is being pressed by his suppliers. Martin agrees to pay £1,000 as he is worried that Ted will go bust and not complete the contract.

Finally the system is completed on Christmas Eve and works perfectly but Ted does not present his bill until January 5th as he is snowed under with work.

Task 3

Ted clearly has both *profitability* problems and *liquidity* problems but is not short of work.

Analyse his problems and suggest ways in which he can improve his business.

9. Operating cycle

The problem of working capital is largely one of the operating cycle. Suppose the trade cycle consists of:

❏ buying a good
❏ holding it in stock
❏ selling it.

So far as *cash* is concerned this can be stated as:

❏ Paying for the good.
❏ Receiving payment after sale.

The further apart these latter two events are, the more the need for working capital. It can be measured as:

Average days held in stock	50
Less: Average creditors period	(45)
Add Average debtors period	72
Conversion cycle	77

The aim should be to shorten this period as much as possible.

In manufacturing, this is more complicated and the conversion cycle is generally longer.

10. Recent developments

The slow payment of bills primarily by large organisations has been seen as major national problem for decades. Many members of parliament have taken up the problem and attempted to introduce legislation using private members bills in parliament. The object of such proposed legislation is to induce companies to pay more quickly, usually by some compulsory interest charge on late payments. So far such attempts to introduce legislation have always failed. Some recent developments which may work include:

❐ A new British Standard has been issued by the British Standards Institution (BS 7890): Method for achieving good payment performance in commercial transactions. It is not a legally binding document unless both parties to a transaction include it in the contract.

❐ There is a CBI prompt payment code and prompt payment requirement in the Government Accounting Rules. These require that all bills are paid within 30 days of supply or of a valid invoice unless the contract specifies differently. Some organisations report compliance. For example, Shropshire's Community Health Service NHS Trust pay some 52% of their bills within target.

❐ Only about 25% of bills are paid promptly in the UK against 40% in Europe and 60% in Germany. Perhaps the Government will fulfil their promise to act.

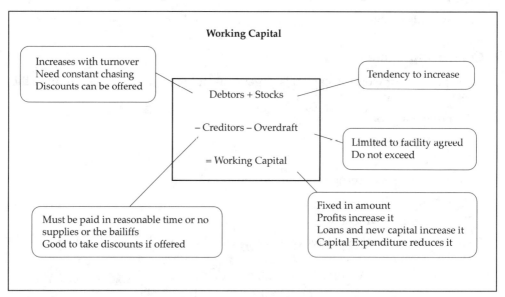

11. Summary of Unit 8

❐ Working capital is defined as current assets less current liabilities or current assets less creditors and overdraft.

❐ The working capital problem arises because of a tendency of working capital as a whole to be limited in amount. The component parts - stock and debtors - tend to increase and overdraft is limited. The result is difficulty in paying creditors. Some people call this phenomenon cash flow difficulties.

- ❐ Stock has a tendency to increase even without an increase in business.
- ❐ Customers have a tendency not to pay unless pressed and not always then.
- ❐ Banks give businesses finite overdraft limits.
- ❐ A monthly analysis of debtors (an age analysis), showing how long accounts have been outstanding, is helpful in highlighting the problem and suggesting solutions.
- ❐ Debtors should be minimised by a range of policies including invoicing promptly and chasing debtors rigorously.
- ❐ Settlement discounts can be offered to customers but turn out to be very expensive.
- ❐ Paying creditors slowly can be construed as being given free finance but can be bad practice both morally and commercially. Taking discounts is generally good.
- ❐ Increasing sales without considering the effects on working capital components can lead to overtrading and disaster.
- ❐ The payment of taxes should not be delayed.
- ❐ The operating cycle of a firm can be measured by observing the time taken from payment for inputs to receipt of cash from outputs.

Exercise 1

Some extracts from the annual accounts of AHM Trading are:

Balance Sheet at 31.12.19x2:

	£		£
Stocks	24,000	Creditors	11,500
Debtors	18,000	Overdraft	12,000

Profit and Loss Account

Sales	104,000
Cost of goods sold	65,000
Purchases	61,000

a. Calculate the working capital.

b. On these figures creditors average payment time is:

$$\frac{11,500}{61,000} \times 365 = 69 \text{ days}$$

Calculate the creditors average payment time if all the figures (including the net working capital) remained the same except as stated with the following independent events:

i. Stocks increase to £30,000

ii. Debtors increased to 90 days average collection time

iii. The bank overdraft was reduced to £8,000

iv. Sales increased by 20% (but debtors collection time remained the same)

v. Stock turnover changed to 160 days

vi. Purchases increased by 20% and stock creditors by a similar monetary amount

Exercise 2

Some extracts from the annual accounts of RP Trading are:

Balance Sheet at 31.12.19x2:

	£		£
Stocks	50,000	Creditors	31,500
Debtors	45,000	Overdraft	12,000

Profit and Loss Account

Sales	270,000
Cost of goods sold	189,000
Purchases	189,000

a. Calculate the working capital.

b. Calculate the creditors average payment time if all the figures (including the net working capital) remained the same except as stated with the following independent events:
   i. Stocks increase by 15%
   ii. Debtors increased to 90 days average collection time
   iii. The bank overdraft was reduced to £10,000
   iv. Sales increased by 15% (but debtors collection time remained the same)
   v. Stock turnover changed to 200 days
   vi. Purchases increased by 1/9 and stock and creditors by a similar monetary amount

c. All figures except the bank overdraft rose by 10% as a result of inflation and stock, debtors and creditors ratios remained the same. Calculate the increase in working capital required.

Exercise 3

The Balance Sheet of AB Ltd at 31.12.19x2:

Share Capital	20,000	Fixed Assets	35,000
Profit and Loss	32,000	Stock	18,000
Creditors	13,000	Debtors	23,000
Overdraft	11,000		
	76,000		76,000

The Profit and Loss Account for 19x2 showed:

Sales (all credit)	92,000
Cost of sales	56,000
Gross Profit	36,000
Overheads	20,000
Net Profit	16,000

At the beginning of 19x3 the directors are planning:
  ❐ to spend £8,000 on fixed assets
  ❐ to increase sales by 20%

a. Explore the consequences of this on cash requirements assuming stock remains at £18,000 and gross profit ratio, debtors payment time, creditors payment time and overheads all remain the same.

b. Suggest some possible sources of finance.

Exercise *4

The Balance Sheet of CD Ltd at 31.12.19x2:

Share Capital	30,000	Fixed Assets	64,000
Profit and Loss	31,000	Stock	24,000
Creditors	28,000	Debtors	56,000
Overdraft	55,000		
	144,000		144,000

The Profit and Loss Account for 19x2 showed:

Sales (all credit)	168,000
Cost of sales	104,000
Gross Profit	64,000
Overheads	20,000
Net Profit	44,000

a. Stock at 1.1.19x2 was £20,000. Calculate:

Debtors average payment time

Stock turnover

Creditors average payment time

b. Discuss the company's apparent good points and its apparent problems.

c. At the beginning of 19x3 the directors are planning:

❏ to spend £10,000 on fixed assets

❏ to increase sales by 20%

Explore the consequences of this on cash requirements assuming stock increases by 20% and gross profit ratio, debtors payment time, creditors payment time and overheads all remain the same. Note that profits will bring in £15,000 of additional working capital in 19x3.

Exercise 5

The working capital sections of the accounts of Swetblud Ltd and Easy Ltd showed:

	Swetblud £	Easy £
Current Assets		
Stock	40,000	76,000
Debtors	54,000	45,000
	94,000	121,000

	Swetblud	£	Easy	£
Current Liabilities				
Creditors	43,000		26,000	
Overdraft	18,000	61,000	2,500	28,500
		33,000		92,500

Other relevant data:

Debtors average credit time	70 days	60 days
Stock turnover	102 days	52 days
Creditors average credit time	91 days	38 days
Bank Overdraft Facility	£16,000	£30,000

Both companies are wholesalers in the same line of business

Required

a. Review all the figures and identify any problems that each company may have.

b. What action would you recommend to each company to remedy any problem?

c. Swetblud has a bill for £10,000 corporation tax to pay. How will this cause difficulty?

d. Easy has a dividend to pay of £15,000. Will this cause any problem?

e. Both companies are looking for an increase in turnover. Discuss the effect this might have on the Balance Sheet extracts above.

Exercise 6

The working capital of two companies is:

	A	£	B	£
Current Assets				
Stock		230,000		360,000
Debtors		23,000		417,000
		253,000		777,000
Current Liabilities				
Creditors	186,000		172,000	
Overdraft	64,000	250,000	213,000	385,000
		3,000		392,000

Other data:

Annual Sales	1,100,000	1,375,000
Annual Purchases	745,000	923,000
Bank Overdraft Facility	100,000	200,000

A Ltd is a warehouse retailing garden things to the public.

B Ltd is a wholesaler of garden furniture. One third of the company's purchases are imported and the whole cost of imports is paid when the goods are released from the docks.

Required:

a. Review these figures, calculate any useful ratios and comment on them.

b. Identify any problems that may be worrying each company.

c. Suggest some solutions to the problems.

d. Do you think that the figures above would change if the year end was changed in each case?

e. Explore the effects of i. an increase and ii. a decrease in turnover.

Exercise *7

LM Ltd have a difficulty in collecting in their debts from customers and are considering offering a settlement discount of 5% for payment on invoice. Data about their sales and collection times includes:

Annual Sales	Average collection time
£	
48,000	1 month
60,000	2 months
120,000	3 months
84,000	4 months

If all the customers took the discount:

a. What would the annual cost be?

b. What would be the reduction in credit granted?

c. Calculate a./b. x100. This gives the effective cost as an interest rate.

d. Discuss how the discount idea would work out in practice.

Exercise 8

JK Ltd have a problem in collecting debts from their customers and are considering offering a settlement discount. Data about their sales and collection times includes:

Annual Sales	Average collection time
£	
30,000	1 month
60,000	2 months
90,000	3 months
50,000	4 months or more

The company estimate that if 3, 4 or 5% were offered for immediate settlement, all the 1 month payers would take it, 60% of the 2 month payers would take it at 5%, 50% at 4% and 40% at 3%, only 20% of the 3 month payers would take it at 5% and none at 3% or 4%. The 4 month payers would never take the discount.

The company can borrow at 14%. What should they do?

Exercise 9

Some extracts from the annual accounts of Chad Trading are:

Balance Sheet at 31.12.19x2:

	£		£
Stocks	44,000	Creditors	21,500
Debtors	38,000	Overdraft	32,000

Profit and Loss Account

Sales	154,000
Cost of goods sold	105,000
Purchases	102,000

Required:

a. Calculate the conversion cycle in days.

b. Calculate the overdraft if the cycle could be shortened by 10 days.

c. How might this shortening be achieved?

Case Study / Assignment 1

The directors of Harbridge Manufacturing PLC are meeting to discuss a cash crisis which is afflicting their profitable company. The problem is that the company is taking an average of 90 days to pay their suppliers and some of the suppliers are threatening to cut off supplies unless the period is shortened. In addition the company wish to pay an interim dividend. The bank have said that the overdraft facility is already larger than the bank would like. The views of the directors are:

Alec, the Chairman: I think we should borrow more money by the issue of some long term loan. Of course, the interest rate will be high but such an issue should solve our cash problem permanently.

Beryl, the works director: the problem lies in debtors. I see these are now £1,440,000 on annual sales of £6,600,000. If they paid more quickly we would solve the problem. We may have to pay to have a better computer system as I know that invoices take a week to process and statements do not go off until the 8th of the month.

Charles, the finance person: we could make the debtors pay more quickly if we offered 5% discount for quick payment. But my opinion is that the problem lies in the stock levels. We have a raw material stock of £400,000 and that is 15 weeks supplies. If that were reduced we would have no cash problem to worry about. Further the work in progress of £300,000 is absurdly large.

Donna, the sales director: we sell as much as we can but do we really need to hold more than 5 weeks supply of finished goods we have in stock? I think we should stop making some of our lines and buy them from Korea.

Required:

Write a report to the Board commenting on each of the director's remarks and recommending actions which would alleviate the cash problem. You may make assumptions but should then state them.

Assignment / Case Study 2

The Pendil Hospital Trust have a financial crisis on their hands. There is three months before the new financial year and they foresee that cash receipts in these three months will be insufficient to make the required payments. The Board realise that the basic problem is that annual expenditure exceeds annual income and that the coming financial year will have to see some economies. However, such economies will not alleviate the short term problem of the next three months. The financial director suggests that the only way she can see to survive in the short term is a working capital solution. She explains this to the Board:

❐ we shall have to run down all our stocks and that means buying only essential supplies (groans from Foodbotham who supplies the hospital with heating oil)

❐ we shall have to insist on early payment from our debtors — other health service organisations and private medical suppliers

❐ we shall have to postpone payments to our suppliers — many of these are other health service organisations and local suppliers (more groans from Foodbotham)

❐ we shall have to negotiate an increase in our overdraft.

Required:

i.   Evaluate the difficulties and disadvantages/advantages of these measures.

ii. From your experience, evaluate the possibilities of extra fundraising by NHS hospitals, and the possibilities of obtaining inputs more cheaply, more economical transformation of inputs into outputs (= treatment of patients) and possible rationing of expensive treatments.

9 Stocks

1. Objectives

This unit begins with the valuation of stock. You will recall from Units 2 and 3 that it is necessary to value stocks for the purposes of preparing Trading and Profit and Loss Accounts and Balance Sheets. This is not a difficult procedure for the stocks of retailers and wholesalers but is for manufacturing companies.

The amount of stocks held is a problem for most enterprises and we look at ways in which stock levels can be optimised using economic order quantities, re-order levels and Just in Time.

The Unit also looks at the accounting convention of prudence.

SCENARIO 1 — Martin values his stocks

Martin is well aware that stocks of the goods he buys from his suppliers are assessed in the annual *stocktake* at the year end. He himself organises the stock take and makes quite sure that:

- [ ] each type of stock is separately identified and counted;
- [ ] each type of stock is counted twice by separate people;
- [ ] the state of each item in stock is assessed for condition and saleability. Any items that are old, slow to sell, obsolete or damaged are noted;
- [ ] all this information is recorded in stock sheets which are numbered on issue and the return of each sheet is carefully recorded;
- [ ] any items not belonging to Martin Padlocks Ltd are not recorded;
- [ ] any items belonging to the company but not physically present (perhaps because they are in transit) are included;
- [ ] *cut-off* is correct. Cut-off means making sure that any goods which are included in purchases in a year are also included in stock if not sold and any goods sold in the year are not included in stock at the year end.

Martin hands the stocksheets to the accountant who takes each item, puts on a price, multiplies the price by the quantity to find the value of each category, adds the individual values to find the grand total and puts this in the Profit and Loss Account and Balance Sheet.

However Martin has not concerned himself with the price to be attached to each category other than knowing that it is the cost price to the company and not the selling out price. Several difficulties present themselves to him and he asks Anne to explain how these items would be valued.

The following categories of stock present special difficulties with valuation:

i. Padlock type G276 is imported from China at £2 each. Martin imports so many that the supplier gives him a trade discount of 20% off the £2 price. Martin pays the shipping cost of £200 a 1,000 units. On arrival at the works, Martin pays June £6 a

100 units to rebox and label them. The boxes cost 3p a unit and the labels 4p a unit. There were 860 type G276 in stock at the December 31st stocktake.

ii. Lock type G726 costs £48 a dozen from a local supplier and by special agreement Martin pays the day after each delivery and receives a 5% cash (another word is settlement) discount for doing so. He has 2,760 in stock.

iii. Lock type G627 contains a component made from a rare mineral which has a cost which varies from week to week. Consequently the price to Martin varies and so he buys from his supplier in small quantities. There were none in stock three months before the stocktake. There has been the following movements in the last three months:

October	14	Bought 500 at £4.90 each
	21	Sold 200 at £7.00 each
	28	Sold 250 at £6.70 each
November	3	Bought 400 at £3.60 each
	8	Bought 600 at £3.50 each
	15	Sold 350 at £6.00 each
	24	Sold 240 at £6.20 each
December	7	Sold 100 at £7.00 each
	15	Bought 200 at £4.25 each
	21	Sold 350 at £7.50 each

Martin Padlocks Ltd value stocks on the FIFO principle.

iv. Lock G400 was bought in July in a job lot of 2,000 for £1.50 each. Since then 200 have been sold but Martin knows that further sales will be made only at a low price as the locks are too flimsy. He has decided to sell off the remaining 1,800 at £1.60 each. Before selling them he will have to fit a replacement part at a cost to each lock of 20p for the part and 5p for labour. He will also have to pay a 10% commission on the sale to his representative.

Tasks 1

1. Show how each of these items of stock should be valued.

2. Explain the effect on profit of 19x2 and 19x3 of the following errors in stocktaking and valuation in the stock at 31 December 19x2:

   i. 35 H13s were counted as 30.

   ii. 43 H14s were included in the stocksheets as 34.

   iii. 100 H15s were omitted altogether.

   iv. 130 H16s were counted and entered twice.

   v. 60 H17s were sold and invoiced on 29th December. However they were collected by the carrier on Jan 2nd only and so were counted in the stocktake.

   vi. 45 H18s were priced at selling price instead of cost price.

   vii. 20 H19s were priced at cost but they are damaged and net realisable value is below cost.

viii. 100 H20s were valued on LIFO principles instead of FIFO. The price of H20s has been rising.

ix. Stock sheet 18 was not handed in and the items on it excluded from the final total.

x. An H21 was in the warehouse for a warranty repair. The stocktaker did not know this and included it in the stocktake.

2. Introduction

Most businesses have stocks. There are several possible kinds:

❑ stocks of raw materials in a manufacturing business

❑ stocks of goods for sale to customers. These may have been manufactured by the business (as in the stocks of new cars held by a motor car manufacturer) or purchased (as in stocks of new cars held by a car dealer)

❑ stocks of consumable items. These may include spare parts for machines, small tools, heating oil, stationery

❑ manufacturers and construction companies also have work in progress which is the stock of products for sale which are still in the course of manufacture.

At a Balance Sheet date all stocks held have to be identified and counted. This is often a major undertaking and unless it is very carefully planned and executed, errors will occur. After booking the items in stock on a listing which is called an inventory, the stocks have to be valued at cost. Some of them may be valued at lower than cost and we will deal with this point later.

3. Valuation at cost

Valuation at input cost may seem easy but in practice major conceptual problems occur with the definition of cost.

The basic principle is that stock should be valued at:

'The expenditure that has been incurred in bringing each item to its present location and condition.'

This is further defined as the cost of purchase + the cost of conversion.

These definitions come from Statement of Standard Accounting Practice (SSAP9) — Stocks and Long-term contracts. This SSAP governs the way stocks are valued for accounting purposes.

Cost of purchase includes the purchase price including import duties, transport and handling costs and any other directly attributable costs, less trade discounts, rebates and subsidies. Most of these costs and deductions are easily identifiable. For example:

i) 25,000 widgets are imported at £10 each from Hong Kong. Carriage to our works cost £4,000 for the consignment.

Cost of each is clearly £10 + £4,000/25,000 = £10.16.

ii) A farmer bought 10 tons of fertiliser at £20 a ton. The government paid him a subsidy of £6 a ton. The cost is thus £14 a ton.

iii) Hugh purchased a widget at £20 less 25% trade discount. He was allowed a 5% cash or settlement discount when he paid for them 3 days after the invoice date.

Cost here is considered to be £20 – £5 = £15. The cash or settlement discount is ignored in computing cost. The theory is that the cost is £15. The cash discount is a financial benefit obtained by financial means (having the cash to pay quickly) and is nothing to do with the goods.

Cost of conversion is more difficult. In general there are two types of cost to be added to purchase price:

i)   Costs which are specifically attributable to units of production, e.g. direct labour, direct expenses, and sub-contracted work.

Example

Guy imported 10,000 door handles from Taiwan. These cost £1 delivered to his warehouse. They were then lacquered by a subcontractor who charged 5p each. They were then reboxed and labelled by Guy's staff at a cost of 7p a box for the boxes and 20 hours labour at £3 an hour. Total cost is then £1 + 5p + 7p + £60/10,000 = £1.18.

ii) *Production overheads*. This is more difficult and is treated in more detail in Unit 12.

Example

Julie makes a single product — plastic cartons of mushy peas. Costs of producing 500,000 in a year of these are:

	£
500,000 plastic cartons	5,000
Peas	4,000
Direct labour	12,000
Production overheads	
(rent, rates, power, supervision etc)	16,000
	37,000

Total cost per carton is thus £37,000/500,000 = 7.4p

In practice, no businesses produce just one product and the production overheads have to be shared between the different products. This is a conceptual problem which is dealt with in Unit 12. However you should now realise that the cost of manufacturing a product must include an appropriate proportion of the manufacturing overhead.

Companies also have non-manufacturing overheads (administration, selling, distribution, finance) but these are not normally regarded as part of the cost of a product.

4. Valuation at net realisable value

Some items in stock may be damaged, old, obsolete or otherwise difficult to sell. It may be that the possible selling price of these is actually lower than cost. In such cases the net realisable value has to be estimated and this value is then used for stock valuation purposes instead of cost.

Essentially stocks are valued at the *lower* of two possible values:

i.   Cost

ii. Net realisable value

Most items in stock can be sold at above cost and so are valued at cost. A few may only be able to be sold at a price which is below cost because they are perhaps damaged or obsolete or because of price changes or bad buying decisions.

Net realisable value is defined in SSAP 9 as the actual or estimated selling price less:

❒ all further costs to completion

❒ all costs to be incurred in marketing, selling and distributing.

The valuation of stocks at the lower of cost and net realisable value is a consequence of the *prudence* convention in accounting. This convention requires that:

❒ revenue and profits are not anticipated (hence valuation at cost)

❒ charges to Profit and Loss Account are made of all known liabilities and losses whether the amount is known with certainty or is a best estimate in the light of the information available.

Thus if the financial statements for 19x2 are being prepared and it is known that most items in stock at the year end will be sold at a profit in 19x3, then the profit recognition will wait until 19x3. However any losses expected in 19x3 will be included in 19x2. So if an item is in stock at the end of 19x2 and will be sold at below cost in 19x3 then the loss in put into 19x2 by valuing at net realisable value in the 19x2 financial statements.

Note that this rule applies to all current assets including debtors as well as stocks. If a debt is expected to be bad, or that the debt will only be paid in part, then the value of such a debt is included on the Balance Sheet at what is expected to be received. The difference (a loss) is included in the Profit and Loss Account as an expense, usually labelled *provision for doubtful debts*. The rule can apply even to bank accounts. Some companies have their money in banks which go bust although this is rare. If the cash at bank is at risk, then the prudence convention requires that *Cash at Bank* is valued at what it is estimated will be recovered after the bank fails.

Examples

20 old model widgets are in Ted's stock. These cost £30 each to buy. They can now only be sold for £15 and Ted will have to pay £1 each carriage and 10% commission on the sale.

The cost is £30 each.

The realisable value is £15 each.

The net realisable value is £15 – £1 – £1.50 = £12.50.

Since £12.50 is below £30, the value for inclusion in the Balance Sheet is £12.50.

5. Like items

Some items in stock are indistinguishable from similar items. For example a dealer has a stock of identical exhausts for 1968 Morris Minors. Each of these is equally good at its function as the others. This means the items are *fungible*. However not all the items had the same cost because they were bought at different times and at different prices.

Example

Wilf bought 5 exhausts in October 19x2 for £30 each

and 7 exhausts in November 19x2 for £40 each.

In December he sold 8 of them.

At 31 December 19x2 he took stock and found he had 4 left and wondered what he should consider the cost of these to be. Remember that they are identical and he does not know from which consignment they came.

Accountants have developed three possible solutions for this problem:

First in first out	— FIFO
Last in last out	— LIFO
Average cost	— AVCO

We will consider each:

FIFO

	In	Out	Balance
October	$5 \times 30 = 150$		$5 \times 30 = 150$
November	$7 \times 40 = 280$		$\begin{cases} 5 \times 30 = 150 \\ 7 \times 40 = 280 \end{cases}$
December		$\begin{cases} 5 \times 30 = 150 \\ 3 \times 40 = 120 \end{cases}$	$4 \times 40 = 160$

In FIFO we consider or assume that the oldest go out first so that what remain in stock are the later deliveries.

LIFO

	In	Out	Balance
October	$5 \times 30 = 150$		$5 \times 30 = 150$
November	$7 \times 40 = 280$		$\begin{cases} 5 \times 30 = 150 \\ 7 \times 40 = 280 \end{cases}$
December		$\begin{cases} 7 \times 40 = 280 \\ 1 \times 30 = 30 \end{cases}$	$4 \times 30 = 120$

In LIFO we consider or assume that the newest go out first so that what remain in stock are the earlier delivered items.

AVCO

	In	Out	Balance
October	$5 \times 30 = 150$		$5 \times 30 = 150$
November	$7 \times 40 = 280$		$12 \times 35.8^* = 430$
December		$8 \times 35.8 = 287$	$4 \times 35.8 = 143$

* This is calculated by $\dfrac{150 + 280}{5 + 7}$

In average cost we assume or consider that a mixture of old and new go out each time there is a sale or a use of the items.

In practice LIFO is rarely used in the UK because it is not an acceptable valuation method for tax purposes and because it is frowned upon in Statement of Standard Accounting Practice No 9 on stocks. It is however used in the USA and other parts of the world.

FIFO and AVCO are both found extensively in the UK. Note that the assumptions for valuation purposes may not correspond with reality. In some real situations FIFO is always the reality. An obvious example is with perishable foodstuffs.

6. Stock costs and standard prices

A fourth common valuation method for stocks is to use a standard price. This is only used where a system of standard costing is in use and this is described in Unit 13. Standard cost cannot be used for financial statement purposes unless it approximates reasonably to actual cost.

SCENARIO 2 — Martin explores economic order quantity

Martin orders 500 type RP padlocks from his usual supplier as the company is out of stock and he has an order from a customer. The supplier is very apologetic but they have run out and their manufacturer in the Far East cannot supply for another three weeks. The supplier's salesperson is especially upset as her company have invested in a state of the art computer system incorporating EOQ and Automatic Ordering when Re-order levels are reached. She cannot understand what has gone wrong. Martin is upset at having to disappoint his customer and cannot understand what the sales-person is talking about.

Task 2

Explain to Martin what the salesperson means by EOQ and Reorder levels and what may have gone wrong.

---

7. Stock holding

Return to the working capital calculation in Unit 8. You will see that if stocks can be reduced, creditors can be reduced if all the other figures remain unchanged.

The amount of stocks carried is of great importance to the management of most enter-prises. Large amounts of stock prevent stock outs and enable all the demands of customers to be met. However holding stock has costs including:

> storage space costs
>
> financing costs
>
> risk of damage or spoilage
>
> risk of obsolescence.

Deliberately carrying small stocks also means buying in small quantities which involves extra handling costs and loss of bulk discounts.

In practice stocks are of many different lines. Some of these sell well and sometimes stock outs occur. Some stocks sell very slowly if at all. The tendency is for stocks of slow selling lines to multiply so that stock becomes too large and consists of the wrong items. Effectively the firm suffers from the penalties of holding large stocks without the benefits of being able to supply popular items to customers. The remedy for this situa-tion is vigilance. All purchasing should be carefully considered and stocks continually monitored. Any that do not move rapidly should be studied and movement hastened by a special promotion or price reductions.

There is a theory about the optimal amount of a particular line of stock. This concerns the economic order quantity (the optimal size of order) and is given in the formula:

$$EOQ = \sqrt{\frac{2BN}{C}}$$

where B = the costs (clerical, transport etc) of making one order.

   N = the number of units used in a year

   C = costs associated with holding the stock in £ per year.

Suppose T Ltd use 5,000 mark 3 widgets a year, the holding cost is 30p a unit a year and the buying cost is £20 an order then:

$$EOQ \text{ is } \sqrt{\frac{2 \times 20 \times 5,000}{0.30}} = 816 \text{ units}$$

Once the economic order quantity has been calculated it is then desirable to calculate the re-order level. This is the level of stock at which an order should be placed.

It is given by:

$$\text{Re-order level} = \frac{DN}{W}$$

where D = the delivery time taken by suppliers in weeks

   W = the number of working weeks in the year.

T Ltd find that the supplier of mark 3 widgets takes 7 weeks from order to delivery and there are 50 working weeks in the year. Then:

$$\text{Re-order level} = \frac{7 \times 5,000}{50} = 700 \text{ units}$$

Thus the purchasing officer should be told to order 816 units every time the stock falls to 700 units. In practice 816 units may be an unacceptable order and an order of 1,000 may be necessary or perhaps 6 gross — 864 units.

This explanation works well in theory but in practice:

a) Estimation of purchasing costs and holding costs is difficult and subjective.

b) The numbers change constantly — demand increases or reduces and delivery times vary greatly.

c) Doing the calculations for perhaps thousands of lines is a formidable task.

but

d) Attempting the calculations keeps the stock constantly under review.

e) Stock records are ideal for computerisation and once EOQs and re-order levels have been input, the computer can re-order automatically.

Note that the most modern manufacturing systems use *'just in time'* stock deliveries so stock levels of raw materials and components are effectively nil.

8. Just in time

Large manufacturers, who use numbers of components which they buy in from suppliers and who have highly automated production lines, used to carry large stocks of components. This required lots of space and heavy costs in storing and caring for the stocks. To avoid these two problems, the Just in Time idea was invented. Essentially, the manufacturer schedules his production and precise demand for components in advance. He then arranges for deliveries of the components to be scheduled at precisely the right time for them to be used on the assembly line. This does depend on the suppliers being able to deliver exactly as required and, indeed, may involve lorries circulating round the factory until delivery time is due.

Just in Time shifts the stock carrying problem from the manufacturer to the supplier. It is possible for the supplier to schedule her manufacture of the components so that as they are finished they are transported to the manufacturer. This requires very tight organisation and well disciplined manufacturing systems. To a large extent this is what usually happens but some stocking is inevitable. You will appreciate that stopping a modern assembly plant because a supply of widgets is an hour late is extremely expensive.

9. Work in progress

Manufacturing companies also have work in progress and stocks of finished goods. To optimise holdings:

a) The work in progress at any one time depends on the cycle time in manufacture. This should be kept as short as possible and constantly monitored. Delays caused by machine breakdown should be minimised by planned maintenance and delays caused by material or component shortages should be minimised by stock controls like the use of EOQ and re-order levels.

b) Finished goods levels are a function of production and sales. Production should be planned in relation to sales forecasts and the up to date position constantly monitored.

SCENARIO 3 — Martin advises on catering stocks

Martin has a sister Martina who is manager of the cafe/restaurant of a major museum. She is complaining to him about her problems. These seem to include:

❑ she has too much stock including bought in frozen dishes and frozen dishes made by her staff

❑ she has to buy large quantities of some dishes in order to get bulk discounts

❑ suppliers ring up to get orders and she has to search through the deep freezes to find what she needs to re-order

❑ some of the dishes go out of sell-by date and she has to sell them off to her staff at a very low price

❑ she has some dishes which fill up the freezers but which sell very slowly

❑ she panics at the year end when the accountants make her do a complete stock take. She does not know how to value all the dishes as the cost prices seem to vary so much.

Martin is very sympathetic as her problems seem to parallel his own.

Task 3

Table a memorandum to Martina suggesting:

❑ how she might optimise her stocks of frozen dishes

□ some new approaches to menu planning

□ how she might go about taking an inventory of her stocks at the year end and how the stocks should be valued.

10. Continuous inventory

Most enterprises do not keep a continuous record of what is in stock and count up the stock only at period ends. However, the advent of cheap computing has made a continuous record a reasonable possibility. A continuous recording of what is in stock in called a continuous inventory. Records can be kept in quantity terms only or in both quantity and value terms. Values will be at cost using usually FIFO or AVCO.

The disadvantage of continuous inventory is primarily the cost of the recording. Also it is important to ensure an accurate record by continuous sample comparison of actual with record and that too is costly. However the advantages are numerous:

□ instant knowledge what is in stock and how many, both on site and at branches

□ details of stock items can be recorded (e.g. supplier, lead time, shelf life etc)

□ application of techniques such as EOQ and automatic re-ordering

□ if values are included then total value of stock can quickly be found for financial statement purposes

□ extent of losses due to theft, mistakes can be determined

□ deterrent against petty pilfering

□ statistical summaries can be prepared of usage, average time in stock and similar data

□ catalogues are easily prepared

□ reviews of items stocked can be made by management.

Stocks

Goods for resale	Economic order quantity	Cost	- purchase
Raw material	Re-order levels		- conversion
Components	Continuous inventory	Fungible	- FIFO
Work in progress	Just in Time		- LIFO
Consumable stores			- AVCO

Service to customers v Holding costs

Prudence convention

11. Summary of Unit 9

□ Stocks are of various kinds: raw materials, work in progress, finished goods awaiting sale, purchased goods awaiting sale, consumable stores.

□ For financial statement purposes stocks are valued at the lower of cost and net realisable value.

- [] Cost is the expenditure incurred in bringing the good or service to its present location or condition.
- [] Cost is the cost of purchase + the cost of conversion.
- [] Cost of purchase includes import duties, transport and handling costs less trade discounts, rebates, and subsidies.
- [] Cost of conversion includes specifically attributable direct costs + an appropriate proportion of production overheads.
- [] Net realisable value is the expected selling price less all further costs to completion and all costs in marketing, selling and distribution of the product or service.
- [] Fungible stocks can be valued at FIFO, LIFO or AVCO. LIFO is not usual in the UK.
- [] Continuous inventory has many advantages.
- [] Techniques for optimising stock levels include economic order quantity, re-order levels and Just in Time.
- [] Stock levels tend to drift upwards as rarely or never used or sold items are added to it. This has cash flow implications. It is essential to continuously review all stocks.
- [] Stocktaking at period ends need to be well organised if it is to be accurate and have correct cut-off.
- [] Stock levels should be as low as is commensurate with uninterrupted production and service to customers.
- [] The prudence or conservatism convention applies to the valuation of stocks and all current assets and liabilities.

Exercise 1

Cheepoh supermarkets plc categorise their stocks as goods for resale and miscellaneous (heating oil, stationery, spare parts for equipment and vehicles). How do you think the following might categorise their stocks?

Giant Civil Engineering and Construction plc

Fork lift truck manufacturing company plc

Shoo pharmaceuticals plc (research, design, manufacture, wholesale and retail)

Mayne car dealers plc

Exercise *2

How would the following stocks be valued:

a. 200 widgets purchased by A Ltd from B Ltd in Taiwan at £50 each. The consignment was for 500 widgets and A Ltd sold 300 before the year end stock take when the 200 were counted. From the price B Ltd allowed a 20% trade discount. A Ltd had to pay £2,000 carriage from Taiwan. On arrival the widgets were painted with A Ltd's Logo at a cost of £2 each and packaged at a cost of £3 each.

b. 100 Things purchased by D Wholesale Ltd from E Ltd at £20 each. E Ltd gave a 15% trade discount and D took advantage of a 5% settlement discount.

c. 50 Grombles manufactured by G Ltd. The cost of manufacture of each Gromble was:

	£
Materials and components	6
Direct Labour	4
Works overheads – estimated at 1.5 × prime cost	

d. A stock of 8 houses built by H PLC in the hope of selling them. Each house was planned to cost:

> Land: the houses will almost fill one acre which cost £270,000. There is room for one more house.
>
> Site works: i.   before building. The whole site is now complete as to these which cost £90,000
>
>   ii.   after build. These will cost £120,000 but have not yet been commenced.

Professional fees. Architects (already paid) £1,000 a house

Construction costs (all sub-contracted) £60,000 a house. The houses are estimated to be just half complete. (note that in practice this would be determined more precisely)

Selling and conveyance costs £1,000 a house. (not yet spent)

Exercise *3

How would the following stock items be valued?

a. 4 gubbins in the stock of J Ltd which are the obsolete mark 2 model. They cost £60 each but can now be sold at 2/3 of the normal selling price of £105. Each sale will cost J Ltd 10% sales commission and £10 delivery costs.

b. Stubby Homes plc have sold an estate of new houses but have in stock just one second hand home which they took in part exchange. The part exchange price was £40,000 but the agent reckons:

     i.   it will require £4,000 repair expenditure before sale.

     ii.   it will sell for only £38,000.

     iii.   the sale will cost £1,000 in professional fees.

Exercise 4

K Ltd deal in car spares. Among these are exhausts for the Rocket mark 1. His transactions in these items in the year 19x2 are:

1 Jan	In stock 15 at cost £20 each
3 Feb	Purchase 23 at £18 each
4 Mar	Sell 8 at £40 each
5 Apr	Sell 25 at £45 each
6 May	Purchase 9 at £26 each
7 Aug	Purchase 10 at £30 each
8 Oct	Sold 3 at £40 each
9 Dec	Sold 9 at £42 each

How should the stock be valued at 31 December 19x2 based on

i. FIFO

ii. Average Cost

iii. LIFO?

Exercise *5

Liz's gift shop stocks, among many other things, a line of identical alpine paintings. Her deals in 19x2 in these were:

4 Feb	Purchase 40 at 10
6 Mar	Purchase 20 at 12
8 May	Sold 22 at 30
9 Oct	Purchase 10 at 15
1 Dec	Sold 35 at 28

a. How should the stock of paintings be valued at 31 December 19x2 based on i. LIFO ii. FIFO iii. AVCO?

b. One painting in stock at 31 December 19x2 is damaged and can only be sold for £5. How should this be valued and why is this value adopted?

Exercise 6

EF Ltd have large stocks of an imported widget for which they have exclusive importation rights. They are considering the size of orders to make. Data collected includes:

❏ The costs of making one order (including clerical costs, banking charges and transport) is £240

❏ Throughput is 10,000 units a year

❏ Holding costs are £2.00 a unit a year

❏ The supplier will only ship in multiples of 200 items.

Calculate the economic order quantity.

The supplier takes twelve weeks from the order to delivery. There are 50 weeks in the year. Calculate the re-order level.

Exercise 7

GH Publishers Ltd have large stocks of a guidebook for which they receive regular orders. They are considering the size of print orders to make. Data collected includes:

❏ The costs of making one order is £80

❏ Throughput is 8,000 units a year

❏ Holding costs are 50p a unit a year

❏ The printer will only print in multiples of 500 items.

a. Calculate the economic order quantity.

b. Discuss the difficulties and imperfections of this model in the real world.

The supplier takes six weeks from the order to delivery. There are 50 weeks in the year.

c. Calculate the re-order level.

d. Discuss the consequences of a stock-out.

Assignment 1

Eli formed his company Eli Ltd to manufacture specialised machinery which it makes for stock and then sells overseas. His first (19x2) year expenditure was:

	£
Materials and components	100,000
Direct Labour	75,000
General Works overheads	160,000
General Overheads	71,000
Interest	15,000
Plant and Machinery	140,000
Vehicles	60,000

Sales in the year were £396,000

His stocks on 31 December 19x2 were:

Raw materials and components valued at £15,000 (FIFO) or £8,000 (AVCO)

Finished goods valued at prime cost £24,000 + works overheads

He calculated his profit as:

Raw Materials and components	x	
Less Stocks	x	x
Direct Labour		x
Prime cost		x
Works Overheads:		
General	x	
Depreciation of Plant	x	x
Total Works inputs		x
Less Finished goods stocks		x
Cost of goods sold		x
Sales		x
Gross Profit		x
General Overheads	x	
Interest	x	
Vehicle depreciation	x	x
Net Profit		x

The Plant and Machinery is expected to last 4 years and have a salvage value of £32,000. The depreciation rate on the reducing balance method would be 30%.

The vehicles are expected to last 3 years and have a salvage value of £12,000. The depreciation rate on the reducing instalment method would be 40%.

The works overheads to be included in the valuation of finished goods stocks is that proportion of the total works overheads as the prime cost of the stock bears to the total prime cost.

Required:

a. Calculate the profit using alternative accounting policies for stock valuation (FIFO or AVCO) and depreciation (Straight line or reducing balance)

    Note that both types of fixed asset should be subject to the same depreciation method because of the consistency convention.

b. Eli Ltd had a large overdraft from the bank to fund the company initially. This is possibly renewable and the survival of the company depends upon its renewal. Eli knows that the bank is not expecting large profits in the early years of the company but is very wary of a loss making company. In view of this:

    i.   Recommend which accounting policies should be adopted.

    ii. Discuss the impact of the alternative accounting policies on subsequent annual profits/losses.

c. Describe the circumstances in which the valuation of raw material stocks can be so different on the two methods. Discuss the effect of the two alternative methods on future profits.

Assignment 2

Grape Ltd manufacture specialised plant to order. A substantial part of the plant items made is a component of which Grape stock about 200 varieties. The input cost of these varies substantially as they are partly made from a rare metal for which demand fluctuates widely.

Customers usually send a specification for a piece of plant to Grape and other suppliers. Grape's estimator then draws up a cost schedule for manufacture, adds a profit margin and quotes a price to the customer.

The stocks of the component are recorded, in quantities only, on a computer system and the estimator obtains his costs from a file of invoices. This system is unsatisfactory and it is proposed to incorporate values into the stock recording system.

The systems analyst has asked the company whether she should value the stocks on:

   FIFO or LIFO or AVCO.

The estimator also wonders if it would help him if information could be incorporated on:

   The highest input price in the previous six months

   The current price charged by suppliers

   The price of the most recent purchase.

Required:

a. Discuss the price that the estimator might include in his cost schedule when preparing a quotation for a customer.

b. The computed values must be used for stock valuation purposes in the annual accounts. Discuss the constraints this may make on the choice of values used by the systems analyst.

Assignment 3

Backus Ltd have an up-market restaurant and carry an extensive stock of wines. In recent months the stock seems to have grown and the cellar is so crowded that staff have been unable to find some wines they know are there. The restaurant is doing well but the high stock is causing cash flow problems.

The company are technologically minded and intend to acquire a computer system which they think may assist them in managing their stock and reducing their cash flow problems.

Explain how computerised stock records may assist the company in overcoming the problems identified above.

10 Investment appraisal

1. Objectives

Firms do not stand still but continually make changes. Most changes involve new capital expenditure on fixed assets. Such **capital expenditure** may be for replacement assets or for more efficient assets or in connection with new products, production methods, factories, branches etc. The acquisition of an entire business or company as in **takeover** situations can also be regarded as capital expenditure.

Clearly decisions on such capital expenditure should not be made without thought and the processes by which possible capital expenditure is considered is called **capital budgeting** or **capital investment appraisal**. There are various techniques for considering such capital expenditure and this unit is about them.

SCENARIO 1 — Martin considers some capital expenditure

Martin has discovered that there is a market for a new type of lock which he calls the Zitron. His manager is asked to design the lock and a production system in detail and consider the feasibility of setting up a production line for it. Martin commissions his local College marketing department to determine the likely demand at various price levels.

The College charge him £1,000 and tell him that demand over the next few years is likely to be:

Year	Units
1	10,000
2	20,000
3	20,000
4	15,000
5	10,000
6	5,000

Price should be about £10 each.

The manager has spent £4,000 on designing the lock and the production system and is ready to go ahead with obtaining firm prices for the production system from suppliers if Martin gives the go ahead.

He estimates that costs will be:

Capital costs:

Market survey (see above)	£1,000
Design (see above)	£4,000
Machinery	£80,000
Working capital	£35,000

Production costs:

Variable:	Labour	£2 a lock
	Material	£4 a lock

	Energy	£0.50 a lock
	Consumables	£0.30 a lock
Fixed:	Labour	£15,000 a year
	Other costs	£6,000

He expects that the machinery will fetch a salvage value of about £10,000 whenever it is sold.

The working capital would reduce as sales fell off in years 4 and 5 but it is reasonable to simplify the calculations to say that the original investment in the working capital will be returned at the end of the project.

Quick Answer Questions 10.1

1. Before considering whether to go ahead with the project, Martin has already spent £5,000. Do you think that in deciding whether or not to go ahead Martin should take the £5,000 into account?

2. Why do you think sales of the product will decline towards the end of the project?

3. What is meant by an investment in working capital? Why will it be returned at the end of the project?

4. What will be the contribution from the sale of one lock?

5. Will it be worthwhile making and selling just 5,000 locks in year 6?

SCENARIO 2 — Martin tries out some capital investment appraisal techniques

Martin is wondering how to appraise the project when he remembers a course he once attended. He recovers the notes and makes himself familiar again with the techniques.

Firstly he has to make some decisions. These are:

a. He will assume that the project will last five years as year 6 promises to be unprofitable. He will of course continue into year 6 and beyond if sales are still keeping up.

b. He has talked about *cost of capital* to Anne and has calculated it at 16%.

c. He reckons that he requires that any project should pay *off* within four years.

Tasks 1

1. Appraise the project by:
   a. Calculating the *payback* period
   b. Calculating the net present value and profitability index.
   c. Calculating the *accounting rate of return* using average capital investment over the life of the project.

2. Write a report to Martin arguing out the correct decision on the project. You should bring in any non-financial arguments you can think of, stating any assumptions you may care to make?

2. Introduction

Capital expenditure is expenditure on fixed assets. Fixed assets are long lived items like land, buildings, plant and machinery and vehicles. These are called tangible assets. For the purposes of this chapter we will include also the acquisition of intangible assets such as goodwill, patents and trade marks.

Fixed assets can be acquired singly as in the purchase of a replacement lorry or lathe or the construction of a factory extension. They can also be acquired as a set as in the setting up of a new branch, a new production line or a whole business.

The important thing is to distinguish between capital expenditure and revenue expenditure. Revenue expenditure is spending on the supply and manufacture of goods and the provision of services charged in the Profit and Loss Account in the accounting period in which they are consumed.

In most companies, revenue expenditure is controlled by systems of budgetary control perhaps with standard costing and variance analysis. Capital expenditure often involves very large sums and is non-routine, so it is very important to have a system to deal with projected capital expenditure. Such systems are called *investment appraisal* or *capital budgeting*.

3. Payback

A simple way of appraising projected capital investment is to use payback. This is simply considering the length of time which is required for a stream of *cash receipts* flowing from the investment to recover the initial investment.

Suppose a replacement machine was being considered. The cost (after deducting the proceeds of sale of the old machine) will be £5,000. The new machine will cost less to run and the annual savings are estimated at £1,500 a year. The payback period is $3\frac{1}{3}$ years $(3 \times £1,500 + \frac{1}{3} \times £1,500)$.

For management, knowing the payback period is useful in deciding whether or not to go ahead with an investment and deciding between possible alternatives. Some managements have a hurdle such that investments are not accepted unless the payback period is say less than three or four years.

Points about payback include:

a) Cash flows are considered, not accounting flows.

b) Future cash flows are not equivalent to current cash flows as current cash held can be invested to earn interest. £1,000 today can be invested at say 10% so that in one years time it is equivalent to £1,100. This important idea is not recognised by payback.

c) Payback prefers short term investments rather than investments which take a long time to pay off. *Short-termism* is a criticism often levelled at British management.

d) In a time of rapid technological change, payback has some obvious benefits.

e) Projects that pay back quickly may present less *risk* and payback is sometimes used as a proxy for the riskiness of the project.

4. Discounted cash flow

This is a more sophisticated approach to capital investment appraisal but is not so simple to understand.

The important concept is that money has a time value.

If you have £1,000 today (the *present* time) then it can be invested to earn say 10% interest. This means that its value grows as:

	£	
now	1,000	
Interest year 1	100	
value after one year	1,100	
Interest year 2	110	(10% of £1,100)
value after two years	1,210	

This is easy to understand. However we can see the process in a different way. We can say that the £1,210 after two years is equivalent in value to the £1,000 now. We can also say that the *present (= now) value* of £1,210 receivable in two years time is £1,000.

If the interest rate was say 15% the figures would be:

	£
now	1,000
Interest year 1	150
value after one year	1,150
Interest year 2	172.50
value after two years	1,322.50

So the present value of £1,322.5 two years in the future at 15% rate of interest is £1,000.

It is possible to calculate the present value of any future sum, given its date and a rate of interest. We can use a formula:

$$\text{Present value} = \frac{\text{future sum}}{(1 + r)^n}$$

where r = the rate of interest. This has to be expressed as a percentage divided by 100 i.e. if the rate is 16% then r = 0.16. and n = the number of years.

If we take the figures already calculated then £1,322.50 at 15% two years in the future:

$$\text{Present value} = \frac{1,322.5}{(1.15)^2} = £1,000$$

Alternatively, tables can be used. This is an extract from a table:

	Interest rate			
Year	10%	12%	14%	16%
1	.91	.89	.88	.86
2	.83	.80	.77	.74
3	.75	.71	.67	.64
4	.68	.64	.59	.55

You can read off that the discount factor for a sum three years away at 14% is .67. So if we need the present value of £4,800 three years away at 14% then the answer is

£4,800 × .67 = £3,216 or as .67 is a rounded figure we should perhaps specify it as £3,200. The formula gives £3,239.86…

An example

Upandaway plc are considering an investment in a company aeroplane. Projected cash flows are:

Cost now £600,000

Resale value after 4 years £100,000

Savings each year on other forms of transport £380,000

Running costs year 1 £150,000, year 2 £180,000, year 3 £200,000 year 4 £200,000.

We can set this up as a table:

(all figures in £'000)

Year	0	1	2	3	4
Outflow	− 600				
Savings		+ 380	+ 380	+ 380	+ 380
Costs		− 150	− 180	− 200	− 200
Resale					+ 100
Net cash flow	− 600	+ 230	+ 200	+ 180	+ 280
Discount factor		.89	.80	.71	.64
Present value	− 600	+ 200	+ 160	+ 130	+ 180

Note:

a) I have used a discount rate of 12%. The discount rate to be used is the *'cost of capital'* to the company. Its calculation is a very large subject and we will not attempt to calculate it in this manual.

b) The original outlay is described as year 0 and subsequent flows as being in year 1, 2 etc. Cash flows in a year are usually considered to be received or paid at the *year end*.

c) The estimates of future cash flows are very *uncertain* and the effect of multiplying an uncertain number say £380,000 by a discount factor which is a rounded fraction of an uncertain discount rate should not be a precise number. I have therefore given the discounted cash flows to two significant figures.

d) The net present value is:

−£600,000 + £200,000 + £160,000 + £130,000 + £180,000 = + £70,000

As this is positive, the project is a good one and should be undertaken. Essentially, we can say that it will earn income which represents a rate of interest greater than 12% which is the cost of capital.

e) It is possible to calculate a profitability index:

$$\frac{\text{Discounted inflow}}{\text{Initial outlays}} = \frac{£670,000}{£600,000} = 1.1$$

This can also be used as a measure of risk as the higher the projected discounted inflows in relation to the initial outflow, the less likely it is that the actual discounted future inflows will return a negative net present value.

f) In order to appraise a project using this method, it is necessary to specify all cash flows and an interest rate. In specifying future cash flows, a *time horizon* has to be specified. In the example I have suggested that the aeroplane will last four years. In practice the life of new projects is uncertain and stating a time horizon adds yet another layer of unreality to the process.

5. Internal rate of return

This is a similar but more difficult alternative to net present value. It actually presents a number of conceptual and practical problems which I will not address here. As a result it is not very commonly used in business.

The objective of this approach is to see what rate of interest a proposed project will *return*. Suppose that Upandaway plc are considering a joint venture project in Poland which will involve an outlay now (year 0) of £65,000 and the expected returns over the three year life of the project are:

Year 1 £20,000 Year 2 £30,000 year 3 £40,000

What rate of return is given by this project? An alternative statement of the problem is: what rate of discount will discount the cash flows in years 1, 2 and 3 back to the outlay in year 0? This can only be found by *trial and error*. Let us start with 14%.

Year	1	2	3
	£'000	£'000	£'000
Cash flows	20	30	40
Discount factor at 14%	.88	.77	.67
Present values	18	23	27

Net present values in total are £68,000.

This is more than the outlay, so we can say the project pays more than 14% and we should try 15%.

This gives figures of £17,000 + £23,000 + £26,000 = £66,000

This is approximately correct and we can say the project will pay about 15%. The company may have a rule that all projects which pay above the cost of capital of 12% are acceptable and then this project would be considered to be acceptable.

Some points about internal rate of return are:

a) Most text books calculate the rate exactly (e.g. 14.63%). However the forecast cash flows are estimates with a large margin for error and it is not really possible to specify the rate of return accurately. In fact it may give management a spurious confidence in the accuracy of the forecasts.

b) The calculations can be tedious and in practice are carried out on a computer.

c) The higher the internal rate of return in relation to the cost of capital, the less risky the project appears to be.

6. Accounting rate of return

The net present value and internal rate of return approaches use cash flows. A disadvantage of this approach is that measurements of cash flows are not made or are not reported so there is often no feedback on the success of the forecasts made. As measurement and reporting is done of accounting flows, some writers advocate appraising projects by using the accounting rate of return. Suppose Upandaway plc are proposing to open a branch in Tipton and expected initial outlays are £30,000. Expected returns are:

Year	1	2	3	4	5
(in £'000)	5	6	8	6	5

These returns are after depreciation.

Average return is $\dfrac{£30,000}{5} = £6,000$

The accounting rate of return is $\dfrac{£6,000}{£30,000} \times 100 = 20\%$

An alternative is to take the *average capital employed* which, assuming that the investment will be steadily depreciated to nil over the five years is

$$\frac{£30,000}{2} = £15,000.$$

In this case the accounting rate of return will be $\dfrac{£6,000}{£15,000} \times 100 = 40\%$.

Points about this method include:

a) It is in effect a rate of return on capital employed.

b) The accounting flows are subject to the vagaries of accounting measurement including different depreciation methods.

c) The method is not intellectually rigorous and there are no universally accepted methods of applying it.

d) I do not recommend it.

7. Practical investment appraisal

There is agreement that some approach to formal capital investment appraisal is desirable if only to clarify thinking. For example management may decide they fancy a company aeroplane but to do so without careful estimates of costs, revenues, savings, alternatives etc may well lead to a bad decision.

However the intellectually rigorous methods of appraisal (net present value and internal rate of return) do have drawbacks including the fact that management do not always understand them.

The simple methods (payback and accounting rate of return) are easier to understand but lack rigour. Many companies adopt a combination of methods. This may mean net present value as a first hurdle and payback as a second hurdle. Also in practice many proposals may pass the tests and be rejected by management and many fail the tests but are adopted anyway!

SCENARIO 3 — Martin sets up a spreadsheet model

Martin thinks that the figures he has prepared for the Zitron are not firm but may be changed. For example he thinks that the price of £10 could be lowered to £9. In that case sales will rise perhaps by about 10%. Or he could raise the price to £11 and then expect sales to fall by say 10%. He would like to know how any changes might affect the overall appraisal.

Tasks 2

1. Set up the problem on a spreadsheet
2. Test the model for *sensitivity* to changes in the data. Changes may be in the initial cost, the discount rate, the time horizon, the volume of sales, the sales price, the input costs etc.

SCENARIO 4 — Martin wonders about double glazing

Martin lives on a main road and is talking one day to a neighbour who tells him that she supplies replacement windows. Martin agrees to consider any quotation that she makes for his house. Being familiar with capital appraisal techniques, he writes down all the relevant data:

Estimate for all front facing windows: £6,000

Savings from reduced energy loss: £900 a year

Addition to value of house (estimated) £4,000

Cost of Capital: 12%

Time Horizon: 5 years

Note:

a. He has worked out the saving in energy from data supplied by his neighbour.
b. The addition to the value of his house was estimated by a friend who is an estate agent. He will realise the extra money only when he sells the house.
c. The cost of capital is the rate he can borrow at.
d. The time horizon is just a guess. He arrived at it by thinking that he would move when his last child left home which will be in five years' time.

Tasks 3

1. Calculate the net present value of this project.
2. Suggest and discuss any factors other than the purely financial that Martin may care to take into account.
3. Advise him on whether to accept or reject the project.
4. Consider how accurate each of the figures are. How variable do you think each of them might be?
5. What addition to the value of the house would make the project exactly viable, that is, have a net present value of zero?

---

8. More advanced capital investment appraisal

Capital investment appraisal techniques such as payback and net present value have been much criticised as being based upon exceedingly unreliable estimates. For example James owns a very successful chain of menswear shops. He is considering opening a new shop in Walsall. To use the proper appraisal techniques, he should estimate the cost of setting up the shop and then estimate likely sales and overheads. The overheads can be estimated fairly readily but likely sales can really only be a guess.

In this case James is a successful entrepreneur and will rely on his own flair in deciding whether to go ahead or not.

In a case where the company is a large corporation and local management want to open the new shop then the company might require that the local management make out a good case. They can do this by:

❏ estimating costs and expenses by getting estimates from suppliers and considering costs levels at other shops

❏ estimate sales by considering comparable existing shops, assessing competition, market research etc. In other words they will have to do their homework and perhaps the benefit of capital investment appraisal lies in the homework rather than in the mathematics.

There are a number of more advanced techniques and we will review some of them.

9. Mutually exclusive projects

Jayne can use the first floor of her hairdressing salon for either:

      A. Starting a beauty business

or   B. Starting a dressmaking business

The capital costs would be   A. £7,000

                                  B. £3,200

and the sales less expenses would be: A. £3,000 a year

                                  B. £1,500 a year

The business can only last the remainder of the lease – 4 years and we will assume a nil scrap value.

Cost of capital is 20%.

The net present values and profitability indeces are:

a. $(£3,000 \times 2.58) - £7,000 = £740$: $\dfrac{£7,740}{£7,000} = 1.1$

b. $(£1,500 \times 2.58) - £3,200 = £670$: $\dfrac{£3,870}{£3,200} = 1.2$

Note that 2.58 = the sum of the discount rates for four years at 20%.

Jayne cannot undertake both projects. She has to choose. The criterion is to select the project offering the highest net present value. Thus in this case she should adopt project A even though project B has a higher profitability index. This is because the higher NPV enriches the firm the most.

10. Capital rationing

In theory, any project that gives a prospective positive net present value should be undertaken. However if a company has a very large number of such projects (it would be very fortunate if it had) infinite capital may not be available to finance all the projects. In theory finance should be available as banks should be willing to finance any project with a positive NPV but in practice infinite finance is not available. Where limited capital is available and all positive NPV projects cannot be undertaken then a capital rationing situation is said to exist.

Other capital rationing situations exist where:
- all projects cannot be undertaken due to limited entrepreneurial energy or limited management time
- groups restrict capital available to subsidiaries.

Suppose Lal Ltd have identified the following projects:

(£'000)	Outlay	Net Present Value
A.	34	8.1
B.	20	4.3
C.	15	2.8
D.	47	8.8
E.	12	1.6

If capital is limited to £50,000, which should be chosen? The answer is to choose the combination of projects which maximises NPV. In theory every possible combination should be considered but in practice it is usually possible to work out the best combination fairly easily by trial and error. I think the answer is A. + C.

11. Cost benefit analysis

In essence capital investment appraisal is simply a comparison of expected costs and expected revenues or benefits. The analysis is made more meaningful by incorporating timing and perhaps risk considerations. In the case of commercial businesses a project is considered viable if the benefits *to the firm* exceed the costs to the *firm*. It is not usual to consider the costs which may be borne by other people. These costs are called externalities. For example, Hedy is considering going down market at her exclusive restaurant and increasing the number of meals sold from 150 a week to 450 a week by offering cheaper meals to a different (and more numerous) type of customer. Estimates show that this would be very profitable. However she does not take into account the impact on the local people of extra traffic, extra noise and extra smells. The cost of these is both difficult to quantify in money terms and would not be borne by Hedy but by her neighbours. To be fair, the benefits to the neighbourhood may include more employment and more purchases from local suppliers. These are also not considered by Hedy.

I leave you to consider whether firms should take external costs and benefits into account!

In the case of not-for-profit organisations, the internal costs of some new venture are often capable of assessment but again there may be external costs. The benefits are often much more difficult to appraise. Consider a potential day centre in a suburb which provides facilities for disabled and elderly people. The costs of running it can be assessed by the council. But what are the benefits? These may include a better life for the disabled and elderly but also it may free carers to engage in economic activity, it may keep some people out of very expensive residential care, it may form a focus for community activity in a crime ridden area and the building and running costs may prime the pump of economic activity in the district. It may be that the economic benefits in total are greater than the economic costs in total.

Local councils and central government engage in many large scale capital projects from road building to airport construction. Before commencing any new project a cost benefit analysis needs to be done. This is very difficult both because it is very difficult to identify all the costs and benefits and even more difficult to quantify them in money terms. Consider the construction of a new runway to an airport. What are the costs? They must include the noise nuisance to local householders. That identifies one cost. But how many householders? At what cost to each? A number of techniques have been developed to estimate these costs. They include measuring the falls in value of each house or the costs of installing double glazing and other noise reducing installations in each house. The benefits are also difficult to measure. A new runway will save numerous journeys to other more distant airports and it will boost economic activity in the region. But how to measure these benefits?

Cost benefit analysis is a fascinating and ultimately very important matter. There is a large literature and I commend it to you.

12. Taxation

In the real world taxation is a fact of life and must be taken into account in all decisions where it has an impact — it has an impact on most decisions. In practice taking taxation into account in NPV and other investment appraisal calculations is very complicated. I feel that it is beyond the scope of this non-specialist manual and is best carried out by experts.

Capital budgeting	
Uses	– Adding to Fixed Assets
	– Replacing Fixed Assets
	– New Products
	– New Branches
	– New Methods
	– Acquisition of businesses
	– Acquisition of companies
	– Investing in Financial Assets
Appraisal Methods	– Payback
	– Net Present Value
	– Internal Rate of Return
	– Accounting Rate of Return
Net Present value	– Initial cost
	– Cash Flows
	– Working Capital
	– Disposal of assets/working capital
	– Discount Rate/ Cost of Capital
	– Profitability Index
	– Time Horizon

13. Summary of Unit 10

- ❑ Capital expenditure is in some ways the most important activity of enterprises.
- ❑ It is vital that projected capital investment should be subject to careful scrutiny and consideration including the use of capital investment appraisal techniques.
- ❑ Capital investment appraisal can also be called capital budgeting.
- ❑ The simplest technique is payback where the time taken by estimated future cash inflows to cover the initial outlay is calculated.
- ❑ The best technique is the calculation of net present value. This is carried out by discounting all cash flows (except the initial outlay) by a rate of interest equal to the cost of capital.
- ❑ A similar, but more difficult, technique is the internal rate of return. This method involves the calculation of the discount rate which will just discount the future cash flows back to the initial outlay.
- ❑ The accounting rate of return involves the calculation of a return on capital employed using the average after depreciation returns and the actual or average capital employed.
- ❑ In practice, enterprises may use none, any or a combination of these or make decisions on other grounds altogether.
- ❑ All figures used are forecasts and estimates. These are not necessarily reliable.
- ❑ Estimates required include the initial capital outlay, working capital requirement, salvage value, cash flows for sales or savings, cash flows of costs, cost of capital and time horizon.
- ❑ Where there are competing mutually exclusive projects then the project with the highest NPV should be chosen.
- ❑ In capital rationing situations, the projects giving the highest total of NPV should be chosen.
- ❑ In the case of public investment, cost benefit analysis needs to be carried out.

Exercise *1

At the beginning of 19x2, Buggins Ltd are considering 5 investments in replacement plant:

Reference Net Cost Savings in year:

Reference	Net Cost	1	2	3	4	5
	£	£	£	£	£	£
A	40,000	5,000	8,000	12,000	18,000	16,000
B	20,000	8,000	8,000	5,000	4,000	2,000
C	29,000	1,000	12,000	23,000	nil	3,000
D	29,000	24,000	6,000	1,000	1,000	1,000
E	30,000	nil	nil	nil	nil	45,000

You can assume that the returns in year 5 include the proceeds of disposal of the plant and that all the projects have 5 year lives.

Required:

a. Calculate payback period for each project.

b. Calculate net present value for each project at

    i. 10%   ii. 12%   iii. 16% cost of capital.

c. Calculate the profitability index for each project.

d. Make reasoned recommendations on acceptance or rejection of each project.

e. Using these projects, discuss the utility of the capital investment appraisal process.

f. Calculate the internal rate of return for each project.

Exercise 2

Yogg Gurt Ltd have a chain of shops selling dairy produce. They are considering opening a branch in Wednesfield and the marketing director with the help of the finance director has produced the following forecasts for the proposal:

Cost of initial ingoing (lease, shop front, fittings, equipment etc)	£65,000
Initial working capital	£4,000
Annual outgoings (rent, wages, rates, heating etc)	£24,000

Annual sales:

year	1	2	3	4	5
(£'000)	60	90	100	100	100

Gross profit to sales ratio 50%

The branch will sell retail and also supply local businesses on credit.

At the end of the lease (after 5 years) the shop will either close and Yogg will get back their initial investment in working capital only or they can continue with a further investment in a new lease etc.

Required:

a. Calculate the payback period for the project.

b. Calculate the net present value and profitability index at 14% the cost of capital.

c. Calculate the internal rate of return.

d. Should the company go ahead?

e. Recalculate a. and b. if:

    i.   Initial ingoing was £68,000

    ii. Annual outgoings were 5% more or 5% less than forecast

    iii. Annual sales were 5% more or 5% less than forecast

    iv. Gross Profit ratio was 45% or 55%.

f. Explain the investment in working capital and why it will be returned at the end of the project.

g. What should the company do at the end of the lease?

Exercise 3

Dream Ltd, a manufacturer of special beds, are considering the purchase of a rival company Reverie Ltd. If the company is purchased, Dream Ltd will close it down and realise about £200,000 from the sale of the assets less the settlement of liabilities including redundancy pay. It is estimated that this will take about a year.

Dream reckon that they will make extra sales as follows as a consequence of this purchase:

Year	1	2	3	4
	£180,000	£140,000	£80,000	£40,000

They make a gross profit of 60% on all sales. They estimate that fixed costs will remain unchanged despite the increase in turnover.

Required:

a. What is the minimum price that Dream could pay to make the purchase of Reverie worth while if cost of capital is i. 14% ii. 20%?

b. Discuss this question from an ethical and public policy point of view.

Exercise *4

It is 19x6 and Doreen is considering the purchase of a new and better machine for her hardwood business. She already has a machine which does the job. She bought the machine in 19x2 for £50,000 and it will work well for at least 5 years. She could sell it now for about £10,000. However the new machine is much more efficient and would save her £6,000 a year in wages and materials over the next 6 years, the life of the machine. In addition the new machine will do some work the present machine will not do and this will bring in a contribution of £6,000 a year.

The new machine will cost £50,000 and like the present one will have no value at the end of its life.

Required:

a. Should she buy the new machine if her cost of capital is

   i. 14% ii. 22%?

b. At what rate of interest is the purchase of the new machine just viable?

c. Assuming a straight line method of depreciation, calculate the depreciation in the accounts if:

   i. the new machine is purchased

   ii. the new machine is not purchased.

d. The extra contribution of £6,000 mentioned above is not certain. How much actual contribution is required to make the project just viable at 14%?

Exercise 5

Labey is considering two investments offered by a financial institution:

a. An investment now of £20,000 with guaranteed payment of £35,000 in 5 years time.

b. An investment now of £20,000 with five annual interest payments of £2,200 + a guaranteed return of £24,000 in 5 years time.

Required:

a. Which investment offers the best return?

b. Which should Labey invest in if a. also offers the guaranteed sum on the death of Labey at any time before the end of the five years if:

    i. Labey is 60 and has no dependants

    ii. Labey is 40, is in work, is married and has 3 young children.

Case Study / Assignment

Things PLC are in a very competitive industry making parts for the motor industry. They are considering the replacement of one production line with a more modern one. Indications are that the cost of the new line less the scrap value obtained from the present one will be £450,000. This figure is fairly certain but the changeover will have substantial costs and these have been estimated as between £50,000 and £150,000. The engineer cannot be more precise than this.

The new line will last 5 years and estimated savings in production costs over the old line are:

Year	1	2	3	4	5
(£'000)	150	150	150	200	250

The higher savings in later years are because the old line would be costing substantial sums in repairs by then and may well be unreliable.

The company fears a takeover bid from a larger company and the chairman has a issued a rather optimistic profit forecast which he is very anxious to adhere to in the short term.

The financial director is uncertain as to the cost of capital but accepts that the current figure is about 14% but fears it may rise to 15% if they need to borrow in the near future.

The marketing director is a natural optimist and considers that the new production line will enable higher production levels in the future should the increased sales which he expects actually happen. Currently sales are running at about 80% of capacity.

Required:

Write a report to the Board

a. Detailing the methods which might be used to evaluate the proposal.

b. Assess the proposal using these methods.

c. Express an opinion on the proposal and make a case for your opinion.

Exercise 6

Stoo can use a field at the back of his leisure complex for either A. a crazy golf course or B. a model boating lake. Estimated figures are:

	A	B
Capital costs	£100,000	£200,000
Annual Profits	£40,000	£70,000

Cost of capital is 18% and Stoo only considers returns for a maximum of 5 years. You can ignore any salvage value to the expenditure.

Which should he choose?

Exercise 7

Phyllis is considering building on the plot of land next to her house. There is planning permission for commercial use and she is considering:

a. Building a bingo club and letting it on a 7 year lease to an operating company (not connected to her) at £10,000 a year.

b. Building an office block and letting it in small units on 7 year leases for a total rent of £7,000 a year.

c. Building a showroom and opening a piano shop of her own. She estimates she will make £20,000 a year for the 7 years before she retires and will have to give up her job as an insurance clerk at £11,000 a year.

Cost of capital is 12% .

At the end of seven years, the whole site will be compulsorily purchased by the development corporation for redevelopment. Site value only will be paid.

Construction costs would be:

    A. £40,000   B. £35,000   C. £30,000

Required:

a. Which should she adopt?

b. Discuss any other factors that she may wish to take into account.

Exercise 8

Chall is considering six projects:

(£'000)		Outlay	Net Present Value
	A.	90	4
	B.	30	11
	C.	52	7
	D.	32	6
	E.	120	19
	F.	21	7

Capital is limited to £150,000

Which projects should be undertaken?

Exercise 9

Bjorn is considering six projects:

(£'000)		Outlay	Net Present Value
	A.	102	12.1
	B.	55	4.3
	C.	32	9.8
	D.	120	14.1
	E.	60	3.1
	F.	80	5.0

If capital is limited to £210,000, which projects should be undertaken if:

a. Each project must be undertaken in full or not at all;

or

b. Each project can be scaled down as much as is necessary (in this case the criteria for selection is profitability index)?

Exercise 10

Tau intends to buy a machine for £10,000. This will last 5 years and attract capital allowances of 25%. At the end of 5 years he will sell the machine for £3,000.

During the 5 years savings made by using the machine will be:

Year	1	2	3	4	5
(£'000)					
Savings	4	4.5	3.9	2.8	2.7

Cost of capital is 8% net of tax

Tau pays tax at a marginal rate of 40%.

Is the project viable?

Exercise 11

A region of the UK has a negative economic growth rate and a noted industrial museum, owned by a charity, which is capable of substantial development. Unfortunately the museum can only be reached by narrow road. The government are considering building a dual carriageway road to improve access to the museum. Identify the costs and benefits of building the road and consider how each may be quantified in money terms. Consider also the time scale of costs and benefits and how timing may be brought into the analysis. List the parties who may bear the costs or reap the benefits of the road.

Exercise 12

Mainchance has a haulage business centred on a small town in a rural area. He keeps, services and maintains his 20 lorries in a depot in the main street. He sees that the business is in long term decline and resolves to build a factory on the site to apply metal and plastic coatings to manufactured products.

How might Mainchance evaluate his proposal? How might the local council evaluate the request for planning permission? What legal constraints are likely to minimise the externalities attached to the industrial processes concerned?

11 Manufacturing and construction

1. Objectives

This Unit begins by explaining how the profit is measured in manufacturing companies. We then consider the difficult problem of measuring the profit in construction companies.

We then include a look at three more accounting conventions — materiality, consistency and going concern.

Finally we look at two perennial problems in accounting measurement — goodwill and research and development expenditure.

SCENARIO 1 — Martin analyses a manufacturing account

Martin is familiar with the accounts of his own company but has relied on Anne going through the Manufacturing Account section with him to really understand what the words and figures mean. He would like to expand his manufacturing and knows that he can do this by building up manufacturing in his own business or perhaps by buying an already existing business. He is approached by a fellow member of the Chamber of Commerce who suggests Martin might be interested in buying her business as she makes a complementary range of products. Before making a decision he asks for a copy of the accounts and is supplied with a copy of the two most recent sets of figures. Here they are:

Bukkeyball Lock Manufacturing Company

Manufacturing, Trading and Profit and Loss Account

For the year ending 31 December

	19x1		19x2
	(£'000)		
Raw materials			
Opening Stock	23		17
Purchases	223		195
	246		212
Less Closing Stock	17		16
Consumed		229	196
Direct labour		431	420
Other Direct Costs		20	18
Prime Costs		680	634
Production Overheads		145	152
Factory Inputs in the year		825	786
Opening Work in Progress		13	17
		838	803

	19x1 (£'000)		19x2	
Less Closing Work in Progress		17		45
Works Cost of Finished Goods Output		821		758
Opening Stock of Finished Goods		105		68
		924		826
Less Closing Stock of Finished Goods		68		143
Cost of Finished Goods Sold		856		683
Sales		1,050		840
Gross Profit		194		157
Administration Costs	94		82	
Repair to roof	80		–	
Selling and Distribution Costs	89		75	
Financial Charges	12	275	18	175
Net Loss		(81)		(18)

Task 1

Martin wants to form a general impression of the company and its performance over the last two years. Comment on the following matters which Martin thought about:

a. Does the company carry much raw material in stock?

b. How has the relative proportions of the three elements of prime cost changed over the two years?

c. Is Bukkeyball a hi-tech company or a rather old-fashioned manufacturer?

d. The size of work in progress at the year ends.

e. The stock of finished goods at the year ends.

f. The trend in sales.

g. Gross Profit as a percentage of sales.

h. Containment of overhead costs.

i. Why repairs to roof is shown separately.

j. Financial charges.

k. Depreciation of machinery, the computer and the delivery van must be included under headings somewhere. Which headings?

l. The accounts have been typed in a hurry and it is possible that they contain an error. Can you find one?

2. Manufacturing accounts

The measurement of profit in a manufacturing business requires a long financial statement called a 'Manufacturing, Trading and Profit and Loss Account'. Though long, its layout is very logical and the train of thinking usually very clear.

A common format is:

		(£'000)	(£'000)
a)	Widget Manufacturing Company		
b)	*Manufacturing, Trading and Profit and Loss Account*		
c)	*for the year ending 31 December 19x2*		
d)	Raw materials		
e)	Opening stock	67	
f)	Purchases	534	
		601	
g)	Less closing stock	74	
h)	Consumed		527
i)	Direct labour		445
j)	Other direct costs		62
k)	Prime costs		1,034
l)	Production overheads		690
m)	Factory inputs in the year		1,724
n)	Opening work in progress		180
			1,904
o)	Less closing work in progress		201
p)	Works cost of finished goods output		1,703
q)	Opening stock of finished goods		299
			2,002
r)	Less closing stock of finished goods		350
s)	Cost of finished goods sold		1,652
t)	Sales		2,311
u)	Gross profit		659
v)	Administration costs	128	
w)	Selling and distribution costs	243	
x)	Financial charges	102	473
y)	Net profit		186

Considering this financial statement line by line:

a) It is customary to identify the enterprise.

b) It is also customary to identify the financial statement.

c) And the period covered.

d) Manufacturing starts with raw materials and so do we.

e) There was a stock of raw materials (valued at cost, of course) at the beginning and

f) We must add the deliveries of raw materials that arrived during the year.

g) However not all were used so we take away that part of (f) and perhaps (e) that were still there at the year end. This gives us —

h) — the raw materials consumed in the year.

i) Raw materials have to be worked on and so we add the costs of working on them which will include the wages of the workers who work on the raw materials and

j) Any other costs directly associated with particular products. These may include royalties payable on production, work done on the products by sub-contractors and other outside firms.

k) This gives us a total of direct costs and is usually termed the prime cost.

l) Product cost is not just the direct costs but must also include the production overheads. So we add these. They would include rent, rates, insurance, supervisory and management salaries, telephone, repairs, machinery depreciation, power and numerous other headings of cost.

m) Total inputs to the cost of products in the factory in the year.

n) (m) gives us the total cost of inputs in the year but there was also some part-finished products at the beginning of the year which presumably were finished during the year by some of the inputs (d) to (l).

o) Some of the inputs did not result in finished goods in the year but part finished goods which will be completed in 19x3. The costs included in (d) to (l) attributable to work in progress must be identified. This is actually a considerable task.

p) Finally we arrive at the total cost of the products completed in the year and actually or metaphorically transferred into the warehouse and ready for sale.

q) The products made in the year are not the only ones which could be sold. There were also some left over from the year before.

r) Some of (p) and perhaps (o) were not sold in 19x2 and we take off the costs included in (p) and (o) for them as closing stock. This also is a formidable task in practice.

s) We finally arrive at the cost of the finished goods which actually left the warehouse. These will have been sold but some may not have been sold but have been scrapped or stolen.

t) The amount we sold them for.

u) Gross profit is then the selling price of the goods sold in the year less the production cost of those goods.

v) There are some non-manufacturing overhead costs and we summarise these over three headings (v), (w) and (x).

w) These like the administration costs and financial charges could be itemised under sub-headings, e.g. reps' salaries, reps' expenses, advertising, sales office costs etc.

x) Financial charges could include interest and settlement discounts.

y) Finally the bottom line which is the net profit.

A Manufacturing, Trading and Profit and Loss Account has three sections which are not usually so labelled. These are:

❐ The Manufacturing Account (d) to (p).

❐ The Trading Account (p) to (u).

❐ The Profit and Loss Account (u) to (y).

3. Conventions

The conventions used in preparing Manufacturing etc accounts are the same as those used in preparing Trading and Profit and Loss Accounts. See Units 2 to 4.

These conventions include:

i) The realisation convention. All sales made in the year are included irrespective of the date of payment. This applies also to the purchases of materials.

ii) The accruals convention. All costs and expenses are included in the period to which they relate irrespective of the date of payment.

iii) Prudence/conservatism. Stocks are valued at the lower of cost and net realisable value. Suppose the total cost of product X was £100 and was included in line (p).

It is in stock at the year end and has to be valued. It is damaged and can only be sold for £80 and as this is less than the cost of £100, £80 is included in line (r).

This means that £20 is included in line (s) but nothing in line (t) (it will be in sales in 19x3 hopefully). Consequently (u) and (y) are £20 less than they would have been. This means that the expected loss is taken this year and not in the year of sale.

Next year £80 will be in lines (q) and (s) and £80 in line (t) so there is nil in lines (u) and (y).

4. Stocks and work in progress

The value of stocks and work in progress is often very large. As an example consider the 1996 accounts of Triplex Lloyd plc. Stocks and work in progress are valued at £20 million and the profit after tax is only £6.8 million. The effect of differing methods of valuing stocks, or indeed of errors, on profit can easily be seen.

The actual method of valuing stocks and work in progress follows the methods outlined in Unit 9. The important principle to grasp is that the valuation of stock and work in progress takes out expenditure (e.g. from lines (h) to (l)) from 19x2 and puts it into lines (e), (n) and (q) of 19x3.

SCENARIO 2 — Martin marvels at the riskiness of construction companies

Martin is now happy that he broadly understands how profit is measured in retail, wholesale and manufacturing companies. Driving to work one morning he waits in the traffic queue along a partly completed section of the new by-pass as he has done every morning since construction commenced. He recalls that construction commenced over a year ago and completion is not due for another eight months. He muses that he measures his company's profits every year and wonders how this can be done by construction companies when their trading cycle is so long. He resolves to ask Anne when he next sees her.

Anne tells him that she is currently dealing with a construction company which has gone into receivership and shows him how the annual profits (or losses!) were measured.

Quick Answer Questions 11.1

1. What is meant by the business cycle?
2. What is meant by receivership?

SCENARIO 3 — Martin finds out how to measure profit in a construction business

Anne explains that her client had two contracts. At the year end before it went bust, the positions of the two contracts were: (in £s)

	A	B
Value of work done	19,450	34,762
Cost of work done	16,900	38,434
Payments received	14,200	26,000
Total contract price	28,200	50,700
Estimated costs to completion	7,120	19,400

Martin muses on this and says ' I think I understand this. Contract A was tendered and accepted at a total price of £28,200. The work done to date has been certified by a surveyor at £19,450 and that leaves £8,750 still to be done. The work to date has cost £16,900 to do, and will cost a further £7,120 in order to finish it. The customer has paid £14,200 so far, on account. So this contract is profitable but how much of the profit will be counted in this year's Profit and Loss Account?'

Tasks 2

1. Show how these two contracts would appear in the financial statements.
2. Discuss why the company went bust in the following year. Why do you think construction companies take on contracts which ultimately show a loss?
3. Consider whether the application of the prudence concept here leads to a true and fair view of what the actual position is.

---

5. Long term contracts

The realisation convention requires that the profit on a sale is recognised in the Profit and Loss Account in the period when the sale was made regardless of the date when the payment was received. The date of sale is usually fairly easy to determine in the case of sales of things as most sales of things are evidenced by a dated invoice. The date of sale of a service is not quite as clear. For example, Anne prepares and audits Martin's accounts. This takes her some three or four weeks. If her year end occurs during this period, in which period is the profit earned? Most accountants recognise the profit on supplying accounting services when they invoice so that the profit would fall in the period in which the service was completed. It does not make very much difference either way.

In the case of long term contracts the date of recognition can make a very large difference. As a consequence SSAP 9, Stocks and Long-Term Contracts, allows an abandonment of the strict realisation convention and the profit is recognised on each contract in proportion to the work done in each accounting period. Sadly some contracts are unprofitable and then the prudence convention is applied. This requires that if, at the end of a financial year, a loss is expected on a contract then the whole estimated loss on the contract is put into that year. Suppose a company starts two contracts in year 1 and each contract will take three years. Contract A is profitable and the profit will be spread over the Profit and Loss Accounts of all three years. But B is loss making, the whole of the estimated loss will go in year 1. No profit or loss will appear in years 2 and 3 except for adjustments to be made as the actual loss is measured and any difference from the estimated loss written off to Profit and Loss Account.

Some examples: (All figures in £'000)

Project	A	B	C
Total costs incurred	564	730	35
Value of work done	620	720	45
Cumulative payments on account received	430	525	-
Expected costs to completion	240	134	920
Contract total price	915	835	1,200
Include in turnover in the Profit and Loss Account	£620	720	
Include in cost of sales	£564	749	
Thus profit/loss taken =	£56	(29)	
Include in debtors	£190	195	
Include in Current liabilities		19	

Notes to all three contracts:

a. The figures are as at a year end when each contract was still in progress.

b. The contract price is as tendered and is for the whole contract.

c. Total costs incurred are all the costs incurred on the contract to the year end.

d. It is possible to value the work done to date. This is at selling price. That is, it is that part of the contract price already completed. Valuation is by quantity surveyors.

e. It is customary for the client (the highways agency, local authority or other body or company) to pay on account as the work progresses.

f. It is possible to estimate the total costs yet to be incurred, from the current state to the end of the contract.

Project A:

This project is about 2/3 through and appears to be profitable. So a portion of the profit can be taken to Profit and Loss Account. You will see that the remainder of the contract price (£295) is greater than the cost of work to be done (£240). Note that in example A, the amount to be included in the turnover (i.e. in sales) is the value of the work done to date. This can normally be ascertained on a long term contract. The profit to be included is the profit earned to date, that is, the value of work done to date less the cost of carrying out that work. Ultimately, the remaining turnover and profit on the contract will be included in the years when the work is done. The value on the Balance Sheet (in debtors) is the work done to date less money already received. It is usual for customers to pay for long term contracts as they go along and not wait until completion. In accordance with SSAP 9 the part finished contract A, which is expected to make an overall profit, is included in turnover and debtors and not as work in progress.

Contract B is expected to make a loss of £29 (£835 - £730 - £134) and the whole of this loss, not just the £10 (£730 - £720) lost so far, must be included in the Profit and Loss Account immediately. The cost of sales figure is the costs so far £730 + the loss expected to be incurred in the future £19 (£835 - £720 - £134). The expected future loss is included in the Balance Sheet as a current liability and labelled provision for loss on contract.

Contract C has hardly started and it is thought inappropriate to include any profit yet. So the accounting in the financial statements is to include work-in-progress at cost £35 in both Profit and Loss Account and Balance Sheet. The sales figure is not included at all.

In estimating costs to completion, all expected costs must be considered including rectification and guarantee work and bearing in mind the effects of inflation on future costs. Many contracts are agreed at a total price for the job and a sale price, for the work done so far, can only be estimated. However some jobs do have separate prices for separate stages and usually, for stage payment purposes, quantity surveyors certify the value of the work done. It is customary for contractors to tender high prices for the first part of a contract and low prices for the latter parts. This way, they receive the actual profit on the contract in the earlier stages!

SCENARIO 4 — Martin delves deeper into accounting conventions

Martin thinks he now understands the way Profit and Loss Account is measured in construction companies but considers that including all expected losses as soon as they are known about rather a gloomy approach. Anne concedes that it is but insists that all accountants are not gloomy people but a rather conservative approach to measuring profit and loss does mean that financial statements show a position that is at least as good as any theoretical 'true' position.

Anne goes on to explain that the following year the construction company failed and Martin is concerned that despite the impending failure in the following year the accounts did not reveal any expectation of failure. Anne explained that this was as a result of the going concern convention in accounting. While on the subject of accounting conventions, Martin asks for an explanation of two others - consistency and materiality.

Tasks 3

1. Explain how the measurement of the following assets and liabilities might change in Martin Padlocks Ltd's financial statements if the going concern convention was abandoned.

    Plant and machinery   Stocks

    Redundancy pay   Long term loans

2. Explain how the following assets and liabilities in Martin Padlocks Ltd's financial statements are affected by the materiality and consistency conventions: debtors, stocks, plant, creditors.

6. Going concern

The going concern convention assumes that the enterprise will continue in operational existence for the foreseeable future. The Balance Sheet and Profit and Loss Account are drawn up on the assumption that there is no *intention* or *necessity* to liquidate or *curtail* significantly the scale of operation. The justification for this convention is simply that it is true. If it were not so, then liquidation values would need to be substituted for the historical cost based figures.

Most businesses continue for many years. However some firms do cease trading shortly after publication of accounts drawn up on the going concern basis. It is not always possible to forecast the failure of a company and the final collapse may be very sudden.

The consequences of this convention include:

(i) Fixed assets are valued at unamortised costs.

(ii) Current assets are valued at lower of cost and net realisable value in the normal course of business.

(iii) Liabilities that will arise only in the event of liquidation (e.g. redundancy pay), are ignored.

(iv) Liabilities are divided between current and long term.

(v) Information about the consequences of liquidation is not given.

To consider a specific case of a construction company. Normally the company will continue for many years but some construction companies go bust. If a construction company continues then it will complete its contracts and ultimately receive and pay out any sums receivable or payable. However if it fails then it will be unable to fulfil its contracts. Each customer will need to get another contractor to finish his contract - probably at a higher price. He will pay to the liquidator of the failed company only sums which are currently due less the extra cost of finishing the contract - probably he will pay nothing!

The company may have plant and machinery and some stocks of materials etc. These will be sold at auction and will probably fetch a lot less than book values. Any staff will have to be made redundant and redundancy money paid.

How can an accountant decide if a company is a going concern? Usually this is no problem, but in borderline cases it can be difficult. Note that if the accountant decides that it is not a going concern and includes all assets and liabilities at realisable values then the creditors will surely put the company into liquidation.

7. Consistency

This convention requires that there is consistency of accounting treatment of like items within each accounting period and from one period to the next. For example, the straight line method of depreciation once chosen for vehicles, should be used for all vehicles and for all periods.

The justification for this convention seems self evident if comparability over time is to be achieved.

However, its extension to all businesses seems desirable, but has not been achieved.

Sometimes the accounting policy adopted may, as a result of experience, seem inappropriate. It is possible to change it, despite the consistency convention, but the money effect and the fact of a change must be made clear in the financial statements — accountants say that the change must be disclosed and quantified.

8. Materiality

Accounting is a process of summarising and presenting information in a digestible form. The Balance Sheet shows, for example, a single figure 'Debtors £2,468,500'. It does not list the names and amounts due of the 546 individual debtors. The reader of the Balance Sheet knows that it is a summary figure. However the summarising can go too far. Suppose the debtors included one debtor for £500,000 being, not a normal trade debt, but a sum due for the sale of a part of the business. Readers may compare the magnitude of the debtors in this Balance Sheet with that in previous Balance Sheets. Clearly the magnitude this year is not comparable with those of previous years which were all just trade debtors. In such cases, it is necessary to *disclose* the £500,000 separately. Accountants say that the item is *material*. An item is material if it is sufficiently significant enough to affect evaluation of the financial statements or the making of decisions based on them.

It is very difficult to make materiality decisions. One approach, is to consider each item in the financial statements and compare it with previous years. If what is included has changed then perhaps the change needs to be disclosed. Would knowledge of the change affect the evaluation or decisions of the reader of the financial statements? If yes, then the item is material and needs to be separately disclosed.

***

SCENARIO 5 — Martin researches research and development expenditure

Martin meets an old friend who is a teacher at his local University. His friend explains that he is doing research into a new type of electronic lock. The lock interests Martin who feels he might be able to develop a variant which he could sell. Martin is finally persuaded to put £6,000 of the company's money into supporting a research student who will specifically develop a lock for Martin to make and sell. Martin turns down a suggestion that his company might contribute funds to enable the University to do general research into electronic security.

Martin considers that he will need to spend some few thousands of pounds to develop the new lock for production in his works after the research student has done her work.

His friend also tells him of a competitor of Martin who is retiring and selling the patent of a new lock. Martin meets the competitor and they negotiate a possible sale of the assets of the business. The plant and stock are worth very little and Martin agrees to a nominal payment for them. However the value of the business as a whole is much greater. The reason for this is that the business owns some patents and trade marks but also has a number of loyal customers including one large customer for the new patented lock.

Martin wonders how any payments for research, development, goodwill, patents and trade marks will be reflected in his financial statements and resolves to ask Anne.

Task 4

How would the following payments be accounted for:

❐ supporting the research student £6,000

❐ supporting general research

❐ buying the business including plant, stocks, patents, trade marks and goodwill.

9. Research and development

SSAP 13 - Accounting for research and development. Many companies (e.g. companies in pharmaceuticals, chemicals, electronics, aerospace) engage in expenditure on research and development. The accounting rules are:

a. The cost of fixed assets acquired or constructed in order to provide facilities for R. and D. activities over a number of accounting periods should be capitalised (= treated as fixed assets) and written off over their useful lives through the Profit and Loss Account.

b. Expenditure on pure and applied research should be written off in the year of expenditure through the Profit and Loss Account.

c. Development expenditure should be written off in the year of expenditure except in the following circumstances:

❐ there is a clearly defined project

❐ the related expenditure is separately identifiable

❐ the outcome of such a project has been assessed with reasonable certainty as to its technical feasibility and its ultimate commercial viability considered in the light of factors such as likely market conditions (including competing products), public opinion, consumer and environmental legislation

❐ the aggregate of the deferred development costs, any further development costs, and related production, selling and administration costs is reasonably expected to be exceeded by related future sales or other revenues

❐ adequate resources exist or are reasonably expected to be available, to enable the project to be completed and to provide any consequential increases in working capital.

In these circumstances, development expenditure may be deferred to the extent that its recovery can reasonably be regarded as assured. Deferred means the cost is not put in the Profit and Loss Account as an expense but is treated as an asset on the Balance Sheet. It does not remain on successive Balance Sheets for ever but is put in successive Profit and Loss Accounts as an expense. Amortisation (= depreciation) to Profit and Loss Account should be systematic, beginning with the period of first commercial production or use, and be allocated to successive periods by reference to sales or use.

There should be reviews of each project and in any that seem doubtful or unviable, any deferred expenditure written off immediately.

d.   The accounting policy adopted towards research and development and all relevant figures should be disclosed.

These rules on deferring R. and D. are very conservative and, as a consequence, very little R. and D. expenditure is actually deferred. One effect of this is that companies that do R. and D. show lower profits than companies that do not. And yet, on balance, one would expect that companies doing R. and D. would have a better future than those that do not. Hopefully, investors will be able to evaluate company performance and future prospects by reference to all the facts disclosed and not simply to measured profits. It is worth noting that investors and industry generally in the UK are often accused of 'short-termism'.

10. Goodwill

FRS 10 - goodwill and intangible assets. Intangible assets are non-financial assets that do not have physical substance but are identifiable and are controlled by the entity through custody or legal rights. Examples are goodwill, copyrights, trademarks and franchises. Only purchased goodwill is relevant. Purchased goodwill arises when a company buys another company, as in a take-over. The amount paid over and above the fair value of the net assets acquired is an intangible asset and should appear on the Balance Sheet and be amortised. Created goodwill should not appear in Balance Sheets but readers of Balance Sheets should remember that the entity will usually have goodwill, often of great value.

FRS 10 requires that:

a.   Purchased goodwill and other intangibles should be capitalised (treated as an asset and not as an expense).

b.   Capitalised goodwill should be amortised (depreciated) by annual charges to the Profit and Loss Account over a period not exceeding 20 years.

c.   If the economic life of the goodwill is more than 20 years, then the period may be longer, or even infinite, but this is exceedingly unlikely. At the end of the first year after acquisition there should be an impairment review. This is to see if the goodwill has a recoverable amount less than its carrying value.

FRS 10 appeared in December 1997 and is a change from its predecessor SSAP 22. It is no longer acceptable to write off valuable acquired goodwill direct to reserves.

11. Summary of Unit 11

❐   Profit measurement in manufacturing companies is done using a financial statement called the Manufacturing, Trading and Profit and Loss Account.

❐   The valuation of work in progress and finished goods stocks is a vital part of the preparation of the financial statement.

❐   Profit measurement in construction is different from other companies as the profit on long term contracts is accrued over the life of the contract instead of being at the point of sale. Such measurement is governed by SSAP 9.

❏ Long term contracts should be valued to include that part of the expected profit which has been earned to date as *attributable* profit. This should occur only if the outcome of the contract can reasonably be foreseen.

❏ If an attributable profit is included then the work done to date should be included in turnover and (the cost + attributable profit - amount received to date) should be included as a separate item in debtors.

❏ If a loss is expected on a contract then the whole expected loss should be included in the accounts. The work done to date should be included in turnover and the value of work done less the cash received on account should be included in a separate item in stocks. Further the provision for the loss should be included in current liabilities.

❏ Failed companies go into receivership or liquidation.

❏ Construction companies have a long business cycle.

❏ The going concern convention assumes that a company will continue into the future and allows measurement of assets and liabilities to be at cost derived figures instead of realisation values.

❏ The consistency convention requires similar accounting treatment of like items within each accounting period and from one period to the next.

❏ The materiality convention allows figures on financial statements to be summary figures. However items which are sufficiently significant to affect evaluation, assessment or decision making should be disclosed.

❏ Research and Development expenditure is usually written off as it is incurred but can be deferred in certain very carefully defined circumstances. SSAP 13 applies.

❏ Goodwill appears in Balance Sheet only when purchased. Usually it is written off as it is purchased but it can be capitalised and written off by instalments. SSAP 22 applies.

Construction companies		
Profitable contracts	—	attributable profit in years during which contract is performed
Unprofitable contracts	—	whole loss in year in which probable loss is recognised as likely

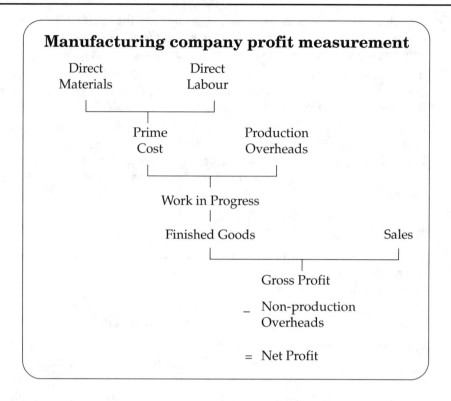

Manufacturing company profit measurement

Direct Materials — Direct Labour

Prime Cost — Production Overheads

Work in Progress

Finished Goods — Sales

Gross Profit

− Non-production Overheads

= Net Profit

Exercise *1

The following sums are relevant to the measurement of profit for Stubby Furniture Manufacturing Co Ltd:

(all figures are in £'000)

	19x1	19x2	19x3	19x4
Assets at 31 December (the year end)				
Raw Material stocks	132	144	156	180
Work in Progress	89	201	128	145
Finished Goods stocks	360	380	529	602
Plant and Machinery at cost	1,680	1,680	2,450	2,480
Delivery vehicles at cost	240	280	350	350
Expenditure in the year				
Raw Materials		520	540	602
Factory direct wages		720	730	702
Royalties payable on manufacture		74	68	170
Production Overheads		530	489	470
Rates (2/3 Works,				
1/6 Office, 1/6 Distribution)		294	330	384
Administration Costs		332	370	290
Selling and distribution costs		448	502	540

	19x1	19x2	19x3	19x4
Financial Charges		39	80	140
Revenues in the year:				
Sales		2,800	2,950	3,420

Note: Depreciation is 10% per annum on the cost of the Plant and Machinery held at the year end (straight line method) and 20% on the cost of the vehicles held at the year end.

a. Prepare Manufacturing, Trading and Profit and Loss Accounts for the years ending 19x2, 19x3 and 19x4.

b. After the preparation of the accounts of these years, the following errors were found:

   i. The raw material stock at 31 December 19x2 omitted some components which had cost £24,000.

   ii. The finished goods stock at 31 December 19x3 included some tables which had been valued at materials only instead of at prime cost + works overheads. The difference is £38,000.

   iii. A royalty payable on the sale of some desks in 19x3 was not recognised (and therefore not included in the accounts) until 19x5 when a court case was settled. The amount involved is £16,000.

   iv. Sales of £17,000 were made in December 19x2 but due to holidays the invoices were not typed until January 19x3 and as the wrong dating was not spotted the sales were actually included in the 19x3 accounts.

   v. A fire insurance premium for the year ending 30 April 19x4 £12,000 was entirely included in the accounts for 19x3. The corresponding premiums for other years were correctly treated.

The accounts cannot normally be altered retrospectively but you are required to state the effect on individual figures and the net profit of each year for each of these items.

c. The company sells its products to retailers and guarantees its products for one year after sale by the retailer. The average retailer holds in stock furniture bought from Stubby for an average of four months. Any item returned is normally replaced from finished goods stock free of charge and the returned items re-used in the manufacturing process if possible.

   Stubby do not make a provision for expected returns at each year end so that the cost of replacing a faulty item falls into the year when the return is made instead of in the year when the item was originally sold.

   Calculate the effect on profits for the years 19x2 to 19x4 of making a provision so that the cost of replacing faulty furniture falls in the year of sale. You can assume that 2% of sales are returned as faulty and that the cost of replacement (less re-usable parts) is 1/3 of the selling price from Stubby to its customers.

   Which of these two alternative accounting policies do you think is most appropriate?

d. Look at the following items in the three years of Stubby's activities and suggest a plausible explanation of changes between the years:

Work in progress	Production Overheads
Finished goods stocks	Administration costs
Plant and Machinery	Selling and Distribution costs
Factory Direct Wages	Financial Charges
Royalties	

Case Study / Assignment 1

Keith is the newly appointed managing director of Stubby Widgets Ltd a subsidiary of a major group. The company make a range of three widgets — the deluxe, the special and the super and they supply the European market. The company accountant has produced a Manufacturing, Trading and Profit and Loss Account for the year just ended and this shows a loss. It is Keith's primary job to make the factory more efficient and he is looking for ways of achieving this. With this in mind he has been able to obtain a copy of the accounts of a fellow subsidiary, Lee Widgets Ltd, which makes a similar range of products to sell in North America. This subsidiary is located in the Far East and is reputed to be extremely efficient. Following are the two sets of accounts:

	Stubby Ltd (in £'000)		Lee Ltd (in local currency)	
Raw Materials:				
Opening stock	146		103	
Purchases	541		870	
	687		973	
Closing Stock	171	516	99	874
Direct Labour		782		207
Prime cost		1,298		1,081
Works Overheads				
Rent, rates, insurance	480		280	
Plant Depreciation	32		180	
Energy	249		200	
Staff Salaries	521		320	
Other overheads	178	1,460	190	1,170
		2,758		2,251
Opening Work in Progress		212		46
		2,970		2,297
Closing Work in Progress		280		54
		2,690		2,243
Opening Finished Goods Stock		401		208
		3,091		2,451

		Stubby Ltd (in £'000)		Lee Ltd (in local currency)
Closing Finished Goods Stock		441		160
		2,650		2,291
Sales		3,100		3,900
Gross Profit		450		1,609
Administration Costs	390		340	
Selling Costs	270		360	
Warehousing Costs	246		90	
Distribution Costs	180	1,086	238	1,028
Net Profit (Loss)		(636)		581

Keith makes a few enquiries and finds that:

i.   The raw material unit costs are similar for the two companies.
ii. Selling prices are higher in the European market as there is, as yet, less competition.
iii. Due to environmental and legal factors, the companies produce products of very marginally different specifications.
iv. There are no financial costs as Group supply all capital requirements (but require a commensurate profit to be earned on the use of the capital).

Required:

Write a report as from Keith to the Group Chief Executive:

i. Detailing the problems of the company.
ii. Giving proposals to turn the company round.

You can make any reasonable assumptions but must state them.

Assignment 2

A summary of the Manufacturing, Trading and Profit and Loss Account of Revpen Manufacturing Co Ltd for the year ending 31 December 19x2 is:

(All figures in £'000)

Raw Materials:		
Opening stock	56	
Purchases	345	
	401	
Closing Stock	36	365
Direct Labour		582
		947
Works Overheads		
Rent, rates, insurance	232	
Plant Depreciation	52	
Energy	180	
Staff Salaries	241	
Other overheads	103	808
		1,755

Opening Work in Progress		240
		1,995
Closing Work in Progress		379
		1,616
Opening Finished Goods Stock		180
		1,796
Closing Finished Goods Stock		193
		1,603
Sales		2,600
Gross Profit		997
Administration Costs	401	
Selling Costs	240	
Distribution Costs	49	690
Net Profit		307

Part A

Note each statement is either true or false. Tick those that are true.

A1 *Re Closing stock of raw materials:*

    a.   These are mostly valued at cost

    b.   These are mostly valued at replacement price

    c.   Some of these may be valued at below cost

A2 *Re Purchases of raw materials:*

    a.   Goods purchased on 16.12.19x1 and paid for on 16.1.19x2 is included in this sum

    b.   Goods purchased on 30.6.19x2 (£4,100) and stolen on 18.7.19x2 are included in this sum

    c.   Heating Oil purchased and paid for on 13.11.19x2 is included in this sum

A3 *Re prime cost:*

    a.   Prime cost was   £947,000

    b.   Prime cost was   £582,000

    c.   prime cost was   £1,755,000

A4 *Re Work in Progress:*

    a.   Work in progress was valued at cost

    b.   Work in progress was valued at prime cost

    c.   Work in progress was valued at a percentage of the selling price

    d.   Work in progress was valued at prime cost + an appropriate proportion of all overheads

e. Work in progress was valued at prime cost + an appropriate proportion of works overheads

A5 *Re Rent, Rates and Insurance £232,000*

a. Rent for the quarter ending 31 March 19x3, paid on 27 December 19x2, is included in this sum

b. Rates paid in October 19x1 for the half year ending 31 March 19x2 is included in full in this sum

c. Insurance of the delivery vans is included in this sum.

A6 *Re Plant Depreciation* (note that the straight line method is used and items of plant are depreciated over 8 years)

a. Depreciation includes the total cost of a new machine purchased in the year

b. Depreciation includes depreciation on a machine purchased ten years ago

c. Depreciation includes the loss on sale of a machine sold in the year

d. Depreciation includes depreciation on the sales director's secretary's word processor

A7 *Re finished goods stock:*

a. This is mostly valued at prime cost + an appropriate portion of works overheads

b. This is mostly valued at selling price

c. This is mostly valued at prime cost + an appropriate portion of all overheads

d. This is valued at prime cost

e. This may include some items valued at net realisable value

A8 *Re administration costs:*

a. This includes £2,000 paid in December 19x2 for stationery to be delivered in January 19x3

b. This includes the salary of the cost accountant

c. This includes depreciation on the office photocopier

d. This includes the cost of a new computer system acquired to record shareholdings

A9 *Re net profit:*

a. This measures the increase in the company's bank account in the year

b. This measures the net increase in net assets in the year from manufacturing and trading activity.

Part B

The Manufacturing, Trading and Profit and Loss Account is a very detailed and comprehensive document. In fact the above document is somewhat summarised, as works and other overheads are divided into more categories in the original. (For example selling costs are categorised into advertising, reps' salaries, reps' expenses, selling overheads.) Also the original contains the corresponding figures for the previous year. However the works manager says that the document is:

a. available only to senior management
b. not understood by all of them
c. useless as a diagnosis of what went well/wrong in the year
d. useless as a guide to action.

Comment on the works manager's views and suggest ways that these accounts could be made more useful to him and others.

Case Study 3

a. Speckless Ltd makes different kinds of vacuum cleaners. Its Manufacturing, Trading and Profit and Loss Account for the years ending 31 December 19x1 and 19x2 showed:

(All figures in £'000)

Raw Materials:				
Opening stock	680		720	
Purchases	3,100		3,240	
	3,780		3,960	
Closing Stock	720	3,060	840	3,120
Direct Labour		3,580		2,900
		6,640		6,020
Works Overheads		5,700		7,100
		12,340		13,120
Opening Work in Progress		950		1,280
		13,290		14,400
Closing Work in Progress		1,280		1,350
		12,010		13,050
Opening Finished				
Goods Stock		2,040		1,950
		14,050		15,000
Closing Finished				
Goods Stock		1,950		2,200
		12,100		12,800
Sales		15,800		17,100
Gross Profit		3,700		4,300
Administration, Selling				
and Distribution Costs		2,480		2,750
Net Profit		1,220		1,550

You can assume that there was no inflation in the two years.

Review the performance of the company so far as you can from this data. Consider each figure in relation to the other figures and to the figure for the other year. Suggest reasons for changes between the years.

b. The management felt that the performance shown in the manufacturing accounts was satisfactory considering that trading was very competitive.

However Timothea, the Chief Executive, asked for a breakdown of the figures over the four products. This produced this schedule:

	Giant		Large		Small		Special	
	19x1	19x2	19x1	19x2	19x1	19x2	19x1	19x2
Raw Materials								
Opening stock	128	132	152	146	230	250	170	192
Purchases	660	698	1,100	1,185	800	940	540	417
	788	830	1,252	1,331	1,030	1,190	710	609
Closing Stock	132	160	146	131	250	290	192	259
	656	670	1,106	1,200	780	900	518	350
Direct Labour	480	490	990	780	840	950	1,270	680
	1,136	1,160	2,096	1,980	1,620	1,850	1,788	1,030
Works Overheads	1,290	1,490	1,200	2,890	1,500	1,620	1,710	1,100
	2,426	2,650	3,296	4,870	3,120	3,470	3,498	2,130
Opening WIP	200	320	166	340	340	232	244	388
	2,626	2,970	3,462	5,210	3,460	3,702	3,742	2,518
Closing WIP	320	280	340	350	232	600	388	120
	2,306	2,690	3,022	4,860	3,328	3,102	3,354	2,398
Opening FGS	450	430	510	290	380	120	700	1,110
	2,756	3,120	3,532	5,150	3,708	3,222	4,054	3,508
Closing FGS	430	500	290	720	120	180	1,110	800
	2,326	2,620	3,242	4,430	3,588	3,042	2,944	2,708
Sales	2,560	2,940	5,200	6,300	5,200	4,960	2,840	2,900
Gross Profit	234	320	1,958	1,870	1,612	1,918	(104)	192

Review the schedule and make comments on the performance of each of the four products over the two years.

What changes might be made?

Construction accounts

Exercise 2

Sheinton Construction Ltd have the following contracts on hand at 31 December 19x2:

Project	A	B	C	D
Total costs incurred	648	880	1,900	230
Value of work done	723	930	1,880	259
Payments on account received	550	800	1,700	0
Expected costs to completion	230	440	800	860
Contract total price	1,024	1,330	2,980	1,220

How would these contracts appear in the financial statements?

Exercise 3

Rising Buck Construction Ltd have the following Balance Sheet extracts at 31 December 19x2:

£

Fixed assets	Land	50,000
	Buildings	90,000
	Plant	68,000
	Vehicles	120,300
Current assets	Stocks	44,500
	Work in progress	52,000
	Debtors	349,000
Current Liabilities	Trade creditors	212,000
	VAT, PAYE etc	104,200
	Bank overdraft	180,000
	Provision for loss on contracts	98,000

Requirement

a. Explain how each item has been valued. The Balance Sheet has been drawn up under the going concern convention.

b. The company have found that they cannot pay their creditors and a liquidator has been appointed. Explain what would happen to the values in the Balance Sheet when the assets were sold/collected and the liabilities paid off by the liquidator.

Exercise 4

Yipee biochemicals PLC are a fast growing company. In 19x4, their spending included:

	£		£
New production plant	140,00	New lorry	23,000
New research building	50,000	Development costs of Covicum	66,000
New research plant	38,800	A patent to make Gogum	20,000
Grant for pure research to Sheinton University	5,000	All the shares in Cressage Ltd, a rival company	134,000

Note: a. Covicum has been approved for agricultural use and sales commenced in 19x5. It expected that very profitable production will continue for many years.

b. Gogum started to be manufactured profitably in 19x4 and the patent has another ten years to run.

Required:

How will these items be included in the financial statements?

12 Total absorption costing

1. Objectives

This Unit introduces the system of cost finding called total absorption costing and shows how product costs can be found in manufacturing and service industries but also in not-for-profit enterprises.

SCENARIO 1 — Martin finds out about total absorption costs

Martin is aware that finished goods stocks are valued at the lower of cost and net realisable value in his own and Bukkeyball's Accounts but has not had time to research in depth how his accounting staff and Anne have measured cost bearing in mind that both businesses make a range of products – they are multiproduct firms. He has also accepted their estimates of production costs when fixing selling prices. He now thinks it is time he investigated this area more fully.

Some costs, known as direct costs, are traceable to particular products but some costs, known as indirect costs, are shared by more than one product. You will remember the concept of direct and indirect costs from Unit 5. In building up the cost of a product it is relatively easy to find the direct costs which relate to it. This will primarily be the materials and components which compose it and also labour where a worker spends time exclusively on the product. However the rent and rates of the factory are equally costs of manufacture with some portion of them having to be included in pricing decisions and stock valuation.

Martin markets a special lock which he has made by pieceworkers in a part of his factory. His costs of manufacture for this product are:

For each lock:

Materials and components	£2.80
Labour of worker (piecework)	£1.40

Overall annual costs relating to the lock:

Supervisor	£12,000
Licence to use patent process	£4,000
Rent and Rates	£3,000

Quick Answer Questions 12.1

1. Divide these costs into:
    a. Material, labour, services
    b. Fixed, Variable
    c. Direct, Indirect

2. Calculate the total cost and the cost per unit if
    a. Total output is 5,000 units
    or b. Total output is 10,000 units

SCENARIO 2 — Martin derives some absorption rates after some allocation and apportionment

Martin has developed a range of special locks which he is making in a bay of his factory. He has estimated the costs attached to the bay which is divided into three shops: machining, assembly, and, packing. The overheads for a year of the whole bay are:

	£
Rent	8,800
Rates	3,700
Fire Insurance	1,200
Supervision	15,800
Repairs to machinery	3,000

In addition the overheads which can be allocated to specific shops are:

	Machining	*Assembly*	*Packing*
Depreciation of			
Machinery	13,000	1,500	2,400
Energy	2,600	350	600
Labour on fixed rates	12,200	9,150	–
Some information about the three shops is:			
Area in square metres	40	30	40
Number of employees	5	6	5

Martin recognises that the principal activity in the Machining shop is machining and that activity can be measured in *machine hours*. He reckons that output will be large enough in the next twelve months to require 10,000 hours. In the Assembly shop, *labour hours* are the important factor and that output will require 12,000 hours. In the Packing shop also, labour hours are the relevant output and that production will require 8,000 hours.

Tasks 1

1. Produce an overhead summary allocating and apportioning the expense items to the three shops and derive a total overhead cost for each shop.
2. Suggest absorption rates for each department.

---

2. Multiproduct overhead costing

No firm produces just one product. Students often suggest water supply as a single product company but pricing by water rates or by differential tariffs effectively are the supply of separate products.

It is relatively simple, at least in principle, to determine the *prime cost* of each product produced but *apportioning the overheads* is more difficult.

The method normally adopted is to divide the firm into separate *cost centres*. A cost centre is any location, function or items of equipment in respect of which costs may be ascertained and related to cost units for control purposes. Examples of the division of a firm into cost centres may include a factory which is divisible into shops or departments e.g. welding shop, plating shop, assembly shop etc or each route covered in an airline, each department in a department store; each classroom in a school.

The procedure is then to list the overheads. As an example we will take a widget factory and the overheads are:

	£
Rates	200,000
Electricity	180,000
Management salaries	300,000
Canteen subsidy	60,000

There are three departments — welding, assembly and packing which have statistics as:

	Welding	Assembly	Packing
Floor area (m²)	900	600	500
No of workers	40	80	30
Total HP of machinery	600	100	200

The second procedure is to apportion the overheads to the cost centres in accordance with some appropriate criteria. In this case these might be:

Overhead apportionment schedule

Cost	Method	Total	Welding	Assembly	Packing
Rates	Floor area	200,000	90,000	60,000	50,000
Electricity	HP of machines	180,000	120,000	20,000	40,000
Management	No of workers	300,000	80,000	160,000	60,000
Canteen	No of workers	60,000	16,000	32,000	12,000
		740,000	306,000	272,000	162,000

Note: The methods chosen here are common but would depend on the circumstances. For example electricity could be split and part apportioned by floor area representing heating and lighting and that part that is power divided up in accordance with machine HP or hours used or hours used × HP.

Some overheads are known to be for specific cost centres. Examples are the salaries of supervisors who work exclusively in specific cost centres. Such costs are not apportioned but are simply *allocated* to the appropriate cost centre to be added to the *apportioned* amounts to find the total overheads of each centre.

The next procedure is to find a method of dividing each cost centre overhead over the products which use it. There are several methods including the *machine hour rate,* the *labour hour rate, the percentage on direct wages.* To illustrate, suppose the welding department was primarily a machine using department and total machine hours available in a period were 5,100. Then the machine hour rate would be

$$\frac{£306,000}{5,100} = £60.$$

If job No 341 required 4 hours of machining in the welding shop then the overhead cost of the that machining would be 4 × £60 = £240. Job 341 is said to absorb £240 of the overheads. If enough jobs were available in the department to use all the 5,100 hours then all the overheads would be absorbed.

Note that the overhead total apportioned is a function of the apportioning method which may vary with different accountants and the extent of factual information (e.g. how much electricity used for heat and how much for power) and as such is imprecise. The total hours actually supplied may be less in a recession and more in a boom or may vary for other reasons. Thus a machine hour rate is not an exact scientific figure and so also a product cost is not either.

3. Overhead recovery

An objective of a firm may be to make full recovery of all its costs, including its overheads, in its selling prices. If the total costs of the assembly department are £272,000 and the total direct labour hours available in the department in a period are 12,000 then a labour hour rate for absorption of overheads will be $\frac{£272,000}{12,000}$ = £22.67 per hour. Full overhead recovery will depend on:

❑   All the 12,000 hours actually being available in the period.

❑   Enough work being available in the period to absorb all these hours.

Each job done is priced out at prime cost + absorbed overheads + profit. Thus each sale can be seen as recovering part of the overheads. Clearly in practice either under or over recovery of overheads always occurs.

SCENARIO 3 — Martin's product costs are rather elusive

Martin has two products, the VX and the WY, which he can sell at prices which are restricted by competition. They are made in the factory bay discussed above and he needs to know what it would cost to make them.

He reckons the costs will be:

	VX	WY
Materials and components	£2.40	£2.60
Piecework Labour	£1.80	£3.30
Machine time (Machining)	20 mins	30 mins
Labour Time (Assembly)	15 mins	10 mins
Labour Time (Packing)	25 mins	20 mins

Tasks 2

1.   Calculate the total cost of manufacture of each item.

2.   Martin is worried that demand for the products may be less than the demand used in the estimates above (for example he thinks that demand may be such that less than 10,000 hours will be worked in the Machine shop). He suspects that output will be only sufficient to require 75% of the hours stated for the three shops.

   Recalculate the costs for the two products on the 75% assumption.

3.   Discuss the relationship between the costs obtained under tasks 1 and 2.

4. Martin deliberately arranged to pay most of the workers on piece rates and is slightly put out when he realises that the cost of production is still partly dependent on the time taken to make an item. Explain why this is so.

5. Martin has assumed that all the machines in the machine shop are the same but actually there are three different machines of different sizes. Clearly product costs will be differ depending on the machine used. How can this be handled in the cost accumulation process?

6. Martin feels that, if the calculated costs of production of the products manufactured in the three shops are less than the selling prices, he must make a profit. Anne explains that there are several reasons why that is not so. Explain what Anne means.

SCENARIO 4 — Martin revisits selling prices

Martin estimates that in his factory as a whole the relative magnitudes of overheads will be:

Manufacturing Overheads	3
Administrative Overheads	1
Selling and Distribution Overheads	1

He has calculated the cost of making a lock called the TU at:

	£
Direct Costs	1.60
Manufacturing Overhead Absorbed	1.20
Total Manufacturing Cost	2.80

Martin aims to sell that product at a price which will cover all costs (Manufacturing and non-manufacturing) and give a profit of 10% of the selling price.

Tasks 3

1. Calculate the selling price required.

2. Explain why Martin may actually set the price either higher or lower than the price you have calculated.

SCENARIO 5 — Martin advises a school on selling prices

Martin is talking with a neighbour who is the bursar of a local fee paying school. The bursar is full of a new idea to boost revenue for his school and at the same time to do some good for the local area where the school is situated. The school want to open some A level courses to adults. The benefit to the school would be to add to revenues with only a tiny increase in costs. This is because all A level courses could take more students without increasing staff or using extra rooms. The benefit to the local people would be the supply of high class educational opportunities locally.

The bursar explains that his difficulty is working out how to price the courses.

Tasks 4

1. Explain to the bursar three approaches to pricing.
2. Show in principle how the calculations might be done.

4. Pricing

How prices are determined in practice and in theory is the subject of economics text-books. Accountants are often involved in real life pricing decisions both by supplying relevant data and also by supplying techniques such as total absorption costing and marginal costing. Ultimately pricing decisions are an important part of management decision making. We will consider three approaches:

Market prices

For many products there is a market price. All firms charge about the same price. To charge less would be to lose the opportunity for profit and possibly lead to a loss. To charge more would be to lose sales. If the market determines the prices that can be charged then the way of charging a different price is to have a different or slightly different product which is differentiated from others. Effectively there is a market for every product, with competing suppliers (there are also a few monopoly situations) and management need to consider what price would be acceptable and what sales might be made at various prices.

Marginal cost pricing

If it is possible to sell a product at more than marginal cost then a benefit is gained. We considered this in Unit 7. For example an Army unit may have a firing range which is never used at weekends. If the range can be let out to a local rifle club at a price which is more than the marginal costs, then the Army unit benefits. The costs of opening specially are likely to be mainly the time of personnel opening and closing and super-vising. Since the people involved are serving personnel and are paid a fixed salary with no overtime, the actual **extra or marginal** cost will be nil. The only actual marginal cost will be electricity and gas for heating and lighting. Thus the price to the rifle club can be very low but as long as it is more than the cost of energy it benefits the Army finan-cially.

It is important to realise that mainstream activities must be priced at full or total absorption cost (plus a profit margin!). However additional or marginal opportunities can be priced by reference to marginal cost. In practice there are frequent opportunities for additional revenues in all enterprises.

Total absorption cost

Most pricing decisions are made by calculating total absorption cost and adding a margin. Even if the price must be fixed in relation to market forces it is desirable to ensure that products are sold at above total absorption cost. This applies equally to service sector firms as well as to manufacture. For example a college that sells a range of courses should price them in accordance with total absorption cost per course. It is readily apparent that courses involving extensive laboratory work are going to be much more expensive than courses in economics or English literature. However the techniques of total absorption costing translate easily to a college situation with perhaps the class room as the main cost centre. Currently total absorption costing is being applied also to not-for-profit areas like hospitals (what possible cost centres are there in a hospital?) with the setting up of internal markets.

Total absorption costing has a long history. It is interesting to note that the success of Josiah Wedgewood's pottery factory in the eighteenth century was partly due to the careful measurement of the total absorption cost of each product.

5. Total absorption costing and not-for-profit

The technique of finding a total absorption cost for a product can work quite well for not-for-profit activity. As an example consider a hospital. Its products are treatment of patients in wards, in out-patient clinics, surgical operations, and investigative activities. There are a range of supporting or ancillary activities including the pathology department, the mortuary, the laundry, the grounds, the car park, the offices and many others. The division of costs between direct and indirect is probably necessary and detailed investigation may suggest that the costs of some products (e.g. an operation or an X-ray) may be considered as both types of cost. In general the approach would be to divide the whole hospital up into cost centres — each ward, each operating theatre, the kitchen, the plaster room etc and determine the cost of each including labour, materials and services. Some of these costs can be allocated (a nurse who works in one ward only) but many will need to be apportioned (e.g. electricity). After the primary allocation and apportionment there will need to be further re-apportionments. For example the laundry cost need to be apportioned over the cost centres which use the laundry.

Once the costs of each cost centre have been determined, then an absorption rate needs to be found for each cost centre. This might be an hourly rate for an operating theatre or a daily rate for a bed in a ward. Finally the cost of a particular treatment should be assembled. For example the cost of an operation may include costs of n days in a ward, drugs and dressings, X-rays, endoscope, m hours in an operating theatre, x hours of out-patient treatment etc.

This kind of accounting exercise is expensive and its benefits must be greater than its costs. Some uses include:

❐ charging out rates for an internal market — higher costs in Hospital A than in Hospital B will mean that Hospital B gets all the work

❐ budgeting — budgets can be in total absorption costing form

❐ control — actual costs can be compared with budgets and any necessary action taken to correct variances

❐ motivation — staff will perhaps be inclined to be aware of, and take account of, the financial implications in making decisions

❐ statistical comparison — government, ever mindful of money, can point to disparities in costs between hospitals

❐ external policy — government can make rational decisions on resource allocation once costs are known

❐ internal policy — in times of restricted resources, hospital administrators can make rational choices on which treatments to offer bearing in mind cost benefit matters.

Shall we spend £200,000 treating old Fred's rare condition or offer all the local community a screening for early signs of some cancer?

6. Service departments

The principle of allocating and apportioning costs to cost centres is defensible and practical if arbitrary but there can be complications. One of these is the problem of service departments. In Saturn's factory there are 5 departments and here is a list of them with some statistics:

	Prod 1	Prod 2	Stores	Maint'nce	Canteen
Area (Sq M)	300	250	80	24	120
Number of employees	30	20	8	10	6
Machine Hours	4,000	2,000			

Overheads budgeted are allocable:

	£	£	£	£	£
Depreciation	8,000	5,000	1,000	2,000	2,500
Indirect costs	28,000	9,000	7,000	8,000	16,000

Overheads to be apportioned are:

Rent, rates etc	£46,440
Management	£29,600

There would be more expense headings and probably many more departments in a real situation but the principle is illustrated with just a few.

So, overheads can be summarised as:

Overhead apportionment schedule

	Prod 1	Prod 2	Stores	Maint'nce	Canteen	Total
	£	£	£	£	£	£
Depreciation	8,000	5,000	1,000	2,000	2,500	18,500
Indirect	28,000	9,000	7,000	8,000	16,000	68,000
Rent, Rates	18,000	15,000	4,800	1,440	7,200	46,440
Management	12,000	8,000	3,200	4,000	2,400	29,600
	66,000	37,000	16,000	15,440	28,100	162,540

You will notice that the rent and rates have been apportioned on floor area and management on number of employees.

So far we have produced a schedule in much the same way as before but at this point we have to realise that although the total overheads are £162,540 only £103,000 have been apportioned to production departments. And it is from production departments that products absorb overheads. Consequently the next step is to apportion the overheads of the three service departments to the two production departments. We will do this as:

❐ Stores in proportion to usage as evidenced by numbers of stores requisitions which are 960 to 1 and 640 to 2.

❐ Maintenance in proportion to depreciation.

❐ Canteen in proportion to number of employees.

Thus:

	Production 1	Production 2	Total
	£	£	£
Brought forward	66,000	37,000	103,000
Stores	9,600	6,400	16,000
Maintenance	9,502	5,938	15,440
Canteen	16,860	11,240	28,100
	101,962	60,578	162,540

All the overheads have been effectively located in the two production departments and we can now derive an absorption basis. Suppose we use machine hour rates, then the machine hour rates will be:

❒ Production 1 $\dfrac{£101,962}{4,000}$ = £25.50

❒ Production 2 $\dfrac{£101,962}{4,000}$ = £30.30

We have done this in steps and the method is called the step down method.

Management are often led into thinking that the £25.50 is a scientifically accurate measure. The process, as you have seen, is full of assumptions (for example, that maintenance expenditure is proportional to machine depreciation) and guesses (for example, that machine hours in Department 1 will be 4,000). So the figure is a practical usable sum and the true cost cannot actually be measured except after the event and even then only with the assumptions.

You may also have noticed that the stores department overheads were apportioned just between the two production departments whereas in practice they should be divided up into the production and the other service departments. The same applies to the other two service departments. The problem can be that having apportioned the stores, stores acquire new overheads from an apportionment of the canteen. The canteen then has an apportionment of this from maintenance. The problem is called the *reciprocal service department problem*. We need not detain ourselves with it.

7. Activity based costing

Product costing systems have generally been of two types — total absorption costing and marginal costing. Total absorption costing is required for determining the cost of inventory in preparing the annual financial statements and it is used in long run pricing decisions and in control and evaluation in budgetary control and standard costing systems. Marginal costing tends to find its uses in short term decision making.

A new concept of product cost which is really a new approach to total absorption costing has been developed in recent years and this is activity based costing (ABC).

The system is based on the following set of ideas:

❒ the decision to manufacture a product is a seen as a long term commitment which should take into account all costs both fixed and variable

❒ in modern manufacturing variable costs are a decreasing proportion of total costs

- ❏ methods of absorbing overheads onto products by labour hour rates (which is the commonest way) are inequitable as direct labour forms only a small proportion of total cost. Machine time is a more appropriate method but has many limitations for some categories of overheads.
- ❏ ABC concentrates on what causes overhead expenditure
- ❏ ABC views all costs as variable, that is they vary with some measure of activity
- ❏ even traditional long term costs, usually regarded as fixed are in fact variable with some measure of activity although changes are not usually immediate. As an example quality control inspectors are not going to vary in number and hence cost with short term changes in output but in the long term numbers will be a function of output.
- ❏ ABC tries to relate costs to products by understanding the forces which cause costs — the so-called cost drivers. Examples include material handling costs being driven by the number of parts in a product, packing costs being driven by the number of orders, machine maintenance by machine hours.
- ❏ many cost drivers are transaction based. For example, material handling, packing, inspection, set-up costs for machines.
- ❏ product costs should be measured using absorption methods which take account of cost drivers.

A simple example of activity based costing

Tops Ltd assemble two products from bought-in components — the A and the B. Details of manufacture are:

	A	B
Output in units	10,000	15,000
Component numbers	8	4
Components cost (£)	4.5	3.6
Number of production runs	200	50
Machine hours per 100 units	2.6	5.3
Items packed in cartons of	10 units	50 units

You will notice that output of A is smaller but that it has more components, is produced in relatively frequent production runs with small numbers per production run and is packed in relatively small numbers per carton.

Overhead costs are budgeted at:

	£
Component purchasing and handling	14,000
Production control	18,000
Machine set-up costs	25,000
Machine running costs	64,355
Packing	31,200

Calculation of overhead rates:

Component purchasing and handling (driven by component numbers)

$$\frac{£14,000}{8 \times 10,000 + 4 \times 15,000} = 10\text{p per component}$$

Production control (driven by number of production runs)

$$\frac{£18,000}{200 + 50} = £72 \text{ per production run}$$

Machine set-up costs (also driven by number of production runs)

$$\frac{£25,000}{200 + 50} = £100 \text{ per production run}$$

Machine running costs (driven by machine hours)

$$\frac{£64,355}{2.6 \times 100 + 5.3 \times 150} = £61 \text{ per machine hour}$$

Packing (driven by number of cartons packed)

$$\frac{£31,200}{1,000 + 300} = £24 \text{ per carton}$$

Thus the cost of manufacture of the two items:

	A	B
	£	£
Direct Materials (components)	4.50	3.60
Purchasing and handling	0.80	0.40
Production control (i)	1.44	0.24
Machine set-up	2.00	0.33
Machine running (ii)	1.59	3.23
Packing (iii)	2.40	0.48
Total	12.73	8.28

i. $^{(a)}$ $\dfrac{10,000}{200} = 50$ are made per production run.

Therefore the cost per item is $\dfrac{£72}{50} = £1.44$

ii. $^{(m)}$ $\dfrac{2.6}{100 \text{ units}} \times £61 = £1.59$

iii. $^{(q)}$ 10 units in a carton therefore cost is $\dfrac{£24}{10} = £2.40$

$^{(b)}$ $\dfrac{15,000}{50} = 300 \text{ per run}$

$\dfrac{£72}{300} = £0.24$

$^{(s)}$ $\dfrac{5.3}{100} \times £61 = £3.23$

$^{(h)}$ $\dfrac{24}{50} = £0.48$

Note:

❏ Overheads are a mixture of conventional fixed and variable costs but will vary in the long term with cost drivers.

❏ This example is simplified. For example, the cost driver for component purchasing and handling should include size of components and size of orders

❏ This example illustrates that long runs do not drive overheads as much as short runs. For example, A is run more often than B and consequently costs per unit such as production control and machine set-up are higher.

❏ Costs are very much transaction driven as you can see from purchasing and handling, production control, set-up and packing.

❐ The overhead absorption system still has two stages:

allocating and apportioning costs to cost centres

finding absorption methods.

An ABC system is likely to be expensive to set up but will produce more appropriate product costs which in a competitive market will give a firm an edge in its pricing and product mix policies. Further, knowing the underlying driving force behind costs enables management to anticipate the cost change effects of decisions and hence enables them to make better decisions.

Activity Based Costing has only been around since the mid 1980's so it is too early to judge its impact. There is no evidence as yet that its adoption increases corporate profitability despite its apparent superiority over traditional systems. There are some difficulties in installing an ABC system. It is necessary to identify the cost driver for each cost and then to place all the costs driven by a particular cost driver into a pool. This is difficult and the tendency is to find that there is a very large number of cost pools.

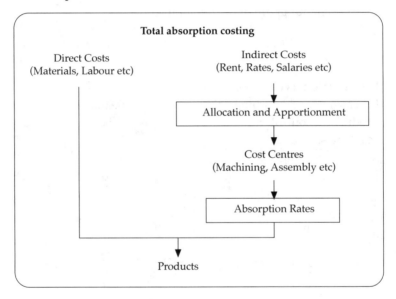

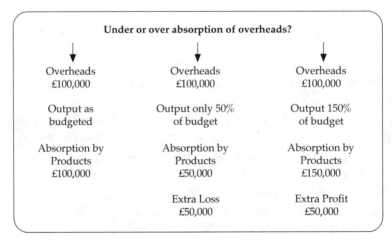

8. Summary of Unit 12

❐ A product cost under Total Absorption Costing principles is the sum of direct costs and an appropriate proportion of indirect costs.

❐ Direct costs form the prime cost of a product.

❐ The overheads to be included will be production costs only if a cost is to be found for stock valuation purposes.

❐ For other purposes, including selling price determination, administrative and selling and distribution costs may be added.

❐ In multiproduct firms ascribing overheads to individual or batches of products involves:

i)   Listing overheads;

ii) Allocating and apportioning the overheads to cost centres;

iii) Developing an absorption method such as a machine hour rate, a labour hour rate or a percentage on materials, labour, or prime cost.

❐ If activity is less than budgeted under-absorption of overheads takes place.

❐ The computation of product costs can be complicated by the reciprocal service department cost problem.

❐ A relatively new but potentially very powerful technique is Activity Based Costing (ABC).

Exercise 1

Wedd makes mass produced machine parts by sophisticated machinery. The principal costs are the overheads associated with the machines except in the packing shop which is largely labour oriented. All the workers in the machine departments are regarded as indirect but most in the packing department are direct. There are 3 manufacturing departments and information about them is:

	Machine 1	Machine 2	Packing
Floor area (Sq M.)	400	300	400
Number of workers	30	12	60
Value of machinery	£400,000	£150,000	£25,000

Overheads expected in 19x2 (in £'000) to be apportioned to departments:

Rates	£240
Property Insurance	£60
Works management Costs	£300
Power	£180
Depreciation	10% of value

Overheads (in £'000) to be allocated to specific departments:

	Machine 1	Machine 2	Packing
Indirect labour	£320	£160	£60
Machine Spares	£34	£40	£4

221

Required:

a. Prepare an overhead schedule to determine the total overheads for each department.

b. Budgeted machine hours in 19x2 are:

in Machine 1 dept	20,000
in Machine 2 dept	30,000

Budgeted direct labour hours for the packing department are 100,000.

Calculate overhead absorption rates for the three departments.

c. Use these rates to produce a cost for a batch of machine parts which will consume:

Material costs	£600
Direct labour packing	£400
Machine 1 hours	30
Machine 2 hours	25
Packing Labour hours	60

d. Calculate a price for the batch on the basis that Wedd expects a profit of 20% of the sales price.

e. Calculate the under recovery of overheads assuming that actual production consumed only:

Machine 1	18,600	hours
Machine 2	25,500	hours
Packing	90,000	hours

Exercise *2

Thor is a manufacturer of shelving to order. Budgeted data for period 6 are:

	£
Direct materials	30,000
Direct Labour 10,000 hours at £6 an hour	
Rates	20,000
Machinery Depreciation	14,000
Electric Power	30,000
Supervision	22,000

Statistics about the three manufacturing departments (Cutting, Making, Finishing) are:

	Cutting	Making	Finishing
Area in square metres	100	200	160
Machinery value	£60,000	£30,000	£10,000
Number of employees	10	20	25
Machine hours	600	300	100

Required:

a. Prepare an overhead apportionment schedule for the three production cost centres.

b. Calculate absorption rates (machine hour rates) for the three departments.

c. Calculate an alternative absorption rate (a labour hour rate) for the finishing department using labour hours — budgeted at 4,500 hours.

d. Calculate a selling price for a product whose estimated costs are:

Materials	£300
Direct Labour	
Cutting	30 hours
Making	12 hours
Finishing	36 hours
Machine hours	
Cutting	12 hours
Making	6 hours
Finishing	22 hours

Profit margin should be 25% on cost.

Initially you should use machine hours for all departments and then use a labour hour rate for the Finishing department.

e. How might a manager decide on whether a labour hour rate or a machine hour rate (or some other method) might be most appropriate for his department?

Exercise 3

Fry makes cakes for the retail trade. His costs are budgeted for period 8 as:

Materials	£10,000
Direct Labour	£30,000
Overheads	£36,000

He makes a wide variety and is continually trying out new recipes. All cakes are made in batches in one single cost centre.

He has to fix a selling price for each batch of cakes and finds he can determine the materials and direct labour cost of each batch but is unsure of how to include overheads in the cost calculation. Suggestions include:

❒ a percentage on material cost

❒ a percentage on labour cost

❒ a percentage on prime cost

❒ a baking hour rate

The last would depend on the total baking hours available which are estimated for period 8 at 4,000 — there are various ovens of different sizes.

Required:

a. Calculate a cost for batch AX using each method assuming costs will be:

Materials	£50
Labour Hours	£200
Baking hours	25 hours

b. Discuss which method might be most appropriate.

c. Calculate a selling price on the basis of:

❏ Profit is 25% on cost

❏ Profit is 20% of selling price

d. Discuss the viability of fixing a selling price based on total cost + a percentage for profit. What alternative pricing methods might be adopted? If cost + is not used, is there any purpose in calculating cost?

Exercise 4

Sheinton Primary School has resolved to let some rooms in the evenings for community activity. A charge out price has to be determined and the Head feels that the rate should be sufficient to cover costs, something for his and the Administrative Officer's time (say 20% on cost) and to make a small profit (say 25% on total cost). The intention is to let out the lecture theatre (100 m²), two equal size classrooms (50m²) and a small tutorial room (20m²).

The actual costs for term one are expected to be: Caretaking £420, Heating and lighting £800, Cleaning £260 and repairs and maintenance £400.

It is expected that letting demand in term one will be Lecture Theatre 140 hours, each classroom 70 hours and the tutorial room 70 hours.

Required:

Determine a charge out rate for each room per hour based on some rational apportionment scheme.

Exercise 5

Davina has a factory making a wide variety of jars of molluscs. There are four departments in the process: preparation, steam cooking, steam production, stores. Statistics are:

	Preparation	Cook	Steam	Stores
Employees	10	6	4	3
Floor area (m2)	30	15	6	12
Value of Plant (£'000)	4	6	6	2
For period 12 overheads allocated are:	£4,200	£2,900	£3,800	£3,000

Overheads to be apportioned are:

	£
Rent, Rates	24,800
Supervision	36,000
Repairs and Maintenance	12,000

Required:

a. Prepare an overhead apportionment schedule for the four departments and then reduce it to the two production departments. Steam is 100% cooking and stores are divided equally.

b. Preparation is a largely manual process although the staff do use machines. In period ten 2,000 hours will be available. Steam cooking is largely a machine operation although much direct labour is involved. Machine hours in the period will be 800. Calculate suitable absorption rates.

c. A batch of mollusc jars is to be produced. Costs will probably be:

Materials	£180
Direct Labour	
Prep 18 hours at £4	£72
Cook 10 hours at £5	£50
Machine hours	12

Calculate a cost and also a selling price if profit is to be 15% on Cost.

Assignment 1

Upmarket Stores PLC have paid a premium on a 21 year lease on a department store in a newish development in a county town. The intention is to spend a considerable sum on a new shop front and on complete redecoration and refurbishment. The store will hold a number of departments operated by Upmarket and will let some parts as concessions to a number of interested firms.

Required:

a. In the context of the store explain the difference between direct and indirect costs.

   The Chief Executive has a provisional idea on which parts of the store to put each department and where to place the concessions. He now wants to know the costs associated with each area.

b. Explain why it is desirable to know the costs of each area.

c. Explain in detail how the costs could be calculated.

d. Explain the consequences of getting the calculations in c. wrong.

Case study / Assignment 2

Stubbee PLC manufacture widgets. They have three major products, A, B, and C. Some data about manufacture are:

	A	B	C
Annual number of production runs	50	20	30
Component numbers	3	10	12
X Type Machine hours	4	2	9
Y type Machine hours	9	7	2
Manual Polishing time in hours	8	4	8
Packing — units in each carton	12	24	6
Cartons per lorry	20	25	30
Number of customers	6	150	200

All products are delivered to customers in the company's own vans.

The X type machine is much more expensive to set-up and run than the Y type.

The company have been hit by competition and are considering introducing a small range of additional products using small production runs but with the products tailored to the needs of specific customers. The company currently work 5 daily shifts and the additional products would require 2 night time shifts.

Discussion

The company currently use a simple Total absorption costing system based on manufacturing overhead recovery by machine hour rates and labour hour rates. How might an ABC system assist the company in formulating a pricing policy for their existing and proposed products which might assist it to compete more strongly in the widget market?

13 Standard costing

1. Objectives

The objective of this Unit is to introduce **Standard Costing**. Firms can examine the cost of a product and establish a **standard cost** for it. The **actual cost** of making the product can then be compared with the standard and any difference noted. The difference can be broken down into separate causes known as **variances**.

Thus management have an objective standard against which actual costs can be compared and can take action to investigate variances and correct any adverse cost movements.

SCENARIO 1 — Martin classifies some costs

Martin is worried about the costs of manufacture of a range of keys which are made in a corner of his factory called the key department. These keys are made by stamping them out of sheets of metal. They are then polished and packed. An investigation of the annual cost of the department reveals:

	£
Materials:	20,000
Labour: Stamper	8,000
Polisher	10,200
Packer	7,500
Energy and consumables	3,800
Depreciation of Machines	18,000
Apportionment of rent etc	9,000

Quick Answer Question 13.1

Which of these costs are likely to be:
Direct
Indirect
Fixed
Variable?

SCENARIO 2 — Martin creates a standard cost

Martin asks his general manager to measure a standard cost for a batch of type 433 keys made in the department.

The manager comes up with the following:

Standard Cost of one batch of type 433 Keys

	£
Materials:	
10 Kilos of Metal at £5.20 a kilo	52.00
Packaging	2.00
Labour :	
Stamper : 3 hours at £4.00 an hour	12.00
Polisher: 3 hours at £5.00 an hour	15.00
Packer : 3.5 hours at £3.90 an hour	13.65
Variable Overheads : 6 hours at £1.50 per Stamper and Polisher hour	9.00
Fixed Overheads : 9.5 hours at £6 a direct labour hour	57.00
Total	160.65

Martin is perplexed by the way that the variable and fixed overheads are expressed.

The manager explains that the amount of electricity and consumables like lubricating oil that are used depends on how long the machines are used. Since the machines are used by the Stamper and Polisher, the amount of variable overhead will depend on how many hours they operate the machines. It is the stamper and polisher which *drive* the variable overheads.

He also explains that the fixed overheads of the department have to be divided over the output of the department. The department do not make a single type of key but a range. It is thus necessary to express the output in some common form. The method chosen is to take a view that the department provides a quantity of direct labour hours in a year. Production can then be expressed in terms of direct labour hours. Thus it is possible to say that output in a period is n *thousand standard labour hours.* Suppose that Lock 555 should take under standard conditions, 5 hours and lock 666 should take 7 hours then total output is two locks but can also said to be 12 standard hours of output.

In this case the fixed costs were budgeted as:

Depreciation of Machines	£18,000
Apportionment of rent etc	£9,000
	£27,000

The total direct labour hours budgeted are 4,500.

So the fixed costs are 27,000 ÷ 4,500 = £6 per direct labour hour. A batch of type 433 keys should take 9.5 hours of direct labour. Therefore it will absorb 9.5 × £6 = £57 of fixed overheads.

Quick Answer Question 13.2

What would you expect the standard cost of type 501 keys to be using the following data:

Materials:

6 Kilos of Metal at £4 a kilo

Packaging £3.00

Labour :   Stamper : 2 hours at £4.00 an hour

Polisher: 2.5 hours at £5.00 an hour

Packer :2 hours at £3.90 an hour?

SCENARIO 3 — Martin finds uses for standard costs

Martin now understands that he has a standard cost for type 433 keys and can similarly find a standard cost for all the keys produced in the department. He still wonders whether this will be useful to him and the manager gives him several possible uses:

a. In *pricing*. Suppose a selling price was required for a job that included a batch of type 433 keys. He has at least a cost for the keys which he can incorporate in his estimate.

b. In *monthly accounting*. If Martin wished to prepare a Profit and Loss Account and Balance Sheet monthly, he would be put off by the labour of finding the costs of items in stock. However if he counts up 4 batches of type 433 keys in stock, he can use the standard cost. For the annual accounts however he should not use standard costs as these may not coincide with actual costs which are required for accounts prepared under the requirements of the Companies Act.

c. In *variance analysis* which we explore later in the Unit.

Some months later, Martin picked out a batch of type 433 keys and enquired what the actual cost of making them was:

Records had been carefully kept and the costs were collected as:

Materials: 11 Kilos at £6 a kilo

Packaging £2.60

Labour: Stamper : 3.25 hours at £3.60 an hour

Polisher: 2.75 hours at £6.00 an hour

Packer : 4 hours at £4.20 an hour

Quick Answer Question 13.3

Why do you think the actual costs of overheads were not recorded for the batch Martin picked out so that we can compare them with the actual costs?

Tasks 1

1. Calculate *material* and *labour* variances.

2. Suggest reasons for the variances.

2. Introduction

Standard costing is an extension of budgetary control. It began in manufacturing but it can be applied in all industries. The objective is to set up *predetermined* standards of cost and other aspects of performance such as sales. The actual outcome can then be compared and *variances* between *standard* and *actual* can be computed. If a variance is significant then it can be investigated and if necessary corrective action taken. The setting up of standards is the essential since they supply objective criteria against which performance can be measured.

Standards must be set up realistically using all available technical knowledge. For example if the standard cost of making a widget is to be established then the material quantities must be evaluated by production personnel and prices established by purchasing personnel. Labour time must be evaluated by work study engineers and cost by wages staff. The standards to be adopted should be *attainable* standards. That is those standards of performance that are achievable if machinery is operated efficiently, material properly used and appropriate allowances are made for normal losses, waste and machine downtime. *Ideal* standards which can only be achieved in exceptional circumstances are not normally adopted.

Once set up, standard costs have several uses. Measuring *profit* for regular internal performance reports is much easier if standard costs are used for valuing stocks of raw materials, work in progress and finished goods rather than determining the actual costs. Note that actual costs have to be used for external profit reporting. Standard costs are also used for cost measurement when determining the *price* to be quoted to potential customers. However the principal use of standard costs is in *variance analysis*.

3. Variance analysis — material variances

The standard material cost of one mark IV widget is 24 kg of Hedonite at £2.40 a kg.

In period twelve 420 widgets were made. The actual material cost of these was 10,710 kg at £2.30 a kg.

The standard material cost of making 420 widgets is:

$$420 \times 24 \times £2.40 = £24,192$$

The actual cost turned out to be:

$$10,710 \times £2.30 = £24,633$$

The difference at £441 is an *adverse* variance as the actual cost was more than the standard cost.

Now we can break this variance down into two sub-variances:

a) Material price variance:

$$10,710 \times 10p = £1,071 \text{ FAV}$$

Obviously the Hedonite was bought at a slightly cheaper price than the standard and we have a *favourable* variance. How can we interpret this? Possibly the price of the material has simply changed and the firm have to accept the price given by the market. This might be called a planning variance since effectively the standard is now wrong as the market price has changed. An alternative possibility is that the buying department were successful in securing the material at a lower price or perhaps deliberately bought an inferior grade of material. These interpretations would imply that the variance was a *performance* variance.

Generally the objective of calculating of variances is not to explain but to alert management to the existence of non-standard costs so that they can enquire the reasons from the persons responsible.

Now that we have extracted the price variance we can calculate any further variances at standard cost.

b) Material usage variance:

$$[(420 \times 24) - 10{,}710] \times £2.40 = £1{,}512 \text{ ADV}$$

Std Usage   Actual

Clearly more material was used than standard and the explanation is likely to be caused by *adverse* performance. Perhaps supervision was lax or perhaps the process results vary naturally and this was one of the bad periods. It may be that the adverse usage variance was connected with the price variance as poorer quality material (favourable price variance) caused excessive usage. Different variances are often *connected*. Management are now alerted to determine the cause and if necessary take some action to prevent recurrence.

The two variances are now

$$£1{,}071 \text{ FAV} + £1{,}512 \text{ ADV} = £441 \text{ ADV}$$

so we can check our calculations.

4. Labour variances

The standard labour cost of making one Mark IV widget is 9 hours at £3.50 an hour = £31.50.

Therefore the standard labour cost of making the 420 widgets was:

$$420 \times 9 \times £3.5 = £13{,}230$$

The actual cost of making the 420 widgets was 3,600 hours at £3.72 an hour = £13,392.

The variance is thus £162 ADV

This variance can broken down into sub-variances:

a) Labour rate variance:

$$3{,}600 \times 22\text{p} = £792 \text{ ADV}$$

The cause of this may be planning in that the standard is now out of date following an agreed wage increase. Or it may be a performance variance as the mix of labour (skilled, semi-skilled or unskilled) was slightly more skewed, than standard, toward the skilled. Another alternative may be some overtime working.

Having extracted the rate (equivalent to price) variance, all further variances will be at the standard rate of £3.50 an hour.

b) Efficiency variance:

$$[(420 \times 9) - 3{,}600] \times £3.50 = £630 \text{ FAV}$$

Std Usage   Actual

The explanation for this may be that conditions were just right or that fewer breakdowns or hold-ups occurred than the standard foresaw. There may be a connection with the rate variance if that was caused by a higher than standard proportion of more skilled labour.

The two sub-variances are £792 ADV and £630 FAV = £162 ADV

SCENARIO 4 — Martin reviews some variances

Martin is very interested in the schedule of variances and seeks an explanation for them from the manager. After due enquiry the manager produces a schedule of reasons as:

Materials:

Metal: Price — the price has gone up from the supplier as the price of the metal has increased on world markets.

Usage — the stamper is newly appointed and has not yet mastered the knack of getting the maximum number of keys from a sheet.

Packaging: the price has gone up and on this batch some materials were torn during use and had to be replaced. Martin finds that splitting the cost of packing into price and usage variances would cost more than any benefit.

Labour:

Stamper: Rate — the stamper is new and is paid less than the old stamper

Efficiency — she takes a little longer than the old one

Polisher: Rate — a wage increase was given above the normal rate as he now supervises the others as well as doing his own work.

Efficiency — this varies from batch to batch and he was on form in this batch.

Packer: Rate — she has been given the usual annual wage increase.

Efficiency — she had a bad cold on that day and took a little longer.

Tasks 2

1.   Suggest which variances are planning variances and which are *operating* variances.
2.   What actions might Martin take as a result of investigating the variances?

SCENARIO 5 — Martin learns from overhead variances

After a month designated as operating period 5, Martin enquired about overhead variances. He was told that budgeted standard direct labour hours (the measure of output) were 375. Actual output was measured as 340 hours only. This output included 110 hours of Stamping, 125 hours of Polishing and 105 hours of Packing.

Expenditure was:

	Budgeted	Actual
Variable		£402
Fixed :		
Depreciation	£1,500	£1,500
Rent etc	£750	£800

The hours spent on production were:

Stamper	125
Polisher	130
Packer	105

Tasks 3

1. Calculate overhead variances.
2. Suggest reasons for the variances.

---

5. Variable overheads

The variable overheads are costs such as power and consumable stores which vary linearly with output. Suppose that the standard variable cost for the production of one widget was £27 then the standard variable overhead cost for 420 widgets is £11,340. In period 12 the actual variable overheads were £12,743. The total overhead variance is thus:

$$£11,340 - £12,743 = £1,403 \text{ ADV}$$

The total variance can be broken down:

a) Efficiency variance. The variable overheads are associated with labour hours. Cost accountants say the variable overheads are *driven* by the labour hours. In fact the standard labour hours required for 420 items of output are $420 \times 9 = 3,780$. We have seen that the standard variable overheads per widget are £27 or £3 a labour hour. Therefore we might expect the variable overhead cost to be $3,780 \times £3 = £11,340$. However the actual labour hours were 3,600 and if variable overheads are driven by labour hours then the variable overheads should be $3,600 \times £3 = £10,800$. By using less labour hours than standard on our output, we would expect a saving on variable overheads of:

$$£11,340 - £10,800 = £540 \text{ FAV}$$

This is called the efficiency variance.

b) Expenditure variance.

The standard variable overhead cost driven by labour hours is:

$$3,600 \times £3 = £10,800$$

The actual expenditure was £12,743 and so the expenditure variance is:

$$£10,800 - £12,743 = £1,943 \text{ ADV}$$

The total variance is:

$$£540 \text{ FAV} + £1,943 \text{ ADV} = £1,403 \text{ ADV}$$

The cause of the efficiency variance is simply the efficiency of labour and the cause of the expenditure variance is probably that prices of the variable overhead constituents have risen or that the outlays were excessive in relation to standard. Perhaps excessive lubricating oil was used.

In practice the variable overheads are not simply driven by labour hours and meaningful variances are best obtained by looking at each variable overhead expenditure heading in turn.

6. Fixed overheads

Fixed overheads are those that do not vary with output and the standard will be a lump sum not an amount per unit of output. We will suppose the lump sum is £16,000. A standard cost per widget is calculated and must include an amount for fixed overheads. This can only be done by having a budgeted output. Suppose this was 400 widgets. Then the fixed overhead cost per widget is:

$$\frac{£16,000}{400} = £40$$

In period 12, the actual fixed overhead expenditure was £15,700.

The total fixed overhead variance is:

$$(420 \times £40) - £15,700 = £1,100 \text{ FAV}$$

The idea is that by including £40 a widget in the standard cost every unit produced (and sold) recovers £40 from the customer. As 420 units were produced then recovery is $420 \times £40 = £16,800$. Since actual expenditure was only £15,700, £1,100 more was recovered than was expended.

The total variance is broken down into:

a) Expenditure variance. This is:

$$£16,000 - £15,700 = £300 \text{ FAV}$$

Fixed overheads should be the same regardless of output and at standard are £16,000. In fact they were £15,700 so some savings were made. Perhaps less than standard was spent on maintenance or a supervisor left and was not replaced.

b) Volume variance. This is:

$$(420 - 400) \times £40 = £800 \text{ FAV}$$

The calculation is the extra output over budget viz 20 widgets at standard cost.

This is a very useful measure because the effect of output over budget is to increase profit not only by the profit margin on the extra output but also by the recovery of fixed overheads that have already been recovered by the budgeted output.

SCENARIO 6 — Martin extends variance analysis to sales

Martin reads the schedule of variances and asks for investigations to be made. The reasons brought out were:

Variable:

Efficiency: the temperature in the department had been unseasonably hot in the month and as the department was always too hot anyway output had been even lower than normal as a consequence.

Expenditure: Electricity prices had risen.

Fixed:

Expenditure: this was nothing to do with the department as it was an apportionment of the fixed costs of the factory as a whole.

Efficiency: see under variable above.

Volume: both of the machines had broken down and production was lost as a result.

As a result of these explanations, Martin dug deeper and found that the temperature of the department varied considerably but that it was usually too hot and that efficiency suffered as a consequence. He agreed to investigate ways of maintaining a more comfortable temperature. He also found that the machines often broke down and that output was lost. He agreed to look at the possibility of new machines or a programme of preventative maintenance.

Martin feels that standard costing and variance analysis have a lot to offer and decides to extend his experiment.

The company have an agent in Canada who sells just one type of lock – the AZ500. The standard cost of this was worked out at £20 each and the Canadian agent is expected to sell them at £30 each. In fact the price he gets depends on the prices charged for a similar lock sold by a competitor. In addition the sales in Canada are in Canadian Dollars.

For month 9, Martin has set a budget for Canadian sales as:

Number of units to sell	2,000
Selling Price	62 Dollars
Exchange rate	2.1 Dollars to the pound sterling

The actual sales in the month were:

Sales	2,200 units
Selling Price	58 dollars
Exchange rate	2.05 dollars to the pound

Tasks 4

1. Calculate suitable *sales variances*.

2. Write a report explaining precisely what the variances mean.

7. Sales margin variances

The variances so far have been concerned with costs. Clearly these variances affect profit. So also do sales volume and prices.

We will first summarise the position with the standard cost per widget which is:

£

Materials	24 Kg at £2.40	57.60
Labour	9 Hours at £3.50	31.50
Variable overheads		27.00
Fixed overheads		40.00
		156.10

Suppose the selling price is £180 then the standard *margin* of profit per widget is:

$$£180 – £156.10 = £23.90$$

In period 12, actual sales were 420 units at £175 = £73,500

The total sales margin variance is:

$$[(400 × £23.90) – (420 × £18.90] = £1,622 \text{ ADV}$$

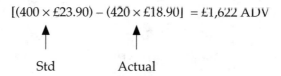

Std   Actual

235

This is the budgeted profit less the actual sales at actual sales margin assuming standard costs. Clearly the actual costs were not standard but the variances from standard are dealt with as cost variances and we have already done this. Since the selling price is £5 less than the standard the actual margin is £18.90.

This total variance can be broken down as:

a) Sales margin price variance.

This is:

$$420 \times £5 = £2,100 \text{ ADV}$$

The sales margin achieved was less by 420 (the actual output) at £5 which is the reduction in price.

The reduction in price of £5 caused a reduction in profit of £2,100.

b) Sales margin volume variance. This is:

$$(400 - 420) \times £23.90 = £478 \text{ FAV}$$

This isolates the effect on profit of the extra 20 units sold over budget.

Notice that this is a sales margin variance not a sales variance.

The total variance is thus confirmed as:

$$£2,100 \text{ ADV} + £478 \text{ FAV} = £1,622 \text{ ADV}$$

8. Reconciliation of actual and budgeted profit

In period 12, the budgeted output is 400 units and so the budgeted profit is:

$$400 \times £23.90 = £9,560$$

The actual costs were:

	£
Materials 10,710 Kg at £2.30	24,633
Labour 3,600 hours £3.72	13,392
Variable overheads	12,743
Fixed overheads	15,700
	66,468

As sales were 420 units at £175 = £73,500 then the profit was:

$$£73,500 - £66,468 = £7,032$$

This is different from the budgeted profit of £9,560 and we can now produce a statement reconciling the standard with the actual profit as:

	£			
Budgeted net profit				9,560
Sales variances				
Sales margin price	2,100	A		
Sales margin volume	478	F	1,622	A
Material variances				
Price	1,071	F		
Usage	1,512	A	441	A

Labour variances

Rate	792	A				
Efficiency	630	F	162	A		

Variable overhead variances

Expenditure	1,943	A			
Efficiency	540	F	1,403	A	

Fixed overhead variances

Expenditure	300	F					
Volume	800	F	1,100	F	2,528	A	
Actual profit					7,032		

9. Planning and operating variances

Calculating variances is best left to accounting staff who have the necessary expertise. However, managers are the people who take action on variances and consequently they need to know how a variance is calculated in order to understand the message given by the variance. It is important to realise that some variances arise out of changes in circumstances which in effect make the standard out of date. For example, a wage rise will mean that the labour cost standard for a task should be higher. Variances arising out of these sorts of causes are called planning variances. Essentially the need is to eliminate them by constant updating of standards. Modern computer systems generally allow this. The remaining variances can be called operating variances and they are genuine variances which may require investigation.

10. Sales mix variances

Suppose the budgeted sales for X and Y components Ltd were:

	Product X	Product X
Unit Selling price	£100	£160
Unit Standard Cost	£80	£100
Unit Margin	£20	£60

Budgeted sales are 400 X and 200 Y giving total sales of £72,000 and a gross margin of £8,000 + £12,000 = £20,000.

Actual sales were 480 X and 150 Y giving total sales of £48,000 + £24,000 = £72,000 (as budgeted) but sales margin was only £9,600 + £9,000 = £18,600.

The loss of margin and profit comes, not from a drop in turnover, but in a change of sales mix with more of the lower margin X and less of the higher margin Y. The calculation of sales mix variances is best left to cost accountants but you will appreciate that they are very important in practice.

11. Summary of Unit 13

❑ Standard costs are established as the costs of production of products. They are usually attainable but should also be challenging and stimulating.

- Standard costs can be compared with actual costs and variances extracted.
- Significant variances can be investigated to determine the causes and take corrective action.
- Causes can be planning which indicates that the standard is now unrealistic or out of date or performance which means that they are caused by operations which were different from standard.
- Variances are usually analysed as:

material	price:	actual usage × price difference
	usage:	(std – actual usage) × std price
labour	rate:	actual usage × rate difference
	efficiency:	(std – actual usage) × std rate
variable overheads	efficiency:	(std – actual labour hours for output) × std rate
	expenditure:	(std labour hours for output × std rate) –
		actual expenditure
Fixed overheads	expenditure:	Std – actual expenditure
	volume:	(Std – actual output) × std rate
Sales margin	price:	Sales volume × price difference
	volume:	(budget– actual volume) × std margin

- Once the variances have been extracted it is possible to draw up a reconciliation between budgeted profit and actual profit.
- Price variances are usually extracted first and subsequent variances are calculated at standard prices.
- Sales margin variances are extracted not sales variances. Sales margins are calculated assuming standard costs.

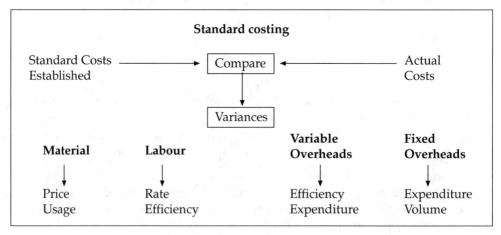

Exercise 1

Jerry Boam PLC are manufacturers of electronically controlled robotic manufacturing systems to special order. Most systems are composed of a selection of discrete components drawn from an extensive selection kept in the warehouse. Some are made in the factory and some are bought in. Enquiries are received from potential customers and specifications are drawn up by the design department. The actual price quoted to the customer is estimated by the estimation department. The company have full order books and have achieved record turnover but return on capital employed has been disappointing. The company currently measure profit only twice a year owing to the difficulty of determining stocks of components, work in progress and finished goods.

How might the adoption of a system of standard costing assist the company?

Exercise 2

The standard material cost of one of Moises's widgets is:

> 30 grams of Green Metal at £12 a gram
>
> 10 grams of Epson's salts at £500 a kilo

In period one, 260 widgets were made. The material used was:

> 7,500 grams of Green Metal at £13 a gram
>
> 2,700 grams of Epson's salts at £496 a kilo

a. Calculate material usage and price variances for period 1.

b. Suggest possible causes for the variances.

c. Might the variances be related?

Exercise *3

The standard material cost of one of Jaime's costumes is:

> 12 yards of cloth at £2 a yard
>
> 20 buttons at 30p each

In period two, 300 costumes were made. The material used was:

> 4,000 yards of cloth at £1.89 a yard
>
> 6,400 buttons at 35p each

a. Calculate the total variance and the material usage and price variances for period 2.

b. Suggest possible causes for the variances.

c Might the variances be connected?

d. What might the works manager do about the variances?

Exercise 4

The standard direct wage cost of making one of Davis's wooden souvenirs is:

> 6 skilled worker hours at £6.50 an hour
>
> 4 unskilled worker hours at £4.20 an hour

In period three, 800 souvenirs were produced costing:

> 4,500 skilled hours at £6.40
>
> 3,500 unskilled hours at £4.50

a. Calculate rate and efficiency variances for period 3.

b. Suggest possible causes for the variances.

c Might the variances be connected?

d. What might the works manager do about the variances?

Exercise 5

The standard direct wage cost of making one of Chip's chairs is:

    3.5 skilled worker hours at £5.50 an hour

    4 unskilled worker hours at £4.70 an hour

In period three, 420 chairs were produced costing:

    1,300 skilled hours at £5.40

    1,500 unskilled hours at £4.50

a. Calculate total, rate and efficiency variances for period 3.

b. Suggest possible causes for the variances.

c Might the variances be connected?

d. What might the works manager do about the variances?

Exercise *6

Pip produces plastic components in his factory. The budget and actual for period 1 is:

	Budget	Actual
Variable overheads	£20,400	£23,900
Direct labour hours	4,500	4,650
Units of output	13,500	13,100

Variable overheads are direct labour hour driven.

Required:

a. Calculate variable overhead efficiency and expenditure variances.

b. Suggest reasons for the variances.

Exercise 7

Pippa produces dresses in her factory. The budget and actual for period 1 is:

	Budget	Actual
Variable overheads	£18,600	£17,300
Direct labour hours	3,000	2,900
Units of output	7,000	7,600

Variable overheads are direct labour hour driven.

Required:

a. Calculate variable overhead total, efficiency and expenditure variances.

b. Suggest reasons for the variances.

Exercise *8

Don produces floral displays in his workshop. Part of his budget and actual for period 4:

	Budget	Actual
Fixed Overheads	£10,000	£11,050
Output	4,000	3,870

Required:

a. Calculate fixed overhead expenditure and volume variances.

b. Suggest reasons for them.

c. What might Don do about them.

Exercise 9

Donna delivers parcels in vans for customers.

Part of her budget and actual statistics for period 5 are:

	Budget	Actual
Fixed Overheads	£23,000	£21,600
Parcels delivered	4,600	4,920

Required:

a. Calculate fixed overhead expenditure and volume variances.

b. Suggest reasons for them.

c. Does this calculation seem to you to be informative?

d. What might Donna do about them.

Exercise 10

Washington sells new cars. He has only two models to sell — the Amazing and the Fab. Budgeted and actual sales for period 7 were:

	Budget		Actual	
	Amazing	Fab	Amazing	Fab
Unit sales	40	15	46	13
Sales Price	£10,200	£15,100	£9,600	£13,000
Standard Cost	£8,300	£12,750		

Required:

a. Calculate total, sales margin and volume variances for period 7.

b. Suggest explanations for them.

c. Do you think:

❑ this is a very realistic problem?

❑ the sales margin variances provide a useful explanation of why Washington's profit is different from budget?

Exercise 11

The budget for the furniture department of Randolph's department store and actual performance in period 11 were:

	Budget	Actual
Unit Sales	80	70
Sales price	£210	£190
Standard Cost	£140	

Required:

a. Calculate total, sales margin and volume variances for period 11.

b. Suggest reasons for them.

c. Do you think the variances might be connected?

d. Why is standard cost and not actual cost used in calculating these variances.

Case Study/Assignment 1

Mack makes a single type of widget in his small factory.

His budget for period 1 was:

	£	£
Sales 2,000 widgets at £60		120,000
Materials 4,000 Kg at £6	24,000	
Direct Labour 6,000 hours at £5	30,000	
Variable overheads	18,000	72,000
Contribution		48,000
Fixed Overheads		28,000
Net Profit		20,000

The actual outturn in period 1 was:

Sales	2,400 at £58	
Materials	5,000 Kg at £6.20	
Direct Labour	7,000 hours at £5.60	
Variable Overheads		£22,780
Fixed Overheads		£30,210

Required:

a. Produce an actual Profit and Loss Account for period 1 in the same format as the budget.

b. Prepare a reconciliation of the budgeted profit and the actual profit showing all the standard variances.

c. Prepare a report to Mack explaining the reconciliation giving imagined but plausible explanations for each variance.

Case Study/Assignment 2

The standard cost of producing one of Eddy's wheelbarrows is:

Galvanised steel 2 yards at £1 a yard

Bought in components £3
Consumable stores £1
Direct labour 2 hours at £4.50
Variable overheads   £4
Fixed Overheads £2.50
Budgeted output is 2,000 units.
Selling price is £24
Actual results for period 2 were:
Output and sales 2,200 units at £26 (average)
Galvanised steel used 4,500 yards at £1.20 a yard
Bought in components used £6,700
Consumable stores used £2,170
Direct Labour 4,700 hours at £4.80 (average)
Variable overheads £9,800
Fixed Overheads £4,950

Required:

a.   Calculate and comment on variances.

b.   Prepare a statement of budgeted and actual profit.

c.   Variances have been similar for several periods.

Eddy is very concerned and has asked you to suggest actions he could take to ensure that variances are minimised. Write him a report.

Exercise 12

Lolling sells a range of garden furniture through reps to DIY sheds and caravan shops. There is a range of high margin De Luxe furniture and a range of lower margin standard furniture. Higher prices are obtained from the caravan shops than from the DIY sheds.

Explain the information that could be obtained from a calculation of sales margin variances.

In view of the different margins described, how might you reward the reps?

Exercise 13

Martin is entertaining his friend Amar who sells a variety of cakes to the freezer trade and is telling the friend of his experiments with standard costing. The friend counters this by telling him that he has a very sophisticated system of standard costing in his bakery.

In fact he shows Martin a list of variances which include:

Production of type 11 cakes on 24th June:

Yield variance   £34 ADV

Sales of cakes in week 25:

Mix variance   £131 FAV

Martin is intrigued by these but needs to have them explained by his friend.

Explain the meaning of these variances and why they are useful to Amar.

Case Study/Assignment 3

The Intolerable Assurance Company PLC own a national chain of estate agents. Each branch has a manager and he/she is required to make a profit and to make frequent financial reports to head office. The Intolerable are renowned for tight financial management. In each branch a system of standard costing applies such that the standard cost of each sale of a property for a customer is charged out at 1 1/4% of the selling price to include advertising and incidentals. The standard cost of each sale is:

Negotiator's time 10 hours at £20	200
Advertising	80
Direct Costs (photos, sale board, printing etc)	60
General overheads 10 hours at £35	350
	690

Reflecting different prices and costs the standard costs are negotiated for each branch and these costs are for the branch in Boghampton. The negotiator costs include salary and motoring costs. Negotiators vary in salary and type of motor car. The general overheads are recovered as a function of negotiator time and the general overheads budget (all such costs are assumed to be fixed) for Boghampton in 19x7 is £210,000 which includes unchargeable negotiator time.

We will look at 3 sales in 19x7 when the actual costs were:

	Sale 102	Sale 181	Sale 234
Negotiators' time	15 hrs at £24	6 hrs at £21	9 hrs at £18
Advertising	£140	£65	£42
Direct costs	£85	£63	£38

Required:

a. Calculate variances and suggest possible causes for them.

   Overall in 19x7, the general overheads totalled £234,000, 560 houses were sold and 5,300 negotiator hours were charged out.

b. Calculate suitable variances and suggest possible causes for them.

   Intolerable require each sale to be followed by a variance calculation. Any sale where the cost exceeds 150% of the standard cost must be reported with an explanation to Head Office.

c. Comment on this standard cost scheme. You may consider issues like: Would it work? Would its costs outweigh its benefits? Could it be improved? What would its motivational effects be?

14 Company accounting

1. Objectives

The Accounts of limited companies (including Public Limited Companies – PLCs) are not easy to understand and are full of an amazing amount of detail. As a result even accountants find the Annual Report and Accounts of a PLC somewhat formidable. They are considered very important by the financial community and are highly regulated by the Companies Act 1985 and the Accounting Standards Board.

This Unit gives an overview of published accounts and of some of the detail. It is designed to assist my readers in understanding the accounts of their own companies and of companies that they come in contact with as customers, suppliers, investors etc.

SCENARIO 1 — Martin investigates company accounts

An informal approach has been made to Martin by a *director* of a local *Public Limited Company* suggesting that the PLC might be interested in taking over Martin Padlocks Ltd. She explains that they are interested because Martin's company would fit well into their current business plans and that they would like to have Martin on the Main Board of their company as an executive director. Martin is not really interested but is intrigued to find out that the director seems to know quite a lot about Martin Padlocks Ltd and its accounts.

She explains that her company have searched the file on Martin Padlocks Ltd at Companies House in Cardiff.

Martin feels he would like to know more about the public company and finds that his uncle is a shareholder and has a copy of the latest Annual Report and Accounts.

Following is the Profit and Loss Account and Balance Sheet of the company which is called XYZ Manufacturing and Trading PLC at 31 December 19x8:

Profit and Loss Account for the year ending 31 December 19x8

		19x8		19x7
		£'000		£'000
Turnover		10,500		9,700
Cost of sales		6,700		6,500
Gross profit		3,800		3,200
Distribution costs	1,280		1,270	
Administration costs	1,450	2,730	1,428	2,698
Operating profit		1,070		502
Loss on sale of investments		280		
		790		
Interest payable		220		190
Profit on ordinary activities		570		312
Taxation		250		120

	19x8	19x7
Profit on ordinary activities after taxation	320	192
Dividends	100	80
Retained profit for the year	220	112
Earnings per share	3.2p	

Group Balance sheet as at 31 December 19x8

	£'000	£'000
	19x8	19x7
Fixed Assets		
Tangible assets	4,360	2,190
Investments		500
		2,690
Current Assets		
Stocks	1,300	970
Debtors	2,200	1,684
	3,500	2,654
Creditors: amounts falling due within one year		
Creditors	1,100	838
Bank Overdrafts	350	202
Taxation and Social Security	102	102
Corporation Tax	250	164
Dividends	40	40
	1,842	1,346
Net Current Assets	1,658	1,308
Total Assets less Current Liabilities	6,018	3,998
Creditors: amounts falling due after more than one year		
14% Debentures 1998-1999	1,200	840
	4,818	3,158
Capital and Reserves		
Issued Share Capital (in 10p shares)	1,000	500
Share Premium	380	
Revaluation Reserve	560	
Profit and Loss Account	2,878	2,658
Shareholders Funds	4,818	3,158

Quick Answer Questions 14.1

1. How many words do you recognise from Units 2 and 3?
2. How do you think the fixed assets will have been valued?
3. What is the working capital?

SCENARIO 2 — Martin learns from company accounts

Martin has many questions about these Accounts and asks Anne to help him understand them. Can you help him with the questions?

Tasks 1

1. What is *turnover* and what items will be included in this figure?
2. What is calculated by Turnover less Cost of Sales?
3. Below are seven expense headings:
   ❒ settlement discounts given to customers;
   ❒ the managing director's salary;
   ❒ public relations costs;
   ❒ goods purchased for resale;
   ❒ the auditor's fee;
   ❒ depreciation on a computer system;
   ❒ repairs to forklift trucks.

In which of the following three general expense headings may each be included:

Cost of Sales, Distribution Costs, Administration Expenses?

4. In how many lines of the Profit and Loss Account does the word 'profit' occur?
5. Interest in the Profit and Loss Account relates to which items in the Balance Sheet?
6. To which item in the Balance Sheet does the Taxation item in the Profit and Loss Account relate?
7. How is the Profit and Loss item (loss on sale of investment) related to the Balance Sheet?
8. How many shares have the company issued?
9. What is the *dividend* per share using the Profit and Loss Account figure for dividends?
10. Why is the dividend in the Profit and Loss Account different from that shown in the Balance Sheet?
11. How were the *Earnings per Share* calculated?
12. What are *tangible* assets?
13. What types of fixed asset would this company probably have?
14. What does the expression 'Taxation and Social Security' mean in the Balance Sheet?
15. What rate of interest is paid on the debentures and when are they *redeemable*?
16. What is the significance of the term *'Share Premium'*?

17. Why was the line 'Revaluation Reserve' included?

18. Does the word 'Reserve' in *'Revaluation Reserve'* mean that the company has some money cached away somewhere?

19. How are the Retained Profits in the Profit and Loss Account related to the Profit and Loss Account figure in the Balance Sheet?

20. If all the assets were sold off at their book values and all the liabilities paid off at the amount of their book values, how much money would be left for the shareholders?

21. According to the newspaper city page, one share in XYZ can be purchased for 80p. How does this figure square up with the answer you calculated for question 20?

2. Introduction

Accounting for company results is governed by the Companies Act 1985 (as amended in the Companies Act 1989). The Act specifies:

❒ The financial statements to be produced

❒ The format of the financial statements

❒ The minimum information which must be given

❒ The accounting principles to be followed

❒ The dates by which the financial statements must be laid before the members (= shareholders) of the company in general meeting (at the AGM) and delivered to the Registrar of Companies (where they are filed and can be seen by members of the public).

The financial statements which must be produced are:

❒ a Profit and Loss Account

❒ a Balance Sheet

❒ in addition, there must be notes which are attached to, and form part of, the Profit and Loss Account and Balance Sheet.

There must also be a directors' report with minimum content and an auditors' report.

In addition to the Companies Act requirements, company financial statements also have to comply with the requirements of the Financial Reporting Standard FRS 3: Reporting Financial Performance issued in 1993. FRS 3 requires two more financial statements:

❒ Statement of total recognised gains and losses

❒ Reconciliation of movements in shareholders' funds

Large companies also have to produce yet another financial statement. FRS 1 requires that they produce a Cash Flow Statement.

We will deal with these three statements later and in Unit 19.

All companies have also to abide by the requirements of all the FRSs and SSAPs currently in issue.

In this book, I shall cover the formats of the required financial statements. But I will not consider the information requirements, the directors' report, the auditors' report or the laying and delivering requirements in detail. All these matters could take up an immense volume and the general student does not need to know them.

All companies produce an 'Annual Report and accounts' which is often a glossy product. You are strongly advised to obtain some of these. They are sent to all shareholders and you should have relatives or friends who are shareholders in at least the privatised utilities. They can also be obtained directly from the Secretary of any public company and are often in university and college libraries.

3. The Profit and Loss Account

A common format which complies with the Companies Act is:

a. *Stubby Widgets PLC*

b. *Profit and Loss Account*

c. *For the year ending 31 December 19x2*

d.	Continuing operations 19x2	Discontinued operations 19x2 £'000	Total 19x2	19x1 £'000
e. Turnover	6,500	650	7,150	6,540
f. Cost of sales	4,200	620	4,820	4,320
g. Gross profit	2,300	30	2,330	2,220
h. Distribution costs	1,340	24	1,364	1,232
i. Administration costs	536	17	553	438
j. Operating profit	424	(11)	413	550
k. Interest payable			71	151
l. Profit on ordinary activities			342	399
m. Taxation			102	124
n. Profit on ordinary activities after taxation			240	275
p. Dividends			60	60
q. Retained profit for the year			180	215
r. Earnings per share			6p	6.875p

Notes:

a. The name of the company must be given (i.e in this case Stubby Widgets plc).

b. The title of the financial statement should be indicated.

c. The period which is normally one year should be stated.

d. FRS 3 requires that figures down to the operating profit level are divided into three parts:

❐ continuing operations

❐ discontinued operations

❐ acquisitions.

Most quoted companies are groups. This means that they consist of a holding company and subsidiaries. It is common practice for a group to grow by acquisition, that is to acquire companies from their current owners or from other groups. If you read the financial press you will see reports daily of this happening. Similarly groups often sell off subsidiaries to other groups, to management (management buy-outs), or to the public generally when a subsidiary is separately floated.

Investors use the Profit and Loss Account, amongst other data, to assess the company's future prospects. Consequently it is essential to know how much of the overall profit came from operations that are discontinued and hence will not appear in future years. The rationale for separate disclosure of the results of acquisitions in the year is less clear. But it is does enable comparison to be made between this years profits and last years. Note that last years figures (known as comparative figures) are given in the final column. A similar analysis of last years figures into continuing etc is given in the notes and not on the face of the Profit and Loss Account.

You will not always see the analysis into continuing etc if there have been no material acquisitions or discontinuances. They are rare in private company accounts.

The operating profit can include profit and losses from exceptional items. Exceptional items are those items which, by virtue of their size and incidence, need to be separately disclosed for the financial statements to give a true and fair view. Examples of exceptional items taken from recent accounts include:

- ❏ costs consequent on scrapping, and withdrawing from sale, a major product.
- ❏ costs of withdrawal from a property development
- ❏ abortive acquisition costs
- ❏ release of pension provision no longer required.

FRS 3 requires separate disclosure, after operating profit and before interest, of:

- ❏ profits or losses on the sale or termination of an operation
- ❏ costs of a fundamental reorganisation or restructuring
- ❏ profits and losses on the disposal of assets.

You will see that Stubby did not have any of these.

e) *Turnover* is the word used in the Act. *Sales* is the same thing but turnover can also be used for total fares in a transport company where 'sales' would be inappropriate. Do not forget that all sales made in the year must be included whether the customer paid in the year or not – the realisation convention.

f) *Cost of sales.* This idea has been met in Unit 2. However it is usually wider here and will include all costs except those in lines (h), (i) and (k).

g) *Gross profit* is simply the difference between turnover and cost of sales.

h) *Distribution costs* are undefined in the Act but usually include sales salaries and commissions, advertising, warehousing costs of finished goods, travelling and entertaining of reps and customers, carriage of goods to customers including depreciation of vehicles, overhead costs of sales outlets and settlement discount allowed to customers.

i) *Administration costs* are also undefined in the Act but usually include salary costs of administrative personnel (e.g. in accounting function, directors and general management), overhead costs of administration buildings, professional fees and bad debts.

j) *The operating profit.* You will have realised that the word profit occurs in many lines. So that a question such as 'What was the profit?' can only be answered if the question is specified more precisely. Each 'profit' is significant. The operating profit is significant in that the business can be seen as a set of resources (assets) provided by suppliers of capital (both shareholders and lenders) which the directors have to use to make a profit. The operating profit measures the profit they managed to make in the year from using the resources in their charge.

This represents the reward in total which is available for lenders (who will receive interest), the government (who receive tax) and the shareholders.

k) Resources are supplied to a company both by the shareholders and by long term lenders. The reward to lenders is *interest* and this line measures the amount payable to lenders for the use of capital in the year.

l) What is left is the profit on *ordinary activities* before taxation. This is the reward to shareholders for the use of their capital but is subject to corporation tax.

m) *Corporation tax* is payable on profit at rates decreed by parliament in the annual Finance Act. The calculation of corporation tax can be very complicated and it is enough to know how much will be payable on the profits shown in line (l).

n) This is the reward for shareholders after tax.

p) The shareholders are entitled to all the profits of the company but the custom is to make payments to them which are less than the total profit. The amount paid or payable is called the *dividend*. Directors dislike paying dividends as a dividend means that resources leave the company. Dividends are expressed as so many pence per share.

q) The amount of the profit which has been made but not paid out to the shareholders is called the *retained profit* of the year.

r) This statistic is required for all companies which are quoted on the stock exchange. It is obtained by dividing line (n) by the number of shares which have been issued. There can be, as always, complications but we need not consider them.

Students often think of the annual profit as a sum of money. It is not. To make this clear, consider:

❐ sales are the sales made in the year irrespective of the date of settlement by the customer

❐ capital expenditure costs money in the year but only the depreciation appears in the Profit and Loss Account

❐ expenses follow the accruals convention so that the correct expense of the year is shown irrespective of the payments made.

4. The Balance Sheet

Companies can be listed on the stock exchange but most are not. The larger ones are usually listed and their shares are bought and sold by investors. Another feature of the larger companies is that they are usually holding companies with subsidiaries. They are groups like this:

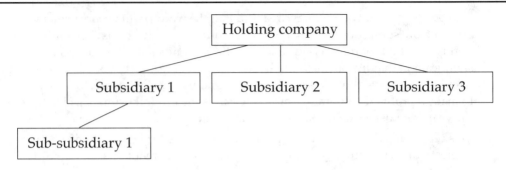

The public hold shares in the holding company and in turn the holding company holds shares in each subsidiary. Sometimes the subsidiary companies own the share in sub-subsidiaries.

Often the holding company holds all (100%) of the shares in its subsidiaries but sometimes it does not own all the shares and there are outside shareholders called *minorities*.

You are most likely to have access to the published Annual Reports and accounts of listed companies and most listed companies are groups so that I shall illustrate the Balance Sheet of a group. In the Annual Reports you will find four Balance Sheets:

❏ The current Balance Sheet of the group
❏ The current Balance Sheet of the holding company
❏ The previous year end Balance Sheet of the group
❏ The previous year end Balance Sheet of the company.

The company Balance Sheets have to be given but are usually of no interest. The important Balance Sheets are the group ones.

Group Balance Sheets are drawn up on the assumptions that:

❏ the group is not a set of separate companies
❏ the group is one single company
❏ the group is owned by the shareholders of the holding company.

The effect is:

❏ that a group Balance Sheet shows the assets and liabilities of all the companies as if they were one company
❏ the capital and reserves sections relates to the holding company as the holding company shareholders in fact own all the group.

A typical group Balance Sheet:

Stubby Widgets plc

Group Balance Sheet as at 31 December 19x2

£'000

a)	Fixed assets	
b)	Intangible assets	87
c)	Tangible assets	1,648
d)	Investments	44
		1,779

		£'000
e)	Current assets	
	Stocks	431
	Debtors	590
	Cash at bank and in hand	32
		1,053
f)	Creditors: amounts falling due within one year	
	Creditors	400
g)	Bank overdrafts	228
h)	Taxation and social security	87
i)	Corporation tax	102
j)	Dividends	40
		857
	Net current assets	196
	Total assets less current liabilities	1,975
k)	Creditors: amounts falling due after more than one year	
l)	Bank and other loans	220
m)		1,755
n)	Capital and reserves	
o)	Issued share capital	800
p)	Share premium	100
q)	Revaluation reserve	200
r)	Profit and Loss Account	652
s)	Shareholders funds	1,752
t)	Minority interests	3
u)	Total capital employed	1,755

The Balance Sheet is similar to the one you have already met in Unit 3 but there are some special company things:

a) Fixed assets are usually divided into the three categories b. to d.

b) *Intangible assets* are those like goodwill, patents and trade marks which have value but no physical substance. They appear in Balance Sheets at cost or less so they only appear if the goodwill etc was purchased. Non-appearance of intangible assets does not mean the company has none but that none has been purchased or any purchased goodwill etc has been written off.

c) *Tangible* fixed assets are the physical ones like buildings, plant and machinery and vehicles. The detail is always given in notes to the accounts.

d) Groups may also own shares in other companies where the holding is less than 50% and these are included using somewhat complex valuations.

e) These are as explained in Unit 3. There may be other headings and prepayments are normally included with debtors.

f) There are more sub-headings for this line than in Unit 3. I have shown 5. You may meet others.

g) Many groups have both overdrafts and cash at bank. This may seem strange but each separate company may have either, and in the group Balance Sheet they are not normally netted off.

h) This is required to be shown separately and shows the amount due but unpaid at the Balance Sheet date of VAT, PAYE Income Tax and National Insurance.

i) This is usually the corporation tax payable on the profits of the year and you will see that it is the same amount as in the Profit and Loss Account. It is payable on 1 October 19x3.

j) The dividends in the Profit and Loss Account are £60,000 divided into:

❐ an interim dividend paid on 30 September 19x2 £20,000

❐ a final dividend to be paid in May 19x3 £40,000

Companies usually make two dividend payments. One is after publication of the abbreviated unaudited results of the first half year and a final one when the full year results are published and the AGM has been held.

k) Most groups have long term liabilities. They are often called 'borrowings' or sometimes simply 'debt'.

l) Details are given in notes. Loans can be termed simply loans but may also be termed stock, notes, bonds, debentures, lease obligations, etc. The interest rates payable and the dates for repayment (repayment may be called *redemption)* are given for each loan. The total amounts owing may be surprisingly large.

m) This line concludes the list of assets and liabilities. Most students find the Balance Sheet up to now reasonably understandable although the valuation methods (based on cost) may be unexpected. The difficulty lies in lines (n) to (u).

n) The next section explains where the resources came from to enable the Group to buy the assets less liabilities. If X is a rich man, it may be reasonable to say how did he get to be rich. The answer may be:

❐ he was left a fortune by his aunt

❐ he has, over his life, spent less than his income

❐ his investments have increased in value since he bought them.

The company 'Capital and Reserves' section explains a Group's wealth in a similar way. It is very important to realise that the word *'Reserves'* is a technical one and its meaning bears no resemblance at all to the normal meanings given to it.

o) Companies obtain their initial resources from the people and institutions who become the shareholders. Each shareholder *subscribes* for so many shares. Each share is given a *nominal* or *par* value which has no real meaning at all. In the case of Stubby Widgets plc each share has a par value of 20p so that the total number of shares is 20p × £800,000 = 4,000,000. You may now work out that the earnings per share given in the Profit and Loss Account are £240,000/4,000,000 = 6p. You could also work out that the dividends per share are:

$$\text{interim } \frac{£20,000}{4,000,000} = 0.5p$$

$$\text{final } \frac{£40,000}{4,000,000} = 1p$$

p) All the share capital may not have been subscribed at the formation of the company. The shareholders may have subscribed for shares later in the life of the company when they may have paid more than the par value for each share. The excess of amount paid over the par value is called the *share premium*. So the total amount of resources provided to the company by the shareholders is the share capital + the share premium.

q) The fixed assets may include land and buildings. These usually increase in value due to inflation and other causes. However accounting practice requires the land to be valued at original cost and the buildings at cost less depreciation. The effect of this is that a major asset of the company is valued at what may be a small fraction of its 'real' value. It is felt that this may mislead readers of the accounts even if an up to date valuation is included in the notes to the accounts. A way out of the problem is to commission a professional revaluation of the land and buildings and substitute this for the historical cost less depreciation. Note that in later years depreciation will continue to be applied to the buildings but at a higher rate as it will be based on the new valuation.

The Balance Sheet is based on an equation:

Assets less liabilities = capital and reserves.

In effect this means that the assets and liabilities are stated and the capital and reserves explains the sources of finance for their acquisition.

By unilaterally increasing the carrying value of land and buildings the equation is unbalanced. To restore the balance and to show the source of the increase in assets less liabilities, a line is included described as *revaluation reserve*.

r) Profit and Loss Account is the amount of profit after tax made *since the company started* less all dividends. Profit is a measure of the increase in assets less liabilities as a result of trading. Every year in which a profit is made there is an increase in the assets less liabilities. The Profit and Loss Account figure on the Balance Sheet measures the total effect of such profits since the company began. It is sometimes called the *accumulated profit*.

Just as profit increases assets less liabilities so dividends decrease them and the accumulated figure shows the effect of profits less dividends.

s) Shareholders put funds into the company (the share capital and share premium) and the funds then grow and profit is the measure of growth. All growth represented by retained profits and revaluations belongs to the shareholders. So this figure represents the shareholders stake in the net assets of the company.

t) If one or more of the subsidiaries companies have minority shareholders then there will be *minority interests* shown here. The assets less liabilities of these subsidiaries are included in the group Balance Sheet in full so it is necessary to show the portion of them which in effect belongs to the minorities.

u) This concludes the explanation of the sources of finance for the assets and liabilities of the group. It can also be seen as an explanation of who owns the assets less liabilities of the group.

5. Shares — par and other values

The capital and reserves section of a Balance Sheet seems to have been designed to mislead and mystify everybody except accountants. We will try to unravel its meanings by considering a series of values — par or nominal values, net asset values and quoted values.

Firstly remember that the Balance Sheet must balance and so the total of capital and reserves must equal the total of assets less liabilities. Thus any change in assets and liabilities must lead to a change in capital and reserves.

When a company is formed it has no assets or liabilities, capital or reserves.

To acquire assets, the company issue shares to persons who become its shareholders. Supposing the first sale of shares is of 10,000 shares of £1 each then the first Balance Sheet will show:

	£
Assets:	
Cash	10,000
Capital and reserves:	
Share capital	10,000

The cash will be spent on fixed assets etc and rapidly will be replaced by a complex mixture of assets and liabilities.

Each share is a £1 share and £1 is known as the par or nominal value. The shares could have been issued at any par price. If par had been 50p then, to raise £10,000, 20,000 shares would have been issued.

After a period of trading at a profit, a Balance Sheet can be drawn up as:

	£
Net assets:	24,300
Capital and reserves:	
Share capital	10,000
Profit and Loss Account	14,300
	24,300

To explain this:

a) The original £10,000 cash has become a complex mixture of assets and liabilities valued at £24,300.

b) The capital and reserves explain where the resources to acquire the net assets came from.

c) £10,000 came from the shareholders originally.

d) The remainder (£14,300) came from profitable trading.

The nominal or par value of each share is still £1. However as the company now has net assets of £24,300 and is divided into 10,000 shares, each share is represented by net assets of £2.43. We can say the net asset value of each share is £2.43.

If a shareholder wished to sell one of his shares to another person, the price would be decided by negotiation between the parties. Suppose this was £3.60 then the value of the share is clearly £3.60. If the company is quoted (another word is listed) on the Stock Exchange then this price varies continuously and potential buyers and sellers can know the current price by consulting a broker or the newspapers.

Thus the par value means very little in reality. The net asset value is useful knowledge (although assets like goodwill may be omitted and accounting values are strange). The really useful value is not given by the financial statements and that is the real value of the share.

Later in its life the company may issue more shares. Probably this will not be at the par value. Suppose our company sold a further 5,000 £1 shares at £3 each. The par value remains at £1 but the market allows the company to sell them for £3 and will receive £15,000 from the new shareholders.

The Balance Sheet will show (presume the new shares were sold immediately after the last Balance Sheet):

	£
Net assets:	39,300
Capital and reserves:	
Share capital	15,000
Share premium	10,000
Profit and Loss Account	14,300
	39,300

To explain this:

a) The net assets have gone up by the extra money (£15,000) subscribed by the new shareholders.

b) The share capital has gone up by the 5,000 shares at par value.

c) The Share Premium is the difference between the cash obtained from the issue and the par value.

When you see a Capital and Reserves section of a Balance Sheet with Share Premium you know that at some time in its history, the company sold shares at a price above par.

Remember that the Capital and Reserves section shows where the resources came from to provide the net assets.

6. Statement of total recognised gains and losses

FRS 3 requires one of these financial statements with all company accounts. An example:

Stubby Widgets PLC

STATEMENT OF TOTAL RECOGNISED GAINS AND LOSSES

FOR THE YEAR ENDING 31ST DECEMBER 19x2

	£'000	Notes
Profit for the financial year	240	1
Unrealised surplus on revaluation of properties	96	2
Currency adjustments on investments	(15)	3
Total recognised gains and losses relating to the year	321	4

Notes:

1. This is line n taken from the Profit and Loss Account — check it!

2. Not all gains and losses go into the Profit and Loss Account. A good and common example is the unrealised surplus arising out of a revaluation of land and buildings. This goes into the revaluation reserve.

3. Another example is the gain or loss on translation of foreign currency assets. This seems to appear in a great number of company accounts.

4. The thinking behind this statement is that the Profit and Loss Account is supposed to record all gains and losses. However some gains and losses (as the two here) do not go into the Profit and Loss Account. Consequently there is a need for a short statement to gather together all gains and losses.

7. Reconciliation of movements in shareholders funds

An example of one of these Financial Statements:

Stubby Widgets PLC

RECONCILIATION OF MOVEMENTS IN SHAREHOLDERS' FUNDS

FOR THE YEAR ENDING 31 DECEMBER 19x2

		£'000	Notes
Total recognised gains and losses for the year		321	1
Dividends		(60)	2
New Share Capital Issued:			
rights issue	450		3
scrip dividend alternative	2	452	4
Goodwill purchased		(75)	5
Net increase in shareholders' funds		638	6
Opening shareholders' funds		1,114	7
Closing shareholders' funds		1,752	8

Notes:

1. You will see that this figure comes from the Statement of total recognised gains and losses.

2. You will also see that this figure comes from the Profit and Loss Account.

3. This is the proceeds of an issue of shares with pro rata rights to subscribe given to all shareholders. The £450,000 is the actual net proceeds (new shares at nominal value + share premium — expenses of issue).

4. Many public companies now give their shareholders a choice between a cash dividend and additional shares. In this case the total dividend was £60,000 with £2,000 being taken as shares and £58,000 as cash.

5. When a company is purchased and becomes a subsidiary the fair value of the actual net assets (fixed and current assets etc) is incorporated in the accounts. However the amount paid for the acquisition is usually more than the fair value of the actual net assets. The difference is goodwill and is written off straight to reserves. Thus, suppose £50 was paid for an acquisition then shareholders funds are reduced by £50 being cash or other consideration leaving the company. Net assets acquired were valued at £39 and these are now owned so the shareholders funds rise by £39. The difference is £11 goodwill and is a net reduction of shareholders funds. Of course the goodwill is a real, though intangible, asset but it is not recognised on the Balance Sheet.

6. This is the total so far — check it!

7. and 8. are self-explanatory

The objective of this statement is to bring together all increases and reductions of shareholders funds which occurred in the year. Other examples of changes you might see include redemption of preference shares and reinstatement of goodwill in respect of businesses sold, previously written off to reserves.

SCENARIO 3 — Martin looks at directors' remuneration

Martin now feels he understands the overall view given by the Accounts and he is now interested in some details.

The first thing he wants to know about is the Board of Directors. He looks at the notes and finds several bits of data:

Directors		Beneficial Shareholdings	
		31.12.19x8	31.12.19x7
Joseph Smith	(1)	600,000	800,000
Edward Crippen	(2)	1,000	1,000
Amanda Burke		30,000	2,000
William Hare	(3)	140,000	50,000
Jean Palmer		6,000	6,000
Paul Pilate	(3)	14,500	4,000
Lord Pott	(3)	5,000	5,000
Jane Ripper		2,300	2,300

(1) – the Chairman; (2) – the Chief Executive; (3) – non-executive

Directors' Remuneration

Aggregate emoluments of Directors including pension contributions:

	19x8	19x7
Fees	£5,000	£5,000
Other emoluments	£300,500	£260,000
Chairman's Emoluments	£20,000	£18,000
Highest Paid Director's Emoluments £85,000		£60,000

	19x8	19x7
All directors:		
£0 – £5,000	3	3
£15,001 – £20,000	1	1
£55,001 – £60,000	1	4
£60,001 – £65,000	2	
£80,001 – £85,000	1	

Quick Answer Question 14.2

What can you conclude from this data about:

a. Directors' shareholdings
b. The ownership of the company
c. The roles of particular directors
d. The remuneration paid to directors?

Note that this information may be extended as a result of the Cadbury and Greenbury Codes — see below.

SCENARIO 4 — Martin appreciates asset appreciation

As he really is not very sure about the revaluation reserve Martin looks at those parts of the Annual Report and Accounts which set out details of the property and other fixed assets. He discovers the following:

Accounting Policies:

Fixed Assets are stated at valuation, for property, and cost for plant. The provision for depreciation of fixed assets is on a straight line basis at rates estimated to be sufficient to write off the assets over the terms of their working lives under normal conditions. The rates of depreciation are:

Land — nil
Buildings — 2%
Plant etc — 12.5%

	Premises	Plant etc
Cost at 31 December 19x7	1,500	2,200
Additions in year	1,202	600
Revaluation	440	
at 31 December 19x8	3,142	2,800
Depreciation at 31 December 19x7	320	1,190
Charge for year	42	350
Revaluation Adjustment	(320)	

	Premises	Plant etc
at 31 December 19x8	42	1,540
Net Book Value 31 December 19x8	3,100	1,260
Net Book Value 31 December 19x7	1,180	1,010

Revaluation

In November 19x8, the premises were independently valued by Slick, Sharp & Co, Chartered Surveyors at £3,142,000. They had previously been carried at cost less depreciation.

Tasks 2

1. Comment on the movements in fixed assets
2. How much of the value of the premises is in the land?

SCENARIO 5 — Martin attends an AGM

Martin has invested some of his savings in shares in a local *listed* company – Soopertek Manufacturing PLC. He wanted to see how a listed company went about things because he felt he might seek a listing for his own company eventually and because the whole subject of company accounting and finance had begun to fascinate him. He also thought he might make a profit!

He has just received the glossy Annual Report and Accounts for the year ending 31 December 19x8 and eagerly looks for the things he thinks he might understand. Firstly he looks at the notice of the Annual General Meeting:

Notice is hereby given that the annual general meeting of the shareholders will be held at the Hotel Colossal, Birmingham on Tuesday 11 June at 19x9 at 12 noon.

Agenda

1. To approve the Report of the Directors and the Accounts for the year ended 31 December 19x8.

2. To approve the final dividend of 10p a share for the year ended 31 December 19x8.

3. To re-elect as directors:
   Thomas Gilbert
   Andrea Sullivan

4. To re-appoint Puce, Mauve & Co. as auditors and authorise the directors to determine their remuneration.

5. To consider and if thought fit, pass the following resolution:
   That the directors are authorised to allot new ordinary shares of 50p each in the company to shareholders who elect to receive such an allotment as a scrip issue in lieu of all or part of the interim and final dividends for the year ending 31 December 19x9.

By order of the Board

A Smith, Secretary 12 May 19x9.

Quick Answer Questions 14.3

1. Martin knows the company have some 25,000 shareholders. Why do you think the AGM can be held in a hotel?

2. Do you think that Martin will miss his lunch if he attends the AGM?

3. In the Chairman's review he sees that Mr Gilbert was appointed a director by the Board on 4th December 19x8 and that Ms Sullivan retires by rotation but is available for re-election. Do you think that these elections are democratically made by the shareholders?

SCENARIO 6 — Martin considers dividend or shares

Martin realises that as a shareholder he can receive the dividend mentioned in resolution 2 but that he can receive new shares instead as a consequence of resolution 5.

He has 500 shares in the company.

The offer is to receive the dividend or 25 new ordinary shares which are currently quoted at £2 each.

Tasks 3

1. Evaluate the two alternatives from Martin's point of view. Martin has a high salary from his company and is adding to his savings all the time.

2. Evaluate the offer from the point of view of the Incompetent Assurance Co PLC which owns 4% of Soopertek.

3. Some of the shareholders accept shares and some the cash. Explain how the balance of power among the shareholders is changed by this. Explain how in a normal bonus issue the balance of power is not affected.

8. Bonus, rights and other issues

Many companies make bonus issues. These can be called scrip issues, capitalisation issues and in jest, bogus issues.

Suppose Q PLC has a Balance Sheet as:

	£
Net assets:	1,650,000
Capital and reserves:	
Share capital in 20p shares	500,000
Profit and Loss Account	1,150,000
	1,650,000

The directors wish to please the shareholders but do not wish to actually pay money to them in the form of dividends. They can make a bonus issue of new free shares to the shareholders. This might be say a one for two issue, in which case Martin who has 100 shares will receive 50 new shares. The effect on the Balance Sheet will be:

	£
Net assets:	1,650,000
Capital and reserves:	
Share capital	750,000
Profit and Loss Account	900,000
	1,650,000

Note:

a) The net assets remain the same.

b) An issue of one new share for each two held will increase the share capital by 50%.

c) As net assets remain the same, so must capital and reserves and to keep capital and reserves in balance, Profit and Loss Account must be reduced by £250,000.

d) Before the issue each share was quoted at 90p and as the company was divided into 2,500,000 (500,000 ÷ 20p) shares the company was worth £2,250,000. After the issue the company is still worth £2,250,000 but is now divided into 3,750,000 shares. Thus the quotation will go down to approximately 60p.

e) This seems a pointless exercise but shareholders will be pleased at receiving (apparently) something for nothing and the Market sees a bonus issue as a signal of confidence from the directors.

The company may also make a rights issue. This is a real issue of shares for cash. New shares are offered to existing shareholders in proportion to their holdings. They are not obliged to take up the offer and instead may sell their rights to other investors.

Suppose Q PLC make a rights issue of one new share for every three held at 50p each then 1,250,000 new shares will be sold and net the company £625,000.

The new Balance Sheet will look like this:

	£
Net assets:	2,275,000
Capital and reserves:	
Share capital	1,000,000
Share premium	375,000
Profit and Loss Account	900,000
	2,275,000

Note:

a) The net assets will rise because money has flowed into the company.

b) The share capital has risen as more shares have been issued.

c) The new shares have a par value of 20p and were issued at 50p so the share premium is 1,250,000 × 30p = £375,000.

d) The company was worth £2,250,000 before the issue. In theory it will be worth £2,250,000 + £625,000 = £2,875,000 after the issue. It is now divided into 5,000,000 shares so each share may be quoted at 57.50p.

A form of bonus issue is the common practice of offering shareholders new shares instead of dividends. This saves the company paying out cash and is therefore popular with directors.

Q PLC determine to pay a dividend of 2p a share but offer instead one new share for every 30 held. Holders of 1,200,000 shares accept the shares and the remainder opt for the dividend. The Balance Sheet will now look like this:

Net assets:	2,199,000
Capital and reserves:	
Share capital	1,008,000
Share premium	391,000
Profit and Loss Account	800,000
	2,199,000

Note:

a) Net assets have gone down by £76,000. This is the payment of the dividend – $(5,000,000 - 1,200,000) \times 2p = £76,000$.

b) The share capital has risen by the issue of new shares – $\frac{1,200,000}{30} \times 20p = £8,000$.

c) The share premium on the issue of 40,000 new shares, issued effectively at 60p, is $40,000 \times (60p - 20p) = £16,000$. The issue price is effectively 60p because the dividend foregone by the holder of 30 shares is $30 \times 2p = 60p$.

d) The dividend, whether in cash or shares reduces the Profit and Loss Account by $5,000,000 \times 2p = £100,000$.

———————

SCENARIO 7 — Martin studies auditing

Martin is interested in the auditors and manages to find in the notes to the Accounts that their remuneration was £250,000. This seems to him to be a large amount and he wonders what they do for this sum. He is also puzzled by Resolution 4 which seems to make the auditors somewhat less independent as the directors are able to fix the audit fee. He thought that the auditors were completely independent of the company and acted in the interests of the shareholders. He discusses this matter with Anne who tells him that auditors are supposed to be completely independent from the company but in practice:

a. auditors are appointed by the Board although the fiction that they are appointed by the shareholders is maintained in the resolution.

b. the Board fix the auditors' remuneration although this is normally a matter of negotiation between the directors and the auditors.

c. the auditors do work other than auditing for the company and are specially interested in lucrative management consultancy contracts.

d. Boards of directors do shop around for cheaper or more amenable firms of auditors.

This makes Martin think that the auditors are beholden to the directors when they should be taking an entirely objective view of the Accounts. Anne points out that all is not what it seems as:

a. audit firms are very tightly regulated by their professional bodies.

b. failure to perform an audit properly may lead to claims of negligence against the auditors and in many recorded instances auditors (or rather their insurers) have had to pay very large sums to aggrieved persons.

c. if the Board wish to remove an auditor because he goes against their wishes (for example, by insisting on the company revealing full details of directors' remuneration as required by the Companies Act when the Board wish to keep some matters secret) the Companies Act gives the auditor extensive powers of publicity.

d. the whole issue of auditor independence is very contentious and EEC inspired legislation on the subject in the Companies Act 1989 is still being absorbed. Further legislation is expected in the next few years.

Martin finds the auditor's report which reads as:

Report of the Auditors to the Members of Soopertek Manufacturing PLC

We have audited the accounts on pages 36 to 60 which have been prepared under the historical cost convention as modified by the revaluation of certain fixed assets and on the basis of the accounting policies set out on pages 36 and 37.

Respective Responsibilities of Directors and Auditors

As described above, the Company's Directors are responsible for the preparation of the accounts. It is our responsibility to form an independent opinion, based on our audit, on those accounts and to report our opinion to you.

Basis of Opinion

We conducted our audit in accordance with Auditing Standards issued by the Auditing Practices Board. An audit includes examination, on a test basis, of evidence relevant to the amounts and disclosures in the accounts. It also includes an assessment of the significant estimates and judgments made by the directors in the preparation of the accounts, and of whether the accounting policies are appropriate to the Group's circumstances, consistently applied and adequately disclosed. We planned and performed our audit so as to obtain all the information and explanations which we considered necessary in order to provide us with sufficient evidence to give reasonable assurance that the accounts are free from material mis-statement, whether caused by fraud or other irregularity or error. In forming our opinion we also evaluated the overall adequacy of the presentation of information in the accounts.

Opinion

In our opinion the accounts give a true and fair view of the state of affairs of the Company and of the Group as at 31 December 19x8 and of the profit of the Group for the year then ended and have been properly prepared in accordance with the Companies Act 1985.

Puce, Mauve & Co   Chartered Accountants

Birmingham   Registered Auditor

Tasks 4

1. Discuss why is it essential that an annual Report and Accounts is produced for every company.

2. Discuss why it is essential that readers of the Accounts should have confidence in the truth and fairness of the Accounts.

3. Describe the role of the auditor in making the Accounts credible.

4. Discuss what the auditor does if she considers that the Accounts fail to show a true and fair view in some particular or do not comply with the requirements of the Companies Act in some way.

The Annual Report and Accounts of a company is an important document and it is important that it should at the very least:

❐ give a true representation of facts

❐ fairly present information where judgement is required or choices are possible (e.g. on the lives of fixed assets and the depreciation policy)

❐ disclose all facts relevant to a shareholder

❐ comply with the Companies Act 1985 requirements

❐ comply with all the Accounting Standards.

Directors may have a vested interest in producing misleading or incorrect information or in suppressing information. They may perhaps wish to show a small profit when a small loss has been incurred!

To ensure that accounts can be relied upon, the Act requires that every company shall have an auditor who must give an opinion on the accounts. Auditors are qualified accountants who have been trained and licensed by their professional body to do this kind of work. Auditing is a very complex business and the relationship between the company, the shareholders and the auditors is a delicate one. Suffice it to say that you can rely on annual accounts in general despite some well publicised cases where the accounts proved unreliable after a scandal was revealed.

SCENARIO 8 — Martin is disabused about creative accounting

Martin has heard that profits can be increased by creative accounting and wonders if Soopertek have increased their profits in this way. He discusses the matter with Anne who tells him that creative accounting means selecting accounting policies that maximised profits rather than policies that did not. Generally in creative accounting policies are created which are unexpected or not generally accepted. Creative accounting has been almost eliminated by the *Statements of Standard Accounting Practice* and the *new Accounting Standards Board.* New ideas in creative accounting do come up from time to time in the City but these would usually be rapidly defeated by the *Urgent Issues Task Force* which is a subsidiary body of the Accounting Standards Board. Most 'creative accounting' ideas are highly technical and not understood even by other accountants.

Anne urged Martin to forget creative accounting and to concentrate instead on comparability in accounting. She mentioned two issues specifically – Depreciation of property and Goodwill. Martin resolves to do this and looks up what Soopertek have done in this area and what two similar companies – Veni Manufacturing PLC and Vidi Manufacturing PLC, have done.

He finds:

Premises Depreciation:

	Soopertek	Veni	Vidi
Land values	cost	revalued two years earlier	revalued this year

None of the companies depreciate land

Buildings values

	writing off over 50 years	writing off over 25 years	Not * depreciated

* on the grounds that the company spend large sums on maintaining the buildings in order to extend their economic lives indefinitely.

Goodwill

	Written off against reserves immediately	amortised over five years	amortised over twenty years

Quick Answer Questions 14.4

1. What is the effect of depreciation (amortisation is another word for the same thing) on profit and the carrying values of assets in the Balance Sheet?

2. What is the effect on annual profit and the Balance Sheet of an immediate write-off of goodwill to reserves?

SCENARIO 9 — Martin meets accounting standards

Extracts from Statement of Standard Accounting Practice 12 — Accounting for depreciation show:

para 15   Provision for depreciation of fixed assets having a finite useful economic life should be made by allocating the cost (or revalued amount) less estimated residual value of the assets as fairly as possible to periods expected to benefit from their use.

para 17   It is essential that assets lives are estimated on a realistic basis.

para 24   Buildings are no different from other fixed assets in that they have a limited useful economic life, albeit usually significantly longer than that of other types of assets. They should, therefore, be depreciated having regard to the same criteria.

Financial Reporting Standard 10:

Goodwill and intangible assets suggests that only purchased goodwill should appear in financial statements. Usually purchased goodwill arises when a company buys another company as in a take-over. The amount paid over and above the fair value of the net assets acquired is an intangible asset and should appear on the Balance Sheet and be amortised.

FRS 10 is long and complicated and its provisions are both very detailed and yet leave a good deal to the judgement of the Board. All three companies may be obeying the precepts of FRS 10 and yet it would appear that Soopertek see the goodwill purchased as having no value. Veni reckon the purchased goodwill (e.g. the probability that existing customers will continue to patronise the purchased company) will last for five years and Vidi reckon 20 years.

Task 5

Write a report on the comparability of the annual profit measurements and the net assets in the Balance Sheets of these three companies.

9. Related parties' transactions

Users of accounts may reasonably assume that a company has complete autonomy within the law and other regulations to act with complete independence for the good of its shareholders. Users may assume that the company enters into all its transactions at 'arms length'. We can fairly assume that the private interests of persons like directors will not influence the conduct of the company.

However, situations do exist where persons in authority (e.g. directors, senior managers, major shareholders) may be in a position to have private agendas which conflict with those of the company and may be able to cause the company to engage in transactions which are not in the best interests of the company. Such persons are known as *related parties*. In 1995 the Accounting Standards Board issued a Financial Reporting Standard FRS 8 *Related Party Transactions*. The objective was to ensure that financial statements contained the disclosures necessary to draw users' attention to the possibility that the reported financial position and results may have been affected by the existence of related parties and by material transactions with them.

The Companies Act already requires disclosure of many matters. For example, a list of directors, their remuneration and shareholdings and loans to them, lists of major shareholders, lists of subsidiary and associated companies and many other things. FRS goes further and requires and includes particularly a requirement to show the *ultimate ownership* of a company and to give details of *related parties* and any *relevant transactions*. Some companies registered in the UK are owned by companies registered in tax havens and the ultimate ownership was not clear. Now it should be.

It is worth looking through Annual Reports to find mention of related parties and to see the sort of things disclosed. Many Annual Reports contain no mention but some do. As an example (adapted from an actual report): 'On 5 June 19x4 the entire share capital of XYZ Ltd (a subsidiary) was sold to Eyewash Ltd. Mr Smith the financial director of your company is a substantial shareholder in Eyewash Ltd.' You may realise that Mr Smith might wish to influence the price paid to the benefit of Eyewash and full disclosure of the matter has to be made.

It is always possible that transactions do occur with related parties but are not disclosed as the directors do not wish them to be disclosed. However, the auditors have a duty to have procedures to discover and report any related party transactions not reported in the financial statements.

10. Cadbury

By 1991 there was considerable disquiet in financial circles over corporate governance. Corporate governance is the system by which companies are directed and controlled. A number of public disclosures occurred which made people wonder if the system of management of major companies was appropriate to modern conditions. Specifically there was a low level of confidence in financial reporting and in the ability of auditors to provide the safeguards which users of company reports sought and expected. Factors which underlay this low level of confidence included the perceived looseness of accounting standards, lack of a clear framework for ensuring that directors kept under review the controls in their business and competitive pressures both on companies and their auditors which made it difficult for auditors to stand up to demanding boards.

You may find examples of these matters in the city columns (or sometimes the front page headlines) of the newspapers. Recent ones include: reported profits in a major retailer which turned out to be illusory, the failure of a major bank as a result of dealings in the far East and actions against auditors for negligence. Other symptoms of unease included unexpected failures of major companies and a feeling that directors' pay was out of control. The latter problem was compounded by enormous pay-offs to directors who were fired for failure.

Essentially the system is that directors should be appointed by the shareholders in general meeting. In practice, however, Boards tended to be self-perpetuating bodies and the shareholders' meetings are mere rubber stamp processes. Once in office Boards had almost total power including power over their own remuneration. In many companies the Board was controlled by a single dominant individual.

In fact there are many controls over Boards including Companies Act regulation, the Stock Exchange Rules, the Accounting Standards and the Accounting Standards Board and many other regulations. Frequently Boards would prepare accounts using doubtful estimates or doubtful accounting policies and these would be changed before publication at the request of the auditors. But these examples of effective regulation went unreported. Also in private, pension fund managers and other corporate shareholders have considerable influence over the Boards of the companies they invest in.

However, as a result of all this disquiet, the Cadbury Committee on the Financial Aspects of Corporate Governance was set up in 1991 and reported in 1992. They published a Code of Best Practice which most listed companies now comply with: Briefly the Code recommends:

❐ The Board should meet regularly and *monitor* the executive management.

❐ There should be a clearly accepted division of responsibility such that *no individual has unfettered powers* of decision.

❐ The Board should include *non-executive directors* of suitable calibre and number.

❐ The Board should have a *formal schedule* of matters specifically reserved to it for decision.

❐ Non-executive directors should bring an independent judgement to bear on issues of strategy, performance and resources including *key appointments and standards of conduct.*

- ❒ *Directors' service contracts* should not exceed three years without shareholders' approval.
- ❒ There should be full and clear *disclosure of directors' total emoluments* including pension contributions and share options. Separate figures should be given for salary and performance-related elements and the basis on which performance is measured should be explained.
- ❒ Executive directors' pay should be subject to the recommendations of a *remuneration committee* composed of non-executive directors.
- ❒ The Board should present a balanced and understandable *assessment* of the company's position, performance and *prospects*.
- ❒ The Board should establish an *audit committee* of at least three non-executive directors.
- ❒ The Board should explain their responsibility for *preparing the accounts* next to a statement by the auditors about their reporting responsibilities.
- ❒ The directors should report on the effectiveness of the company's *system of internal control*.
- ❒ The directors should report that the business is a *going concern* with supporting assumptions or qualifications as necessary.

The London Stock Exchange has a listing requirement that listed companies make a statement in their report and accounts on the extent of their compliance with the Code.

The committee issued a report on compliance with best practice in May 1995 which makes interesting reading. Essentially a high level of compliance was achieved by the top 500 companies and a smaller level in the smaller companies. A recent survey has found that many companies feel that Cadbury adds yet another burden of regulation on already overburdened companies. Others feel that even more regulation is needed especially on environmental and ethical issues.

11. Greenbury

Despite the Cadbury improvements in corporate governance there was still much public and shareholder disquiet about the pay and other remuneration of company directors in the UK. Specifically these centred on large pay increases and large gains from share options in the recently privatised utility industries. These increases have sometimes coincided with staff reductions, pay restraint for other staff and price increases. There have also been concerns about the amounts of compensation paid to some departing directors. In 1995 the Greenbury Committee reported and published a Code of Best Practice:

Some of the recommendations are:

- ❒ All listed companies in the UK should comply with the Code and include a statement about their compliance in the Annual Report by their remuneration committee.
- ❒ To avoid potential conflicts of interest, Boards should set up *remuneration committees* of non-executive directors.
- ❒ The remuneration committee should make a *report* each year to the shareholders.

- ❏ The report should set out the company's *policy* on executive directors' pay including levels, comparator groups of companies etc.
- ❏ The report should also include *pension entitlements*.
- ❏ The report should include full details on *all elements* of the remuneration package including (for each director) basic salary, benefits in kind, annual bonuses and long-term incentive schemes including share options.
- ❏ Annual bonuses and benefits in kind should generally *not be pensionable.*
- ❏ *Notice periods* for directors should not exceed one year or should be disclosed and the reasons for longer notice given.
- ❏ Shareholders should be invited specifically to approve all new *long-term incentive schemes*.
- ❏ Remuneration committees should have regard for the need to attract and retain directors with the right qualities but judge the position of their company in relation to other companies. They should be sensitive to the wider scene including pay and conditions *elsewhere in the company.*
- ❏ Performance-related remuneration should be designed to *align the interests* of directors and shareholders.
- ❏ Grants of new incentive schemes should be subject to *challenging performance criteria.*
- ❏ Executive share options should never be issued at a *discount.*
- ❏ Remuneration committees should consider what *compensation commitments* their service contracts would entail particularly for unsatisfactory performance.

It is too early yet to know what the effect of Greenbury will be on the amounts and disclosures of directors' remuneration. However it will make company Annual Reports more interesting in the future. Perhaps we shall be even more envious.

You should look out for references to the requirements of Cadbury and Greenbury in all listed company Annual Reports. You should find plenty. Note that the work of these two committees continues in the work of the Hampel Committee. The whole matter is still developing!

12. Accounting regulation

At the time of writing accounting, and in particular company accounting, is very highly regulated. We will now review some of the regulations.

The Companies Act 1985 as amended by the Companies Act 1989.

Accounting and reporting by companies to their shareholders in the form of a Profit and Loss Account and Balance Sheet have been subject to statutory regulation since the mid nineteenth century and successive Companies Acts have added to and refined the requirements ever since. The current Act is very detailed and I have covered some of its requirements in this Unit. Some points of note are:

a. All companies are required to comply in detail with the requirements of the Act as to the production of the Profit and Loss Account, Balance Sheet, Directors' Report and Auditors' Report. This means that they have to be produced in the format required and with all the detailed information which is obligatory in the Act. The

Profit and Loss Account and Balance Sheet also have to be audited and auditing is itself now highly regulated.

b. These accounts have to be laid before the shareholders at the Annual General Meeting and be filed at Companies House where they will be available to be seen by the public. However there are some exceptions which we will discuss below.

c. Private companies can, by elective resolution of the shareholders, dispense with the requirement to lay the Accounts before the members at a general meeting of shareholders but the accounts must still be sent to the individual shareholders so this exemption does not really save very much.

d. Small and medium sized companies need only file abbreviated accounts with the Registrar of Companies. A small and medium sized company is defined as one satisfying two of the three conditions:

	Small	Medium Size
Turnover not more than	£2million	£8million
Balance Sheet total not more than	£0.975m	£3.9m
Average number of employees not more than	50	250

Instead of filing all the accounts a small company need only file an abbreviated Balance Sheet with reduced notes and need not file a Profit and Loss Account or Directors' Report. A medium sized company need only file a slightly abbreviated Profit and Loss Account but must file all the rest.

It is important to note that all accounts and reports must still be produced, audited and sent to shareholders so the saving is only that more limited information is made available to the public.

e. *Listed* public companies (companies quoted on the Stock Exchange) need not send their shareholders the full Report and Accounts but instead may send a *summary financial statement*. The content of the summary financial statement is prescribed by regulation. Any shareholder who wants the full set of Accounts can require that the company supply it to her.

13. The Financial Reporting Council

The Financial Reporting Council is a company limited by guarantee so that in theory it is in the private sector but it was set up by the government who, with the Bank of England, appoint its Chairman and three Deputy Chairmen so that it has statutory backing. Its remit is to give support to its operational bodies and to encourage good financial reporting generally. It has two subsidiaries — the Accounting Standards Board (ABS) and the Financial Reporting Review Panel (FRRP).

The Accounting Standards Board makes and amends and withdraws Accounting Standards. One of its first acts was to adopt the 22 extant Statements of Standard Accounting Practice which were approved by the professional accounting bodies. The previous system of creation of SSAPs by the Accounting Standards Committee and approval by the professional bodies has now been discontinued. The first new Financial Reporting Standard (FRS 1 — Cash Flow Statements) was issued in 1991 and seven more have now been published. Before issuing a new Standard the ABS issues its proposals in the form of a *Financial Reporting Exposure Draft* (FRED) for public comment and sometimes before issuing a FRED it issues a *Discussion Paper*.

Some industries need accounting standards for their particular purposes and they can produce Statements of Recommended Practice (SORPS). The ABS has a role in the approval of these by approving bodies who issue them rather than the SORPS themselves.

The Accounting Standards Board has a sub-committee called the *Urgent Issues Task Force* (UITF). The work of the UITF is to assist the ASB in areas where an accounting standard or Companies Act provision exists but where unsatisfactory or conflicting interpretations have developed or seem likely to develop. A surprising number of matters have been subject to UITF pronouncements, most of them very technical.

14. The Financial Reporting Review Panel

The FRRP is a subsidiary of the FRC. Its role is to examine departures from the accounting requirements of the Companies Act 1985 and if necessary to seek an order from the court to remedy them. As well as having detailed requirements on accounting the Companies Act requires all accounts to show a *true and fair view* and by implication to comply with the accounting standards. The panel does not seek out departures but acts on matters drawn to its attention directly or indirectly. The panel's concerns are with the public companies and small and medium sized companies are outside its ambit.

15. Acts of Parliament

Many businesses are subject to the regulation of specific acts of Parliament and the Acts also regulate the records to be kept and the reporting to shareholders and to regulatory bodies that must be done. Examples include Building Societies, Housing Associations, Solicitors, Friendly Societies and Financial Services companies. Many businesspeople now feel that the amount of regulation is unduly restrictive and expensive. It is often pointed out that legislation to deter rogues causes immense labour and expense for the honest businessperson without deterring the rogue at all.

16. Government agencies

Adequate accounting and record keeping are needed by businesses to accord with the requirements of a number of government agencies. These include the Inland Revenue for income tax, corporation tax and PAYE purposes and by the Customs and Excise for Value Added Tax (VAT) purposes. Records are also required for Statutory Sick Pay purposes and National Insurance. The burden of complying with regulation is considerable on all businesses but is very good for accountants!

17. Accounting for the effects of changing price levels

Traditional accounting measures profit by comparing sales with cost of sales and overheads measured at their historical input cost. This method is objective and, in times of relatively stable prices, works very well. However in recent years inflation has been as high as 20% in the UK and even at rates as low as 4% or 5%, Accounts are distorted. As a result the accountancy profession has tried to introduce adjustments to accounts to counter the effects of inflation.

The major problem lies in the fact that dividends and taxation are based on profits measured using historical costs. The effect of this is that there is a possibility that operating assets will not be maintained and capital will be reduced. This is not easy to see so I will illustrate it in two examples:

	£
a. A Ltd maintains a stock of 10 widgets at cost of £1 each	10
They sell these for £1.50 each	15
and make a profit in historical terms of	5
This permits a dividend (ignoring tax) of	5
But, prices are rising and A Ltd must replace the widgets at £1.20 each	12

If the historical cost profit (£5) is distributed in full, it will not be possible to replace the ten widgets at £1.20 each since the operating capital is only £10. To stay in the same position of stocking 10 widgets, capital must be increased by £2.

b.   B Ltd operate an ice cream van. This cost £4,000 and will last for four years.

Each year —	Sales		10,000
	Cost of sales	3,000	
	Depreciation	1,000	4,000
	Historical cost profit		6,000

If this profit is distributed in full as a dividend, then resources available to replace the van will be £4,000 — cash flow each year is sales £10,000 — cost of sales £3,000 — dividend £6,000 = £1,000.

However because of inflation the cost of replacing the van after 4 years is £7,000. Capital has been maintained at £4,000 but £7,000 is needed so more capital has to be put into the business.

18. Benefits of historical cost accounting

There are limitations to historical cost accounting but there also considerable benefits. These include:

a.   Book keeping is done by recording transactions. It is not really feasible to record transactions (e.g. the purchase of a good) in any way other than at its cost.

b.   Financial statements are drawn up from the book keeping system. Any alternative to historical cost would require much manipulation of the data.

c.   Historical cost accounting is *objective* and *verifiable*. The cost of an asset is clearly stated in the invoice and payment and this can be verified by the auditor. Any other value is inevitably subjective. Users of accounts know where they stand with historical cost accounts and can and do make mental adjustments.

d.   The original raison d'etre of accounts was the report to owners as to 'what has happened to our money?' Historical cost accounting answers this question fairly well. It is only relatively recently that persons other than owners are taking an interest in financial statements.

e.   After many years of development, historical cost financial statements are well understood — this is a doubtful statement!

f.   No acceptable alternative to historical cost has yet been found.

19. Limitations of historical cost

It is easy to pick out weaknesses in the measurement of income and capital under historical cost principles. Some of these are:

a. Fixed assets in a Balance Sheet and depreciation in a Profit and Loss Account bear no relation to real values. The requirement to depreciate buildings worsens this criticism but the tendency to revalue property lessens it.

b. Stock valued at £40,000 at cost may need £50,000 to replace and yet £40,000 is the value used in accounts.

c. The sum of values of assets in a Balance Sheet is a mixture of say 19x2, 19x3, 19x8 pounds etc and because of inflation these are not the same.

d. The capital (= capital and reserves in a company) purports to show the capital tied up in a business but this is nonsense when historical values are used.

e. In a Profit and Loss Account sales at current prices are matched with inputs which will include stocks purchased months earlier and depreciation of assets purchased years earlier when price levels were different.

f. Holding gains are ignored. Inflation increases the money value of assets but this is ignored in Profit and Loss Accounts.

g. The sum repayable on long term loans and debentures may be much reduced in real terms but this is ignored in Profit and Loss Accounts.

h. Dividends and drawings are based on historical value financial statements and may as a consequence be paid partly out of capital. We have already considered this point.

i. Return on capital employed calculations are usually misleading:
   - ❏ capital employed is distorted by using historical cost
   - ❏ return (= profit) is distorted by using depreciation at historical cost.

j. Decision making on out of date values will be sub-optimal. As examples:
   - ❏ X does not really know the profitability of his marginal branch in Darlaston and so does not know whether or not to close it down
   - ❏ Y does not know if selling his product at prices based on historical cost costings is actually profitable
   - ❏ Z, an investor, is unable to evaluate realistically the companies he has shares in.

20. Solutions to the problems of historical cost accounting

a. One partial solution is to *revalue* assets and this approach is widely adopted but applies largely only to land and buildings.

b. Another solution is more comprehensive and is called *Current Purchasing Price Accounting* (CPP). This complete system works by converting the historical figures to current purchasing power by an appropriate price index usually the Retail Price Index (RPI). CPP had a vogue in the 1970s but is not much considered now.

c. The most regarded solution is *Current Cost Accounting* (CCA). This system is also comprehensive and is still found (for example in the Accounts of British Gas PLC).

The basic concepts are:

❐ Profit and Loss Account: the profit is adjusted by charging an extra item against profit. The extra item is the difference between the value to the business of assets consumed and the historical acquisition costs. Value to the business is generally taken as the replacement costs of the assets consumed. Four adjustments are taken in two stages:

Stage i.

a. A depreciation adjustment

b. A cost of sales adjustment being the difference between the value to the business of the stocks consumed and their historical input costs

c. A monetary working capital adjustment to reflect the additional working capital (mainly debtors) required in times of rising prices. Additional resources are needed to finance any increase in debtors caused purely by inflation, less any part financed by increased creditors.

Stage ii.

The gearing adjustment. When part of the net operating assets are financed by long term debt, a proportional reduction of the stage i. adjustments is made to reflect the gain made by the company from borrowing which will be repaid at some future date in depreciated currency.

❐ the Balance Sheet: the Balance Sheet should contain:

i. Fixed Assets and stocks at their value to the business

ii. Other current assets and all liabilities at their historical cost

iii. Shareholders interests divided into

Share capital

Current Cost Reserve — the adjustments made

Other Reserves

CCA is very sophisticated at a detailed level but is not easy to grasp at an intuitive level and as a result has not really commanded the respect of the business community.

The search continues!

21. Escaping from the conventions of accounting

Financial statements offer limited information and are historical in nature. In recent years more people have found a use for them — customers, suppliers, all sorts of government agencies including the tax authorities, banks and other suppliers of finance, employees, managers, buyers of businesses, investors etc. More people now have some understanding of accounting as a consequence of the proliferation of courses in business and management studies.

The limitations of convention bound accounting have become more evident to more people. However no radical attempt to reform accounting to make it more informative has yet appeared. Some suggestions that have been made are:

a. valuing goodwill, especially the value of brands

b. valuing the people who are employed by the business

c. requiring a profit forecast with each set of financial statements

d. listing statistics like orders on hand

e. a review of products and research and development into new products
f. review of ecological progress by the company
g. review of employment practices and health and safety
h. listing of exporting and importing undertaken
i. provision of accurately calculated and detailed ratios
j. a commentary on each line of the accounts with explanations of changes from the previous year
k. a summary of significant activities and contracts affecting the company.

All of these things seem a good idea but have practical difficulties. For example c. requires the directors to put their necks upon the block. Forecasting is very difficult and the directors may be afraid of litigation if their forecasts were not fulfilled.

Bonus, rights and other share issues

Bonus Issues:	Shareholders receive free new shares	
	Company receive no new resources	
	In the balance sheet:	
	Share Capital	— up
	Share Premium or Profit and Loss Account	— down
	Total value remains the same on the stock exchange but each share is worth less as there are more of them	
Rights Issues	Shareholders buy new shares from the company	
	The company receives new resources	
	Bank	— up
	Share Capital	— up
	Share Premium	— up
	Stock Exchange value of a share is weighted average of previous value and issue price	

Issue of shares in exchange for a company (a takeover)	Shareholders of taken over company become shareholders in taking over company	
	Victim company becomes asset (investment) of predator company	
	Goodwill element written off	
	Net Assets	— up
	Share Capital	— up
	Share Premium	— up
	but then: as goodwill is written off:	
	Net Assets	— down
	Reserves	— down

Contents of a company annual report and accounts

Chairman's Statement

Directors   Balance Sheets

Directors' Report   Accounting Policies

Profit and Loss Account   Movements in Shareholders' Funds

Total recognised Gains and Losses   Auditors' Report

Notice of Meeting   Financial Calendar

Principal Companies   Financial Summary

Cash Flow Statement   Notes to the Accounts

Divisions   Share Data

Codes of Best Practice

Profit and Loss Account

Turnover   Continuing Operations

Cost of Sales   Discontinued Operations

Gross Profit   Acquisitions

Operating Expenses   Exceptional Items

Trading Profit

Interest

Profit on ordinary activities before tax

Tax

Profit on ordinary activities after tax

Profit for the financial year

Dividends

Retained Profits for year

Note:

1. The Profit and Loss figure in the Balance Sheet is the sum of this year and previous years profits.
2. The final line is the Earnings per Share.
3. The previous year's figures are also included so that a comparison can be made.

Balance Sheet

Fixed Assets	— Tangible
	— Intangible
	— Investments
+ Current Assets	— Stocks
	— Debtors
	— Cash and Bank
– Creditors: amounts falling due within one year	— Trade Creditors
	— Overdrafts
	— Tax and social security
	— Corporation Tax
	— Dividends
	— etc
– Creditors: amounts falling due after more than one year	— Loans
	— Debentures
	— Provisions for liabilities and charges*
= Capital and Reserves	— Share Capital
	— Share Premium
	— Revaluation Reserve
	— Profit and Loss Account

Notes:

1. * these are rather technical. Only accountants understand them.
2. Four Balance Sheets are usually given. Only the two labelled *Group* are of any real interest.

---

22. Summary of Unit 14

❑ Company Accounts are very complex documents with a very large amount of detail.

❑ Basic information is as in the simple accounts introduced in Units 2 and 3 but simple messages are often obscured by a mass of detail and unfamiliar language.

❑ The relationship between Profit and Loss Account items and Balance Sheet items can often be followed through.

❑ Information on any particular topic can often be found in more than one document in the Annual Report and Accounts.

❑ For such information, search may be made in the Balance Sheet, Profit and Loss Account, notes to accounts, accounting policies, directors' report and yet others.

❑ The Profit and Loss Account shows several different figures for 'profit'. These are not usually difficult to understand but in discussion it is important to ensure that all parties are talking about the same profit.

- ❐ The capital and reserves section of the Balance Sheet is not easily understood. The total is more important than the detail and represents the assets less the external liabilities.

- ❐ The net asset value of one share is usually rather different from the stock exchange quotation.

- ❐ Information about the directors is copious but strangely woolly. It always follows the requirements of the Companies Act 1985.

- ❐ As the corresponding figures for the previous years are also given, changes between the years can be explored.

- ❐ All companies hold an Annual general meeting of Shareholders. Few shareholders attend and the meetings are short. Most of the resolutions rubber stamp the actions of the directors.

- ❐ A bonus issue is a free issue of shares to all shareholders pro rata to their existing holdings.

- ❐ Many companies allow shareholders to take a cash dividend or to have a bonus issue of shares in lieu.

- ❐ Auditors have a vital role in validating the credibility of Accounts.

- ❐ The independence of auditors from a company and its directors is currently a contentious issue.

- ❐ A company can make a rights issue which means that further monies are invested in the company by existing shareholders. Rights can be sold so that the buyer of the rights takes up the new shares and some change occurs in the shareholding.

- ❐ Creative accounting is largely a myth now but was more prevalent in the past.

- ❐ Companies can keep within the Accounting Standards and yet have different accounting policies. This means that comparing the performance of a company with other companies requires careful consideration of what policies have been adopted.

- ❐ Disquiet on a number of matters of corporate governance has led to Codes of Best Practice from the Cadbury and the Greenbury Committees.

- ❐ Company accounting is highly regulated by many rules including the Companies Act 1985 and the Accounting Standards Board.

- ❐ Accounting for the effects of changing price levels has been a big issue in finance but in current low levels of inflation has largely been forgotten.

- ❐ The conventions of accounting are well tried and fairly comprehensive but the limitations of accounting are becoming more apparent.

Exercise *1

From the following data relating to two companies Cain Ltd and Abel Ltd, prepare Profit and Loss Accounts and Balance Sheets. The relevant year is 19x2.

	Cain	Abel
(All figures in £'000)		
Sales	10,300	2,300
Distribution costs	620	120
Tangible Fixed Assets	4,108	1,030
Goodwill	560	200
Interim Dividend paid	70	25
Exceptional items:		
Expenditure (very large bad debt)		28
Stocks	375	430
Trade creditors	680	213
Debtors	980	540
Prepayments	32	17
Cost of sales	7,800	1,240
Administration Expenses	790	135
Debenture loan at 12% payable 19x6	2,400	600
Interest	370	72
Corporation Tax on 19x2 profits	180	201
Taxation and social security due	134	39
Bank Overdraft	621	
Cash at bank		74
Cash in hand	12	18
Final Dividend proposed	140	50
Issued Ordinary share capital		
(20p shares)	700	250
Share Premium	280	80
Revaluation Reserve	239	75
Profit and Loss Account at 1.1.19x2	363	341
Minority Interests		31

Exercise 2

From the following data relating to two companies Samantha Ltd and Damian Ltd, prepare Profit and Loss Accounts and Balance Sheets. The relevant year is 19x2.

	Samantha	Damian
(All figures in £'000)		
Sales	26,000	1,400
Distribution costs	1,380	134
Tangible Fixed Assets	12,567	943
Goodwill, Patents and Trade Marks	500	320
Interim Dividend paid	460	30

	Samantha	Damian
Exceptional items:		
Expenditure		
(settlement of copyright action)	1,200	
Income		23
Stocks	6,390	124
Trade creditors	3,870	67
Debtors	6,800	87
Cost of sales	20,100	470
Administration Expenses	2,512	98
9% Bonds payable 19x7	1,000	
8% Convertible loan 19x4/19x6		250
Interest	135	20
Corporation Tax on 19x2 profits	540	220
Taxation and social security due	967	86
Bank Overdraft	260	
Cash at bank		55
Final Dividend proposed — Ordinary	690	120
— Preference	70	
Issued Ordinary share capital		
(20p shares)	2,300	700
Share Premium	1,678	
Revaluation Reserve	239	
Profit and Loss Account at 1.1.19x2	14,230	(276)
7% Preference Shares of £1 each	1,000	
Minority Interests		31
Capital Redemption Reserve	500	

Note:

❐ 'Bonds' is just another word for loans.

❐ Preference shares are shares where the holders have different rights from the ordinary shareholders. Preference share rights normally include the right to a fixed rate of dividend (here it is 7% of the nominal value of the shares) which can only be paid if there are profits and the right to take preference over ordinary shareholders in a winding up (= liquidation) when they would be paid a maximum of the nominal value of the shares. The ordinary shareholders can only be given a dividend if one is also given to preference shareholders. Preference shareholders normally do not have a vote at meetings of the company.

❐ Many preference shares (and also some ordinary shares in special circumstances) are redeemable (= repayable). When they are redeemed part of the profit and loss balance is renamed Capital Redemption Reserve.

❐ Convertible Loans are loans where the lender has an option at specified times to convert his loan into ordinary shares at a specified rate.

Answer the following questions:

Samantha Ltd

a. Has the company made sufficient profits to cover its dividends relating to the year 19x2? If not, how is it able to pay dividends?

b. What are the rates of dividend per share on each dividend?

c. What are the earnings per ordinary share if earnings are defined as profits after tax and preference dividends?

d. Can you calculate the interest paid on the overdraft?

e. Have any of the preference shares been redeemed?

f. Are any of the fixed tangible assets valued by reference to a valuation?

Damian Ltd

a. What are the rates of dividend on the ordinary shares?

b. Can you calculate the earnings per share?

c. Is the Balance Sheet that of a company or a group? If it is a group, does Damian Ltd own all the shares in its subsidiaries?

Exercise 3

The Profit and Loss Accounts of Jephtha PLC for two years show:

Profit and Loss Account

(All figures in £'000)	19x2	19x3
Turnover	6,300	7,400
Cost of Sales	4,200	4,600
Gross Profit	2,100	2,800
Distribution Costs	450	280
Administration Expenses	340	510
Operating Profit	1,310	2,010
Exceptional item	450	670
Profit before interest	860	1,340
Interest Payable	550	300
Profit on ordinary activities before taxation	310	1,040
Taxation	230	510
Profit of the year	80	530
Dividends	200	220
Retained profit for the year	(120)	310
Earnings per share	1.6p	10.6p

Required:

a. Comment on these two accounts in detail.

b. How might your comments change when you know that:

   ❐ The exceptional item in 19x2 is the closure costs of the loss making wholesale division of the company.

❐ The exceptional item of 19x3 is the loss on disposal of the US subsidiary. This subsidiary made profits but the directors decided that as these were lower than expected when the company was bought, it should be sold again.

Exercise *4

Mixwell PLC have a Balance Sheet as follows at the end of 19x1:

(all figures in £'000)

Net Assets	6,900
Share Capital (50p shares)	2,000
Profit and Loss Account	4,900
	6,900

The company did the following things:

a. Made a bonus issue of 1 share for every 2 held.

b. Then made a rights issue of one share for every four held of the enlarged capital at £2.40 a share.

c. Revalued the property upwards by £6 million.

d. Made a profit of £1.6 million.

e. Paid a dividend of 4p a share.

Required:

a. Show the summary Balance Sheet after each thing.

b. Comment on the fact that the share price moved from £4.00 a share before the bonus issue to £2.70 immediately after the bonus issue.

c. Comment on the fact that the share price moved from £2.70 a share to £2.50 a share immediately after the rights issue.

Exercise 5

Financial Chicanery PLC made a bonus issue at the end of 19x1, a profit in 19x2 and a rights issue at the end of 19x2. The company is divided into shares of 20p each. Its Balance Sheets at various dates were:

(all figures in £'000)	*end 19x1 but pre bonus issue*	*end 19x1 post bonus issue*	*end 19x2 pre rights issue*	*end 19x2 post rights issue*
Net Assets	1,900	a	2,400	3,300
Share Capital	800	1,000	1,000	1,400
Share Premium				500
Profit and Loss Account	1,100	b	c	d
	e	f	g	h

a. Insert figures instead of the letters a to h.

b. How many extra shares were issued to a shareholder with 800 shares as a result of the bonus issue?

c. How many shares were offered to a holder of 1,000 shares as a result of the rights issue? And at what price?

d. Before the bonus issue each share was quoted at 60p. What would you expect the price to be after the bonus issue?

e. Before the rights issue each share was quoted at 84p. What would you expect the price to be after the rights issue?

Assignment 1

The published accounts of Adam PLC, wholesalers of ladies wear for the two years 19x2 and 19x3 are:

Profit and Loss Account

(All figures in £'000)

	19x2	19x3
Turnover	6,700	9,300
Cost of Sales	4,500	6,100
Gross Profit	2,200	3,200
Distribution Costs	680	830
Administration Expenses	1,125	1,350
Operating Profit	395	1,020
Exceptional item	302	60
Profit before interest	93	960
Interest Payable	75	140
Profit on ordinary activities before taxation	18	820
Taxation	80	256
Profit of the year	(62)	564
Dividends	20	200
Retained Profit for the year	(82)	364
Earnings per share	(2p)	9.4p

Balance Sheet as at 31 December

	19x2	19x3
Fixed Assets		
Intangible assets		600
Tangible assets	1,200	2,100
	1,200	2,700
Current Assets		
Stocks	830	1,380
Debtors	1,200	1,590
Cash at bank and in hand	180	20
	2,210	2,990

	19x2	19x3
Creditors: amounts falling due within one year		
Creditors	1,430	1,579
Bank Overdrafts		269
Taxation and Social Security	245	367
Corporation Tax	80	256
Dividends		180
	1,755	2,651
Net Current Assets	455	339
Total Assets less Current Liabilities	1,655	3,039
Creditors: amounts falling due after more than one year		
Bank and Other Loans	500	770
	1,155	2,269
Capital and Reserves		
Issued Share Capital (10p shares)	300	600
Share Premium		200
Revaluation Reserve		250
Profit and Loss Account	855	1,219
	1,155	2,269

Required:

Write a report explaining the happenings to Adam PLC in 19x2 and 19x3 as far as it is possible to do so from the accounts. You should deal with:

Increase in business from 19x2 to 19x3

Interest

Exceptional (19x2 re closure of three branches) (19x3 re sale of a subsidiary company)

Dividends

Earnings per share

Intangible assets

Tangible fixed assets

Cash at bank/Overdraft

Bank and Other loans

Share capital and share premium

Revaluation

Profit and Loss Account on the Balance Sheet

Assignment 2

Obtain a copy of the Annual Report and accounts of a public company (or preferably several) and write a report on the following matters:

Profit and Loss Account

i. How much are the auditors paid?

ii. How much is the depreciation (and amortisation) charge?

iii. Are any research and development costs charged?

iv. How much interest is paid?

v. Is segmental information given on activities and geography?

vi. What is the rate of corporation tax?

vii. Are there any minority interests?

viii. Summarise the exceptional items.

ix. What are the rates of interim and final dividend?

x. Relate the rates of dividend with the amounts payable and the share capital.

xi. How is the earnings per share calculated?

xii. What are the accounting policies on the valuation of stocks?

Group Balance Sheet

i. Are there any intangible assets?

ii. If yes, how are they valued?

iii. What are the categories of tangible fixed assets?

iv. Are land and buildings depreciated?

v. Are any tangible fixed assets at a valuation?

vi. Can you reconcile the depreciation to the Profit and Loss Account figure?

vii. Are there any fixed asset investments?

viii. If yes, how are they valued?

ix. What are the categories of stocks?

x. Do debtors include any advance corporation tax? (This is a tax paid at 1/4 of the net dividend, when a dividend is paid. It is recoverable by deduction from later corporation tax payments.)

xi. What types (if any) of current asset investments are held?

xii. What are the categories of creditors due in less than twelve months?

xiii. Do they include advance corporation tax and obligations under finance leases (finance leases arise when the company leases equipment in such a way that the lease transfers substantially all the risks and rewards of ownership of assets to the lessee — they are in effect very similar to hire purchase contracts).

xiv. What are the names given to obligations included in creditors: amounts falling due after more than a year?

xv. What is the nominal value of one share? What is its present stock market value?

xiv. Have any new shares been issued in the past year? Do any issues relate to executive share option schemes, scrip dividends (many companies allow shareholders to take dividends in the form of new shares instead of cash), a bonus issue, a rights issue, an issue in connection with an acquisition of another company?

xvi.   Is there a share premium account and has it changed in the year?

xvii. Is there a revaluation reserve?

xviii. Does the profit retained in the Profit and Loss Account reconcile with the increase in Profit and Loss Account on the Balance Sheet?

General:

i.   How many directors are there? How many are non-executive? What is their total remuneration?

ii.   How many shares in the company do the directors own? What proportion of the total share capital does this represent?

iii.   Did the company make any charitable or political donations in the year?

iv.   How many people worked for the Group in the year and what was their total remuneration?

v.   Is there any qualification to the auditors' report?

vi.   Has the Group acquired or disposed of any companies in the year?

vii.   What is the time of the Annual General Meeting?

viii. What are the items on the agenda?

ix.   Is there an election for directors?

x.   Can all the shareholders be accommodated in the venue of the AGM?

xi.   How many of the directors are under 50; female; non-executive?

Case Study/Assignment 3

Gedoutovit PLC is a listed company with a number of different activities. Among these are life assurance and pensions broking, speculative housebuilding and brewing. Turnover is around £20 million and total number of employees is about 300.

The company accountant is preparing the annual accounts for the year ending 31 December 19x2. He is not sure what do to about:

a. The company advance substantial sums as interest free loans to organisations such as clubs to induce them to buy the company's beers to the exclusion of other brewers' beers. These are repayable immediately if the club goes into receivership or liquidation or if it revokes the agreement to buy exclusively from Gedoutovit. After 10 years of exclusivity the loans are written off. In recent years a significant number of clubs have failed and Gedoutovit has received almost nothing in the ensuing liquidations.

    The present accounting treatment is to show all outstanding loans by including them in trade debtors in current assets i.e. they are not shown as a separate item although they represent about 15% of trade debtors. When loans are written off either on the time expiry rule or because they are bad debts they are included in the Profit and Loss Account figure of cost of sales.

b. The company have built 50 houses to sell and the average cost of these has been £75,000. Only 10 have been sold as the market has dried up and the agent reckons the houses will only sell at about £50,000. The company decided to let them instead and they have all been let to sound tenants at modest rents. The company's intentions are to sell the houses when the market improves and the tenants leave.

The present accounting treatment is to transfer the houses from current assets to fixed assets at cost. No depreciation will be charged and they will be carried at cost.

Discussion:

a. List the record keeping and financial reporting regulations that may apply to the company. It may help to consult friends who are involved in record keeping for companies and financial services companies.

b. Comment on the accounting treatment of the loans and the houses and suggest alternative policies and the extent of disclosure. As a matter of record both of these issues were raised in UITF information sheet No 2 issued on 15 April 1992 without resolution.

Case Study 4

Nomm PLC and Penn PLC are two rival companies of similar size in the widget trade.

Nomm is very long established and is financed largely by retained earnings. It has a net profit after tax to dividends ratio of 1.5. Its factories and plant are in good repair but not at all new. The factories are carried in the accounts at cost less depreciation of the buildings elements. Nomm carries significant stocks of raw materials and finished goods. Traditionally in the widget trade customers are slow in paying.

Penn is a young company with the very latest in factory design and modern plant. In order to finance the fixed assets, it is heavily geared with short, medium term and long term borrowings. Penn operates a just-in-time system for its raw materials and components and has a very sophisticated computerised system for keeping finished goods stocks as low as possible.

The main component in widgets is the metal Alanium which is traded in the commodity exchanges. Demand and supply fluctuates wildly and the price has varied from 20% to 290% of the mean price over the last five years. Prices of widgets have on the contrary varied little.

Discussion:

Both companies report profits and assets on historical cost principles. What would be the effect on profits and return on capital employed of using Current Cost Accounting principles instead?

Case Study 5

In 1968, Willenhall Metal Bashers Ltd was formed by a group of friends who subscribed at par for the £1 shares. A factory site was acquired and a factory building erected. The company depreciated the factory building over 50 years. Very little profit was made and small losses occurred in the final four years. Most of the profits were distributed as dividends.

In 1988 the factory was sold to a neighbouring company who demolished the factory building as it was in disrepair and obsolete for modern needs. The goodwill and other assets of the company were sold to the son of one of the founders.

As a result of the disposal of the substance of the company, the company was liquidated and the shareholders received £6 a share.

Discuss the relevance of historical cost accounting to the decisions of the directors and shareholders of this company.

Assignment 6

Consider the suggestions in the Unit under the heading 'Escaping from the conventions of accounting' and summarise the practical and legal difficulties that may occur to you.

Exercise 6

Sheinton Daily News PLC has many shareholders and the register of shareholders records them including the 60% shareholding by Daffodil Ltd a company registered in the Bahamas. This is duly reported in the Annual Report. However, Daffodil is in turn owned by other companies in tax havens ultimately controlled by Fred Trevethick, the media tycoon. How might Fred influence the conduct of Sheinton Daily News Ltd to accord with his agendas? What do you think should be disclosed?

Exercise 7

Tera PLC is run by its dynamic chairman and chief executive Richard Marwell. The company trades extensively with companies controlled by Marwell outside the UK. Marwell informs the auditors that all such transactions are at arms length. Marwell has only 3% of the shares in Tera PLC. How might Marwell abuse his position at the expense of Tera PLC?

Exercise 8

Examine the Annual Report of at least one listed company and write a commentary on the company's compliance with the two Codes of Best Practice.

Exercise 9

Upton Parva United FC PLC are a quoted football club currently hoping for promotion to the premier league. Anxious to reverse recent poor performance on the field, the Board want to appoint Jack Fixit as manager. Fixit plays hard to get and insists on:

❏ Being a member of the Board.

❏ A five year contract and a salary of £400,000 a year with a Jaguar car.

❏ A bonus of £250,000 if the team are promoted.

❏ Share options to buy up to 50,000 shares at par at any time during the currency of his contract. The £1 shares in the club are at a low ebb and are currently quoted at £1.30.

❏ A pension scheme based on his total remuneration ex the share options.

The Board has ten members, all part-time except for the Chief Executive, Sid Shuter, and, if he is appointed, Jim Fixit.

Required:

Comment on this scenario in the light of Cadbury and Greenbury.

15 Ratio analysis

1. Objectives

The objective of this Unit is to introduce ratio analysis of Accounts. It is possible to evaluate a company's performance by comparing the Accounts with those of previous years, budgets and the Accounts of other companies. Definitive conclusions cannot be drawn because:

❒ circumstances change over time

❒ actual conditions are always different from those forecast in budgets

❒ other companies operate in different conditions and use different accounting policies.

Ratio analysis does nonetheless assist the management, shareholder or other interested party in asking the right questions.

We shall examine the use of ratio analysis by looking at a part of Martin's company over time and as part of an inter firm comparison scheme.

SCENARIO 1 — Martin analyses some accounts

Martin is concerned about the performance of a particular division of his company which is run from a separate factory in Darlaston which is rented. In fact Martin Padlocks bought the business as a going concern and it is still run by its original general manager and it still exercises autonomous decision making and has a separate sales organisation. The Accounts for the last two years show:

Manufacturing, Trading and Profit and Loss Accounts

(All figures in £'000)

	19x6		19x7		IFC%	
Raw Materials:						
Opening stock	82		105		4.6	
Purchases	270		340		14.7	
	352		445		19.3	
Closing Stock	105	*247	132	315	4.6	14.7
Direct Labour		360		400		22.4
		*607		715		37.1
Works Overheads						
Rent, rates, insurance	130		145		8.6	
Plant Depreciation	34		62		3.6	
Energy	190		252		10.2	
Staff Salaries	87		93		5.2	
Other overheads	102	543	132	684	6.4	34.0
		*1,150		1,399		71.1

		19x6	19x7	IFC%
		*1,150	1,399	71.1
Opening Work in Progress		127	163	5.4
		1,277	1,562	76.5
Closing Work in Progress		163	140	5.4
		*1,114	1,422	71.1
Opening Finished Goods Stock		245	280	11.1
		1,359	1,702	82.2
Closing Finished Goods Stock		280	231	11.2
		*1,079	1,471	71.0
Sales		1,758	1,930	100.0
		*679	459	29.0

	19x6		19x7		IFC%	
Administration Costs	182		154		5.1	
Selling Costs	264		296		9.2	
Distribution Costs	82	528	63	513	1.1	15.4
Net Profit		151		(54)		13.6

Balance Sheet

		19x6	19x7	IFC%
Fixed Assets				
Plant + Vehicles				
Cost at beginning		180	190	17.4
Additions in year		10	160	6.2
		*190	350	23.6
Depreciation at start		123	157	11.1
Depreciation in year		34	62	3.6
		157	219	14.7
		* 33	131	8.9
Current Assets				
Stock		548	503	21.1
Debtors		420	477	21.0
		968	980	
Less *Current Liabilities*				
Creditors	– Materials	65	92	3.3
	– Overheads	54	68	2.4
		119	160	
		*849	820	
Net Assets		882	951	

We have omitted the capital section as it is not relevant to our analysis on this occasion. The final columns, headed IFC%, are from an interfirm comparison. We will look at them later.

Quick Answer Questions 15.1

1. There are six lines in the Profit and Loss Account and three in the Balance Sheet which are marked with an asterisk*. Suggest suitable descriptions for these lines.

2. Has there been an increase/decrease from 19x6 to 19x7 in:

   Work in progress, turnover, other overheads, capital expenditure, stocks?

3. Relate the stocks in the Balance Sheet to those in the Profit and Loss Account.

4. Relate the depreciation in the Balance Sheet to that in the Profit and Loss Account.

SCENARIO 2 — Martin extracts the message from accounts

Martin is disappointed in the results as a loss is shown in 19x7 after a profit in 19x6. He decides to review the 2 years accounts without calculating any ratios and discovers:

❑ Turnover is up (but is it up greater than inflation?)

❑ Gross Profit is down.

❑ Both administration costs and distribution costs are down but selling costs are up. The net effect is a reduction in non-manufacturing overheads.

❑ A net profit of £151,000 has become a loss of £54,000.

❑ There has been capital expenditure of £160,000 in the year 19x7 as against only £10,000 in 19x6.

❑ Stocks are down but debtors are up.

❑ Creditors are also up.

❑ Net assets are up by £69,000.

Martin knows that the last point means that in 19x7 he has invested £123,000 from the rest of Martin Padlocks Ltd. The actual calculation is:

(all figures in £'000)

Capital at end of 19x6	882
less Loss in 19x7	54
	828
New capital invested	123
Capital at end of 19x7	951

Martin considers that the division has spent large sums on new plant and has increased its turnover and yet has managed to make a loss. This clearly needs some investigation and to assist him in the investigation he needs a benchmark or standard which will enable him to compare the division's performance against.

To do this he has enrolled at some expense in an *interfirm* comparison which is run by the National Association. The division has a narrow range of products and there are many other firms in the Industry. Many of these subscribe to the Interfirm comparison and the results are now available to Martin.

The process is:

i.   Each firm completes a set of accounts in standard form. This is necessary as different accounting policies are used by different firms and it is necessary to standardise these. In addition two other major differences between firms exist:

    a.   Some own their own property and some rent. This difference has been eliminated by assuming that all rent and making notional adjustments to accounts of owning firms.

    b.   Financing can be from equity or from borrowings. The interfirm comparison figures used have eliminated all borrowings and interest charges. Financing figures are available but we have ignored them.

ii. The sets of accounts are set out in the form of percentages of turnover. The mean (average) of these percentages are circulated to subscribing members.

This enables ratio comparisons to be made. For example:

The gross profit to sales ratio for the Industry is 29% but for our division the ratio is:

$$19x6\ 679 \div 1{,}758 \times 100 = 38\%$$
$$19x7\ 459 \div 1{,}930 \times 100 = 24\%$$

The rate was very good in 19x6 but has become very poor in 19x7. To find the reason it is necessary to explore the make up of costs.

Tasks 1

1.   Calculate suitable ratios for both years and compare them with the Industry averages. Do not confine yourself to the ratios in the unit but calculate any ratio that seems relevant.

2.   Write a report on the divisions performance detailing:

    ❑   where the division's performance has changed between the two years.

    ❑   where the division's performance is different from the Industry average.

    ❑   which items need attention.

2. Introduction

Financial statements — Profit and Loss Accounts and Balance Sheets — are designed to present *historical information* in a stylised form to *owners* primarily but to other interested parties secondarily. They are not designed to enable detailed analysis of the performance of the business or for a ratio analysis to be carried out on them.

In the light of the warning in paragraph 1, extreme care must be applied in using financial statements for analysing company performance and in doing ratio analysis. The probability of coming to the wrong conclusion is very high. At best, ratio analysis enables the analyst to determine areas where awkward questions can be asked or further information sought.

Ratio analysis has the following components:

a)   *Trends* — a gross profit ratio that is below industry average but is getting better may be more hopeful than a ratio that is above average but getting worse.

b) *Similar companies* — clearly it is helpful to compare a company with other similar companies. However caution has to be taken as no two companies are exactly alike or use the same accounting policies.

c) *Industry averages* — if these are available from inter firm comparisons or other sources

d) Comparisons with *budgets* — a company may have intended ratios and a comparison with actual gives the actual outturn some objective standard for comparison.

Ratios are usually extracted for two purposes:

a) To assess the *performance* of the management

b) To assess *liquidity*. This has three sub-purposes:

    i) to determine how long a company will take to pay a supplier who is considering selling goods or services to the company on credit

    ii) to determine if the company will remain as a *going concern* or go into receivership or liquidation

    iii) to assess the ability of the company to repay a loan.

The persons or institutions who might apply ratio analysis to a company may include *actual* or *potential:*

- management
- owners / shareholders
- lenders
- customers
- suppliers
- employees
- competitors

and also

- companies contemplating takeovers
- government agencies including the taxman and those concerning the control and regulation of business
- the public especially those who belong to pressure groups.

Their purposes in doing an analysis will of course differ and the particular ratios they use will also differ.

Example

Despite my opening paragraphs we will attempt to analyse the performance of Stubby Computers Ltd. The company operate a shop, retailing computer hardware and software from a high street site. They belong to an interfirm comparison scheme whereby many firms in the same industry send in their accounts and mean ratios are extracted which enables all participants in the scheme to compare their performance with the average for the industry.

Stubby Computers Ltd
Trading and Profit and Loss Account
For the years ending 31 December:

	19x2	19x3
	£'000	£'000
Sales	980	1,170
Cost of goods sold	600	750
Gross profit	380	420
Occupancy costs	25	34
Employee costs	110	111
Advertising	30	40
Administrative costs	31	34
Directors' salaries	40	45
Depreciation	30	30
	266	294
Net profit before interest	114	126
Interest	30	35
Net profit after interest	84	91
Corporation tax	23	28
Net profit after tax	61	63
Dividends	30	35
Retained profit for the year	31	28

Balance Sheet as at 31 December

	19x2	19x3
Premises	200	188
Equipment and shop fittings	80	92
Vehicles	50	40
	330	320
Current assets		
Stocks	85	120
Debtors	90	87
	175	207
Creditors: amounts falling due within one year		
Creditors	70	90
Overdraft	20	32
Corporation tax	23	28
VAT and PAYE	18	20
Dividend	30	35
	161	205

	19x2	19x3
Net current assets	14	2
Total assets less current liabilities	344	322
Creditors: amounts falling due after more than one year		
15% Bank loan	150	100
	194	222
Capital and reserves		
Called up share capital (20p shares)	100	100
Profit and Loss Account	94	122
	194	222

The mean ratios supplied by the interfirm comparison are:

Gross profit ratio	35%
Net profit to sales	10%
Overheads to sales	25%
Asset utilisation ratio	2.8 times
Annual sales growth	11%
Occupancy costs to sales	6%
Employee costs to sales	8%
Advertising costs to sales	3%
Return on capital employed	25%
Return on shareholders funds	32%
Dividend cover	1.9
Gearing ratio	40%
Stock turnover	65 days
Debtors average payment time	70 days
Creditors average payment time	60 days
Current ratio	1.6
Acid test ratio	1.1
Operating cycle	75 days

Before calculating any ratios we should extract as much *information* from the accounts as we can *without ratios*. The following points may be made:

a) The company owns its own premises and therefore, presumably, no rent is payable.

b) The property is being depreciated and has not been revalued. Therefore the market value is not known.

c) Equipment increased during the year despite depreciation. The company is investing in improved facilities.

d) Vehicles declined in the year presumably as a result of depreciation. There was no investment in new vehicles including presumably no new directors' cars.

e) The company have borrowed at some time in the past from the bank on a fixed interest loan. This was probably in order to buy the premises. £50,000 has been repaid in the year. The remaining £100,000 is in creditors falling due after more than one year so is not payable until at least 19x4.

3. Analysis of the various ratios

Gross profit ratio

This is $\dfrac{\text{gross profit}}{\text{sales}} \times 100$, so for 19x2 the ratio is $\dfrac{380}{980} \times 100 = 39\%$
and for 19x3: 36%.

This is a key ratio and shows the relationship between the input prices paid by the company and prices obtained from customers. 39% means that on average every £1 of sales, the product sold cost 61p giving 39p to pay overheads and give a profit. The reduction from 19x2 to 19x3 may be due to:

❐ failure to pass on higher prices from suppliers

❐ a change in sales mix to lower margin products

❐ competitive pricing to combat competition or to get sales

❐ a change in the type of customer.

The ratio achieved by the company is better than the industry average.

4. Net profit to sales

This ratio shows the extent to which sales have resulted in a profit.

In this case the ratio for 19x2 is $\dfrac{114}{980} \times 100 = 11.6\%$

and for 19x3 10.8%. A drop of 3% in the gross profit ratio would usually lead to a drop of 3% in the net profit ratio. In this case the drop is only 0.8% so the company have actually done well despite the 0.8% drop. They also have a better return than the industry average.

5. Overheads to sales ratio

The ratio for 19x2 is $\dfrac{266}{980} \times 100 = 27\%$ and for 19x3 25%. The improvement in this ratio has enabled the net profit to sales ratio to fall only 0.8 % despite the fall of 3% in gross profit ratio. Probably the overheads were too high in 19x2 as the ratio has now come down to the industry average.

6. Asset utilisation ratio

This shows to what extent the assets used in the business have generated sales.

It is calculated as:
$$\frac{\text{sales}}{\text{operating assets}}$$

Operating assets are usually defined as total assets less current liabilities. We will take the figures at the year ends.

So for 19x2 the ratio is: $\dfrac{980}{344} = 2.8$ and for 19x3 3.6.

This is a big improvement. We could say that the business managed to generate a substantial sales increase with an actual reduction in net operating assets. It is also better than the industry average.

7. Annual sales growth

Sales growth for 19x3 is 1,170 – 980 = 190 (in £'000) so sales growth as a percentage is $\frac{190}{980} \times 100 = 19\%$.

Sales growth has to be compared with inflation which was running at 8% in 19x3 so that there has been an increase of 11% in real terms compared with an industry growth of 11% in money terms and 3% in real terms. Prices of computer products actually fell in 19x3 so that the growth in volume is actually greater than 11%.

However the sales growth was accompanied by a reduction of gross profit ratio, so a possible hypothesis is that sales were obtained by price reductions.

8. Occupancy costs to sales

Occupancy costs include rent, rates, heat and light, repairs to premises, fire insurance etc.

The ratio for 19x2 is $\frac{25}{980} \times 100 = 2.5\%$ and for 19x3 2.9%. The ratio has worsened but cannot be compared with the industry average as the industry average probably includes rent and our company owns its own property. Be warned against comparing unlike figures.

An alternative ratio for this industry might be sales per square foot but we have no data on this.

9. Employee costs to sales

This ratio tells us how effective the staff are.

In this case the ratio for 19x2 is $\frac{110}{980} \times 100 = 11\%$ and for 19x3 9.5%.

Despite inflation of 8% and presumably corresponding pay increases the company have held their wage bill constant so that we can presume staffing levels have actually reduced. Hence the reduction in this ratio. It is however still well above the industry average and further action to reduce staff seems possible.

An alternative ratio might be sales per employee but we have no data on the number of employees.

10. Advertising costs to sales

This ratio for 19x2 is $\frac{30}{90} \times 100 = 3\%$ and 3.4%. The appropriate amount of advertising is clearly difficult to determine but in this case is about the industry average. It has increased in 19x3 and sales have also increased but any connection must be speculative.

11. Return on capital employed

This is often seen as the key success indicator. The theory is that management have been entrusted with the net assets of the enterprise with a duty to make a profit from them.

There are problems of definition. We shall take the return as being the net profit before interest and the capital employed as total assets less current liabilities.

In our case the ROCE for 19x2 is $\dfrac{114}{344} \times 100 = 33\%$

and for 19x3 39%. This seems very good in comparison with the industry average of 25% and the gross return available from for example building society investments. However there are many difficulties in making comparisons here including:

❏ Profit does not include any increase in value of the property over the year.

❏ Assets include the property at cost less depreciation when its market value may be higher or, of course, lower.

❏ Profit measurement includes property depreciation based on historical cost.

12. Return on shareholders funds

This ratio measures how well the management have turned the return on capital employed into a return on the funds invested by the shareholders.

The return is the net profit after tax and the shareholders funds are the total capital and reserves.

The ratio for 19x2 is $\dfrac{61}{194} \times 100 = 31\%$ and for 19x3 28%. The ratio has declined and in both years was less than the industry average. However note that it is an after tax ratio whereas the return on capital employed was a before tax ratio. The remarks about valuation difficulties apply to this ratio also.

13. Dividend cover

This ratio measures the extent to which profits are distributed to shareholders in the form of dividends.

The calculation is simply:
$$\frac{\text{net profit after tax}}{\text{dividends}}$$

In our case the ratio for 19x2 is 2.03 and for 19x3 1.8.

You can interpret the ratio by saying the in 19x2 just under half the profits were distributed but in 19x3, just over half were distributed. The ratio is in line with the industry average.

14. Gearing ratio

Gearing is also called *leverage*. Gearing measures the extent to which the company is financed by borrowings as against *equity*. Equity is the investment by shareholders.

The calculation is:
$$\frac{\text{Long term loans}}{\text{total capital employed}} \times 100$$

In this case the ratio for 19x2 is $\frac{150}{344} \times 100 = 44\%$ and for 19x3 31%. The theory is that some borrowings (usually called debt) are a good thing as the company can earn a rate of return on capital employed (in our case 39% in 19x3) above the cost of borrowing (15% in this case). However excessive debt can dangerously increase risk as interest and debt repayment have to be made even in times of recession. The company decreased its gearing in 19x3 by repaying part of its long term loan and the gearing ratio is now below the industry average.

15. Stock turnover

Stock is necessary in this as in all retailing companies. Too much stock carries risk of deterioration and obsolescence and also has costs of storage and financing. Too little stock may cause loss of sales. The stock turnover ratio measures the amount of stock in relation to its throughput.

Its measurement is $\frac{\text{stock}}{\text{cost of goods sold}} \times 365$

In our case the ratio is $\frac{85}{600} \times 365 = 52$ days and 58 days in 19x3 as against an industry average of 65 days. The ratio indicates that the average item was in stock for 52 days in 19x2 and 58 days in 19x3. It seems that the company either have excellent stock control or frequently lose sales by not having stock. The ratio is often difficult to interpret as year ends are chosen when stock is low to facilitate counting and some companies postpone purchases for the few days around stocktaking so a true average stock is not determined. Also a large stock may seem to be a good service to customers but may hide shortages of frequently wanted items together with surpluses of obsolete and slow moving items.

16. Debtors average

This ratio measures the ability of the company to collect debts from its customers. In practice debt collection is a major problem with many large companies being very slow payers.

The ratio is measured by:

$$\frac{\text{Debtors}}{\text{credit sales}} \times 365$$

We are not given the credit sales but we shall assume that 50% of the sales in both years are on credit and 50% for cash.

With our company the ratio is:

$\frac{90}{490} \times 365 = 67$ days in 19x2 and 54 days in 19x3 against an industry average of 70 days.

Our company seem to be very good at credit control and collecting debts.

17. Creditors average

This is the critical liquidity ratio. It measures the average time taken to pay suppliers. Firms normally take more time to pay than strictly allowed by their suppliers but taking excessive time (say three months or more) usually indicates inability to pay more quickly and may sooner or later cause the company to fail.

It is calculated by:

$$\frac{\text{creditors}}{\text{purchases}} \times 365$$

In this case purchases are not given but can be deduced as opening stock + purchases – closing stock = cost of goods sold. Three of these variables are known for 19x3 but only two for 19x2. If stocks are not radically different at each year end then an approximation is to use cost of goods sold which is usually available knowledge.

Thus for 19x2 the time is $\frac{70}{600} \times 100$ is 42 days and for 19x3 44 days. This is relatively quick and the company might well take longer to pay and reduce their overdraft accordingly. The industry average is 60 days.

18. Current ratio

This is simply current assets over current liabilities and for our company it is for 19x2 $\frac{175}{161} = 1.1$ and for 19x3 1.0. With industry average at 1.6, our company's ratio is significantly different.

Some writers suggest that any variation from industry average should be subject to enquiry but general feeling now is that this ratio has no value whatever.

19. Acid test or liquidity ratio

This ratio is defined as (current assets less stock) over current liabilities. In 19x2 it was: $\frac{90}{161} = 0.6$ and in 19x3 0.4.

As with the current ratio, I can attach no significance to it.

20. Operating cycle

This is defined as stock turnover + debtors average payment time – creditors average payment time. The idea is that it measures the time taken between cash being paid for goods and the receipt of the proceeds of sale of those goods.

In our case the time is 52 + 67 – 42 = 77 days for 19x2 and 68 days in 19x3 as against an industry average of 75 days. We seem to be doing well.

21. Investment ratios

Analysts apply some additional statistics and ratios to companies whose shares are listed or quoted on the stock exchange. These include:

❏ dividends per share
❏ dividend yield
❏ earnings per share
❏ price earnings ratio

To consider these items we will select Stubby Group plc and its abbreviated accounts:

Profit and Loss Account

	£'000
Net profit after tax	1,420
Dividends	700
Retained profits	720
Earnings per share	4.06p

Balance Sheet

Net assets	12,700
Share capital (20p shares)	7,000
Share premium	1,000
Reserves	4,700
	12,700

Remember that reserves are not assets but an explanation of how the company acquired its net assets of £12,700,000, for example by retaining profits or by revaluing its property.

22. Dividend per share

This is calculated by:

$$\frac{\text{Total dividend}}{\text{Number of shares}}$$

In this case each share has a nominal value of 20p and the share capital is given in £s. So the number of shares is $5 \times 7,000,000 = 35,000,000$ and the dividend per share is

$\frac{700,000}{35,000,000} = 2$p. This statistic cannot be compared with other companies as the

number of shares into which a given company is divided is arbitrary but year on year comparisons can be made.

Some serious newspapers give the dividend per share daily for each quoted company. They do however give it gross which is the net dividend (which we have calculated)

$\times \frac{100}{80}$ to reflect a 20% income tax rate. In our case the gross rate is 2.5p.

23. Dividend yield

The dividend per share cannot be compared with other companies but the dividend yield can be. The dividend yield is calculated by:

$$\frac{\text{Dividend per share}}{\text{Quoted price per share}} \times 100$$

The quoted share price varies all the time but we will assume it to be 68p.

The yield is thus $\frac{2.5}{68} \times 100 = 3.7\%$.

This is much below the gross rate obtainable on building society deposits but remember that the dividend per share in Stubby plc is expected to grow.

24. Earnings per share

This statistic is calculated as:

$$\frac{\text{Net profit after tax}}{\text{Number of issued shares}}$$

In our case it is $\dfrac{£1,420,000}{35,000,000}$ = 4.06p. In practice the calculation is not always this easy

and the last line of the Profit and Loss Account of quoted companies gives it. It cannot be compared with other companies but a year on year comparison is very useful.

25. Price earnings ratio

This is calculated as:

$$\frac{\text{Quoted price per share}}{\text{Earnings per share}}$$

In Stubby's case it is $\dfrac{68p}{4.06p}$ = 16.7

The serious papers give the PE ratio for all quoted companies daily. Its meaning is difficult to assess but in general higher PE ratios imply expected growth and a low PE implies a stagnant company. However a company that has a particularly poor profit in a year will show a high PE.

SCENARIO 3 — Martin reviews accounts purposefully

Martin's company has never dealt with Stade Ltd, a wholesaler of locks in Northumberland. However Stade have now asked Martin to supply them with a significant quantity of locks on credit. Martin suspects that Stade may have difficulty in paying their existing suppliers and that they are asking Martin for goods as existing suppliers have restricted deliveries. Before agreeing to grant credit, he asks for a recent set of accounts. To his surprise Stade supplies these and Martin is able look at them. Here they are:

Profit and Loss Account

(all figures in £'000)

	19x7		19x8	
Sales		2,400		2,950
Opening stock	230		254	
Purchases	1,560		1,930	
	1,790		2,184	
Closing Stock	254	1,536	287	1,897
		*864		1,053
Overheads		624		785
		*240		268
Corporation Tax		65		74
		*175		194
Dividends		100		105
		* 75		89

Balance Sheets

	19x7		19x8	
Fixed Assets				
Cost		462		730
Depreciation		280		345
		182		385
Current Assets				
Stock	254		287	
Debtors	660		740	
	914		1,027	
Current Liabilities				
Creditors				
Purchases	410		580	
Expenses	67		91	
Overdraft	340		359	
Tax	65		74	
Dividends	70		75	
	952		1,179	
		*(38)		(152)
Net Assets		144		233
Capital and Reserves				
Share Capital (£1 shares)		50		50
Profit and Loss Account		94		183
		144		233

The notes indicate:

❐ that the fixed assets are equipment and vehicles. The company rent its premises.
❐ the bank overdraft is secured by a floating charge on all the assets. This means that the bank will be paid before other creditors if the company goes bust.

Quick Answer Questions 15.2

1. Give a title to the items marked with an asterisk*
2. What is the dividend per share?
3. Relate the Profit and Loss Account to the Balance Sheet.

SCENARIO 4 — Martin ponders liquidity

Martin feels that the company seems healthy in that it has increased its turnover, made profits and paid dividends. However he notes that the overdraft seems high and has got even higher in 19x8.

Tasks 2

1. Write a report on the events of 19x8 compared with the events of 19x7.
2. Calculate ratios of interest when assessing liquidity.
3. Explain the liquidity problem and how it arose.
4. Give a justified opinion on whether Martin should grant credit.

Ratio analysis

Gross Profit to Sales

Gross Profit to Cost of Sales (Mark up)

Overheads to sales in detail and in total

Net Profit to Sales

Annual Sales growth

Costs or Sales per square metre

Costs or Sales per employee

Asset Utilisation Ratio

Return on Capital Employed

Return on Shareholder funds

Stock Turnover

Debtors Average Payment Time

Creditors Average Payment Time

Operating Cycle

Dividend Cover

Dividend Yield

Earnings per Share

Price Earnings Ratio

Gearing ratio

Notes:

1. Your author does not include the current ratio or the acid test ratio as he does not consider that these have any diagnostic value.
2. Some writers distinguish some ratios as performance indicators and some ratios as liquidity indicators. For example, stock turnover is often regarded as a liquidity ratio. In fact it really does say something about management's ability to manage stocks and it does have an effect on liquidity in that a worsening stock turnover will tie up money. However it does not say anything to answer the questions of a loan or trade creditor: will I be paid and, if so, when?
3. The ratios which are of interest to loan and trade creditors on liquidity are the creditors average credit time and the gearing ratios.
4. Each Industry and indeed each firm has ratios which are not included above but which are very useful. For example:

    Sales returns to Sales in a foundry

    Cost per mile in a Railway.

    Hotel Costs per patient/day in a private hospital

26. Summary of Unit 15

- ❏ Financial statements are historical and produced as a report to shareholders. They are not designed for ratio analysis to be applied but ratio analysis is applied nonetheless.

- ❏ Accounts can be compared with previous years, similar companies, industry averages, and budgets.

- ❏ Ratios are used to assess performance and liquidity.

- ❏ Parties connected with a company who might be interested are actual and potential managers, owners, shareholders, lenders, customers, suppliers, employees, competitors, predators, government agencies and pressure groups.

- ❏ Ratios of interest include gross profit to sales, net profit to sales, overheads to sales, asset utilisation, sales growth, return on capital employed, return on shareholders funds, dividend cover, gearing, stock turnover, debtors average payment time, creditors average payment time, operating cycle, price earnings ratio, dividend yield etc.

- ❏ Individual companies may have ratios of especial interest such as sales per square foot, sales per employee, hotel occupancy rate etc.

- ❏ Accounts can be appraised without using ratios and much useful analysis can be done without them.

- ❏ Ratio analysis should be used only to trigger the right questions. It can be very misleading!

Exercise 1

The trading account of two companies for the years 19x1, 19x2 and 19x3 showed: (in '£000)

	19x1	19x2	19x3
Company A			
Turnover	8,800	9,700	10,100
Cost of goods sold	6,130	6,596	6,717
Gross profit	2,670	3,104	3,383

Inflation in 19x2 was 6% and in 19x3 8%.

	19x1	19x2	19x3
Company B			
Turnover	4,400	5,250	6,015
Cost of goods sold	3,000	3,702	4,331
Gross Profit	1,400	1,548	1,684

Comment on all these figures using ratios.

Exercise 2

The summarised Profit and Loss Accounts of two companies for 19x2, their budgeted figures for the same year and the average for the industry are:

| (in £'000) | Company C | | Company D | | Industry |
	Actual	Budget	Actual	Budget	%age of sales
Sales	240	230	280	320	100
Gross Profit	91	92	104	128	41
Selling and					
Distribution	23	27	26	22	6
Admin	31	30	35	39	10
Net Profit	37	35	43	67	25

Comment on the figures using ratios.

Exercise 3

Some figures from the accounts of two similar chemical companies, one in the UK and one in another European country:

	UK Company in £'000	European in currency
Turnover	86,000	145,000
Net Profit	6,400	18,400
Land and Buildings	33,700	33,100
Plant and Equipment	18,400	27,000
Current Assets	22,100	34,500
Current Liabilities	19,400	18,200
Long-term liabilities	2,000	21,000

a. Comment on these figures using ratios including an asset utilisation ratio and a measure of return on capital employed.

b. Comment further in the light of knowledge that:

   i. The British company recently revalued upwards all its land and buildings. The European company values all its land and buildings simply at cost without depreciation.

   ii. The British company has financed its recent acquisitions of plant with the aid of bank overdrafts with the intention of replacing the overdrafts with long term loans shortly. Note that replacing short term loans with long term loans is known as funding the short term debt. The European company has access to very long term bank finance.

Exercise *4

The accounts of three companies for the year ending 31 December 19x2 show: (in '000)

	K	L	M
Turnover	35,800	21,000	34,000
Gross Profit	8,700	4,800	6,000
Net Profit	2,400	1,200	1,540
Property	1,600	2,800	10,400
Plant etc	3,520	1,400	8,600
Stocks	1,100	1,800	6,300

	K	L	M
Work in Progress	–	720	2,300
Debtors	340	3,200	4,200
Cash at bank	2,890		
Creditors	3,100	1,400	2,430
Bank Overdraft		2,180	5,900

Required:

a. For each company calculate:

Return on capital employed

Asset utilisation ratio

Debtors payment period

Net profit to sales ratio

Stock turnover

Which, if any, of these ratios are meaningful?

b. One of the companies is a supermarket chain, one is a textile manufacturer and the other is a company in heavy industry making process plant. Which company is which and how do you know?

Exercise 5

Here are some data about three companies, all of whom are in the wholesale widget business:

		S		T		U
(all in £'000)						
For 19x2:						
Sales		8,200		6,200		9,500
Opening stock	1,450		900		1,480	
Purchases	6,170		4,568		5,840	
	7,620		5,468		7,320	
Closing stock	1,820	5,800	880	4,588	960	6,360
Gross Profit		2,400		1,612		3,140
At 31.12.19x2						
Debtors		2,220		1,020		2,980
Trade creditors		1,678		730		930

Required:

a. Calculate ratios which might enable you to compare the performance of these three companies.

b. Comment on the ratios and suggest to each management where improvements in performance may be possible.

c. Would your commentary be different if you knew:

❐   that company U had an exceptionally large turnover in December 19x2

❑   company S purchased a specially large amount in December 19x2 at a very advantageous price?

Exercise 6

The following are the profits after tax and the dividends for four successive years for two companies Zig PLC and Zag PLC:

(all in £'000)

		Zig					Zag		
Year	1	2	3	4	1	2	3	4
Profits	6,700	7,100	2,800	8,600	4,500	4,700	6,200	6,600
Dividend	2,400	2,500	2,500	2,900	1,300	1,350	1,650	1,750

Required:

a.   Calculate the dividend cover for all years.

b.   Comment on the change in cover over the years, suggesting reasons for any change.

c.   Would your commentary be different if you had known that Zag PLC had a large rights issue in year 2?

d.   Which company would you expect to grow the fastest? Justify your opinion.

Exercise 7

The accounts for the year ending 31 December 19x2 of Hyde Ltd are shrouded in mystery. Certain facts only are known. These include:

Gross Profit £1,000,000

Gross Profit to sales ratio 40%

Stock 31.12.19x1 £300,000

Creditors £270,000

Creditors are paid after two months

Overheads 20% of sales

Debenture Interest £100,000

Debentures carry interest at 10%

Corporation Tax 25% of profits

Dividend 1/3 of post tax profits

Fixed assets at 31.12.19x1 at cost £1,200,000 less depreciation of £800,000

Depreciation is at 25% reducing balance method

Debtors take 50 days to pay (use round £'000)

Dividend is 25p per £1 share

Profit and Loss balance at 31 December 19x1 was £312,000

Required:

a.   Reconstruct the accounts

b.   Calculate return on capital employed and return on shareholders funds.

Exercise 8

The accounts for the year ended 31 December 19x2 of Cache Ltd are also very mysterious but some information is available:

Sales   £2,000,000

Gross Profit to sales ratio 45%

Stock 31.12.19x2 £400,000

Stock 31.12.19x1 £300,000

Creditors are paid after three months

Overheads 10% of sales

20% Debentures £800,000 are redeemable in 19x5

Corporation Tax 25% of profits

Fixed assets at 31.12.19x1 at cost £2,100,000 less depreciation of £900,000

Depreciation is at 10% straight line method

Half the sales are for cash, the remainder pay after three months

Dividend is 10p per 20p share and takes 1/2 of post tax profits

Profit and Loss balance at 31 December 19x1 was £205,000

Required:

a. Reconstruct the accounts.

b. Calculate return on capital employed and shareholders funds.

Exercise *9

Some extracts from the accounts of four companies for 19x2:

(all figures in £'000)

	A	B	C	D
Net profit before interest	168	240	398	231
Interest	93	25	120	68
Corporation Tax	18	62	106	45
Share capital	54	200	530	89
Profit and loss balance	728	480	790	180
Long term Finance	800	170	640	480

Required:

a. Calculate for each company: gearing, return on total capital employed and return on shareholders funds.

b. Comment on the ratios including a commentary on each company's performance and the risks to lenders and shareholders.

Exercise 10

Some extracts from the accounts of four companies for 19x2:

(all figures in £'000)

	E	F	G	H
Net profit before interest	657	813	923	475
Interest	320	64	320	380
Corporation Tax	84	160	144	23
Share capital	1,200	900	2,900	1,700
Profit and loss balance	780	733	540	2,300
Long term Finance	2,000	390	1,800	1,750

Required:

a. Calculate for each company: gearing, return on total capital employed and return on shareholders funds.

b. Comment on the ratios including a commentary on each company's performance and the risks to lenders and shareholders.

c. Would your remarks be different if you knew that H had a property valued at cost less depreciation at £2,300,000 when its market value is about £6,000,000.

d. Would your remarks be different if you know that:

❐ company E is a brewery that has just spent large sums on doing up its houses

❐ company F is a manufacturer of motor components which is moving into the European market

❐ company G is a construction company

❐ company H is a hotel.

Exercise 11

The following are data about four quoted companies:

(figures in £'000)	I	J	K	L
Profit after tax	2,700	12,500	870	2,800
Interim Dividend	400	3,700	45	600
Final Dividend	800	5,800	47	1,400
Total Share capital	2,000	40,000	900	12,000
(figures in pence)				
Nominal value of one share	20	25	10	100
Quoted Share Price	280	56	170	300

Required:

a. For each company calculate: earnings per share, PE ratio, dividends per share, dividend cover, dividend yield.

b. Comment on each set of ratios.

Exercise 12

The following statistics are available for these four companies for the year ending 31 December 19x2

(all figures in £'000)	P	Q	R	S
Profit after tax	3,900	320	2,400	15,900
Interim Dividend	500	200	–	7,000
Final Dividend	600	250	1,000	–
Total Share capital	2,000	900	13,000	77,000
Total Reserves	18,500	450	32,000	4,500
(figures in pence)				
Nominal value of one share	50	10	25	20
Quoted Share Price	1,250	70	70	19

Required:

a.   For each company calculate: earnings per share, PE ratio, dividends per share, dividend cover, dividend yield, net assets per share, return on shareholders funds.

(note that net assets per share is calculated by net assets divided by the number of shares or as net assets = share capital + reserves by share capital + reserves divided by the number of shares)

b.   Comment on each set of ratios.

c.   Would your comments be different if you knew that:

❒   P's directors have announced that earnings in 19x3 will be much reduced from those in 19x2.

❒   Q's directors have announced that following a scheme of cost reduction the company will return to its normal productivity and make in the region of £900,000 in 19x3.

❒   the City are expecting a takeover bid for R.

❒   S is highly geared and is having liquidity problems.

Case Study/Assignment 1

The following are the accounts of Ketone Ltd, who retail commercial vehicle components, for the two years ending 31 December 19x1 and 19x2. The company are members of a trade association which operate an interfirm comparison scheme and the percentages which have been obtained from this scheme are also given. In addition the company operate a budgetary control scheme and produced a forecast set of accounts for 19x2 at the beginning of that year and these are shown also.

Trading and Profit and Loss Account

(all figures in £'000)

	19x1	19x2	Budget 19x2	Inter Firm %age sales
Sales	2,450	2,970	3,200	100
Cost of goods sold	1,470	1,841	1,920	58
Gross Profit	980	1,129	1,280	42
Occupancy Costs	140	156	160	3.5
Employee Costs	270	280	240	6.8
Advertising	135	158	150	6.2
Administrative costs	234	220	200	5.5

(all figures in £'000)

	19x1	19x2	Budget 19x2	Inter Firm %age sales
Directors' Salaries	80	80	80	4.0
Depreciation	74	104	110	4.1
	933	998	940	30.1
Net Profit before interest	47	131	340	11.9
Interest	31	50	40	1.1
Net Profit after interest	16	81	300	10.8
Corporation Tax	4	19	75	2.6
Net Profit after Tax	12	62	225	8.2
Dividends	–	10	50	4.0
Retained profit for the year	12	52	175	4.2

Balance Sheet

	19x1	19x2	Budget 19x2	Inter Firm %age sales
Plant and vehicles at cost	434	502	500	20.6
less Depreciation	306	108	106	5.4
	128	394	394	15.2
Current Assets				
Stocks	420	410	350	8.4
Debtors	590	730	650	21.2
	1,010	1,140	1,000	
Creditors: amounts falling due within one year				
Creditors	330	370	300	14.8
Overdraft	146	122	20	6.2
Corporation Tax	4	19	75	2.6
VAT and PAYE	20	23	27	.8
Dividend	–	10	59	4.0
	500	544	481	
Net Current Assets	510	596	519	
Total Assets less current liabilities	638	990	913	
Creditors: amounts falling due after more than one year				2.0
Bank Loan	–	100	100	
	638	890	813	

	19x1	19x2	Budget 19x2	Inter Firm %age sales
Capital and Reserves				
Called Up share capital				
(20p shares)	100	200	100	
Share Premium		100		
Profit and Loss Account	538	590	713	
	638	890	813	14.4

Required:

Write a report:

a. Summarising the events of 19x2 in relation to fixed assets, borrowings and share capital.

b. Preparing a list of ratios for 19x1, 19x2 and the forecasted 19x2.

c. Commenting on the performance of the company in 19x1, and 19x2 in relation to the forecast and the interfirm comparison.

Case Study/Assignment 2

Misleading ratio analysis

Things are rarely what they seem to be. Consider the accounts of two companies:

Profit and Loss Account

(all figures in £'000)	Matthew	Mark
Turnover	6,800	4,000
Cost of goods sold	5,200	3,000
Net Profit	568	432
Fixed Assets	500	550
Stocks	1,400	460
Debtors	900	34
Cash at Bank	–	90
Creditors	1,300	680
Overdraft	900	330
Capital and Reserves	600	124

a. Calculate for each company:

Return on capital employed
Asset utilisation ratio
Net Profit to sales ratio
Debtors turnover in days
Creditors turnover in days
Stock Turnover
Current Ratio
Liquidity ratio

b. Try to draw some conclusions about these companies and their performance and liquidity.

Before jumping to conclusions some further information would have been helpful:

Matthew: This is a construction company and it occupies its own headquarters building which is valued at £2,400,000 although it is in the Balance Sheet at cost less depreciation.

Stocks are of raw materials and of work in progress including a property which has since been sold at a good profit.

The overdraft is secured on the property and is for normal operational requirements + £550,000 for the property mentioned above.

Creditors include £300,000 tax not payable for nine months and £200,000 dividend not payable for six months.

Mark: This company is a retailer of babywear with several branches. Sales are for the most part for cash.

The fixed assets are mostly leasehold properties which were recently acquired.

The company are expanding fast and have agreed an overdraft facility of £500,000.

How does the view given by the ratios now appear?

Exercise 13

Prethan PLC own a chain of high class elderly persons' residences. Profits are in decline and the management intend to review and compare the annual financial statements of each residence to see whether best performance characteristics can be identified. Data for 19x7 include:

Residence number	1	2	3	4	5
Number of residents	10	7	24	18	21
Turnover	210	121	520	315	456
Percentage void	4.1	8.2	2.1	5.4	1.6
Staff numbers	6.2	5.6	15.2	12.9	9.8
Staff costs	64	55	161	142	123
Food	18	14	44	37	44
Heating and lighting	8.1	11.2	11	16	9.8
Repairs and maintenance	9	13	14	12	9
Current value of residence	440	400	876	540	1,035

Notes:

❏ Each residence manager is responsible for seeking new residents, pricing, staffing and wage rates and all expenditure except major capital expenditure.

❏ The number of residents row is the maximum occupancy and the void row indicates the percentages of rooms unoccupied in 19x7.

❏ Financial figures are in £'000.

❏ Staff numbers are measured as full-time equivalents.

❏ Repairs and maintenance include the gardens.

Required:

a. Calculate a series of ratios which you think might assist the management in making decisions about the residences and individual managements. Can you discern any relationships between the ratios.

b. The manager of residences 2 and 4 do not seem to come out well. Prepare defences of their performances inventing plausible scenarios.

c. These ratios bring out comparative performance ratios in the financial sense but do they say anything about *economy* (the ability of the managers to obtain necessary resources at lowest cost), about *effectiveness* (maximising outputs for a given set of inputs) and about *effectiveness* (how well the residences achieve their aims as set out in their mission statements)?

16 Sources of finance

1. Objectives

As we saw in Unit 1, starting a business requires some initial capital. Starting a business as small as a window cleaning round may require money to buy ladders, buckets etc and perhaps even a van. Starting a motor car factory would require hundreds of millions of pounds.

Most people start a business with their savings. If more is required then money can be obtained from relatives and friends and money can be borrowed from the Bank. The high street banks are the primary source of capital to the small business. However there are many other sources and we shall look at the main ones in this Unit.

All sources of money have a cost. This cost is the interest payable and the rate varies from source to source. The actual interest rate is not always made explicit but today lenders are required by the Consumer Credit Act 1974 to state the Annualised Percentage Rate (APR) which is the true rate of interest charged.

SCENARIO 1 — Martin looks at sources of finance

Martin Padlocks Ltd has now concluded six years in business and has reached a turnover of £2,000,000. The Balance Sheet at the end of year six can be summarised as:

Fixed Assets		
Cost		300,450
Less Depreciation		128,300
		172,150
Current Assets		
Stocks	330,000	
Debtors	304,000	
	634,000	
Creditors: amounts falling due within one year		
Trade Creditors	248,000	
Bank Overdraft	201,000	
Corporation Tax	35,000	
Taxes and Social Security	189,000	
Dividend	20,000	
	693,000	
Net Current Liabilities		(59,000)
Total Assets less Current Liabilities		113,150

Capital and Reserves	
Share Capital	15,000
Profit and Loss Account	98,150
	113,1150

Quick Answer Questions 16.1

1. The company has total assets of £172,150 + £634,000 = £806,150. Explain how these have been financed.

2. Financing can be considered to be from external sources and from internal sources. Which of the sources in this Balance Sheet are internal and which are external?

SCENARIO 2 — Martin reviews his financing needs

Martin understands his Balance Sheet and its implications and is explaining it to his son who is studying business at school. His son is having difficulty in seeing how profit is a source of finance. Martin consults Anne and comes up with this explanation:

❐ profit enables the company to pay a dividend up to the amount of the profit.

❐ imagine that the company paid the full dividend by writing cheques to the shareholders.

❐ at the same time the company need finance from the shareholders so the shareholders are prevailed upon to write cheques of the same amounts as the dividends in favour of the company.

❐ all the cheques are torn up.

In practice, most companies find that *retained profits* are insufficient for their desired expansion and Martin Padlocks is no exception.

Martin is still attempting to expand the business and he realises that involves the acquisition of new assets and that involves finding some money.

Among the assets he wants to finance are:

a. The factory has been rented up to now but the landlord has offered to sell it to the company for £200,000.

b. The company need three new large vans. The vans will cost about £20,000 each.

c. An increase in turnover of 30% will require an increase in stock, debtors and trade creditors of the same percentage.

d. The company needs some additional machinery which will cost £75,000.

He talks to Anne and to his bank manager and finds out some sources of finance. These include:

❐ *Hire Purchase* is available on most fixed assets over three or four years. He is quoted 16% APR.

❐ The Bank will offer *mortgage loans* over ten or fifteen years at a negotiable fixed rate of $1\frac{1}{2}$ % over base rate.

❐ The Bank will be willing to increase the *overdraft* by £50,000 at a cost of 4% over base rate. The overdraft is already *secured* by a *floating charge*.

319

❏ A *factoring* company are willing to factor up to 50% of approved debts at a rate of 4% over base rate + a 1½% service charge.

❏ A cousin of Martin has just won a large sum on the football pools and is willing to offer a long term loan of up to £50,000 at 12% with *convertibility* after a few years into ordinary shares.

❏ A *venture capital* company is willing to offer an investment of up to £100,000 of which half would be in *equity* and the loan rate would be long term at 3% over base rate.

Martin finds that the current base rate for most banks is 6%.

Tasks 1

Martin decides to investigate the alternatives. Set out the results of his investigation in the form of a report:

1. Summarising the amount of finance needed.

2. Suggesting which sources of finance might be suitable for each new investment. You should summarise the advantages and disadvantages of each.

3. Suggesting some sources of finance not reviewed in the scenario.

2. Introduction

Companies have sources of finance under three general headings:

> Retained profits
>
> Equity
>
> Debt

Each have different costs and we will consider these as we review each type.

3. Retained earnings

The principal source of finance for companies is retained profits. This can be illustrated by Stubby Ltd buying a widget for £50 and selling it for £75. There may be time delays involved as credit is given by the supplier and taken by the customer and there will be a delay between purchase and sale when the widget is in stock. However the effect of the transaction is that the company has £25 more cash. The total cash gains of this kind will be reduced by the payment of overheads and subsequently by tax and dividends. However if the company makes a profit there will be a net increase in financial resources.

It appears that retained earnings have no cost to the company but in fact the expansion in the company, which retained earnings are, will give shareholders expectations of higher dividends. Dividends are the cost to the company of all forms of equity finance.

4. Equity

Equity is the investment in the company by persons and institutions who become shareholders. Such investment is normally for the long term and is risk bearing. If the company does well, the equity shareholders receive large dividends but if the company fails, the equity shareholders lose all their investment.

In company law, the money invested by shareholders is not normally returnable. If a shareholder wants his money back he cannot look to the company but has to find a buyer for his shares. Shareholders in private companies often find themselves locked into their shares and can only find buyers amongst the other shareholders or when the company as a whole is sold. Shareholders in companies quoted on the stock exchange can always sell their shares as the stock exchange provides a market for them.

Companies obtain finance by issuing shares:

a) In exchange for a business, usually because the company is formed to take over a business.

b) By a general issue of shares to the public by a prospectus. This usually happens only when a private company becomes a public company and obtains a listing on the stock exchange.

c) By a rights issue. This means that new shares are issued for cash to existing shareholders in proportion (the usual expression is *pro rata*) to their existing holdings.

d) In a takeover of another company. Sometimes a takeover does not involve buying another company for cash but issuing new shares in the predator company to the shareholders of the victim company in exchange for their shares in the victim company. The predator company does not get cash for the new shares but does get a subsidiary company.

The cost of equity is a difficult concept. Essentially, when a company obtains finance by issuing shares it incurs at least a moral obligation to pay dividends. The dividends are the cost to the company of obtaining equity finance. Investors have expectations of increasing dividends as the years go by.

The cost of borrowing can be expressed as a rate of interest. You may have already compared the interest rates charged on mortgages, bank loans, HP etc. The cost of equity can also be expressed as an interest rate by the formula:

$$\text{Cost of equity} = \left(\frac{\text{Dividend}}{\text{Share price}} \times 100 \right) + \text{growth rate}$$

Suppose Halcyon PLC pay a dividend of 3p a share and each share is quoted at 80p and the dividend is expected to grow at 5% a year, then:

$$\text{Cost of equity} = \left(\frac{3}{80} \times 100 \right) + 5 = 8.75\%$$

This simple model begs the question of how you measure the expected growth rate but it does give at least some idea of the cost of equity.

5. Preference shares

Preference shares are shares which have many of the characteristics of loans. R plc issued 1,000,000 7% £1 preference shares in 1995. The shares are redeemable at par at the company's option at any time after 2006 and the dividends are cumulative.

The redeemable arrangement means that the company can repay the shares at any time after 2006. Par means that each £1 share will be repaid at £1. It is also possible to repay at a premium, for example repayment at £1.20 a share or at a discount, for example at

90p a share. The law requires that preference shares can only be redeemed if profits are available greater than or equal to the redemption. Once used for redemption, the profits are not then available for dividend.

The company can pay dividends on the shares but the annual dividend will always be 7p a share (or less). Cumulative means that if the dividend is missed in a year it should be made good in subsequent years. Dividends on ordinary shares can only be paid if preference dividends are up to date. No dividends, ordinary or preference, can be paid unless the company has a credit balance on Profit and Loss Account greater than the amount of the dividend. The company have no legal obligation to pay dividends.

In a winding up or liquidation, preference shareholders are paid out in full before any payment to ordinary shareholders. However, in most liquidations no funds are available to either type of shareholders!

Preference shares were once common but are now relatively rare.

6. Debt

Debt means borrowing. Borrowing can be in the short term, in the medium term (2-5 years) and for the long term. Borrowing can be *unsecured, secured* by operation of law, secured by a *floating charge* or secured by a *fixed charge* on a specific asset (see later in this Topic). Costs are usually expressed as an interest rate.

7. Short-term debt

Most companies obtain supplies on *credit*. This means they have the supplies and can use them before they pay. Payment can be anything from a few days to several months after receipt of the goods. The exact time depends on the policy of the payer and the tolerance of the supplier. Large companies are notoriously slow in paying small suppliers.

In effect trade credit is a form of finance which companies see as free. In fact it may not be free as:

a) better prices may be negotiated if long credit is not taken

b) settlement discounts are lost by taking credit. If the terms offered are nett, one month or 5% discount for immediate payment then the taking of credit implies a cost of the lost discount.

The other common form of short-term finance is the *bank overdraft*. This is normally regarded as short term as technically the terms of the loan are that the loan is repayable on demand. In practice overdrafts are renegotiated at intervals and often go on for many years so that companies see them as medium-term or even long-term finance. The cost of an overdraft is the interest rate agreed with the bank and often appears extortionate to the business borrower.

There are other forms of short-term finance available including *bills of exchange* which we will not pursue further and factoring.

Factoring involves the following procedures:

❒ Stubby Ltd (the borrower) sells goods on credit to A Ltd, a customer and invoices them at £1,000.

- Natmid Factors Ltd (a factoring finance company) advances 80% of the value, that is £800 to Stubby Ltd on the same or the next day.

- When A Ltd pay three months later, £800 goes to Natmid in repayment for the advance and £200 to Stubby Ltd

- In due course, Natmid charge up Stubby with interest on the £800 loan which was lent for three months.

Factoring finance is only used on sales so that the borrowings only occur to the amount needed to finance debtors.

Factoring companies usually offer other optional services to the lenders including:

- customer accounting

- credit control (assessing whether or not to give credit to a potential customer)

- chasing slow payers.

8. Medium-term debt

We will consider two forms of medium-term debt: hire purchase and leasing. Other forms exist including bank lending which we will consider under long-term debt.

Hire purchase is much used by small companies who often acquire assets such as machines and vehicles on hire purchase. You may be familiar with the concept as it is very common domestically. The parties to the contract are:

- the seller of the goods (say a car) who sells the goods to the company who want the car (known as the hirer) and get paid by the finance company. The seller is then no longer involved in the transaction;

- the hirer company who has use of the car and is in effect (but not in law) the owner;

- the finance company. In law they own the vehicle and receive payments (instalments) from the hirer over the term of the HP agreement. The agreement normally requires the hirer to pay monthly equal instalments over a period of one, two or three years. The instalments are partly repayment of the amount lent and partly interest.

On payment of the last instalment ownership of the car passes to the hirer. The law gives the finance company some rights of repossession which we will not consider here.

The rate of interest is usually high and is given as an annual percentage rate (APR) which is equivalent to the internal rate of return.

Leasing is a rapidly expanding form of finance. If Stubby Ltd need a new machine, they can seek the aid of a leasing finance company who will buy the machine and then lease it to Stubby Ltd. Stubby Ltd as lessees pay equal monthly sums as agreed to the finance company who are the lessors. Failure to pay instalments gives the finance company rights of repossession and the problem of disposing of the repossessed asset.

The essence of the deal is that Stubby do not own the asset but lease it. However many such lease agreements are effectively finance leases and the reality of the matter is that the deal is the same as a hire purchase transaction.

9. Long-term debt

Companies are able to borrow in the long term with repayment required only after a period which can be twenty years. Lenders can be banks, other institutions such as insurance companies and members of the public.

Such borrowings can be termed loans, *unsecured loan stock*, notes, *bonds* or *debentures*. They always pay interest at a specified rate called the *coupon* rate.

Some loans are simply by a single institution which receives interest every year and final repayment when specified. Some loans are made by numerous individuals and are quoted on the stock exchange. Suppose that in 1992 Giant plc raised £10,000,000 by a public issue of 15% loan stock repayable in 2012. Small was a member of the public who subscribed for £2,000 worth of the stock. In 1997 he wished to dispose of the stock. Giant plc will not repay until 2012 but he was able to sell his holding to another investor through the medium of his broker. He would not receive £2,000 but whatever the stock was quoted at on the date of sale which may be more or less than the £2,000. The actual quotation depends on the prevailing interest rates and if interest rates generally had fallen, he would actually sell his holding for more than £2,000.

Loans can be *secured* by a *fixed* charge. Supposing B Ltd wish to raise £50,000 by a loan from Unutterable Assurance plc. B Ltd own a property valued at £100,000 and offer this as a security. This means that the deeds of the security will be deposited with the lender. If B Ltd default on the loan then the lender can appoint a *receiver* to seize the property and sell it. The proceeds of sale will firstly be used to repay the loan and only any remainder will be available to other creditors. The lender cannot lose providing the property is worth more than the loan. The property is said to be subject to a mortgage and my readers will be aware that this is exactly what happens when houses are bought through a building society or bank mortgage.

Loans can also be secured by a *floating charge* on all the assets. C Ltd borrow £20,000 from the Natmid Bank who take a floating charge. If C Ltd default on the loan then the bank can appoint a receiver who must be a qualified insolvency practitioner. The receiver's duties will involve trying to save the company but if this is not possible then the assets will be sold and the loan repaid from the proceeds. Only any remainder is available for other creditors.

10. Convertible loans

Lending long term is not very attractive as interest rates may change and inflation reduces the capital in real terms. In order to attract investors to subscribe for loans, it is common to offer loans with rights to convert the loan into ordinary shares at specified dates. For example D plc issued £1,000,000 of 10% convertible loan stock in 1990. In any August from 1995 to 1999 each £100 of loan stock can be converted into 50 ordinary shares of 20p each. In 1995 Mrs P who has some stock finds the share price is £1.30 so that the value of 50 shares is $50 \times £1.30 = £65$ so she does not convert. However in 1996, she finds the share price is £2.40 so that the value of 50 shares is £120 and she does convert. On conversion she finds she has 50 shares of 20p each instead of £100 of loan stock. Instead of receiving interest she will in future receive dividends. You will see that she has made a capital gain and it is the possibility of this which makes convertibles attractive. This is especially true as she avoids the possibility of loss as the loan will eventually be repaid if it is not converted.

11. Warrants

Another way of attracting investors to loans is to attach warrants, which are rights to subscribe for shares, to the loan. E plc issued £2,000,000 of 12% loan stock in 1994 with warrants giving lenders of £100 rights to subscribe for 5 new 50p ordinary shares at a price of £1.80 at any time after 1998. In 1999, Ella who has £100 of the stock finds that the shares are quoted at £1.60 and does not exercise her warrants. But in 2,000 she finds that the shares are quoted at £2.50 and so she exercises her warrants and subscribes for the 5 shares at £1.80 and thus acquires shares worth £2.50 each. She still has her loan stock but of course no longer has the warrants.

12. Gearing

Gearing is called *leverage* in the USA and the term is now common also in the UK. Gearing describes the relative amounts of investment in a company of *debt* and *equity*.

The theory is that companies should have at least some borrowings because they can borrow at one rate say 15% and invest the money in productive assets to yield a higher rate say 20%. Failure to have some borrowings is to deprive the equity shareholders of this opportunity.

However too large an amount of debt (= too high gearing) can be dangerous. Debt interest has to be paid and debt capital repaid. Too much debt can be an impossible burden in bad times and lead to company failure. The optimum gearing ratio is a matter of much controversy but clearly depends on the type of company. There is a theory associated with two American economists, *Modigliani* and *Miller,* that the cost of capital is independent of the gearing ratio. This implies that high gearing does not increase the risk attached to debt and equity. Their arguments are seductive but most observers take a view that high gearing does increase the risk accepted by both debt holders and equity holders.

13. What sources of finance to use?

There are no golden rules on this. Some debt is desirable as we saw in the last paragraph but too much debt puts the company into danger. There is a theory that *financing* is a *separate function* from investment in productive assets. Thus the directors of F plc should decide what investment in assets to make and then use a range of appropriate financing sources to finance the company. Clearly the two are connected but specific assets should not be associated with specific financing sources.

Clearly leasing, hire purchase and the factoring of debtors are sources of finance which are associated with specific assets but the decision on the amount of investment in the assets which are leased or hire purchased and the debtors should be taken independently of the finance available. Similarly these financing sources should be seen as just some of the range available in selecting the company's mix of financing sources.

Another theory is that short-term assets should be financed with short-term finance and long-term assets with long-term finance. I do not find this theory attractive as it contravenes the theory on the independence of financing and investment. However a mix of short-term, medium-term and long-term finance is probably most appropriate.

14. Repayment and security

All borrowings have ultimately to be repaid. Most companies find that borrowings are repaid by further borrowings. Jason is considering supplying goods on credit to W Ltd. What should he look for in the Balance Sheet? He should look at the repayment dates for all borrowings as it may be that the company have to borrow soon to make a repayment and that replacement borrowing may be difficult. Cash flow difficulties may then follow making payment of creditors tricky. He should also look to see if any of the borrowings are secured. Hire purchase and leasing means that most or all of the value in the corresponding assets will go to these lenders. Some of the lenders, especially bankers, will have fixed or floating charges.

Many loan stocks have redemption dates as 2002–2004. This means that the company must repay the loans at some time between these dates. G plc have £10,000,000 of 12% loan stock 2002–2004 outstanding. If interest rates are less than this, say 9%, they will borrow at 9% and repay the loan early in 2002. But if interest rates are higher, say 14%, they will postpone borrowing until the end of 2004 and repay then.

SCENARIO 3 — Martin measures an interest rate

Martin is interested in buying a small second hand cruising boat. The price is £12,000 and Martin would need to borrow all but £3,000 of this. The boat yard tell him that they are willing to lend him the money at 10% interest and that they are willing to offer this low rate as a concession in order to make the sale. Martin asks for a written quote and takes it to Anne for appraisal. The terms are:

The loan is for 3 years

The loan is repaid in 3 equal instalments, together with interest, on the anniversary of the loan.

The annual interest is 10% on the whole £9,000.

(Thus each instalment will be £3,900.)

Task 2

Calculate the approximate APR of this loan. It can be calculated as the internal rate of return of the arrangement.

---

15. Risk in investment in companies

Investment in companies carries risk. A shareholder in XY Construction PLC may find the company goes into receivership and then liquidation and that his shares are worthless. The investor takes this risk because there is also the possibility of gain. He may buy his shares at 15p each and sell them a year or two later at 100p each as the company has prospered.

Investors can invest not only in ordinary shares but also in other securities. Here are some of the securities and the risks attached both downside and upside:

Loans secured on fixed assets

(usually land and buildings)

Upside	*Downside*
Cannot lose unless company goes bust and property sells for less than loan. Interest very unlikely to be unpaid. Eventual repayment.	Modest interest rate No chance of capital gain. Boring.

Loans secured on floating charges

Upside	*Downside*
Cannot lose unless company goes bust and all assets sell for less than amount of loan and unpaid interest. Interest very unlikely to be passed. Eventual repayment	Modest interest rate No chance of capital gain. Dull

Unsecured loans

Upside	*Downside*
Regular interest. Interest rate slightly better than secured loans. Eventual repayment	No chance of capital gain. Modest interest rate. Chance of losing money if company goes bust. Dreary

Convertible loans

Upside	*Downside*
Regular interest. Chance of capital gain if shares do well. Eventual repayment if not converted Interesting	No capital gain unless shares do well. Low interest rate. Chance of losing money if company goes bust.

Preference shares

Upside	*Downside*
Dividend payable before ordinary dividend. Usually cumulative. Usually redeemable	No capital gain. Low rate of dividend Chance of losing money if company goes bust.

I have suggested that there is no chance of making a capital gain on these securities. This is not quite true. Suppose prevailing interest rates are 12% on company loans. AB PLC issue a loan in 19x2 at that rate for repayment in 20 years. In effect the investor in £100 worth gets assured interest of £12 a year for twenty years and then his money back. Suppose in 19x3 interest rates have fallen to 8%. If he wishes to sell his loan stock, another investor may see £12 a year and looking for an investment paying 8% may be willing to pay £150 for £100 worth.

This gives him $\frac{12}{150} \times 100 = 8\%$.

In practice he will pay slightly less than £150 as he will ultimately be repaid only £100.

Of course if interest rates rise then the £100 nominal may fetch less than £100.

16. Business risk and financial risk

The risk accepted by investors in companies can be considered as coming from two sources:

❏   Business Risk

This is simply the risk that the company may trade profitably or unprofitably. One particular risk is called operating gearing. Suppose FA PLC makes and sells a particular building material. Each batch of the material gives a contribution of £2,000 and fixed costs in its highly capital intensive process are £10,000,000 a year.

If the company sells 6,000 batches the company makes £2,000,000 profit and gives record dividends. But if the company sells only 4,000 batches it loses £2,000,000 and goes bust.

❏   Financial Risk

This is the risk that arises when companies are highly geared. Suppose part of the Balance Sheet of C PLC showed:

(all figures in £'000)	
Share capital 20p shares	4,000
Profit and Loss Account	1,560
Loans at 15%	5,000

If profit before interest is £1,000,000 then interest takes £750,000 and the shareholders have a good dividend. But if the profit before interest is only £500,000 the company has lost £250,000 and may run into difficulty in paying its creditors.

Further if the company has to repay the loans it can only do so by borrowing a similar amount but it cannot do so if it is unprofitable.

Gearing confers benefits on a company that can earn business returns on capital greater than the interest paid on loans. But gearing can be very risky and even disastrous.

17. Not-for-profit enterprises and sources of finance

Investors invest their money in profit seeking companies in the hope of dividends and because they hope that the value of the companies and their investments will rise. There is no such incentive with not-for-profit enterprises and other sources of funding have to be discovered.

Borrowing is a major source of funding in both the profit seeking and not-for-profit sectors. Most of the sources of funds explored in this Unit apply to both and not-for-profit undertakings borrow on mortgage, bank loan and overdraft in much the same way as profit seeking businesses.

In practice not-for-profit enterprises are able to tap an immense variety of sources of money. These include:

Central Government	Grants	Gifts
Local Government	Fees	Legacies

Charities	Rents	The European Community
The National Lottery	Charges for services	Collections
Sales of property	Appeals	Trading
Fund raising activities	Supporters organisations	Sponsorship
Subscriptions	Entrance fees	Lotteries and draws
Covenants	Admission fees	Investment income

Examine the accounts of any not-for-profit enterprises you come across to see what sources they draw on.

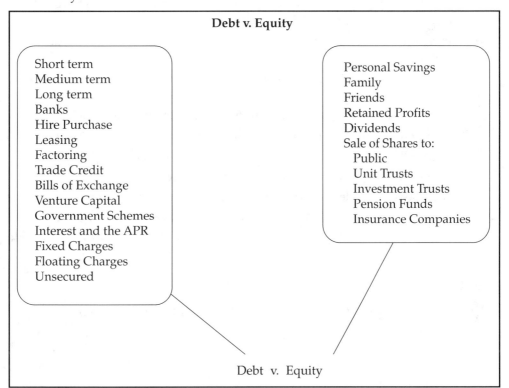

Debt v. Equity

Short term
Medium term
Long term
Banks
Hire Purchase
Leasing
Factoring
Trade Credit
Bills of Exchange
Venture Capital
Government Schemes
Interest and the APR
Fixed Charges
Floating Charges
Unsecured

Personal Savings
Family
Friends
Retained Profits
Dividends
Sale of Shares to:
  Public
  Unit Trusts
  Investment Trusts
  Pension Funds
  Insurance Companies

Debt v. Equity

18. Summary of Unit 16

❏ Expansion usually involves the acquisition of assets.

❏ Acquisition of assets usually means obtaining finance.

❏ Sources of finance can be internal. This means the owners putting up the money either from their private sources (if any) or from retained earnings.

❏ Other sources are external. These include relatives, friends, banks, HP companies, leasing companies, factoring companies, suppliers and venture capital companies.

❏ Some forms of finance are secured by fixed or floating charges or by operation of law (as HP).

❏ Interest rates vary from source to source depending on security and term.

❏ Interest rates may be fixed at the outset of the loan or vary during the period of the loan according to prevailing market rates.

❏ Repayment periods can be short, medium term or long term.

❏ Interest rates quoted can be misleading and it is important to recognise the APR.

❏ Companies finance themselves by a mixture of retained earnings, equity and debt.

❏ Retained earnings are the major source of company finance. Their cost is the higher dividends expected.

❏ Equity comprises the interest in the company of its owners, the shareholders. Equity arises from retained earnings and from new issues.

❏ Shares can be issued in exchange for businesses, companies or cash. New cash issues are nearly always rights issues.

❏ Preference shares pay fixed rates of dividend and are usually redeemable and cumulative.

❏ Trade credit, debt factoring and overdrafts are the principal forms of short-term debt.

❏ Hire purchase and leasing are common forms of medium-term debt.

❏ Long-terms loans are often called debentures, bonds, notes or other terms.

❏ Loans can be quoted.

❏ Loans can be convertible or have warrants attached.

❏ Gearing is desirable but too high gearing can be very dangerous.

❏ Financing and investment in productive assets can be seen as separate activities.

❏ Risk is implicit in company securities. Some securities are more risky than others.

❏ Companies exhibit business risk and financial risk.

Exercise 1

Financial Chicanery PLC have a Balance Sheet at 31 December 19x1 as:

(all figures in £'000)	£	£
Fixed Assets		
Land and Buildings		830
Plant etc		945
		1,775
Current Assets		
Stock	1,250	
Debtors	643	
	1,893	
Creditors: amounts falling due within one year		
Creditors	436	
Midwest Factors Ltd	583	
Bills Payable	120	
Bank Overdraft	371	
Obligations under leases	168	
Corporation Tax	124	

(all figures in £'000)	£	£
Dividends	60	
Taxation and Social Security	238	
Hire Purchase Commitments	89	
	2,189	
Net Current Liabilities		(296)
Total Assets less Current Liabilities		1,479
Creditors: amounts falling due after more than one year		
15% Unsecured Loan Stock 19x6-7	200	
11% Mortgage Debentures 20x4	600	
10% Convertible Loan Stock	100	
Floating Rate French Franc Loan 19x9	100	1,000
		479
Capital and Reserves		
Ordinary Share Capital (20p shares)		54
10% Cumulative Redeemable		
Preference Shares of £1 each		60
Share Premium Account		27
Capital Redemption Reserve		100
Profit and Loss Account		238
		479

Notes:

1. The bank overdraft is secured on a floating charge on all the assets.
2. The mortgage debentures are secured by a fixed charge on the freehold property.
3. The unsecured loan stock is redeemable at a premium of 10%

Required:

a. Assuming no interim dividends are paid, what rate of dividend is paid on the ordinary shares?

b. What was the original amount of preference shares issued, assuming all were issued at par?

c. All the ordinary shares were issued at one go and one price. What was the price?

d. What is the maximum dividend per share that the company could, in law, pay in addition to the dividend already proposed? Why could this not be paid in practice?

e. The company have agreed a maximum overdraft facility. Can you see how much this is?

f. If the company failed and the freehold property was sold for £550,000, would the mortgage debenture holders be paid in full?

g. The French Franc Loan is for 850,000 francs. What would happen to the loan if the pound fell against the franc?

h. The convertible loan is convertible into ordinary shares at a rate of 1 share for each £1 of stock in 19x7. If all the loan stock was converted what would be the amount in the Balance Sheet of:

   Convertible Loan Stock; Ordinary Shares; Share Premium?

i. How much interest does a holder of £100 nominal of the unsecured loan stock receive in a year and when will she be repaid the loan? How much will she receive?

j. List and explain all the sources of finance used by the company.

Exercise 2

The Balance Sheet of Simple Sid Ltd at 31 December 19x2 showed: (all figures in £'000)

Fixed Assets		
Premises		875
Plant etc		660
		1,535
Current Assets		
Stock	546	
Debtors	1,650	
Cash at Bank	132	
	2,328	
Creditors: amounts falling due within one year		
Creditors	430	
Dividends	100	
Corporation Tax	230	
Taxation and Social Security	134	
	894	
Net Current Assets		1,434
Total Assets less current Liabilities		2,969
Capital and Reserves		
Ordinary 20p shares		500
Share Premium		1,200
Profit and Loss Account		1,269
		2,969

Required:

a. Assuming no interim dividend is paid, what rate of dividend per share is paid?

b. The company originally started with 500,000 shares of 20p each issued at par. These shareholders were later given a bonus issue of one for one. Later still there was a rights issue. At what price were those shares sold for?

c. The company now wish to expand rapidly by acquiring new premises, vehicles and plant and doubling sales. The existing shareholders have no resources available for

new investment in the company but wish to retain control at least in the short term.
Review and suggest possible sources of finance for the expansion.

Exercise *3

Livy PLC have a summarised Balance Sheet as:
(all figures in £'000)
Fixed Assets

Freehold Premises at recent valuation		900
Plant etc		700
		1,600
Current Assets		
Stock	1,280	
Debtors	1,220	
	2,500	
Creditors: amounts falling due within one year		
6% Unsecured Loan Stock	1,000	
Bank Overdraft	940	
Creditors	860	
Corporation Tax	130	
Taxation and Social Security	178	
	3,108	
Net Current Liabilities		(608)
Total Assets less Current Liabilities		992
Capital and Reserves		
Share Capital: 10p shares		100
Profit and Loss Account		892
		992

Note that the bank overdraft is secured by a floating charge on all the company's assets.

Required:

a. Explain why you think the company is profitable.
b. Explain why the company did not propose a dividend.
c. The company have a financial problem. What is it?
d. The bank have indicated that they do not wish to advance any further sums to the company.

   Review possible sources of finance to allow the company to continue and prosper.
e. The company is listed on the stock exchange and its shares are quoted at 56p. Comment on this value.

Assignment 1

Orgkem Ltd sells special chemicals to industry. Some of these it imports, some are bought in the UK and some are made in the company's modern factory. It distributes the chemicals in its own vans in order to offer a very rapid service. Opportunities for expansion have occurred and the company is looking for finance for:

> an extension to the factory
>
> new plant
>
> new vehicles
>
> increased turnover

The company is owned by the extended Jones family who lack the resources to further finance the company. The directors are considering:

> leasing
>
> HP
>
> a mortgage
>
> bank loans and overdrafts
>
> factoring
>
> any other sources

Required:

a. Approach financing institutions to find out the terms of issue and the interest rates payable on the various sources of money available to the company.

b. Write a report to the directors reviewing the possible sources of finance.

Assignment 2

Fortune has been left a more than modest sum by an aunt. He wants to invest this in company securities.

Required:

a. Explore the rates of interest (both flat and redemption yield) offered by different types of company securities. This information can most easily obtained by consulting a stockbroker or your high street bank.

b. Write a report contrasting the risks and rewards of these different types of security and contrasting them with the risk and rewards offered by investing in High Street financial institutions.

Assignment 3

Scan the city pages of the newspapers for reference to borrowings, gearing, refinancing packages and the like.

Write a report on your findings incorporating information on why companies get themselves into difficulties and how they attempt to get out of them.

Assignment 4

Some extracts from the Profit and Loss Accounts of four companies and from their Balance Sheets are:

(all figures in £'000)	A	B	C	D
Profit before interest	5,560	3,240	6,400	8,100
Interest	360	2,950		3,600
Shareholders funds	21,000	8,000	32,000	24,000
12% Debentures	3,000	20,000	–	30,000

Required:

a. Comment on the interest paid by B

b. Comment on the risks borne by the debentureholders and the shareholders

c. Comment on the degree of gearing of each company

d. What might B do about its financial problem?

e. How might D raise more money for expansion?

Exercise 4

The Telford Industrial Museum has two acres of spare land. The trustees want to clear the land and use part of it as car park and part of it for a museum devoted to the history of the products of nearby local manufacturers. Suggest a wide variety of ways in which the project could be financed.

17 The Stock Exchange

1. Objectives

The **Stock Exchange** is a market where **investors** can buy and sell shares in companies and trade in other financial assets. It is essentially a **second hand market**. However companies can use the Exchange to raise money for development by selling new shares to investors but investors will only be willing to buy these shares when they know that a **secondary** (= second hand) market exists and that they can sell the shares again later to other investors.

This Unit is about the Stock Exchange and the advantages and disadvantages for a company of having its shares listed or quoted there. The Stock Exchange is important to Martin because of personal investment in quoted securities and because he is contemplating having his company **listed**. My readers may note that much information is available on listed companies. A reader may work for a listed company and will no doubt have business contact with many listed companies.

SCENARIO 1 — Martin reviews the future of his company

After ten years Martin Padlocks has become a relatively large company but Martin still has ambitions and sees many opportunities for further expansion. These include:

❐ Updating his plant, machinery and vehicles

❐ Buying premises where he currently rents

❐ Increasing sales of his current products

❐ Introducing new products and production lines

❐ Opening branches

❐ Increasing exports

❐ Acquiring existing businesses in order to:

   complement his own products

   eliminate competition

   acquire suppliers

   acquire customers.

Martin realises that all of this will require lots of money and that at the present time the company is short on money. He looks at his Balance Sheet:

(all figures in £'000)		
Fixed Assets		4,400
Current Assets		
Stock	3,580	
Debtors	2,560	
	6,140	

Creditors: amount falling due within one year		
Creditors	2,890	
Bank Overdraft	1,450	
Obligations under finance leases	450	
Factoring Companies	410	
Hire Purchase Commitments	120	
Corporation Tax	280	
Dividends	50	
Bills Payable	240	
	5,890	
Net Current Assets		250
Total assets less current liabilities		4,650
Creditors: amounts falling due after more than one year		
Bank Loans	700	
Mortgage Debenture		
Impressionable Assurance	800	1,500
		3,150
Capital and Reserves		
Share Capital (£1)		400
Share Premium		280
Profit and Loss Account		2,470
		3,150

Martin thinks about his Balance Sheet and remembers that:

❒ the fixed assets include property at a carrying value of £1,900,000 which is probably worth over £4 million.

❒ Martin and his wife and children own most of the shares but 40,000 shares are owned by an uncle who would like to sell them in order to buy a farm in Wales.

❒ The Mortgage is secured on a property and all the bank lending is secured by a floating charge on the assets.

Quick Answer Questions 17.1

1. Identify the forms of finance so far used by the company.
2. Calculate the net assets value of one ordinary share. One share is certainly worth much more than this. Explain why.
3. What privileges are available to the secured creditors?

SCENARIO 2 — Martin contemplates flotation

Martin reckons his shares must be worth at least £5 million and probably much more. However he feels that although he lives well and has some private assets he is unable to enjoy the fruits of his ten years hard work in building up the company. He has taken out of the company reasonable directors' remuneration and some dividends but much of the profit earned has been retained in the company.

He would like to:

❏ realise some of the capital which is tied up the company in order to buy a country estate he knows of that is going cheap.

❏ allow his uncle to buy the farm in Wales.

The company cannot give him or his uncle any cash as the company needs cash for expansion.

Anne mentions that flotation of his company on the stock exchange may allow all of these things to be done.

Task 1

Write a report on the ways that flotation may enable Martin to achieve all the ends that have been mentioned so far in this chapter.

---

2. Introduction

The stock exchange is a market. A market is a place where things are bought, sold and exchanged. The things traded on the stock exchange are financial securities and we will review these later in this chapter. Originally the stock exchanges were places in London and other cities, containing a floor where the actual trading took place.

Today trading is not done on the floor of the exchange but through the medium of electronic communications and especially the *computer screen*. The stock exchange is now a world wide market.

3. Investors

The most important people on the stock exchange are the investors. Investors are people and institutions who buy and sell financial securities. Several million people in the UK now invest through the stock exchange directly and nearly everybody invests through the stock exchange indirectly.

Private investors now account for a diminishing proportion of stock exchange investors but private investment has received a boost through the eighties due to the privatisation issues. People who never considered stock exchange investment now have shares in British Gas, British Telecom and the others. There is however a tendency for buyers of privatisation issues to hold these without further dealing. If they do sell there is a tendency for the shares to be sold to *institutions* so that the long term trend is still away from private shareholders towards institutional investors.

The principal institutional investors are:

Pension funds

Insurance companies

Unit trusts

Investment trusts

Large numbers of people in the UK are in occupational pension schemes. Pension schemes often work as:

Deductions are made from salaries and wages.

Contributions are made by the employer.

These two sums are handed by the company to pension fund trustees (who can be representatives of the company and unions).

The trustees invest these sums in securities or other investments using professional advice.

Pensions are paid as agreed.

The essential points are that pension fund investment outside the sponsoring company ensures that pensions are safe even if the sponsoring company fails. In general, pension fund investment is well done but occasional scandals occur such as the Maxwell and Daily Mirror pension fund disgrace. Pension fund investment is now megabillion.

Insurance companies receive premiums from their policyholders and invest them. At a later date claims will be met. This is true of accident insurance but the principal investment is from life assurance and pensions. Premiums on life assurance, endowment, personal pensions and other policies are collected by the assurance companies and invested. Payment on maturity, death or pensionable age may be decades later.

Unit trusts work like this:

❑ A management company forms a trust and appoints a trustee.

❑ The trustee is usually an institution such as a bank or insurance company. It holds the securities in safe custody.

❑ The management company advertise the units for sale and members of the public send in their money.

❑ The money is invested in securities and the whole portfolio is regarded as so many units.

❑ The value of each unit varies according to the value of the underlying portfolio.

❑ New units are sold to the public continuously and the money collected adds to the portfolio and the number of units it is divided into.

❑ Investors can sell their units back to the trust at the quoted rate. If more investors sell than buy then the trust will have to sell securities to fund the buying back from investors.

❑ Unit trust investment can be in shares generally or in specific sectors e.g. Fixed interest, high income shares, European shares, smaller companies etc.

❑ Units are sold to investors at the offer price and bought back at the bid price which is less.

❑ The advantages of unit trust investment are that they are professionally managed and a diversity or spread of investment is obtained.

❐ The disadvantages are that the management of the trust has to be rewarded with fees.

Unit trusts are very popular as a form of investment for the small investor. There are numerous management companies (including the high street banks) and thousands of unit trusts. Latest prices are given regularly in the newspapers.

Investment trusts are not trusts but limited companies whose business is investment in securities. The operation is:

❐ A company is formed (usually a plc);

❐ Shares in it are sold to the public in a public issue advertised in the press (only PLCs can do this);

❐ The sums collected from the shareholders are invested in securities or other investments (e.g. property);

❐ Investment trusts are permanent companies and invest for the long term although they do change their investments as they are professionally managed;

❐ Investment trust companies can borrow money (unlike unit trusts) and so can engage in gearing;

❐ Shareholders cannot recover their money from the company but can sell their shares to other investors as the shares are quoted on the stock exchange.

Investment trusts are a useful medium for investors as a shareholding in an investment trust is in effect an investment in a *diversified portfolio.*

4. Operators on the stock exchange

The principal operators on the stock exchange are the investors. Investors include private citizens like you and me and the institutions. Institutional investors are managed by *fund managers.*

When investors buy or sell securities on the stock exchange they actually buy or sell to *market makers.* A market maker is a firm that maintains a portfolio of specific securities and holds itself out as a dealer in those securities. Its profit comes from changes (which can be up or down) in the value of its portfolio and also from dealing as it buys from the investor at a lower price than it sells to the investor. The difference is known as the *turn.*

Investors do not deal direct with market makers but through stockbrokers who arrange the deals. Stockbroking firms are remunerated by *commissions.* Firms can offer various services as well as arranging deals for investors including advice and portfolio management. You can deal direct with a broker or deal with a firm through your bank. Firms can now be both market makers and brokers.

5. What is traded on the stock exchange?

The stock exchange provides a market for:

    Government securities

    Shares in companies

    Debentures and other securities of companies

    Overseas securities

    etc.

Government securities are usually called gilt-edged securities. An example of a gilt-edged security is $3\frac{1}{2}$ % War Loan. This was issued during the 1939-1945 war when £100 worth was sold to investors for £100. The holder of £100 worth will receive £3.50 a year in interest for ever. As this is an *undated stock* the *capital* is not likely to be repaid. £100 worth of the stock is being bought and sold at the date of writing at about £42. As a result an investor who has held the stock since the war has made a *money* loss and a much greater *real* loss on the stock. The reason why it sells at 42 is that at that price its *yield* is:

$$\frac{£3.5}{£42} \times 100 = 8.3\%$$

and that is the going rate of interest on this relatively risk free security.

Another gilt-edged security is Treasury $13\frac{1}{4}$ % 1997. £100 worth of this stock pays £13.25 annual interest and will be redeemed at par in 1997. This is known as a short as it will be repaid in less than five years from 1995, the time of writing. The stock is quoted at about £109 so the yield on this stock appears to be:

$$\frac{£13.25}{£109} \times 100 = 12.1\%$$

However investment in 1992 is £109 and repayment in 1997 will be only £100. Taking this into account the redemption yield is actually 7.63% which is much the same as the war loan.

There are billions of pounds of gilt-edged securities and new ones are issued from time to time to fund the public sector borrowing requirement which is the difference between the amount spent by government and the amount raised in taxation.

Shares in companies offer investors an exciting medium of investment and many people enjoy much pleasure in receiving dividends and seeing how the quoted price of their investment has risen. Conversely, a company may pass (= omit) its dividend and the share value may go down and the company may go into liquidation.

Other company securities listed on the stock exchange include preference shares, loan stocks, convertible loan stocks and warrants.

Some overseas company shares are quoted and some foreign government stocks. Investors can buy these stocks directly or through the medium of unit or investment trusts. Direct investment through foreign stock exchanges is also possible.

6. Other forms of investment

There are an enormous range of investments available for investors including:

Securities listed on the stock exchange

Unit Trusts

Life assurance

Pension schemes

National Savings

Deposits in Building Societies and Banks

Property (including the home)

Chattels (including stamps, antiques etc)

The best form of investment for a particular person depends on many factors and professional advice should be sought if more than a simple bank or building society deposit is contemplated. The choices are usually between:

Income and capital growth

High risk and low risk

Shares in companies generally offer low income (gross yield on ICI is about 5%) and fixed interest securities like gilt-edged stocks yield higher income. However shares offer a chance of *capital gains* and fixed interest securities generally do not.

Investing in shares offers some risk of loss. This is less in *blue chip* shares. Blue chip shares are those in large reputable well established companies like ICI and Unilever. Investing in National Savings offers little risk of loss. In general the higher the risk, the higher the yield and vice versa.

7. Primary and secondary markets

The exchange also acts as a primary market. This refers to the sale of securities to the public by a company or other institution (including the government) raising new money from investors. New issues can be:

new shares in companies

new gilt edged or local authority stocks

existing shares sold by a single or a few investors.

Many issues appear to be issues of new shares in a company but are in fact sales by one or more investors. As an example, the sale of the privatisation issues have been the sale by one investor (the government) of existing shares to the public.

New issues can be sold by:

a prospectus issue

an offer for sale

a placing.

A prospectus is an advertisement offering the shares for sale. A prospectus must be in the form required by the Companies Act and the Stock Exchange. It contains an amazing amount of detail.

An offer for sale is similar and also involves a prospectus. However an offer for sale comprises the sale of the shares firstly to an issuing house (a bank or a stock exchange firm) and it is the issuing house which offers the shares for sale to the public.

A placing is usually a relatively small issue and the securities are placed with (= sold to) the clients of a stock exchange firm. The firm also make some available to interested members of the public.

8. Alternative Investment Market

The main market for quoted companies is the Stock Exchange. Before being listed on the Stock Exchange a company has to satisfy numerous criteria about length of time it has traded, size, financial performance and prospects and immense amounts of data have to be disclosed. However, the Stock Exchange also run a sort of second division listing called the Alternative Investment Market, usually abbreviated to the AIM. The criteria for achieving listed status on the AIM are fewer and easier and many newer, smaller or more speculative companies are listed on the AIM. Nearly 300 companies are currently listed on the AIM and similar information about current share prices, yield and price/earnings ratios is given regularly in the press. Investment advisers generally see AIM companies as more risky than those listed on the Stock Exchange proper but your author does not entirely agree with this view.

9. Benefits and drawbacks of flotation

Businesses are started by one or a few people with an idea and a little capital usually supplemented by family and bank loans. Initially the legal form of the enterprise is sole trading, a partnership, or like Martin Padlocks Ltd as a small private limited company. The main advantage of trading as a company is limited liability. If the company goes bust the owners do not go bust with it unless they have guaranteed the bank overdraft in which case their liability extends as far as having to repay the bank. The shareholders in a company do not usually have any liability to pay the company's creditors. Taxation advantages are minimal unless very large profits are earned and trading as a company has disadvantages in terms of taxation and strict regulation under the Companies Act.

Most businesses either fail or remain small. However some grow and become large enough to seek quoted status on the stock exchange. There are some advantages in this:

a) The shareholders can sell some or all of their shares to investors

b) The company has access to finance

c) The company can finance the takeover of other companies (see later)

d) The company will have a larger public profile

e) The company can reward and motivate its employees with share option schemes.

The main disadvantages are:

a) Requirements to keep investors and the Stock Exchange informed of all significant developments

b) The need to maintain performance and make dividend payments

c) Vulnerability to takeover.

Nonetheless flotation offers a company substantial benefits and brings with it prestige both for the company and for its directors.

10. Procedures for flotation

Suppose Adam Ltd, a dealer in widgets has reached a size which is large enough to seek a listing on the Stock Exchange. The company has 12 shareholders, all members of the Eden family. The company is currently divided into 10,000 share of £1 each. Procedures might be:

a) Make a bonus issue of 39 new shares for each share held. There will now be 400,000 shares.

b) Split each share into 10 shares of 10p each. There will now be 4 million shares.

c) Create 3 million new shares.

d) Sell shares to the public by an Offer for Sale at £1.30p each.

The shares to be sold will be:

all the new shares

30% of the existing shareholders' shares.

You may be able to calculate that:

i)   The company will gain £3,900,000 from the sale of the new shares.

ii) Eve Eden who held 1,200 shares in the company will gain £187,200 and still hold 336,000 shares worth £436,800.

iii) The original shareholders still own 2,800,000 shares out of 7,000,000 — 40%.

11. Takeovers

A feature of the Stock Exchange is the extent of takeovers of companies by other companies. Suppose Adam PLC has now been trading as a listed company for two years and its shares are now quoted at £2.00. It would like to buy Abel Ltd from its existing shareholders. Adam has agreed to buy the 20,000 shares at £30 each — a total of £600,000. It can pay for the shares in several ways:

a)   Pay cash — this is possible only if Adam PLC have cash or can borrow it. Abel's shareholders may not like cash as they will have to pay capital gains tax.

b)   Create 300,000 new shares in Adam PLC and issue these to the shareholders of Abel. The Balance Sheet of Adam will change by:

adding an asset — investment in Abel Ltd £600,000 — to its net assets

adding: Share Capital 300,000 × 10p   = £30,000

Share Premium 300,000 × £1.90   = £570,000

to the Capital and Reserves.

c)   Creating and issuing loan stock or, more likely, convertible loan stock in Adam PLC to Abel's shareholders.

You will realise that it is possible to issue shares or loan stock as a consideration instead of cash.

It is possible for a large company (often a sluggish one) to be taken over by a small one (usually a thrusting one). This is achieved by the large company creating and issuing new shares to the shareholders in the small one (as with Adam and Abel) such that the old shareholders in the small company have a commanding holding in the large company. Commanding can be 10% or more if the shares in the large companies are diversely held. This is called a reverse takeover as the reality is the taking over of the large by the small whereas the appearance is the reverse.

12. Insider dealing

Much money can be made on the stock exchange by dealing in shares as the prices of shares go up or down as new information becomes available. For example Wulfrun Airlines PLC moved down from 340p a share to 315p a share on news that the price of aviation fuel had risen 20%. A person who has advance news of price-sensitive information can make money. For example Mary works for Stubby PLC and attends a Board Meeting at which the Board agree to make a bid for Adam PLC. Mary left the meeting and rang her Broker to buy some shares in Adam before the news was announced to the public and the price of Adam shares rose.

Mary is an insider in that she is privilege to price sensitive information about Adam PLC before it is known by the investing public at large. Insider dealing is illegal.

13. Bulls, bears and stags

The stock exchange contains many mythical animals including:

Bulls are optimistic investors who buy shares in the expectation of a rise in price. Bears are pessimistic. A bear investor will sell shares in the expectation of a fall in price.

Stags are investors who deal in new issues. The idea is that new issues are often over-subscribed. For example 1,000,000 shares may be offered and ten times that number may be subscribed for by the public. If this happens, the available shares are allocated by some fair process which discriminates in favour of the subscriber for small numbers. If a stag gets an allocation, he will rapidly sell them and make a profit as the price will go to a premium over the issue price as demand clearly exceeded supply.

SCENARIO 3 — Martin values a company

Martin consults a member of the Stock Exchange who tells him that she could arrange a flotation on the Alternative Investment Market. A vital consideration would of course be the price at which the shares could be sold to investors.

The broker suggests that the price would mostly depend on the profits earned by the company and perhaps by the dividends paid.

Martin looks up a number of companies quoted on the AIM and finds that PE ratios in his sector average about 12 and that dividend yields average about 4%.

He notes that his Profit and Loss Account shows:

Net Profit after tax	£650,000
Dividends (interim and final)	£70,000
Retained	£580,000

Quick Answer Questions 17.2

1. What is the company worth if it can be sold at a Price Earnings Ratio of 12?
2. What is the company worth if the company is valued by reference to the dividend yield?
3. Can you account for the discrepancy between the two values?

SCENARIO 4 — Martin considers floating the company

Martin feels that he would like to float the company and with this in mind a procedure like this is proposed:

i.   Split the 400,000 £1 shares into 4,000,000 shares of 10p each
ii. Create 2,000,000 new 10p shares
iii. Sell to the public 3,000,000 shares at £1.80 each

   The shares to be sold will be:

The 2,000,000 new shares

400,000 shares owned by Martin's uncle

600,000 shares owned by Martin

Tasks 2

1. Calculate:
   a. How much money the offer for sale to the public will raise if all the shares are sold.
   b. How much money will go to the company.
   c. How much money will go to Martin.
   d. How much money will go to his uncle.
   e. What proportion of the shares will remain in the hands of the original shareholders.
2. Describe the benefits that the company will enjoy as a listed company.
3. Describe the disadvantages that a listing will bring to:
   a. Martin
   b. the company.
4. Who would buy the shares in Martin Padlocks PLC?

SCENARIO 5 — Martin launches a take-over

Martin successfully floats his company and the shares settle down at a price fluctuating around £2. Martin is introduced to the principal shareholder, Gordon Oldee, in a private company Goldee Locks Ltd and he agrees that Martin Padlocks PLC will takeover the company for a consideration of £600,000. This agreement was made of course after due investigation by Anne and other professionals.

The problem that arises is the nature of the consideration. Three possibilities are considered:

1. Cash
2. 300,000 new shares in Martin Padlocks PLC
3. £600,000 convertible loan stock.

Cash is undesirable as it will involve Oldee in paying lots of capital gains tax.

The convertible loan stock will carry a coupon of 8% and be redeemable at a premium of 10% in 10 years time. The stock will be convertible at a rate of 40 shares for each £100 of stock at any time after 5 years from the date of issue.

Tasks 3

1. Discuss the advantages and disadvantages to Oldee of selling his company and of each form of consideration. He will be given a one year contract as an adviser after the sale at a reasonable salary and thereafter will leave the group.

2. Discuss the effect on Martin personally if Martin Padlocks PLC took over the private company of Ted Keen of which Ted owns 98% of the shares. The consideration is £15,000,000 to be settled entirely in ordinary shares in Martin Padlocks PLC.

SCENARIO 6 — Martin invests his money

Martin finds that he has received a very large amount of money from the flotation of his company. He has firstly to pay some capital gains tax but then realises that he needs to invest the rest. His income is large so he is mainly interested in capital gains to preserve and enhance his estate which will descend to his children and grandchildren.

Task 4

List possible investments and evaluate each from the point of view of capital growth in preference to income.

SCENARIO 7 — Martin encounters insider trading

Some of the shares in Martin Padlock were bought by the company's general sales manager Harold Sligh. Sligh is an excellent salesman and is able to secure a megadeal selling secure door locks to 5 motor car manufacturers at a very good price. Before telling the Board the good news he rings his widowed aunt Mary and asks her to buy, in her name, 200,000 shares in Martin Padlocks PLC. As soon as the Board hear of the deal they make a public announcement of the deal through the Stock Exchange and the price of the shares rises from £2 to £2.40.

Task 5

Comment on this scenario. Would you behave like Sligh? Who suffers from his crime?

14. Real investment

Students of finance are strongly advised to become real investors. Investing involves the student in the real world of investment and with the mechanisms and paperwork of the stock exchange. There is of course a risk of loss but also a chance of gain. Many people seek out companies which give concessions to shareholders. I myself have enjoyed many years of half price channel crossings thanks to a modest investment in P and O.

15. Individual Savings Accounts

UK residents have been entitled in recent years to invest some of their savings in Personal Equity Plans (PEPs). These had tax advantages in that any dividends and capital gains on PEP investments were entirely free of tax providing the rules were obeyed. These PEPs have proved enormously popular and have been heavily advertised in the press. However from April 1999 both PEPs and TESSAs are to be replaced by Individual Savings Accounts (ISAs).

The regulations on these had not been finalised at the time of writing, but they will include regulations on charges by the financial service company which must have a 1% or less annual fee and no initial charge. Essentially ISAs must be for the benefit of investors, rather than for the enrichment of the financial services industry, as charges must be reasonable, access must be for all (not just the rich) and terms must be fair and clear.

16. A world wide market

Investment in shares and other company securities by UK investors was at one time more or less confined to UK companies. The stock exchange was a fair market with a wide variety of companies and substantial activity. UK investors have been well served by the Stock Exchange and few shares have such a thin market that buying or selling is difficult. A similar situation has prevailed in many foreign stock exchanges notably those in the USA. As a result many sophisticated investors have spread their portfolios across the world. This is both more exciting and probably safer as a wide spread of geographical investment will mean that while one area droops others will prosper.

Investment in non UK securities is now open to all through Unit Trusts and Investment Trusts and direct investment is possible. New stock exchanges are opening in the former Eastern Bloc countries and my readers may care to watch the future of stock exchange investment with wonder and perhaps profit.

17. Share prices

Share prices change frequently, even minute by minute. I noted that Tesco shares had a low in a period of twelve months of 207p and high of 299p. What causes a share price to change? The first reason is that the market in general changes. An announcement is made that the trade gap is twice as bad as expected and all shares tend to move down. This tendency of the whole market to move can be seen in the indeces such as the Financial Times Ordinary Share Index. In addition an individual share may change price due to factors intrinsic to the share. This may be a change of market sentiment about the share or its sector. For example the announcement of a road building programme may push up the shares of construction companies. The change may also come about as a result of new information. For example the announcement that profits were less than expected will depress a share price.

Is it possible to predict share price changes? There is a theory called the *efficient market hypothesis* which suggests not. This theory states that the market is efficient in setting prices. The implication of this is that shares are neither underpriced nor overpriced. In effect the price of a share is the market consensus of what its price should be. In practice the market is not perfectly efficient and academic argument usually centres around the degree of efficiency. Another form of the hypothesis is that a share price reflects all available, relevant information. The implication of this is that any new information which bears on the firm will be instantly incorporated into the price of the share. For example the price will change if the firm announces it is negotiating to buy a competitor or if the half year's profits are less than expected. The hypothesis has three levels of efficiency:

a. The *weak* form — this implies that any information which might be contained in past price movements is already reflected in security prices. This strange idea comes as a refutation of the ideas of chartists. Chartists draw charts of the price of a share over time and might produce something like this.

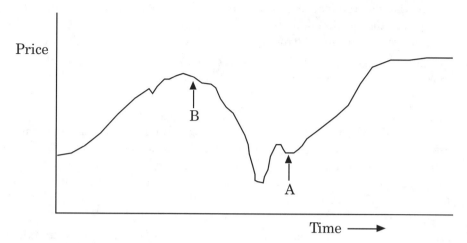

They then predict that in the future there will be similar patterns of movement, allowing perhaps the share to be bought when it is at a similar position to A and sold when it is in a similar position to B and thus making a profit. The logic of this idea is easily refuted and statistical tests show that movements in share prices are randomly distributed and cannot be predicted. Punters always tell you of their gains and never of their losses!

b.   The *semi-strong* form — this implies that all publicly available information is encompassed in the share price. So it is pointless looking through endless Annual Reports and Accounts looking for undervalued shares. Despite this most intelligent investors believe with all their hearts that they can find undervalued shares but doubt with all their minds! Stock exchange firms employ researchers to look into companies and assess their worth as investment. In effect this research process is aimed at finding undervalued shares but by so doing ensures that shares are not undervalued.

c.   The *strong* form — if this is true then all information, publicly available or not, would be incorporated in the share price. Insiders who are privilege to information not made available to the public (for example knowledge of the intention to make a takeover bid or of the results before they are announced) could not make a profit if this form is true. The general feeling is that insiders can make a profit although to do so is illegal. However an interesting piece of logical thinking is that if several *insiders* have secret information they will buy or sell and thus incorporate the information in the price by creating demand or supply.

18. Capital asset pricing model

If an investor wishes to invest in equities what should he do? Try and follow the following bit of logic:

a.   an investor, in investing in a particular share takes two risks:

❒   the risk intrinsic to that share, for example, that profits will fall more than expected or that the managing director will have an aeroplane accident. Such events will probably change the share price but are unpredictable.

☐ the risk that the market as a whole will rise or fall due to unpredictable events such as the election of a liberal democrat government or an increase in interest rates. All shares tend to move to a greater or less extent with the market.

b. The intrinsic risk can be avoided by investing in a range of shares. Ideally the whole market should be invested in but as this is impossible about a dozen shares is considered reasonable.

c. The market risk cannot be avoided. However each share has a unique reaction to movements of the whole market. Some move more than the market because they are especially prone to changes in the whole economy (e.g. housebuilders) and some move less because they deal in necessities (e.g. food processors). It is possible to use statistical means to find the degree of *correlation* of a share with the market movements. The degree of correlation is called the Beta and Betas for all quoted companies are published by the London Business School.

d. An investor can thus avoid intrinsic risk by *diversifying* and select the degree of exposure to market risk he requires by selecting companies with the appropriate Betas. Risk averse investors will select low Betas and risk seekers will choose high Beta companies.

The use of Betas is part of a theory called the Capital Asset Pricing model.

The CAPM is also used in capital investment appraisal. Projects which do not change the company's Beta should be discounted at the cost of capital which already includes the effect of Beta. Projects which change the company's Beta should be discounted differently. This is beyond the scope of this book and indeed nearly all financial directors!

19. Crest

Until 1996, holders of shares in companies had their names registered in the company's share register and consequently received the company's Annual Report and financial statements. Shareholders also had share certificates issued by the company. From 1996, a new computerised system, called Crest, came into use. This system is used for settling sales and purchases of shares. Its use is *optional and voluntary* but its use or non-use may have cost implications for investors. Please enquire on this from your broker. The idea of Crest is that the record of your shareholdings is held in electronic form by Crest instead of by share certificates. The advantages of this are greater security (you cannot lose your share certificates) and ease of transfer as there is no costly and time consuming sending of certificates through the post. Private investors can use Crest in two ways:

a. Sponsored membership whereby you are personally registered with Crest and your holdings are registered with the companies you hold shares in. You receive the Annual Report but have the advantages of electronic transfer of share ownership. You will need a sponsor (a broker or other intermediary) to operate your membership of Crest on your behalf. This arrangement will be for the larger investor who deals relatively frequently.

b. Holding your shares through a nominee company. Your shares are held by a nominee company (your broker or banker) which is a member of Crest. You are not directly a member of the company. It should be possible to ensure that you still receive the Annual Report and any perks available to shareholders. The company and the broker should operate in accordance with the ProShare Nominee Code.

20. Summary of Unit 17

❐ The Stock Exchange is a second hand market for shares and other securities. It is also a market where companies can raise money from investors who know they can sell the new shares to other investors because there is a secondary market.

❐ Expansion as a private company is limited by limitations in finance availability.

❐ Flotation as a listed company makes finance available to a company and also makes money available to individual shareholders.

❐ The value of a private company can be assessed in many ways including by reference to its net assets value, its earnings and its dividends. The most usable data in a flotation is an assessment of future earnings.

❐ Being a listed company gives advantages including access to capital and the ability to offer shares as a consideration in a takeover.

❐ Disadvantages include being in the public eye, having to maintain profits and dividends, and fear of takeover.

❐ Consideration in takeovers can be cash, shares or convertible loans or a combination of these.

❐ Insider trading is common, immoral and illegal. It is sometimes called a victimless crime and may have economic justification in bringing about a true and fair value for the share.

❐ Individual investors have an immense choice for investing their savings. Each type of investment can be characterised by the risks attached and the returns expected.

❐ The stock exchange is a market for financial securities.

❐ Investors can be individuals or institutions.

❐ The principal investing institutions are pension funds, insurance companies, unit trusts and investment trust companies.

❐ The principal players on the stock exchange are investors, market makers and brokers.

❐ The stock exchange provides a market for the securities of the government, foreign governments, local authorities and public companies whose shares are quoted (= listed).

❐ Securities can usually offer above average income or capital growth but not both.

❐ Higher returns (income and capital gains) usually accompanies higher risk.

❐ The stock exchange is primarily a secondary market but new issues are made. These can be of new securities or previously owned securities.

❐ New issues can be sold by prospectus issue, offer for sale or a placing.

- ❏ Bulls are optimistic, bears are pessimistic, and stags hope for a quick capital gain on new issues.
- ❏ Takeovers and mergers are a feature of British financial life.
- ❏ Insider dealing is profitable but illegal.
- ❏ Flotation has advantages and disadvantages.
- ❏ Students may like to engage in real investment on the Stock Exchange.
- ❏ PEPs are very popular.
- ❏ Share prices may be subject to the Efficient Market Hypothesis.
- ❏ The Capital Asset Pricing Model is a somewhat speculative but very elegant idea.

Exercise 1

David is a manager with a major company and his wife is a primary school head. They have a house with an endowment mortgage and both have life assurance. Both are averse to gambling and would not dream of investing in the stock exchange which they see as a casino.

Comment on this scenario.

Exercise 2

Freda invested some £10,000 in 5,000 units of Infinite Life's Smaller Companies Unit Trust. She notices that these have a bid price of 154.7p and an offer price of 166.2p. She reads in the paper that this is one of the best performing unit trusts in the sector.

Explain this statement to Freda and also to Joan who is thinking of buying some units.

Exercise *3

Lee is considering putting all his savings which he has in a building society into an investment trust. He has selected the Pacific and Oriental Trust PLC which specialises in Pacific Basin companies. In the Telegraph he finds that the company is quoted at 192 and has net assets per share of 217. Yield is 0.9% and high and low in the past year are 221 and 158.

Required:

a. Explain all this.

b. Do you think this is a suitable investment for Lee if:

   i.   He is married and 61 and retires soon with a very small pension

   or

   ii. He is unemployed, disabled and has a wife and three children.

   iii. He is married with no children, aged 52 and has a very large salary with a brewery.

Exercise 4

Louie invested £50,000 in £46,000 nominal of Treasury $12\frac{3}{4}$% 19x6 three years ago. It is now 19x1.

She sees in the Times that the stock has an entry as:

19x0/19x1		Price	+/–	Interest	Gross
High	Low			yield % yield	Redemption
111	105	$109\frac{3}{16}$	$+\frac{1}{32}$	11.68	9.54

Explain all this to her. Has this been a good investment?

Exercise 5

Doddery inherited some £12,000 of $3\frac{1}{2}$% War loan from his grandfather. This has a high/low of 38 and 33, a quotation of $37\frac{5}{8}$, and a yield of 9.3%. There is no gross redemption yield given.

Explain all this. Do you consider this to be a great fraud on the part of the British Government?

Exercise 6

Tweed has some shares in a building company and a supermarket group. Data are

19x1/19x2		Company	Price	+/–	Net	Yield	P/E
High	Low		(p)		Div	%	
256	123	AB Constr	123	...	11.2	12.2	14.1
280	200	CD Stores	245	+ 2	5.2	2.9	14.4

Explain all this to Tweed.

Can you explain the disparity in statistics given that at the time he read these statistics there was a very deep depression especially in the building trade. Supermarkets were doing comparatively well.

Exercise *7

Judy has £2,000 Nominal of 8% convertible loan stock 19x9 in EF PLC. The stock is convertible into 20p ordinary shares of the company at the 50 shares per £100 of stock. Conversion dates are all of August in all years 19x3 to 19x7. The current price (19x2) of a 20p share is 120p. The stock is quoted at 86.

Comment on:

a. the future possibilities of this investment.

b. the price of 86.

Exercise 8

Tell has £100,000 in cash, inherited from his mother. He is considering investing it in one of:

a seaside cottage

a building society

shares in ICI

antiques.

Discuss what are the benefits and drawbacks of each.

Assignment 1

Cringe Ltd make and supply a range of widgets from their freehold factory on a trading estate in Walsall. They also have a number of warehouses round the country. Most of these are also freehold or on long leases. The company is very profitable but most of the profits have been retained in the company for expansion. Current profits are in the region of £4 million a year before tax but dividends are only £10 a share.

The share capital is held by a small number of people:

Jack Cringe (56)	3,000
Mrs Cringe (54)	2,000
Albert Cringe (Jack's father)	2,000
The Cringe Foundation	3,000

Jack is still very ambitious and wants to expand much further, including building a new factory and moving into Europe. He also wants to buy a country estate as his hobby is pheasant shooting.

Mrs Cringe wishes to support her husband but she also wants some money to finance her son-in-law's new venture into film production.

Albert is a life long Methodist and has an ambition to donate a very large sum to build a replacement for his crumbling local Church.

The Cringe foundation was set up with the shares left by Jack's son who died of Ping's disease. The ultimate aim is to finance research into the disease.

Jack has seen an opportunity to acquire three companies:

Pierre Widgettes — a French company which has a widget distribution chain throughout Europe. The owners will sell but require cash.

Flounce Ltd — a local company which provides a complementary range of widgets. The owners would like to throw in their lot with Cringe and Jack is willing to make Phil Flounce a director of a combined group. However Flounce is advised by his accountants not to accept shares in a private company as consideration for his company.

Rhubarb Widgets PLC — this is an old established company which has made losses in recent years. To stem the losses the company has sold properties and now is cash rich but is still making losses. The shares are quoted in the penny share category. It needs new blood in the management team.

Required:

Write a report to Jack explaining how the ambitions of all the parties mentioned might be met if Cringe Ltd were to obtain a listing on the stock exchange. You should include a section on how the issue price should be calculated and any alternative way of seeking quoted status that may be possible.

Assignment 2

Note this assignment is best done by a number of students but can be written up individually for personal assessment.

Each student is given a paper sum of £10,000 and asked to 'invest' it a portfolio of shares. Possible portfolios are:

i.   A single blue chip company.

ii.   12 companies with low PEs

iii. 12 companies with high PEs

iv.   12 companies with low dividend yields

v.   12 companies with high dividend yields

vi.   12 companies with low dividend cover

vii. 12 companies with high dividend cover

viii. 12 investment trusts

ix.   a single investment trust

x.   a single unit trust

xi.   12 unit trusts

xii   12 companies recommended in the financial press

xiii. 12 AIM companies

No doubt other possible portfolios will occur to teachers and students.

Record the progress of the portfolio over a period of time. Dividends will need to be included in gains as these will vary from portfolio to portfolio. Contrast the progress of each portfolio with the indeces.

Write a report on findings and put forward any theory that may suggest itself from the figures.

Assignment 3

Find out the rules as to how much can be invested in ISAs. Critically review a number of ISAs advertised especially in respect of initial charges, annual fees, access for all and fair statement of terms. Consider who might invest in them.

Exercise 9

Examine the city pages of the serious newspapers and see their coverage of overseas stock exchanges. Note details of any indeces given for these markets and note how they change over time and in relation to the UK and other market indeces.

Exercise 10

Danielle is drinking in the Pub one Sunday morning and expresses a need for advice on which shares to buy:

Len works for a major PLC and has seen in his horoscope that he will prosper in his work. This seems a good reason to him to buy shares in his employer.

Den subscribes to a journal which recommends penny shares. They never fail he says and suggests she buys shares in this month's recommendation.

Ken has seen a chart which suggests that Wen PLC's share price is at the same position on the chart that it was in two years ago before it rose 20%.

Penny operates a system where she buys and sells Mega PLC. She buys when the price is 10% below her 'norm price'. She sells when it is 10% above. Made a fortune she says. She bought some yesterday.

Xen says that his broker recommends MacroBig PLC which the firm's researchers find to be undervalued.

Yen suggests buying Whopper Construction PLC as he notes that they have just landed a big contract to build the new motorway.

Ben who works for a merchant bank and has drunk too much whispers that he has heard in his office that F.M.Errall PLC are going to be subject to a takeover bid that week.

Hen advises her to invest her money in equal amounts in twelve different companies and hold for the long term.

Comment on all these ideas.

Exercise 11

Kate has 10,000 shares in Mediocre PLC which she bought for 96p each. She has seen the share price rise over the last three months from 120 to 160. Then the company receive a takeover bid from Superior PLC. Superior are offering four shares in Superior for 6 shares in Mediocre.

She notes in the FT that the news has caused Mediocre's price to rise to 180 and Superior's to fall from 250p to 235p.

Explain what might be happening.

Exercise 12

Eric and Paul are partners in a firm of insurance brokers. They have done well and both now have some funds that they wish to invest in shares for the long term. Eric is a very solid, cautious person. Paul is a born gambler. How might information on company betas be useful to them?

Exercise 13

You are considering investing in units of the European Growth Trust managed by Harbridge Fund Managers Ltd. You see that the selling price is £53.88 and the buying price is £57.55.

You discover that the trust deed allows management charges of:

a. a preliminary charge of 5% which is included in the offer price of the units and that the manager will pay a maximum commission of 3% to authorised intermediaries

b. an annual charge not exceeding $1\frac{1}{2}$ % of the value of the trust.

Required:

Explain all these things, discuss the size and appropriateness of the charges, consider whether or not this trust may be a good short-term or long-term investment for you.

18 Accounting in the not-for-profit sector

1. Objectives

Martin's company manufactures and trades and, so far, it has made profits. Profit making is not its only goal but it is clearly the principal objective. The alternative to profit is loss and losses eventually lead to extinction! Increasingly, employment in advanced countries is in activities that have no intention to make a profit. These activities include central and local government services, the health service, education, charities, clubs and societies. While a profit is not an aim of these enterprises, it is essential that in the long term, income should cover expenditure. This lesson is being learnt by the staffs of hospitals, schools, charities hit by lower donations caused by the success of the national Lottery and many other organisations.

This Unit looks at accounting in the not-for profit sector. The sector produces financial statements in the same way as profit seeking businesses but these have some differences which we will investigate. In addition, the sector have to make decisions and use management accounting as one of the inputs to the decision making process.

SCENARIO 1 — Martin encounters some club accounts

Martin is a keen hockey and tennis player and is a member of the Sheinton Hockey and Tennis Club. He has never taken much interest in the finances of his club but takes an interest when he is asked for an increased subscription and an interest free loan to help finance some new developments. He looks up the latest financial statements and finds:

Sheinton Hockey and Tennis Club

Income and Expenditure Account for the year ending 31 December 19x9

	19x8	19x9	Budget
Income	£	£	£
Profit on bar	6,400	6,200	7,000
Profit on discos	5,200	5,100	5,500
Subscriptions	9,670	11,100	13,600
Profit on Catering	987	1,205	900
	22,257	23,605	
Deficit for year	2,115	2,401	
	24,372	26,006	

	19x8	19x9	Budget
Expenditure	£	£	
Wages	12,800	13,600	15,000
Insurances	2,220	2,490	2,500
Water rates	730	760	800
Depreciation of equipment	1,120	1,120	1,430

	19x8	19x9	Budget
Expenditure	£	£	
Stationery and sundries	470	540	550
Loss on sale of clothing	302	632	120
Consumables	1,950	1,870	2,000
Repairs to building	2,400	2,200	1,600
Professional charges	760	860	900
Heat and Light	1,620	1,934	2,100
	24,372	26,006	

Balance Sheet as at 31 December 19x9

Accumulated Fund	46,666	Land and buildings at cost	50,000
Sundry creditors	3,760	Equipment at book value	3,280
Subscriptions in advance	2,100	Stock of consumables	439
		Bar stock	2,864
Prize fund	4,600	Cash at bank	543
	57,126		57,126

Quick Answer Questions 18.1

1. How many words can you recognise?
2. Did the Club make a 'profit' in 19x9?
3. Does the Club depreciate the land or buildings?

SCENARIO 2 — Martin reviews the club accounts

Martin meets the treasurer of the club in the bar and asks for some explanation of the items in the financial statements.

Tasks 1

1. List the items in the financial statements for which you think some explanation and enlargement of detail is required.
2. Comment on the differences between 19x8, 19x9 and the budget for next year.

SCENARIO 3 — Martin reviews the club budget

The treasurer gives Martin some explanations:

a. The Profit and Loss Account of a Club is called the Income and Expenditure account.

b. The bar profit is calculated as:

	19x8	19x9	Budget
Sales	30,500	30,900	30,900
Gross profit	10,200	9,400	9,400
Wages and sundries	3,800	3,200	2,400

The treasurer is a rather timid banker and tells Martin that he thinks that the bar committee are afraid to pass on increased prices from suppliers for fear of adverse member reaction to rising prices. Wages have been held down by using volunteer member labour and low paid students.

c. Discos are very profitable but unpopular with members.

d. There are only three categories of members - full members, under 21 members and life members. Life members pay a subscription at the beginning of membership and pay no more after that. Such subscriptions are taken straight to Income and Expenditure Account.

e. Catering consists in providing teas for team members and visiting teams and charging the team members.

f. Wages are for part timers involved in grounds maintenance, caretaking and property repair.

g. Equipment is depreciated over five years straight line.

h. Sports clothing is sold to members at cost + 5%. Some is not sold and has to be sold off cheaply or is scrapped.

j. Consumables are items like hockey balls and tennis nets.

k. The building requires a lot of repair and maintenance. The committee are proposing to give it a major refit, if money can be raised, which will save on repairs.

l. The prize fund came from a legacy many years ago. A small amount of money is charged to the fund each year when the prizes for the tennis tournament are purchased.

Tasks 2

1. Does the budget for next year indicate that a surplus will be achieved?

2. Comment on and provide a convincing explanation for:
   - ❐ the budget for bar profit
   - ❐ the budget for profit on discos
   - ❐ the budget for subscriptions
   - ❐ the profit on catering.

3. Do you think that the building should be depreciated? If there had been such a policy in the past, what would have been the effect on deficits, levels of subscription and the availability of funds for replacement of the building?

4. The Secretary has asked the treasurer if £1,500 could be taken from the Prize fund to provide prizes for silver anniversary hockey and tennis tournaments. How might the treasurer answer him?

5. Martin suggests that the policy of taking life member subscriptions straight to Income and Expenditure Account offends against generally accepted accounting principles. Explain.

6. Martin thinks that the materiality convention has been carried to far in these financial statements. What does he mean?

2. Financial statements in not-for-profit enterprises

It is usual for all not-for-profit enterprises to prepare financial statements every year. Indeed many are required to because of Acts of Parliament such as the Charities Act 1990. The financial statements prepared are usually the Income and Expenditure Account, which is the equivalent of a Profit and Loss Account, and a Balance Sheet.

The Income and Expenditure Account lists the income and the expenditure. Both are included using the accruals convention so that the amounts are included as they are earned or incurred and not as money is paid or received. Income is listed under suitable headings and may include grants and subsidies (e.g. in a school or hospital), subscriptions (in a club), donations (charities), admission charges (e.g. the National Trust), fees earned (by colleges etc), sundry income and profits. Many clubs have a bar and the bar profit is measured as in a normal trading account. Expenditure is listed under suitable headings. It should include depreciation in accordance with SSAP 12.

The accounting conventions should be adhered to including the realisation, going concern and prudence conventions. A common feature is the matching convention. This can be interpreted in two ways:

❐ Income like life member subscriptions should be put in the income of the Income and Expenditure Account over the expected membership periods of life members. For example if John pays £500 for life membership in 19x1 and is expected to be a member for five years, then £100 will be in the Income and Expenditure Account of each year 19x1 to 19x5. In the Balance Sheet of each year the unexpired portion (£400 in 19x1) will be included in liabilities and labelled unexpired life member subscriptions.

❐ The income and expenditure of particular activities should be put together and the net amount shown. Suppose the discos involved ticket sales £x and expenditures (e.g. on the disc jockey and ticket printing) £y then the Income and Expenditure Account will show a profit (or loss) of £x - £y = £z. The detail may be omitted or shown as a separate statement or in a note. The level of disclosure of detail is a difficult judgement. Try not to obscure the wood with the trees!

Income and Expenditure Accounts should also comply with any relevant accounting standard. For example the bar stock will have been valued at the lower of cost and net realisable value in accordance with SSAP 9.

The Balance Sheet lists assets, liabilities and capital as in any Balance Sheet. In not-for-profit enterprises the capital is usually called the Accumulated Fund or the Unappropriated Surplus. Liabilities may include items like Unexpired life member subscriptions and Subscriptions in advance. They are liabilities because at the Balance Sheet date the Club has an obligation to provide, in the future, facilities which have already been paid for.

A special feature of many not-for-profit undertakings is separate funds. Consider my local church. It has some assets (mainly cash at bank and investments) and some liabilities (mainly unpaid bills). This much is easy to understand. However the difference between assets and liabilities is not just the Unappropriated Surplus (= capital) but a range of three capitals. The three are the Choir Fund, the Organ Fund and the balance which is the Unappropriated Surplus. What this means is that the net total of assets less liabilities is available to be used:

❐ for the choir up to the amount of the choir fund

❐ for the organ up to the amount of the organ fund

❐ for the general purposes of the church up to the amount of the Unappropriated Surplus.

The existence of a fund means that some of the net assets are earmarked for the purposes of the fund but does not necessarily mean that the net assets are in a form which will allow actual expenditure. The net assets may not include any actual cash! An example of separate funds: the Sheinton Primary School Parents Association have a Balance Sheet as:

Assets:		Capital and Liabilities:	
Cash at bank	12,069	Creditors	1,290
		Unappropriated surplus	5,209
		Swimming Pool Fund	3,100
		Minibus Fund	2,470
	12,069		12,069

This Balance Sheet shows that the net assets (£12,069 - £1,290 = £10,779) are held or earmarked for three separate purposes - the swimming pool, the minibus and the general purposes of the association. If a jumble sale was held for the benefit of the minibus and raised £100 then the assets (Bank) would rise by £100 and the minibus fund by the same amount. If a site survey for swimming pool purposes was carried out and cost £60 then assets (bank again) would go down and the swimming pool fund likewise. The annual financial statements would have an Income and Expenditure Account, to show movements in the Unappropriated surplus and separate accounts to show movements in the other two funds. In this case, the only asset is cash at bank but this may not be so and cash management may be as important as having a surplus of income over expenditure.

3. Property valuation

We will consider firstly the problem of property values in non-profit accounting. Many profit seeking enterprises own properties — factories, shops, offices, warehouses etc. These are valued at cost and the buildings part is usually depreciated in accordance with SSAP 12. Sometimes properties are revalued. This is not conceptually difficult although arriving at value is as much guesswork as science. Valuing business properties is normally done by considering what it might fetch in the open market if its existing use was continued. An alternative method of valuation is to consider what it might fetch if given an alternative use. As an example a property used as a warehouse might be worth rather more if it could be used as retail premises but that may depend on planning permission being obtained.

In the not-for-profit sector enterprises may also have properties. These may be capable of revaluation in a similar way to commercially owned premises. For example the Church owns clergy houses and these can be valued at open market values as houses — more or less existing use as residential properties. However some properties may have no obvious sale value in existing use and even no value in any alternative use. Examples are college buildings, hospital buildings, sports pavilions, stadiums etc. Revaluation may be seen as an academic exercise but modern accounting thinking suggests that:

— current values of resources used should be reported so that rational economic allocation of resources can be considered.

— buildings have limited, if long, lives and resources should be retained in order to finance replacements. Consequently depreciation should be charged into Income and Expenditure Accounts on some rational basis which takes into account current values.

One valuation method which meets these criteria is depreciated replacement cost. The method is to estimate the replacement cost of a building and then make some allowance for its age and condition. For example the Cressage College gained its independence from the local authority and commissioned a valuation of its properties. This was carried out using either open market value or depreciated replacement cost which ever was appropriate for each building. The depreciation policy was then to write off the buildings over sixty years straight line.

4. Valuation of gifts

Charities are often given money by way of donation or legacy. Sometimes they are given things (the accounting word is that they are given things in *kind)*. The things might be land, buildings, furniture, pictures, objets d'art or clothing and books etc to sell. In reporting the income and expenditure of the charity for a year, should gifts in kind be reported? One approach is simply to attach a note to the financial statements stating the fact of donations in kind. Another is to value them and incorporate them in the financial statements at the values assumed. The latter is the preferred option but raises the difficulty of how to value such gifts. Once valued and incorporated in the accounts, depreciation may have to be applied on some gifts.

SCENARIO 4 — Martin takes office as treasurer

Martin feels that the Sheinton Hockey and Tennis Club affairs are not being run as well as they might be and gets himself elected as assistant treasurer with special responsibility for future planning. His first priority is next year's budget. He feels that the breakeven budget proposed is inadequate and the club needs to make a surplus to recover from recent deficits and to have cash available for future projects. In any event breakeven would not occur if depreciation on the building were charged and the life member subscriptions were accrued. He has a questionnaire done on the bar and its prices, and finds that the relationship between prices and sales might be:

| Increase in price (%): | 5 | 10 | 15 | 20 | 25 |
| Decline in sales volume (%): | 0 | 5 | 10 | 15 | 25 |

Martin then looks at the subscriptions. He finds that there are actually more than the three types of member. Possible categories of member include Full members (both sports), Hockey players, Tennis players, and Social members (who do not play sport). He is convinced that differential subscriptions would be fairer and would possibly raise more money if a lower subscription attracted many more social members. A side effect of this would be considerably greater bar takings. If there were differential subscriptions, then it would be essential to look more carefully at the costs of supplying services to each category of member and fix subscriptions accordingly.

The wages of part time staff who maintain the grounds, engage in caretaking and property repair are a major expense. Martin wonders if contracting out these activities might save money. Currently there is some dissatisfaction with old Ted who has rolled the tennis courts for many years and who refuses to listen to any criticism of his work.

Tasks 3

1. Summarise the benefits that might arise from a formal budgeting process for the Club.

2. The treasurer points out that the change in accounting policy to accruing life member subscriptions would probably have no material effect on the annual surplus or deficit shown. Why is this?

3. Suggest the optimal pricing policy for the bar. What would the effect be on the annual bar profit?

4. If separate subscription categories were introduced what investigations might be necessary to fix them at realistic levels? What side effects might subsequently be observed?

5. Make a list of the benefits and disbenefits that might accrue from out-sourcing the grounds maintenance, caretaking and property repairs.

5. Management accounting in the not-for-profit sector

The benefits of using management accounting in the not-for-profit sector are as many as in the profit seeking sector. We will look at some of the techniques and see if they have anything to offer the not-for-profit sector.

Budgeting

It is clearly essential that income should match expenditure and that resources should be available for capital expenditure. It is also essential that cash flows over time should match or borrowing resources arranged to smooth out any disparities in timing. A secondary school needs to match the income which it will receive from the local authority with its expenditure. In recent times income has declined so every item of expenditure has to be looked at carefully and priorities established. Any cut backs need to be acceptable to all concerned (difficult if redundancies are called for!) and explained to all affected. Subsequently actual income and expenditure must be compared with the budget and any variances investigated.

Standard costing

It is possible to apply standard costing and variance analysis in the not-for-profit sector although, as a technique, it is not appropriate everywhere. One possible application is in hospitals with treatments. Standard costs may be established for particular treatments and variances established for each application of a treatment. Variances may indicate areas where improvements may be instigated. In fact the actual establishment of standards, with the very detailed investigations required, often brings rewards in itself. Sales variances can also be useful in many enterprises. Variances may include sales price, sales mix and sales volume.

Total Absorption Costing

Most not-for-profit enterprises have a range of different outputs (what are the outputs of a school, a hospital, a museum, a theatre ?) and knowing the costs of providing each output is essential if priorities need to be established. For example, a school may establish its outputs as subject/class hours. Thus if one hour of eighth year English teaching is £x and one hour of A level Chemistry teaching is £y then decision making can at least be informed. From a subject/class hour, a subject/pupil hour can be established once pupil numbers are known.

Marginal costing

Decisions such as make or buy, product mix in scarce resource situations, special orders, optimal pricing etc can be assisted by knowing the financial effects of different courses of action. All not-for-profit organisations are looking at the cost and other implications of in-house supply and out-sourcing. A charity which raises money by having paid organisers in rented offices in large towns might find that economies may be made by reducing the number of such organisers and centralising activities in the most profitable towns. However each closure will mean the loss of some support and careful assessment has to be made of the loss of income v. the reduction in expense. A theatre group might assess the marginal income and costs of taking a successful production on a foreign tour. The pricing of seats at a concert has implications for the number of seats sold. At price £x every seat will be sold. Good, but at what is the highest price at which every seat will just be sold? If even higher prices are charged what will be the price at which total revenue is maximised?

Decision making in the not-for-profit sector

It is essential that financial effects of decisions are known (or at least reasonably forecast) so that decisions are made with awareness of financial implications. Other considerations always enter into decisions. Some of these relate to public policy. For example high price concert seats may exclude a sector of the public which subsidy bodies may see as important. Some may have unknowable financial effects. An example is our theatre group which might find that the publicity surrounding a successful foreign tour may improve box office sales next season or attract new sponsorship.

6. Financial Accounting and Reporting

In the past, the procedure for most organisations, companies, local authorities, the health service, educational institutions, charities and so on, was for the members or other responsible bodies to elect or appoint a management body and let them get on with it. In the 1990s trust in management bodies has somewhat diminished and much emphasis is now given to rules and regulations and especially to *accountability* of management to those who appointed them but also to the *public at large.*

Regulation can be by statute and by individual constitutions and also by accounting and audit regulation. We have considered the regulation of companies by the Companies Act 1985, the Cadbury and Greenbury Codes, the Financial Reporting Standards and there also comprehensive Auditing Standards.

Charities are now ruled by statute (the Charities Act) which prescribes accounting and audit regulations. These regulations imply that accounting and audit must follow the rules of the Financial Reporting Standards, Statements of Recommended Practice (accounting recommendations for particular sectors) and Auditing Standards.

The Charities Act now requires that charities:

Requirement	Income not over £1,000	Neither income nor expenditure over £10,000	Income not over £100,000	Neither income nor expenditure over £250,000	Income or expenditure over £25,000
Receipts and payments	If preferred	If preferred	If preferred	No	No
Accruals accounting	If preferred	If preferred	If preferred	Yes	Yes
External scrutiny of accounts	None	Not generally required	Audit or independent examination	Audit or independent examination	Audit
Annual returns to Charity Commission	Not applicable	Yes; in simplified form	Yes	Yes	Yes
Annual report and accounts to Charity Commission	Not applicable	Only if requested	Yes	Yes	Yes

Notes:

❒ The making of an Annual Report and the making of a return to the Charity Commission is only required of *registered* charities. Registration is voluntary unless annual income is greater than £1,000 or there is a permanent endowment or it has the use or occupation of land.

❒ An audit must be by a registered auditor.

❒ An independent examination must be by a competent person but need not be by a qualified accountant.

❒ All charities must maintain and retain proper accounting records.

❒ All charities must make their accounts available to the public on written request.

❒ Some charities are registered under other Acts of Parliament (e.g. the Companies Act) and must also obey the rules therein required.

Other sectors also have accountability regulations which ensure that:

❒ governing bodies prepare or have prepared comprehensive accounting statements which comply with appropriate legislation or other regulation

❒ the financial statements are audited

❒ the financial statements are made available to the public at large.

I recommend that my readers approach their local authorities, their local hospital trusts and their local colleges and request copies of their Annual Reports and accounts. At first sight these documents may seem dull and difficult to follow. However you should by now be able to understand much of the information included. A detailed read may give you some surprising and perhaps disturbing facts. Accountability and indeed democracy requires that the public take an interest in these matters.

7. Financial accounting and reporting in the Health Service

The NHS Trusts are required to produce annual accounts and these accord with the National Health Service Act 1977 and the National Health Service and Community Care Act 1990. Because the accounts conform to the regulations it is possible to make comparisons between the different trusts after a fashion. Full comparisons would require the accounts to show a level of detail which is unnecessary for ordinary accountability purposes. The financial statements will consist of an Income and Expenditure Account, a Balance Sheet, a Cash Flow Statement, a Statement of Total Recognised Gains and Losses and numerous notes amplifying the data in the main financial statements. The notes will include a Statement of Accounting Policies.

A full example is best seen by obtaining a set from your local Trust but this very abbreviated set will give you something of their flavour:

Loamshire Community Health Service NHS Trust

Income and Expenditure Account for the year ending 31 March 19x9

	£	
Income from activities:		
Health Authorities	18,005	
General Practice Fundholders	1,580	
NHS Trusts	165	
Other income	2,386	22,136
Operating expenses		
Services from other NHS bodies	740	
Staff costs	13,800	
Other	6,700	21,240
Surplus before interest		896
Interest payable		360
Surplus for the year		536
Public Dividend Capital dividends payable		130
Retained Surplus		406

Balance Sheet

Fixed assets (tangible)		9,200
Current assets	738	
Creditors: within one year	1,490	
Net current liabilities		(752)

	£
Total assets less current liabilities	8,448
Creditors: more than one year	(4,200)
Total assets employed	4,248
Financed by:	
Capital and Reserves	
Public dividend capital	3,188
Revaluation reserve	260
Donation reserve	87
Income and expenditure reserve	713
	4,248

The things you might care to look out for in a set of financial statements from a Trust include:

❐ accounting policies especially on fixed assets and clinical negligence costs

❐ the detail of operating income and expenses

❐ staff numbers

❐ financial target performance

❐ the degree of compliance with Public Sector Payment Policy. This measures how quickly the Trust pays its suppliers.

❐ the auditors' report

❐ pension provision.

8. Financial accounting and reporting in education

Colleges and universities are required to produce annual financial statements. They should conform to the Instrument and Articles of Government of the institution, the SORP: Accounting in Higher Education Institutions, generally accepted accounting principles and the Accounting Standards.

The best way to get to grips with these accounts is to obtain a set from your local college (or better still several sets from different colleges and thus to make comparisons) and examine them in detail looking out for:

❐ the report of the governing body

❐ the Income and Expenditure Account, Balance Sheet and Cash Flow Statement

❐ accounting policies especially on fixed assets

❐ detail of income and expenditure

❐ staff costs, number and occupations

❐ pension provision.

9. Management accounting in the not-for-profit sector

Management accounting techniques were developed in the profit seeking sector especially in manufacturing. It is only fairly recently that management accounting techniques have been adopted in the not-for-profit sectors. However budgeting has been in the not-for-profit sector for a very long time on an annual basis. My readers may recognise the procedures for departmental budgeting as:

❐ heads of department take the current year's budget, add something on for inflation, make some optimistic adjustments and submits the result as the coming year's budget to the finance staff

❐ finance staff impose arbitrary cuts to the budget and it is then adopted

❐ in February or March much expenditure is embargoed because the year's budget allowance has already been reached

❐ alternatively, there is a frantic rush to spend in those months to ensure that the budget allowance is fully spent.

More sophisticated management accounting techniques were slow to reach public sector institutions until the late 1980s and 1990s. Then there was a rush to develop them because of tight financial constraints, the need for external funding, internal markets, accountability and other factors. In general management accounting can be adapted fairly well to not-for-profit enterprises and techniques like Total Absorption Costing, standard costing, marginal costing and capital appraisal techniques are now being applied. Activity based costing sits particularly well in the not-for-profit sector.

10. Management accounting in the Health Service

Management accounting in the Health Service can be used to answer questions like: What does it cost to perform an appendectomy? What should it cost to perform an appendectomy? Why did this operation cost more than standard or more in Hospital A than in Hospital B? How much should the hospital charge other hospitals for services? How can expenditure be controlled?

In principal a Total Absorption Costing system seems made for a hospital. Unit 12 has already discussed this problem. However, attempts at applying these techniques in actual hospitals has thrown up a number of problems.

Total Absorption Costing is concerned to find *product* costs. In a hospital what is the product? One possibility is the individual patient. It has been found that this is too expensive as the detailed calculations would require an army of cost accounting personnel. Another possibility is per department/specialty or consultant teams. This has been found to be too general. The probable best product is the individual procedure (e.g. a treatment) and the cost of elective procedures by fundholders. Hospitals price out their products in contracts which can be:

❐ an annual sum for access to a defined range of services

❐ a fixed sum for a given number of treatments + a cost per case.

There is much controversy about management accounting in the Health Service and it is seen by many as a conflict between bureaucracy (or financial efficiency and the rational allocation of resources) and good health care. The following quotations may illustrate the point:

❐ prices should be set with no cross subsidisation

❐ I am willing to accept the discipline of living within budget but the counter is that savings I make should be mine as well

❐ the bottom line is that you have done very well but we will now take away any underspend — there is no incentive

❐ the purposes of formal accounting information are resource planning, controlling performance and evaluating results

❐ the qualities of accounting information are confined to vital especially controllable items, in appropriate detail, reflecting performance, timeliness, user friendly and congruent with goals

❐ the goals of hospital management are not the same as medical staff

❐ close team spirit and professionalism tend to override financial stringency

❐ my personal goal is to provide a high quality service — this is being constantly constrained by the budget

❐ I rarely see patients these days — I spend my time in committees. If I don't my department loses resources.

I think you will see that a comprehensive and detailed costing and budgeting system in a hospital would be feasible to install but would cost a great deal to create and administer. Cost would include cost accountant time but also exceedingly expensive medical staff time. Anything less than a fully detailed scheme would be much less useful. It is general axiom of management accounting that any scheme must not cost more than its benefits.

11. Management accounting in the educational sector

This area is in its infancy but is developing very fast. Universities and colleges have expanded very rapidly in recent years and are exceedingly expensive to run and yet the actual total costs of their individual outputs are not really known. For example, Salop University runs full time courses, post graduate courses, short courses, part time courses, engages in research, engages in consultancy, runs hostels and catering, lets its facilities for conferences, supplies computer and other services to local industry and has many other activities. It is does know not the cost of each individual activity, e.g. the cost of one part time student on an arts course or a science course or cost of undertaking a research project sponsored by a local firm.

This subject is a large one and whole books have been written on it. I will confine myself to a brief outline of an approach to cost determination in this sector. The major procedures are to take the whole cost of running the institution and to divide them into direct costs (e.g. staff time on a course) and overheads (these will include building use, central administration, libraries and many others). The central problem is then how to allocate and apportion overheads to the various activities. A possible approach is:

a. *Determine the cost objective.* Fundamentally this is to attribute infrastructure, central and administrative support services to organisational units (e.g. academic departments, the refectory etc). This will enable the cost of outputs (e.g. a course or a research project) to be determined such that it includes all the pertinent overheads, i.e. that it is a true *full* cost.

b. *Identify the outputs.* These may include courses, research projects, consultancy, residences, catering services, conferences, computer and services provided to other organisations.

c. *Identify the related activities*. This means that the overheads are identified by attributing appropriate direct and indirect costs to the activities (e.g. general administration which support the organisational units (e.g. academic departments) which actually produce the outputs). So it is necessary first to identify these units. In a college these are many and various but would include: building use, equipment use, general administration (for example the cost accountants!), computer department, print unit, student administration and services, library, faculty support etc.

d. *Attribute resource costs to activities*. The total resource costs must be obtained from the financial statements and the costs assigned to the support units. Examples of such costs include premises costs (e.g. depreciation and maintenance), the cost of academics' time spent in administrative and support activities, libraries, student records.

At the end of this stage the overhead costs have been assigned to the support activities — administration, libraries etc.

e. *Link activity costs to outputs*. It is now necessary to assign the support costs to the producing departments (academic departments, residences etc). This can be done scientifically (e.g. by sampling library use) or by rational approaches such as:

❐ building use: space occupied

❐ general administration: total direct costs

❐ student administration and services: student numbers

❐ research administration: total direct costs of research.

f. *Determine total costs of each output*. This involves associating the overheads applied to the producing departments together with the direct costs so that full costs can be determined for each output.

This is likely to be a mammoth task and very expensive. It will however only be worthwhile if a great deal of effort is put into it so the data upon which it is based is known to be reasonably accurate.

12. What are the benefits of full cost determination?

These may include:

❐ Improving the understanding of the costs of activities and outputs across an institution to provide for better information and decision making and resource allocation.

❐ Improving cost awareness throughout the institution so that resources are not wasted.

❐ Identifying cross-subsidisation. So that for example management are aware of the extent that an output (perhaps short courses) is subsidising another output (say research contracts).

❐ Providing a basis for accurate pricing of outputs e.g. research or consultancy contracts.

❐ Assessing value for money in teaching.

❐ As a basis for performance assessment in relation to planned costs, past performance and similar performance in other institutions.

❐ To provide information on costs for variable pricing in different types of course — full time, part time, short, elementary, advanced, classroom based (e.g. economics) or laboratory based (e.g. biomedical sciences).

Your author remembers bitter wars of words over the relatively low weighting given to part time courses which took immense amounts of administration and teaching compared with full time courses and the low weighting given to course administration. It appeared to Heads of Departments that large courses could be run comfortably in an hour a week. The reality was very different and you will see that cost collection can enable proper understanding of the full costs of each product. Better resource allocation and decision making should inevitably follow.

Fees Grants Subsidies Charges Trading Income	**Income and Expenditure Account**	Expenses Depreciation
Unappropriated Surplus Liabilities Separate funds	**Balance Sheet**	Assets
Budgeting Standard costing Marginal costing Total absorption costing	**Decision Making**	Pricing Prioritising Out-sourcing Deletion of activities

13. Summary of Unit 18

❐ Not-for-profit enterprises produce Income and Expenditure Accounts and Balance Sheets.

❐ A range of income sources are usually included.

❐ Expenses are itemised into suitable categories.

❐ Generally accepted accounting principles and the accounting standards should be used.

❐ The profit or loss is called the surplus or deficit.

❐ Balance Sheets may have separate funds.

❐ The level of detail and separate disclosure is a matter for judgement.

❐ Management accounting techniques can profitably be applied to not-for-profit enterprises.

❐ Decision making in not-for-profit enterprises should take into account financial considerations.

❑ Financial facts, forecasts and probable effects should be established before making decisions.

❑ Most of the not-for-profit sector including local and central government, the health service, education and charities are required to produce Annual Reports and financial statements. These should be in the forms prescribed by statute or the appropriate SORPs. These reports should be made available to the public.

❑ Management accounting is now practised widely in the not-for-profit sector but deriving appropriate procedures and methods is proving expensive and controversial.

Exercise *1

The Harbridge Charity was set up many years ago to provide scholarships for impecunious adults who wish to pursue educational courses. The Charity is run by four trustees who are prominent citizens living in Harbridge. The honorary treasurer is a water engineer and he presents his annual accounts as:

Receipts and payments for the period ending 31 December 19x4

Interest	12,765	Purchase of ICI shares	23,000
Dividends	11,061	Stationery and sundries	378
Sale of Treasury Stock	15,700	Travelling expenses	4,960
Donations	2,400	Scholarships	23,367
Fund raising	3,904		
Legacies	6,000		
Balance at bank b/f	246	Balance at bank c/f	371
	52,046		52,046

Required:

a. There is an error. Can you see it?

b. Take an interested reader through this account explaining all that has happened.

c. Do you think that this is an adequate account of the stewardship of the trustees? Suggest additional financial statements and information both financial and non-financial that may be reported.

Exercise 2

John and Jane James run the bookstall at their local church. They buy books, greeting cards and other stationery items at a discount and sell them at full price to members of the Church and others. They rather reluctantly produced this statement to the Church treasurer at the end of the year 19x5 and explain that surplus cash is invested in a building society.

Receipts and payments for the period ending 31 December 19x5

Profit on sale of books etc	£1,680	Donation to Christian Aid	£1,000
		Donation to Organ Fund	£350

The James's make all decisions about the bookshop and its finances. If you were the treasurer of the Church would you be satisfied with these figures? Suggest additional financial statements and information which might be provided. Suggest some ways in which the activities of the James's might be made more accountable. They are difficult people to deal with!

Exercise 3

The Old Sheintonians Club has a bar staffed by Mr and Mrs Joe. It is open evenings from 7 to 11 pm. This is the Joe's only source of income. They take holidays when Mrs Joe's sister fills in for them. They have been there three years. The treasurer takes the stock and prepares an account of the bar profit as:

Bar trading account for the year 19x6

Opening Stock	4,470	Sales	38,100
Purchases	26,780	Closing stock	5,240
Wages	8,400		
Sundry expenses	2,650		
Net profit	1,040		
	43,340		43,340

The committee are disappointed in the low profit and in the discussion a number of points emerge: the prices were set to give an average mark-up of 60%, the till is old and the amount charged on each transaction does not come up on the top of the till as the drawer is always left open, the days takings are counted and banked by Joe. The treasurer remarked that he found a bottle of Scotch in his stocktake that he could not find in the file of purchase invoices. He assumed the cost was the same as the other makes.

How might the trading account be restructured to give more information? Would you be alarmed at the results? How might better control procedures be instituted?

Exercise 4

The Sheinton Community Association produced a Balance Sheet as:

Accumulated surplus	2,680	Sports field	10,500
Footpath fund	5,400	Old railway line	6,000
Rouse's Charity	6,100	Youth Equipment at cost	
		less depreciation	2,200
Sports pavilion fund	2,800	Debtors	1,100
Youth fund	5,320	Deposit on overseas trip	2,300
Sundry creditors	650	Cash at bank	850
	22,950		23,950

Notes:
i.   the sports field was bought this year at a very low price.
ii. the old railway line was purchased to make a country walk. An appeal brought in £5,400.
iii. Rouse's charity is an old charity. It was endowed for the benefit of the community by a former resident and its assets merged with the Association two years ago.
iv. The sports pavilion fund was launched this year to enable a pavilion to be erected on the sports field. The main receipts were from a sponsored walk.

v.   The youth fund was started by taking over the funds of a youth club which closed two years ago and has been enhanced by the profits from youth discos.

Required:

a.   Spot the deliberate mistake.

b.   Explain precisely and in detail what information is conveyed by the Balance Sheet.

c.   Write a critique of the Committee's handling of the affairs of the Association so far as you can from the information given above. Consider the position of different sorts of resident.

Exercise 5

The Librarian of the faculty of Art and Design of the Humpshire College has produced a statement as:

	19x1	19x2	Budget 19x3
Books etc purchased*	24,600	28,200	30,000
Salaries**	17,300	18,480	19,000
Overhead apportionment	5,800	6,200	6,200
Sundries	4,109	4,691	5,000
Telephone	2,506	2,670	2,700
Equipment purchased***	6,700	4,000	8,500
Repairs and maintenance	3,100	3,400	3,500
Charges made	(2,170)	(2,200)	(2,300)
	61,945	65,441	72,600

*   This includes books, prints, CD ROMS etc

**   Mostly part time.

***   The library is proud of its up to date equipment including multi media computers.

The college accountant has told the librarian that the budget must be cut to 19x2 figures less 5%. She also says that the overhead apportionment to the library will be £7,100 in 19x3.

Comment on all this and suggest several things the librarian might do.

Assignment 1

Obtain the accounts of a national charity, a local authority or a health service undertaking and:

a.   Write a commentary on the results of the year and of the previous year.

b.   Comment on accounting words you understand and list matters you do not understand fully.

c.   Suggest ways that the financial statements might be more informative.

d.   Review any information on the probable future prospects given in the report.

e.   Comment on the reliability or otherwise of the financial statements.

f.   Review the accounting policies used.

g.   Review the conformity of the financial statements to any regulations.

Exercise 6

The Sheinton Housing Association Ltd owns a large number of properties which it has acquired or built over many years. All are residential and let to tenants. The Association are concerned to set rents which accord with current tenancy laws and are fair to the tenants but which recover costs and make a modest surplus. It is desired to make a surplus in order to enable the Association to show prospective lenders that the Association is sound financially. Properties are currently valued at cost. Explore alternative valuation measures and how these might impact on a costs and overall surpluses or deficits. Ignore any accounting regulation on Housing Associations (there is some).

Exercise 7

Consider the gifts to the Sheinton Museum (a charity) of a half an acre of ground (for outside displays), a house (a listed building which will house several collections), the Millichamp collection of Coalport China, two tons of old clothes and books for fundraising. How should (if at all) these items be valued and incorporated in the financial statements. What might be the impact of such incorporation on surpluses or deficits and hence on admission prices etc.

Exercise 8

The Head of Department of Classics at Sheinton University has been told that the fee for the part time course in Latin is too low and should be put up to recover the cost. He finds this hard to believe as the students have little contact with the University except being at the classes. He is also worried about recruitment which has been falling.

Explain in detail to him how the costs have been derived. Propose an argument on his behalf that the costs have been wrongly derived for this purpose.

Assignment/Case Study 2

St Martin's College, Sheinton and St Chad's College, Boghampton are two higher education colleges of similar size. After publication of their annual financial statements both principals are concerned to compare the performance of the two colleges. Some details are:

	St Martin's	St Chad's
	£'000	£'000
Funding council grants	17,200	9,600
Full time student fees	7,100	3,200
Part time student fees	1,030	890
Short course fees	475	1,132
Residence, catering and conferences	10,900	6,400
	36,705	21,222
Staff costs	21,580	9,600
Depreciation	1,840	1,600
Residence and catering consumables	3,200	2,200
Academic consumables	2,100	1,540

	St Martin's	St Chad's
	£'000	£'000
Other operating expenses	6,800	3,400
Interest	1,600	880
	37,120	19,220
Deficit/Surplus	415	2,002
Staff numbers:		
Academic	420	170
Non academic	598	310

Depreciation policies on buildings are 1% a year on the revalued amounts by St Martin's and 4% on the revalued amounts by St Chad's. The colleges have similar policies for fixtures etc.

Required:

a. Compare the performance of the two colleges as well as is possible. You may find using ratios assists.

b. The principal of St Martin's is worried about the deficit and is concerned to reconsider the College's policies for the coming year. Using comparisons between the two colleges suggest some changes that St Martin's may adopt to improve financial performance.

Assignment /Case Study 3

Salop University has engaged in a comprehensive cost finding exercise and the Head of Department of Business is considering his options for the future. In particular the study has shown:

❏ the fees for the part time degree in business studies recoup less than half the cost to the University

❏ the cost of administration of courses by full time academic staff is very high and is not always well done

❏ the contract fee for a major project for the local Chamber of Commerce is far too low

❏ the profit made from short courses for local professional people is remarkably high

❏ fees charged to non EC students for tuition on degree courses is very high.

Currently the department have been asked to quote for some consultancy work at the local hospital trust.

Required:

Comment on the findings and suggest how the head of department may make changes and their likely effect. Discuss how she might find a price for the hospital work.

19 Cash flow statements and some international issues

1. Objectives

We began with cash flow forecasts and we end with the reporting of cash flows in the Cash Flow Statement. In this final Unit we include also some issues that often have an international dimension — transfer pricing, segmental reporting and the assessment of subsidiary companies.

SCENARIO 1 — Martin enters the take-over world

Martin Padlocks PLC is now a listed company and Martin is considering how he can use his company's new status to expand both in the UK and internationally. His merchant bank advisers have suggested that he might consider the acquisition of a French company, Fermclef, which manufacture security products and have customers throughout the EC.

Quick Answer Question 19.1

Why might Martin's company benefit from a takeover of this company?

SCENARIO 2 — Martin reviews some foreign accounts

Before entering into negotiations or commissioning an expensive investigation and report, Martin looks at the accounts of Fermclef for 19x3. These are in a different form and in French language and currency but he is able to get Anne to produce a translation. This a summary:

Cash Flow Statement for the year ended 31 December 19x7

Net cash inflow from operating activities		340
Returns on investments and servicing of finance		
Interest paid		(73)
Taxation		(102)
Capital expenditure		
Payments to acquire tangible fixed assets	(930)	
Receipts from sales of tangible fixed assets	105	(825)
		(660)
Equity dividends paid		(50)
		(710)
Financing		
Issue of ordinary share capital		490
Decrease in cash		(220)

Reconciliation of net cash flow to movement in net debt

Decrease in cash in the period	(220)
Net funds at 1.1.19x6	(460)
Net funds at 31.1.19x6	(680)

Notes to the cash flow statement

1. **Reconciliation of operating profit to operating cash flows**

Operating profit	375
Depreciation charges	362
Increase in stocks	(204)
Increase in debtors	(354)
Increase in creditors	161
Net cash inflow from operating activities	340

2. **Analysis of changes in net debt**

	1.1.19x6	Flows	31.12.19x6
Cash in hand/bank	4		4
Overdrafts	(464)	(220)	(684)
Total	(460)	(220)	(680)

Profit and Loss Account		**Balance Sheet**	
Turnover	5,500	Fixed assets	2,100
Operating profit	375	Stocks	615
Interest	74	Debtors	1,100
	301	Cash	4
Taxation	125		3,819
	176	Bank Overdraft	684
Dividends	50	Other current liabilities	785
Retained	126		2,350
		Capital and Reserves	2,350

Anne was able to get the translation done as her firm has merged with an international firm and this firm are also the auditors to Fermclef.

Tasks 1

1. Martin reckons that he should be able to buy Fermclef at about fifteen times earnings after tax. How much is that?

2. The company will need to give consideration for the takeover. List possible types of consideration and the future effects on Martin Padlocks PLC of each type.

3. A possible consideration is loan stock and Martin wonders if cash flows from Fermclef would be sufficient to repay (with interest at about 10%) the loan stock in say five equal annual instalments. Write a report considering this. You should

consider current cash flows as reported and how future cash flows may change. State any assumptions you make.

2. Introduction

Every company needs to make a *profit* and shareholders look to the Profit and Loss Account to determine if a profit has been made. It is however not necessary for a profit to be made every year but in the long term the company must have a *surplus of profits over losses* or it will be in danger of receivership or liquidation.

Companies also pay dividends and a company can pay a dividend in a year in which it makes a loss and many do. However in the long term the company can only pay *dividends* up to the amount of any profit.

Thus companies must make profits and these profits must exceed any dividends declared. Profit is not the only requisite of long term survival. In addition the company must not run out of cash or must have the ability to obtain money (e.g. by borrowing) to enable it to settle its obligations as they fall due. Failure to *manage cash resources* can lead to receivership or liquidation even in profitable companies.

Consequently directors of companies are *accountable* to shareholders not only for the extent of their profit making capabilities but also for their *cash management proficiency*. This proficiency or lack of it is evidenced by a financial statement called the *cash flow statement*. This is a fairly sophisticated statement and is not very easy to understand although it is easier than its predecessor the statement of source and application of funds. The requirement for a cash flow statement was the first pronouncement of the new Accounting Standards Board and it is embodied in Financial Reporting Standard 1 'Cash Flow Statements'. All companies (except small ones and subsidiaries of Groups) are required to produce one each year starting with accounting periods ending on or after 23 March 1992. A revised version of FRS1 appeared in October 1996.

Example

The easiest way of understanding these statements is to follow the production of one from the data in a Profit and Loss Account and Balance Sheet and this we will do.

Here are the Balance Sheets of Cashflow Ltd as at two dates a year apart and also the summary Profit and Loss Account for the year ending 31 December 19x2:

Cashflow Ltd

Balance Sheet as at 31 December

	19x1	19x2
(all figures in £'000)		
Fixed assets		
Cost	2,560	2,720
Less depreciation	1,435	1,710
	1,125	1,010
Current assets		
Stocks	976	1,378
Debtors	1,450	1,769
	2,426	3,147

	19x1	19x2
Creditors — amounts falling due within one year		
Creditors	830	860
Overdraft	234	117
Taxation	88	123
Dividends	40	47
	1,192	1,147
Net current assets	1,234	2,000
Total assets less current liabilities	2,359	3,010
Creditors: amounts falling due after more than one year		
16% Debentures	400	600
Net assets	1,959	2,410
Capital and reserves		
Share capital (£1 shares)	600	700
Share premium	350	500
Profit and Loss Account	1,009	1,210
	1,959	2,410

Profit and Loss Account for the year ending 31 December 19x2

Turnover		6,462
Cost of sales		4,040
Gross profit		2,422
Overheads (including depreciation)		1,920
Operating profit		502
Interest		101
Net profit before taxation		401
Taxation		123
Profit after tax		278
Dividends		
Interim	30	
Final	47	77
Retained profit		201

The cash flow statement is now given with supporting notes which are a part of the statement:

Cash Flow Statement for the year ended 31 December 19x7

a.	**Net cash inflow from operating activities**	243
b.	**Returns on investments and servicing of finance**	
c.	Interest paid	(101)
e.	**Taxation**	(88)

f. **Capital expenditure**

g.	Payments to acquire tangible fixed assets	(360)	
h	Receipts from sales of tangible fixed assets	43	(317)
			(263)
d.	**Equity dividends paid**		(70)
			(333)

Financing

i.	Issue of ordinary share capital	250	
j.	Issue of debenture loan	200	450
k.	**Increase in cash**		117

Reconciliation of net cash flow to movement in net debt

l.	Increase in cash in the period	117
m.	Cash inflow from increase in debt	(200)
n.	Change in net debt	(83)

Analysis of changes in net debt

	At 1 Jan 19x2	Cash Flows	At 31 Dec 19x2
Overdraft	(234)	117	(117)
Debt due after one year	(400)	(200)	(600)
	(634)	(83)	(717)

3. Notes to cash flow statements

Reconciliation of operating profit to net cash inflow from operating activities

Operating profit	502
Depreciation charges	415
Loss on sale of tangible fixed assets	17
Increase in stocks	(402)
Increase in debtors	(319)
Increase in creditors	30
Net cash inflow from operating activities	243

Not included as a note to the cash flow statement but necessary for you to see what has happened is a reconciliation of fixed assets:

		Cost	Depreciation	Book value
r)	at 1 January 19x2	2,560	1,435	1,125
s)	Sold in year	200	140	60
		2,360	1,295	1,065
t)	Addition in year	360		360
u)	Depreciation in year		415	(415)
v)	at 31 December 19x2	2,720	1,710	1,010

The items sold fetched £43,000 so the loss on sale was £60,000 less £43,000 = £17,000.

Line (r) shows the position at the beginning of the year. The company had fixed assets which had originally cost £2,560,000 and which had been depreciated by £1,435,000.

Line (s) removes from line (r) the fixed assets which were sold in the year.

Line (t) adds the fixed assets which were bought in the year.

Line (u) adds the depreciation for the year (which appears as an expense in the Profit and Loss Account). Note that this is depreciation on both the old and the newly acquired fixed assets.

Line (v) shows the fixed assets held at the end of the year and the total or accumulated depreciation on them.

Firstly we will explore how the statement is constructed and then we will consider the story that it tells.

a) Operating profitably usually produces a positive cash flow measured here at £243,000. This is obtained from the Profit and Loss Account but first some adjustments have to be made as the Profit and Loss Account measures value flows not cash flows. The adjustments required are given on page 380. Depreciation is not a cash flow but is in the Profit and Loss Account so it has to be added back. Similarly with the loss on sale where the actual cash flow is shown separately in line (h). Intuitively you will realise that cash flow from sales is less than sales if debtors have increased as they have. Similarly increase in stocks must involve a reduction in cash resources and an increase in creditors means an increase in cash resources.

b) This company has no income from investments as it has no investments but these will appear in many statements.

c) Interest paid is on the debentures and the bank overdraft.

d) Dividends paid are the final dividend from last year (£40,000) + the interim of this year (£30,000). This year's final dividend will be paid in the year ending 31 December 19x3.

e) The tax paid in the year is the tax on the previous year's profits as corporation tax is paid nine months after the year end.

f) These are the acquisition of fixed assets. The acquisition or disposal of subsidiary companies in groups would have a separate heading.

g) During the year £360,000 was spent on fixed assets.

h) Some assets were sold and fetched £43,000.

i) 100,000 new ordinary shares of £1 each nominal were sold for £2.50 each and as a result the company raised £250,000 and share capital increased by £100,000 and share premium by £150,000. New issues of ordinary shares for cash are normally issued to existing shareholders in proportion to their holdings and are called rights issues.

j) A further issue of debentures raised £200,000.

k) Cash and cash equivalents includes cash, bank balances, overdrafts. In this case the only relevant item is the bank overdraft.

In addition to the Statement and the Note there are two other items: the reconciliation of net cash flow to movement in net debt and the analysis of changes in net debt.

In the case of the Reconciliation the three lines indicate:

l)   This is from the Cash Flow Statement.

m) The issue of further debentures raised £200,000 and increased the sums due to debentureholders by that amount.

n)   The net effect of the above to increase net debt by £83,000.

The analysis is I think self-explanatory.

So what does this cash flow statement tell us:

i)   The company made a profit of £502,000 but after adjusting for depreciation and loss on sale of fixed assets the positive cash flow from trading was (£502,000 + £415,000 + £17,000) no less than £934,000.

ii) An increase in stocks of £402,000 and of debtors £319,000 was partly financed by an increase in creditors of £30,000. The net effect of these three things was an absorption of cash of £691,000 and so the net contribution of operations to cash was only £243,000.

iii) Finance was also obtained from shareholders £250,000 and by long term borrowings at £200,000.

iv) Total cash inflows are thus £243,000 + £250,000 + £200,000 = £693,000.

v)   Outgoings of cash were:

	£
on interest	101,000
on dividends	70,000
on tax	88,000

and on fixed assets £360,000, partly financed by sales of old fixed assets £43,000.

vi) Total outgoings are therefore £576,000

vii) Income less outgoings is £693,000 less £576,000 = £117,000. As a result the bank overdraft has come down by this amount.

4. Cash flow statements in practice

The compilation of cash flow statements is difficult and is best left to accountants. However the statements are intended to be used by investors, managers and other people who may not be accountants.

The example I have given is relatively simple and the actual statements of public companies tend to be more complex. The complications do not necessarily obscure the basic message and with some practice it is possible for a non-accountant to obtain much information about a company from its cash flow statement.

The things to watch for are:

i)   The major financing experience of companies is that most cash comes in from operations and most goes out on new fixed assets. Observe the extent that this is so.

ii)   Frequently the positive cash flow from operations is diminished by absorptions from increases in stock and debtors only partly financed by increases in creditors.

iii) Interest is a large absorber of cash and the effect of high interest rates has become a cliché in analysing the ills of business.

iv)   Dividends do not usually absorb major amounts of cash.

v)   Tax payments are also not usually great absorbers.

vi)   New financing in the form of rights issues or borrowings are sometimes found. If the borrowings are relatively large then see if the company has reached dangerous levels of gearing.

vii) The net effect on cash and cash equivalent can be seen.

viii) Many groups buy or sell subsidiaries and the effect of this on cash flow can be traced. Sometimes the effect is large borrowings or rights issues and sometimes there is no effect on cash as the consideration is new shares or loan stock.

ix)   Some companies show net cash flow from operations as I have in line (a) but some companies will give more detail as:

Cash received from customers

Cash payments to suppliers

Cash paid to or on behalf employees

Other cash payments.

SCENARIO 3 — Martin discovers residual profit

Martin Padlocks PLC goes ahead and buys Fermclef using a mixture of cash and loan stock with warrants as consideration. Once the purchase has gone through, Martin gives some consideration to how he can control the French subsidiary. He arranges for monthly reports to be prepared and sent to him but allows the Board of Fermclef to run their own affairs as far as possible. He cannot give too much time to reading the reports and asks Anne if there is any quick way to appraise subsidiaries rapidly. She suggests the use of *residual profit.*

Tasks 2

1. Explain how residual profit might be calculated and how it might be useful to the company and motivate the French management.

2. Calculate residual profit based on the figures in the 19x3 figures. Use 15% gross as cost of capital.

5. Residual profit

Many listed companies are groups with many separate companies each with some degree of managerial independence. It is impossible for a Head Office team in London to plan and control the detailed activities of all its separate subsidiaries which may be in many different countries. The local management must be given some local autonomy to make decisions on both long term and day to day matters. The extent of local autonomy varies from group to group. However whatever the extent of local autonomy, Head Office must have some means of appraising the performance of each separate enterprise in the group. Detailed monthly returns of accounting information are usually required for all subsidiaries.

Appraisal can involve detailed inspection of the returns but some simple criterion to distinguish the successful from the not so successful is desirable. One possible statistic which might assist is the calculation of Return on Capital Employed and the calculation of ROCE has already been discussed in the Unit on ratio analysis. Suppose Mega PLC has a subsidiary - Nano Limitada in Portugal. Nano send in a monthly Profit and Loss Account and Balance Sheet. The November 19x7 return shows Profits after tax of Esc. 4 million and net assets of Esc. 240 million. ROCE (annualised) can be calculated as:

$$\text{ROCE} = \frac{4 \times 12}{240} \times 100 = 20\%.$$

Mega PLC's cost of capital is 8% after tax. So this rate of return seems very good. However, it is essential that valuations are up to date and that accounting policies are uniform throughout the group.

The management of Nano are very pleased with their results and are considering asking Head Office for funds to enable them to expand by engaging in a new project. The best estimates for the new project suggest that a ROCE of 14% after tax can be achieved. Let us consider the likely behaviour of the Portuguese management. They will see that the proposed project is good for the group as it pays much more than the cost of capital. However it will reduce the average ROCE achieved by their company. They may therefore not pursue the project and that will be a loss to the group. This shows that the ROCE criterion may have behavioural defects. An alternative criterion is residual profit. This is calculated as:

Residual profit = profit - (Capital employed × Cost of capital). So, for Nano Lda:

Residual profit = Esc. 48 - (240 × 0.08) = Esc. 28.8 million.

The new project, because it pays better than cost of capital, will enhance residual profit. If absolute value of residual profit is the criterion for success then the Nano Lda management will favour the proposed project.

SCENARIO 4 — Martin ponders transfer prices and motivation

Martin decides to make some of his products in France and some in the UK. This will involve transferring products made in England to the French company either for incorporation in products or for onward sale to EC customers. The reverse will also happen. Some of these finished and intermediate products can be purchased from or sold to third parties. Some cannot. Martin is mindful of the need to motivate the French management (and also the UK managers) and of the requirement to give them autonomy.

Task 3

Review possible methods of fixing prices for goods transferred between the companies and make recommendations. You should state any assumptions made.

6. Transfer pricing

Many companies are vertically integrated. This is means that they have one or more separate divisions and manufactured goods are transferred between the divisions. For example Division A may make a component which is used by division B to make a product which is used by division C ..... and so on.

From the perspective of the whole company, internal transfer prices are irrelevant but companies like to give individual divisions some *autonomy*. This is because *decentralisation* generally works better than autocratic decision making from the top. Each division is seen as a separate *profit centre* with divisional managers making most of the decisions. The problem with decentralisation is that it may be *sub-optimal*. This means that a decision that is best for the division may not be best for the company as a whole. *Goal congruence* is not achieved. However many companies see the benefits of decentralisation as outweighing the disbenefits.

We will look at the advantages and disadvantages of some possible ways of fixing transfer prices:

Prices imposed by top management

This way of fixing prices takes away decentralisation but can be used in certain circumstances. Suppose Division A is in country C and Division B is in country D and intermediate products are transferred from A to B. Top management want to appraise the performance of each division and might feel that one of the transfer price fixing methods below would be best. However suppose company tax rates are 20% in country C and 50% in country D. It pays to have the profits in country C. This is done by having a high transfer price which has the effect of:

❐ giving high profits in Division A - because the high transfer price is their sales price.

❐ giving low profits in Division B - because the high transfer price is a cost.

Market prices

These are ideal but can only be used when a market price exists. If Division A's product can be sold to Division B or sold on the open market and Division B can buy it from Division A or on the open market, then there is an open market. In practice, a price slightly lower than market would be used to reflect the cost savings from internal transfers. For many products there is no external market. For example Division A's product is specially designed as part of Division B's product and cannot be sold or purchased elsewhere. However even in these situations Division B could probably get it made elsewhere but Division A could not sell it anywhere else.

Marginal cost prices

These can be shown by economic analysis to be optimal for the company as a whole in many cases. However, it will mean Division A showing a loss (as fixed costs are not passed on) and Division B showing a super profit. This negates the benefits of decentralisation. A partial way of restoring them is to transfer at marginal cost and then share the profits made from the ultimate product among the divisions contributing to its manufacture.

Full (Total Absorption) cost prices

This may be a full cost or at full cost + a mark up percentage. This is thought to be the commonest method. There are a number of disadvantages. These can be summed up by realising that passing on full costs (perhaps + a profit margin) gives Division A no incentive to be efficient and reduce costs. Division B may have an incentive to purchase outside the company if lower prices can be obtained which may be good for Division B but not necessarily for the company as a whole. Also if Division B has an opportunity to sell its product at over marginal cost and still make a profit, it will not know marginal cost of that part of its product which is the product of division A.

Negotiated prices

This may require much management time, leave some managers dissatisfied and still lead to sub-optimal pricing.

This is a very complex subject and optimal prices are rarely used because of faulty economic and behavioural analysis but also because of incomplete information.

SCENARIO 5 — Martin gets into segmental reporting

Martin is now very ambitious for his company and is considering acquiring both manufacturing and distribution companies in other countries including the former Soviet bloc. He realises that he has to report the Group results in the annual accounts and wonders whether having overseas interests changes the way that the company prepare the Annual Report and Accounts. To find out he inspects the accounts of a local PLC which he knows has international interests. This company make building products and fabrics for use in motor vehicles. He finds:

Segmental analysis (£million)	Turnover		Profit		Net assets	
	19x1	19x2	19x1	19x2	19x1	19x2
By class of business						
Building products	15.6	14.3	1.2	(0.2)	12.6	11.4
Vehicle fabrics	12.8	14.0	1.9	3.4	16.2	18.4
By location of operation						
UK	21.2	19.7	2.0	1.4	17.8	16.6
EC	7.2	8.6	1.1	1.8	11.0	13.2
Turnover by geographical location						
UK	15.6	13.9				
EC	6.3	7.1				
Asia	2.7	2.8				
North America	3.8	4.5				

Tasks 4

1. Analyse this data and see if you can find any clues as to the profitability, growth prospects and risk profile of the PLC as a whole.
2. Discuss why the segmental information is useful to investors and others.
3. Is the information given adequate? (It is adapted from real PLC accounts). What additional information might be given?

7. Segmental analysis

As a PLC may be a group of companies with diverse activities, from manufacturing widgets to retailing Life Assurance all carried out in many different countries, it is clearly difficult to assess the accounts of a PLC in respect of profitability, opportunities for growth and degrees of risk. However investors and investment analysts need to assess the results and, to do this, they need details of the performance etc of each part of the group.

In 1990 SSAP 25: *Segmental reporting* was published and this requires PLCs and certain other companies to include details of the performance of each major segment of activity. The SSAP requires that if the company has two or more classes of business or operates in two or more geographical segments which differ substantially from each other then it should define its classes of business and geographical segments in its financial statements. It should report with respect to each class of business and geographical segment:

❏   turnover, distinguishing between turnover derived from external customers and turnover derived from sales to other segments

❏   results before accounting for taxation and minority interests

❏   net assets.

Most financial statements of PLCs have some segmental analysis and you should try to inspect the Annual Reports of some PLCs to see how they do it. You will realise that should be possible to derive figures for returns on sales and ROCE for each segment.

SCENARIO 6 — Martin dreams of the future

Martin has come a long way from starting a small business with a few pounds to being the boss of a public company and a millionaire. Not all new businesses go this way but, as Napoleon said, every soldier has a Field Marshal's baton in his knapsack.

Where might Martin go from here? His company may grow larger and larger by internal growth or acquisition. His company may be taken over, Martin given a seat on the Board of the larger company and he eventually becomes boss once again. He may get a knighthood.

But of course his company may go bust. As Napoleon also said 'it is only one step from the sublime to the ridiculous'.

---

8. Summary of Unit 19

❏   A way of expansion is through takeovers. Benefits of takeovers include acquisition of desirable facilities and knowledge, elimination of competition, economies of scale, spreading of risk, synergy and others.

❏   Consideration for takeovers can be cash, equity, loans, convertibles or a mixture of these.

❏   Public companies are required by FRS 1 to produce Cash Flow Statements.

❏   A useful way of appraising subsidiaries is by using Residual profit which is the net profit after deducting interest at a standard rate on capital employed. Subsidiaries are required to maximise residual profit.

❏ Transfer pricing is difficult when the goals of maximising group returns conflict with local autonomy.

❏ International transfer pricing can be a device for reducing taxation and circumventing exchange control.

❏ Segmental analysis is required in the financial statements of larger companies. Segments can be classes of business or geographical areas. Turnover, profits and net assets should be revealed segmentally.

Exercise 1

Cash Flow Statement for the year ended 31 December 19x3

Net cash inflow from operating activities		458
Returns on investments and servicing of finance		
Interest received	12	
Interest paid	(109)	(97)
Taxation		(43)
Capital expenditure		
Payments to acquire intangible fixed assets	(145)	
Payments to acquire tangible fixed assets	(265)	
Receipts from sales of tangible fixed assets	15	(395)
		(77)
Equity dividends paid		(65)
		(142)
Financing		
Issue of ordinary share capital	77	
Issue of 12% Unsecured Notes 19x7-19x9	48	125
Decrease in cash		(17)

Notes to the cash flow statement

1. Reconciliation of operating profit to net cash inflow from operating activities.

Operating profit	454
Depreciation Charges	68
Loss on sale of tangible fixed assets	4
Increase in Stocks	(35)
Increase in Debtors	(51)
Increase in creditors	18
Net cash inflow from operating activities	458

Required:

Explain what the company has done during 19x3 as far as can be discerned from the statement.

Exercise *2

The Balance Sheets of three companies at one year intervals are:

(all figures in £'000)	Jonah		Micah		Nahum	
	19x1	19x2	19x1	19x2	19x1	19x2
Fixed Assets						
at cost or valuation	87	102	97	151	34	76
Depreciation	21	39	63	78	10	22
	66	63	34	73	24	54
Current Assets						
Stock	20	24	45	43	16	19
Debtors	31	38	23	27	18	15
Bank and Cash	–	12	21	–	–	–
Current Liabilities						
Trade Creditors	15	31	54	46	11	10
Overdraft	2	–	–	4	2	6
Taxation	5	8	12	14	10	8
Dividend	5	6	13	11	14	17
Net Current Assets	24	29	10	(5)	(3)	(7)
Total Assets less Current						
Liabilities	90	92	44	68	21	47
15% Debentures	30	20	–	10	12	–
	60	72	44	58	9	47
Capital and Reserves						
Share Capital	20	25	12	18	6	9
Share Premium	5	10	–	6	1	7
Revaluation Reserve	–	–	–	–	–	30
Profit and Loss Account	35	37	32	34	2	1
	60	72	44	58	9	47

Profit and Loss Accounts for 19x2 for the three companies showed:

	Jonah	Micah	Nahum
Net Profit	24	29	29
Interest	4	2	2
Net Profit after Interest	20	27	27
Taxation	8	14	8
	12	13	19
Dividends	10	11	20
Retained	2	2	(1)

Note:

Jonah: Fixed Assets costing £16,000 (Net Book Value — £11,000) were sold for £7,000.

Micah: Fixed Assets at cost £12,000 less depreciation £7,000 were sold for £8,000.

Nahum: No fixed Assets were sold but the property (Cost £20,000 less Depreciation £4,000 was revalued to £46,000).

Required:

Prepare a cash flow statement for each company for 19x2.

Case Study/Assignment

The Financial Statements of Wednesfield Wholesale and Importing PLC for the two
years 19x2 and 19x3 show:

Profit and Loss Accounts

(All figures in £'000)	*19x2*	*19x3*
Turnover	14,500	16,800
Cost of Sales	7,900	9,350
Gross Profit	6,600	7,450
Distribution Costs	2,100	2,160
Administration Expenses	2,870	3,260
Operating Profit	1,630	2,030
Interest Payable	620	850
Profit on Ordinary activities before taxation	1,010	1,180
Taxation	300	360
Profit on ordinary activities	710	820
Dividends	350	550
Retained profit for the year	360	270
Earnings per share	1.04p	1.21p

Balance Sheet as at 31 December

	19x2	*19x3*
Fixed Assets		
Tangible assets	10,300	13,510
Current Assets		
Stocks	2,400	2,900
Debtors	2,100	2,570
	4,500	5,470
Creditors: amounts falling due within 1 year		
Creditors	1,200	1,430
Bank Overdrafts	340	760
Corporation Tax	300	360
Dividends	250	450
	2,090	3,000
Net Current Assets	2,410	2,470
Total Assets less Current Liabilities	12,710	15,980

Creditors: amounts falling due after more than one year		
15% Debenture 19x5	2,200	2,200
13% Debenture 19x3	3,000	
	10,510	10,780
Capital and Reserves		
Issued Share Capital (10p shares)	6,800	6,800
Share Premium	500	500
Profit and Loss Account	3,210	3,480
	10,510	10,780

Notes to Profit and Loss Account and Balance Sheet

1. Fixed Assets

	Land	Buildings	Plant	Total
Cost at 31.12.19x2	3,000	5,500	4,970	13,470
Disposals at cost			850	850
Additions at cost		800	4,250	5,050
Cost at 31.12.19x3	3,000	6,300	8,370	17,670
Depreciation to 31.12.19x2		1,690	1,480	3,170
Depreciation on disposals			470	470
Depreciation in year		210	1,250	1,460
Total Depreciation at 31.12.19x3		1,900	2,260	4,160
Book Value 31.12.19x3	3,000	4,400	6,110	13,510

2. The 15% Debenture is secured on the company's freehold properties. The 13% Debenture is secured by a second mortgage on the properties. The directors estimate that the open market value in existing use of the properties is about £10 Million.

Cash Flow Statement for the year ended 31 December 19x3

Net cash inflow from operating activities		2,800
Returns on investments and servicing of finance		
Interest paid		(850)
Taxation		(300)
Capital expenditure		
Payments to acquire tangible fixed assets	(5,050)	
Receipts from sales of tangible fixed assets	330	(4,720)
		(3,070)
Equity dividends paid		(350)
		(3,420)

Financing

Issue of ordinary share capital	3,000
Decrease in cash	(420)

Note to the cash flow statement

Reconciliation of operating profit to net cash inflow from operating activities.

Operating profit	2,030
Depreciation Charges	1,460
Loss on sale of tangible fixed assets	50
Increase in Stocks	(500)
Increase in Debtors	(470)
Increase in Creditors	230
Net cash inflow from operating activities	2,800

Notes:

1. The plant that was sold was an obsolete production line. This was replaced with new plant costing £1,600,000. The remaining capital expenditure was on a new building on the old sports field with plant designed to produce an entirely new product.

2. One share in the company is quoted at 16p.

Required:

Write a report on the company including:

a. What occurred in 19x3

b. Performance ratios

c. Liquidity ratios

d. Investment ratios.

Exercise 3

The Gargantua Group have subsidiaries in many countries. The accounts of some them show:

Company	A		B		C	
	19x1	19x2	19x1	19x2	19x1	19x2
Profit before tax (£000)	2,300	2,700	1,240	1,321	870	1,230
Net assets	16,432	21,600	8,500	8,800	6,700	9,840

Required:

a. Calculate ROCE and residual profit if group cost of capital is 11% before tax.

b. Comment on the figures.

Exercise 4

The Pantagruel Group have subsidiaries in Mexico, the Virgin Islands and the USA and Gombozia. Goods are transferred between the subsidiaries both to sell on in their own markets and to incorporate in manufactured products. Some items are unique and some have external competitors. Transfer prices are calculated in one of three ways: a. to put profits in low tax countries b. to extract profits from countries with exchange controls and c. at full cost + 10%. At a conference of top management in Nice several executives complain that they make all the decisions in their companies and yet because of imposed transfer prices they appear to be unprofitable.

Comment on this and suggest ways of overcoming the problem.

Exercise 5

Subsid GMBH is a German subsidiary of Major PLC and is largely autonomous. The company shows a loss, but in the opinion of Helmut the MD, is actually very successful. One complaint he has is that he sells to other group companies and they are very tardy in paying him.
Discuss Helmut's problem and suggest some solutions.

Exercise 6

Tophole PLC have manufacturing facilities in Scotland, France, Turkey, Hungary, Brazil and Canada. They have wholesale companies in those countries and also in Germany, India, Japan and Korea. They export to over 120 countries. Their products are mainly agricultural equipment and tools, domestic hardware and office furniture.

Design a matrix to show the performance of each segment of their business.

Exercise 7

Petunia Petals PLC have financial statistics as:

	19x4 (in £million)	19x5 (in £million)
Net Assets	64.3	56.4
Operating Profit before tax	10.7	8.6
Turnover	88.9	78.8
Cost of capital pre-tax	12.4	12.4

Assess their performance as far as you can.

The notes to the accounts show also:

	19x4 Defence related	19x4 Leisure industry	19x5 Defence related	19x5 Leisure industry
Net Assets	44.1	20.2	32.0	24.4
Operating Profit before tax	7.6	3.1	1.9	6.7
Turnover	50.2	38.7	43.2	35.6

How does this change your view of the groups' performance, future prospects and risk profile?

Appendix A
Answers to selected exercises

Unit 1 Cash flow forecasting

2. Capital £5,500, Fixed assets £4,000. Maximum overdraft - immediate £2,500, end Jan £1,650, end Feb £700.

Unit 2 Profit and Loss Account

1. C Gross profit = £100,200. A is the supermarket (cash sales!). C is the fish wholesaler (low stock!)

2. F Cost of goods sold £540,000. Gross Profit £440,000

7. £15,000 + £1,200 + (10.4% of £16,200) = £17,884.8

8. Alpha. Gross profit £561,000. Wages £207,000. Rates £13,200. Net Profit £151,050.

Unit 3 Balance Sheet

1. B Fixed Assets £148. Current Assets £311. Curent Liabilities £250. Net Assets £209. Capital £188 + £51 − £30 = £209.

2. Alan. Gross Profit £234. Rent etc £35. Net Profit £20. Fixed Assets £206. Current Assets £259. Current Liabilities £42. Net Assets £423. Capital £438 + £20 − £35 = £423.

Unit 4 Depreciation

1. c. Straight Line £1,167 a year. Written down values: 1992 £4,833, 1993 £3,666, 1994 £2,500.

   e. i. Depreciation £4,833 − £1,500 = £3,333. Not on Balance Sheet at end of 1993!

   g. Depreciation will be charged in the years 1994 through 1996. But no depreciation after that with straight line. Generally reducing balance would however continue.

3. a. Lorry £7,000 a year. Copier 1992: £667, 1993: £1,333, 1994: £1,333 1995: £667.

   b. Fax Machine 1992 £200, 1993 £150, 1994 £112. Written down values: 1992 £600, 1993: £450, 1994: £338.

5. At the end of 19x8 the old Warehouse will have a written down value of Land £10,000 + Buildings £38,750 = £48,750. As it was sold for £100,000 the gain is £51,250. The depreciation on the new warehouse in 19x9 is £3,000. Clearly the gain has a large impact on profit!

   It might be shown as:

	£
Net Profit before exceptional item	31,000
Exceptional item: Profit on sale of warehouse	51,250
Profit after exceptional item	82,250

Unit 5 Costing and pricing a product

3.   a. £294,000 b. £14.70 c. £394,000 d. £19.70 e. £56,000

8.   a. At 600,000, cloth is 54p a metre + 10p + $\dfrac{200,000}{600,000}$ = 97.3p

     At 1,200,000 cost is 74.7p.

   b. Material costs are non-linear. Fixed overheads are spread over more output thus lowering unit costs.

11. Ken: Breakeven – 2,000 batches. Relevant range – 2,000(?) to 4,000.

    Margin of Safety 20%. Statistic is: number of batches sold must exceed BE point (BE sales are £100,000). Period is not specified but if figures are annual then sales of £8,333 a month.

Unit 6 Budgeting

2.   a. Reduce staff by one and work overtime if necessary.

     Reduce training, reduce Margaret's management and training time.

     Keep the old vans.

     You can visualise the consequences of these measures in reduced efficiency, stress and sickness.

     An alternative may be to improve efficiency by more preventive maintenance or scheduling client visits more scientifically to reduce travelling time and costs.

6.   On conventional approaches: as last year + %age for inflation + extra for new initiatives.

    Zero-based: Do we need any PR? If yes, how much? Do we have the right approach, cost structure, people? Can we get it more efficiently by using outside firms?

Unit 7 Uses of marginal costing

4.   a. She has to pay out on overheads before cash is received from customers. Also she pays her friend 20% up front.

   b. Fixed costs are £6,000 + interest £2,000 = £8,000. This means turnover (of which 20% goes to her friend) will need to be £10,000.

     Viability means making more than £8,000 a year as that is the opportunity cost of going on her own. Turnover would need to be £20,000 a year.

   c. Risk, fear, excitement, upside possibilities, personal satisfaction.

7.   Profit and Loss Accounts

(all figures in £'000)	£300SP Make	£300SP Buy	£320SP Make	£320SP Buy
Sales	1,500	1,500	1,440	1,440
Variable	650	1,000	585	900
Fixed	600	200	600	200
Profit	250	300	255	340

    Best is to buy in and sell at £320.

Problems of control over production, supply, quality, stability of pricing etc. Desire to give employment in the UK.

14.

	A	B	C
Contribution	5	6	7
Contribution per minute	1	3	1.17
Rank	3	1	2
Make	2,760	3,000	2,700
Usage (max 600)	230	100	270

Unit 8 Working capital

4. a. Debtors average payment time 121 days. Stock Turnover 84 days. Creditors average payment time 94 days.

   b. Seems to have a high ROCE. Problems are a very long debtors payment period and a dangerously long time taken to pay creditors.

   c. Working Capital will rise by £15,000 and fall by £10,000. Components will change as: debtors + £11,200, stocks + £4,800 and creditors + £5,600.

   Consequently overdraft may increase by £5,400.

7. a. £15,600. b. £72,000. c. 21.7%

   d. The one and two month people would mostly take the discount. The 3 and 4 months people would mostly not. So the cost would actually be much more than 21% and would not reduce the debtors much.

Unit 9 Stocks

2. c. Value at £6 + £4 = £10 Prime cost + Overheads £15 = £25.

3. b. Cost = £40,000 but net realisable value = £38,000 − £4,000 − £1,000 = £33,000 so value at £33,000.

5. FIFO 10 × £15 + 3 × £12 = £186. LIFO 13 × £10 = £130. AVCO 13 × £11.57 = £150.40.

Unit 10 Investment appraisal

1. Project B: Payback 3 years. NPV at 12% £20,770. Profitability index £20,770/£20,000 = 1.0385. Internal rate of return 14% gives £19,950 so that is the IRR as near as can be calculated with tables.

4. a. NPV at 14% is £46,656 − viable. At 22% £38,004 − not viable

   b. Approximately 20%

   c. If new machine is purchased then £50,000/6 = £8,333 a year + loss on sale of old machine in first year.

   If not purchased then £8,333 for next 5 years on the old machine.

   d. £4,288 a year.

Unit 11 Manufacturing and construction

1. a. 1993: Raw Materials £528. Prime Cost £1,326. Works Overheads £954. Gross Profit £746. Admin £425. Selling £627. Net Loss £386.

b. ii. Decrease 19x3 loss by £38,000 and decrease 1994 profit by same amount.

d. Factory Direct Wages: Remained relatively stable (gone slightly down in 19x4) despite inflation and increased turnover. Conclusion labour force reduced. Perhaps big increase in Plant and Machinery in 19x3 is connected.

Royalties: big increase in 19x4. Possibly new products being made under licence, perhaps with the new machinery.

Unit 12 Total absorption costing

2.

		Cut	Make	Finish
	Rates	4,348	8,696	6,956
	Machinery Depeciation	8,400	4,200	1,400
	Electric Power	18,000	9,000	3,000
	Supervision	4,000	8,000	10,000
	Total	34,748	29,896	21,356
	Machine hour rates	£57.91	£99.65	£213.56
d.	Materials	300		
	Labour (78 × £6)	468		
	OHDs Cutting	695		
	Making	598		
	Finishing	4,698		
		6,759		
	Profit	1,690		
	Sales Price	8,449		

Clearly, finishing overheads on this basis is nonsense and a labour hour rate would seem to be more appropriate!

Unit 13 Standard costing

3. a. Cloth – Total variance   Std $300 \times 12 \times £2 = £7,200$

Actual $4,000 \times £1.89 = £7,560$

Variance   £360   ADV

Price $4,000 \times 11p = $ £440   FAV

Usage $400 \times £2 = $ £800   ADV

b. Price: Price change, lower quality, special deal, bulk purchase.

Quantity: Natural variation, wastage, damage to cloth, poorer quality cloth, poor supervision or labour practice.

c. Low price and high usage may both be a function of quality.

d. Consider quality of cloth, labour practices, supervision.

6. a. Total Variance is Actual £23,900 compared with $13,100 \times \dfrac{£20,400}{13,500} = £4,104$ ADV.

Efficiency: 13,100 should require $\dfrac{13,100}{3} = 4,367$ labour hours but took 4,650.

So 283 extra hours were worked. They would drive $\dfrac{£20,400}{4,500} = £4.533$ per hour overheads.

Ergo variance is $£4.533 \times 283 = £1,283$ ADV.

Expenditure. 4,650 labour hours should drive $4,650 \times \dfrac{£20,400}{4,500} = £21,080$ but actual was £23,900 so variance is £2,820 ADV

Note that £1 is lost in rounding.

6. b. Variable overheads are thought to be driven by labour hours. Too many labour hours were used. Possibly due to breakdowns, sickness, accidents, poor supervision, use of lower grade/inexperienced labour.

Actual were more than expected from labour hours. Possible causes are natural variation (e.g. repairs, lubricants), price rises, inefficiencies (low grade labour?), price rises.

8. a. Standard Overhead recovery is $\dfrac{£10,000}{4,000} = £2.50$ per unit.

Actual cost	£11,050
Recovered 3,870 × £2.50	£9,675
Total Variance	£1,375 ADV

Expenditure variance is simply £11,050 –£10,000 = £1,050 ADV

Volume variance is volume shortage 130 units × £2.50 = £325 ADV

b. Expenditure may be price rises or natural variation (e.g. preventive maintenance).

Volume may be inability to produce for reasons such as accidents, breakdowns, need for maintenance downtime, inefficiencies in the labour force etc. Volume may also be deliberate underproduction due to lack of sales.

Unit 14 Company accounts

1. Cain: Gross Profit £2,500. Profit after Interest £720. Dividends £210. Retained Profits £330. Fixed Assets £4,668. Current Assets £1,399. Current Liabilities £1,755. Net Assets £1,912. Profit and Loss Account £693. Capital and Reserves £1,912.

4. a. Balance Sheet at end: Net Assets £17,800. Share Capital £3,750. Share Premium £2,850. Revaluation Reserve £6,000. Profit and Loss Account £5,200.

Unit 15 Ratio analysis

4. a.

		K	L	M
i ROCE K is $\dfrac{2,400}{6,350}$		38%	19%	6.6%
ii AUR L is $\dfrac{21,000}{6,340}$		5.6	3.3	1.45
iii DPP M is $\dfrac{4,200}{34,000} \times 365$		–	55 days	45 days
iv NPTS K is $\dfrac{2,400}{35,800}$		6.7%	5.7%	4.5%

v Stock K is $\dfrac{1,100}{27,100} \times 365$ 15 days   40 days   82 days

b. K is the Supermarket. L is the textile company and M is the process plant manufacturer.

ROCE is not really meaningful for supermarkets but is for the other two. However valuation differences are important. AUR is also less meaningful for supermarkets (especially those with high spare cash) and in any case must be considered in relation to similar companies.

Supermarkets sell for cash! The other DPPs are relevant. NPTS must be compared only with similar companies. Stock turnover (against cost of sales!) is the relevant bit. In the case of the manufacturers separate figures for raw materials, work in progresss and finished goods are needed.

9. B. Gearing $\dfrac{170}{170 + 200 + 480}$ = 20%

ROCE $\dfrac{240}{170 + 200 + 480}$ = 28% (before tax)

ROSF $\dfrac{240 - 25 - 62}{200 + 480}$ = 22.5% (after tax)

Unit 16 Sources of finance

3. a. Positive balance on Profit and Loss Account. This is not conclusive – losses may be have been incurred in recent years. Better evidence is that Corporation Tax (payable on profits) is payable.

b. It has a large overdraft and has to repay the Unsecured loan stock in the near future.

c. Lack of cash and (b) above.

d. Mortgage of premises, rights issue, issue of more loan stock (perhaps convertible to make it attractive), factoring debts.

e. Net Assets value is Net Assets/number of shares i.e. $\dfrac{£992,000}{1,000,000}$ = 99.2p. The actual quote is way below this. The cash crisis seems to have scared investors!

Unit 17 The Stock Exchange

3. a. Each share is priced at £1.92. If the assets were realised at their book value (unlikely!) and the liabilities paid off £2.17 would be available for each share. Dividends will be received and in the past the annual dividends paid represent only 0.9% of the Share price. The share price has been fairly volatile in the last year so unless care is taken over the time of disposal a capital loss could be sustained. Current price is at the higher end.

b. i. No, as he needs income and, at his age, a capital gain is not so essential.

ii. No, as he also needs income.

iii. Yes, he needs no income, needs a capital gain to maintain his capital on eventual retirement. He would also probably like the risk.

7. a. If the share price stays at or near 120p, then conversion will change an investment valued at 86 into one valued at 60. So conversion will depend on a substantial rise in the share price. There are five years in which this can happen. If conversion does not take place then redemption (presumably at par, giving Judy a capital gain over current price) will be in 19x9 and, in the meantime, Judy will receive annual interest of £160.

   b. The price of convertibles is a complex function of several variables and one of these is prevailing interest rates. If rates fall the value of the convertible will rise.

Unit 18 Accounting in the not-for-profit sector

1. a. Both sides add up to £52,076

   b. Various sorts of income (interest, dividends, donations, fund raising, legacies), very small admin costs, expenditures on students' travelling and fees, a change of investment from gilt edged to ICI - higher risk but higher returns. Income totals £36,130 but outgoings are only £28,705.

   c. Clearly not! Balance Sheet is required. Income and expenditure account is required using accruals accounting. Number of students helped etc, number turned down.

Unit 19 Cash flow statements

2. Micah

Operations $(27 + 22 - 3 + 2 - 4 - 8)$	36
Dividend paid	(13)
Tax Paid	(12)
Fixed Assets $(66 - 8)$	(58)
Debenture	10
Share Issue $(6 + 6)$	12
Net Outflow $(21 + 4)$	25

Appendix B
Glossary of accounting terms

Absorption: the sharing out of the costs of a cost centre among the products which use the cost centre.

Account: a record in a double entry system that is kept for each (or each class) of asset, liability, revenue and expense.

Accounting equation: an expression of the equivalence, in total, of assets = liabilities + equity.

Accounting period: that time period, typically one year, to which financial statements are related.

Accounting policies: the specific accounting bases selected and followed by a business enterprise (e.g. straight line or reducing balance depreciation).

Accounting rate of return: a ratio sometimes used in investment appraisal but based on profits not cash flows. Not recommended.

Accounting Standards Board: a quasi-statutory subsidiary of the Financial Reporting Council which makes, amends and withdraws accounting standards.

Accounting standards: Prescribed methods of accounting. The original set (Statements of Standard Accounting Practice – SSAPs) were issued by the Accounting Standards Committee and adopted by the professional bodies. Currently Financial Reporting Standards are issued by the Accounting Standards Board.

Accruals: (that which has accrued, accumulated, grown) expenses which have been consumed or enjoyed but which have not been paid for at the accounting date.

Accruals convention: the convention that revenues and costs are matched with one the other and dealt with in the Profit and Loss Account of the period to which they relate irrespective of the period of receipt or payment.

Accumulated depreciation: that part of the original cost of a fixed asset which has been regarded as a depreciation expense in successive Profit and Loss Accounts: cost less accumulated depreciation = net book value.

Acid test: the ratio of current assets (excluding stock) to current liabilities.

Acquisitions: operations of a reporting entity that are acquired in a period. Separate disclosure of turnover, profits etc must be made.

Activity based costing: cost attribution to cost units on the basis of benefit received from indirect activities. The idea is that overhead costs are driven by activities (e.g. setting up a machine) not products.

Allocation: the charging of discrete, identifiable costs to cost centres or cost units. A cost is allocated when it is unique to a particular cost centre.

Amortisation: another word for depreciation: commonly used for depreciation of the capital cost of acquiring leasehold property.

Apportionment: the division of costs among two or more cost centres in proportion to estimated benefit on some sensible basis. Apportionment is for shared costs.

Assets: resources of value owned by a business entity.

Assets utilisation ratio: a ratio which purports to measure the intensity of use of business assets. Calculated as sales over net operating assets. Can be expressed as sales as a percentage of net operating assets.

Asset value: a term which expresses the money amount of assets less liabilities of a company attributable to one ordinary share.

Avoidable costs: the specific costs of an activity or sector of a business which would be avoided if that activity or sector did not exist.

Auditing: the independent examination of, and expression of an opinion on, the financial statements of an enterprise by an appointed auditor in pursuance of that appointment and in compliance with any relevant statutory obligation.

AVCO (average cost): a method of valuing fungible assets (notably stock) at average (simple or weighted) input prices.

Bad debts: debts known to be irrecoverable and therefore treated as losses by inclusion in the Profit and Loss Account as an expense.

Balance Sheet: a financial statement showing the financial position of a business entity in terms of assets, liabilities and capital at a specified date.

Bankruptcy: a legal status imposed by a court. Usually a trustee is appointed to receive and realise the assets of the bankrupt and to distribute the proceeds to his creditors according to the law.

Benefits in kind: things or services supplied by a company to its directors and others in addition to cash remuneration. The best known is the provision of and free use of a motor car. The value of benefits in kind are taxable.

Bond: a formal written document that provides evidence of a loan. Bond has mainly American usage. Its UK equivalent is debenture.

Bonus issue: a free issue of new shares to existing shareholders. No payment is made for the shares. Its main effect is to divide the substance of the company (assets less liabilities) into a larger number of shares.

Book value: the amount at which an asset is carried on the accounting records and Balance Sheet. The usual book value for fixed assets is cost less accumulated depreciation. Alternative words include written down value, net book value and carrying value. Book value rarely if ever corresponds to saleable value.

Breakeven chart: a chart which illustrates costs, revenues, profit and loss at various levels of activity within a relevant range.

Breakeven point: the level of activity (e.g. level of sales) at which the business makes neither a profit nor a loss i.e. where total revenues exactly equal total costs.

Budget: a formal quantitative expression of management's plans or expectations. Master budgets are the forecast or planned Profit and Loss Account and Balance Sheet. Subsidiary budgets include those for sales, output, purchases, labour, cash etc.

Capital: an imprecise term meaning the whole quantity of assets less liabilities owned by a person or a business.

Capital allowances: deductions from profit for fixed asset purchases. In effect capital allowances is a standard system of depreciation used instead of depreciation for tax purposes only.

Capital budgeting: the process of planning or appraising possible fixed asset acquisitions.

Capital employed: a term describing the total net assets employed in a business. Various definitions are used, so beware talking at cross purposes.

Capital expenditure: expenditure on fixed assets.

Cash: strictly coins and notes but used also to mean all forms of ready money including bank balances.

Cash discount: a reduction in the amount payable by a debtor to induce prompt payment (equivalent to settlement discount).

Cash flow: a vague term (compare cash flow difficulties) used for the difference between total cash in and total cash out in a period.

Cash flow forecast: a document detailing expected or planned cash receipts and outgoings for a future period.

Cash flow statement: a formal financial statement required by Financial Reporting Standard (FRS) 1 and showing a summary of cash inflows and outflows under certain required headings.

Committed costs: those fixed costs which cannot be eliminated or even cut back without having a major effect on the enterprise's activities (e.g. rent).

Common stock: the US equivalent of ordinary shares.

Companies Act 1985: the major Act of Parliament which regulates companies. Was modified and extended by the Companies Act 1989.

Company: a body corporate regulated by the Companies Act 1985.

Conservatism: (also known as prudence) the convention whereby revenue and profits are not anticipated, but provision is made for all known liabilities (expenses and losses) whether the amount of these is known with certainty or is a best estimate. Essentially – future profit, wait until it happens – future loss, count it now.

Consideration: the amount to be paid for anything sold including businesses. May be cash, shares or other securities.

Consistency: convention that there is consistency of accounting treatment of like items within each year and from year to year.

Consolidation: the aggregation of the financial statements of the separate companies of a group as if they were a single entity.

Contribution: a term used in marginal costing – the difference between sale price and associated variable costs.

Controllable costs (also known as managed costs): costs, chargeable to a budget or cost centre, which can be influenced by the actions of the persons in whom control is vested.

Conversion cost: the cost of bringing a product or service into its present location or condition. May include a share of production overheads.

Convertible loan stock: loans where, at the option of the lender, the loan can be converted into ordinary shares at specified times and specified rates of conversion.

Cost behaviour: the change in a cost when the level of output changes.

Cost centre: a location, function, or item of equipment in respect of which costs may be ascertained and related to cost units.

Cost convention: the accounting convention whereby Balance Sheet assets are mostly valued at input cost or by reference to input cost.

Cost-volume-profit (CVP) analysis: the study of the relationships between variable costs, total fixed costs, levels of output and price and mix of units sold and profit.

Credit: commonly used to refer to a benefit or gain also the practice of selling goods and expecting payment at a later date.

Credit control: those measures and procedures adopted by a firm to ensure that its credit customers pay their accounts.

Creditors: those persons, firms or organisations to whom the enterprise owes money.

Creditors payment or settlement period: a ratio (usually creditors/ inputs on credit in a year $\times 365$) which measures how long it takes the firm to pay its creditors.

Cumulative preference shares: preference shares where the rights to dividends omitted in a given year accumulate. These dividends must be paid before a dividend can be paid on the ordinary shares.

Current assets: cash + those assets (stock, debtors, prepayments, bank accounts) which the management intend to convert into cash or consume in the normal course of business within one year or within the operating cycle.

Current cost accounting (CCA): a system of accounting which recognises the fluctuating value of money by measuring current value by applying specific indices and other devices to historical costs. A valid method which is complex and difficult to understand intuitively.

Current liabilities: debts or obligations that will be paid within one year of the accounting date. The Companies Act prefers the expression – Creditors: amount falling due within one year.

Current ratio: the ratio of current assets to current liabilities.

Cut-off: the difficulties encountered by accountants in ensuring all items of income and expense are correctly ascribed to the right annual profit statement.

Debenture: a document which creates or acknowledges a debt. Commonly used for the debt itself.

Debt: a sum due by a debtor to his creditor. Commonly used also as a generic term for borrowings.

Debtors: those who owe money.

Debtors payment (settlement) period: a calculation of the average time taken by credit customers to pay for their goods. Calculated by Debtors/credit sales in a year × 365.

Depletion method: a method of depreciation applicable to wasting assets such as mines and quarries. The amount of depreciation in a year is a function of the quantity extracted in the year compared to the total resource.

Depreciation: a measure of the wearing out, consumption or other loss of value whether arising from use, effluxion of time or obsolescence through technology and market changes. Depreciation should be allocated to accounting period so as to charge a fair proportion to each accounting period during the expected useful life of the asset.

Direct costs: those costs comprising direct materials, direct labour and direct expenses which can be traced directly to specific jobs, products or services.

Discontinued operations: operations of the reporting entity that are sold or terminated in a period. Turnover and results must be separately disclosed.

Discount: a monetary deduction or reduction. Settlement discount (also known as cash discount) is given for early settlement of debts. Debentures can be redeemed at a discount. Trade discount is a simple reduction in price given to favoured customers for reasons such as status or bulk purchase.

Discounted cash flow: an evaluation of the future cash flows generated by a capital investment project, by discounting them to their present value.

Dividend: a distribution of earnings to its shareholders by a company.

Dividend cover: a measure of the extent to which the dividend paid by a company is covered by its earnings (profits).

Dividend yield: a measure of the revenue earning capacity of an ordinary share to its holder. It is calculated by dividend per share as a percentage of the quoted share price.

Drawings: cash or goods withdrawn from the business by a proprietor for his private use.

Earnings: another word for profits, particularly for company profits.

Earnings per share: an investor ratio, calculated as after tax profits from ordinary activities/ number of shares.

Economic order quantity (EOQ): that purchasing order size which takes into account the optimum combination of stockholding costs and ordering costs.

Entity convention: the convention that a business can be viewed as a unit that is a separate entity and apart from its owners and from other firms.

Equity: the ordinary shares or risk capital of an enterprise. Also a system of law and a Trade Union for actors.

Exceptional items: material items which derive from events or transactions that fall within the ordinary activities of the reporting entity and which need to be disclosed by virtue of their size or incidence if the financial statements are to give a true and fair view. Examples are profits or losses on termination of an operation, costs of a fundamental reorganisation and profits and losses on disposal of fixed assets.

Expense: a cost which will be in the Profit and Loss Account of a year.

Exposure draft: a document issue on a specific accounting topic by the Accounting Standards Board for discussion.

Extraordinary items: material items possessing a high degree of abnormality which arise from events or transactions that fall outside the ordinary activities of the reporting entity and which are not expected to recur. They should be disclosed but are very rare indeed.

Factoring: the sale of debtors to a factoring company to improve cash flow. Factoring is a method of obtaining finance tailored to the amount of business done but factoring companies also offer services such as credit worthiness checks, sales and debtor recording, and debt collection.

FIFO: first in first out – a method of recording and valuation of fungible assets, especially stocks, which values items on the assumption that the oldest stock is used first. FIFO stocks are valued at most recent input prices.

Finance lease: a leasing contract which transfers substantially all the risks and rewards of ownership of an asset to the lessee. In effect the lessee is really buying the assets with the aid of a loan and the lease instalments are really payments of interest and repayments of capital. They are accounted for as such in accordance with the accounting convention of substance over form.

Financial Reporting Council: quasi government body which encourages good financial reporting. This is done through the Accounting Standards Board, the Financial Reporting Review Panel and the Urgent Issues Task Force.

Financial Reporting Review panel: a subsidiary of the Financial Reporting Council which reviews accounts of companies and seeks to ensure compliance with the requirements of the Companies Act and the Accounting Standards Board.

Financial statements: Balance Sheets, Profit and Loss Account, Income and Expenditure Accounts, Cash Flow Statements and other documents which formally convey information of a financial nature to interested parties concerning an enterprise. In companies, the financial statements are subject to audit opinion.

Fixed assets: business assets which have a useful life extending over more than one year. Examples are land and buildings, plant and machinery, vehicles.

Fixed cost: a cost which in the short term, remains the same at different levels of activity. An example is rent.

Flexible budget: a budget which is flexed to recognise the difference in behaviour of fixed and variable costs in relation to levels of output. Total budgeted costs changed to accord with changed levels of activity.

Floating charge: an arrangement whereby a lender to a company has a floating charge over the assets generally of the company gives the lender priority of repayment from the proceeds of sale of the assets in the event of insolvency. Banks frequently take a floating charge when lending.

Format: a specific layout for a financial statement. Several alternatives are prescribed by the Companies Act 1985.

Funds flow statement: a financial statement which links Balance Sheets at the beginning and end of a period with the Profit and Loss Account for that period. Now replaced by the cash flow statement.

Fungible assets: assets which are substantially indistinguishable from each other. Used for stocks which can then be valued on FIFO or AVCO principles. LIFO is also possible but not usually in the UK for tax reasons.

Gearing: also known as leverage, the relationship between debt and equity in the financing structure of a company.

Gilt-edged securities: securities and investments which offer a negligible risk of default. Principally government securities

Goal congruence: the situation in which each individual, in satisfying his (her) own interests, is also making the best possible contribution to the objectives of the enterprise.

Going concern: the accounting convention which assumes that the enterprise will continue in operational existence for the foreseeable future. This means in particular that the Profit and Loss Account and Balance Sheet assume no intention or necessity to liquidate or curtail significantly the scale of operation.

Goodwill: an intangible asset which appears on the Balance Sheet of some businesses. It is valued at (or below) the difference between the price paid for a whole business and the fair value of the net assets acquired.

Gross: usually means before or without deductions. For example Gross Pay or Gross Profit.

Gross profit: sales revenue less cost of sales but before deduction of overhead expenses. In a manufacturing company it is sales revenue less cost of sales but before deduction of non-manufacturing overheads.

Gross margin: (or gross profit ratio), gross profit expressed as a percentage of sales.

Group: a set of interrelated companies usually consisting of a holding company and its subsidiary and sub-subsidiary companies.

Group accounts: the financial statements of a group wherein the separate financial statements of the member companies of a group are combined into consolidated financial statements.

HIFO: highest in highest out, a pricing policy where costs are collected for a job on the basis that the cost of materials and components is the highest recent input price.

Historical cost: the accounting convention whereby goods, resources and services are recorded at cost. Cost is defined as the exchange or transaction price. Under this convention, realisable values are generally ignored. Inflation is also ignored. The almost universal adoption of this convention makes accounting harder to understand and lessens the credibility of financial statements.

Hurdle: a criterion that a proposed capital investment must pass before it is accepted. It may be a certain interest rate, a positive NPV or a maximum payback period.

Income and expenditure account: the equivalent to Profit and Loss Accounts in non-profit organisations such as clubs, societies and charities.

Indirect costs: costs which cannot be traced to particular products. An example is rent or management salaries. They are usually shared by more than one product and are called overheads.

Insolvency: the state of being unable to pay debts as they fall due. Also used to describe the activities of practitioners in the fields of bankruptcy, receivership and liquidations.

Intangible assets: assets which have long term value but no physical identity. Examples are goodwill, patents, trade marks and brands.

Interim dividend: a dividend paid during a financial year, generally after the issue of unaudited profit figures half way through the year.

Internal rate of return: the rate of discount which will just discount the future cash flows of a proposed capital investment back to the initial outlay.

Inventory: a detailed list of things. Used by accountants as another word for stock.

Investment appraisal: the use of accounting and mathematical methods to determine the likely returns for a proposed investment or capital project.

Key factor: a factor of production which is in limited supply and therefore constrains production.

Labour hour rate: a method of absorption where the costs of a cost centre are shared out amongst products on the basis of the number of hours of direct labour used on each product.

Leverage: an American word for gearing.

LIFO: Last in first out – a valuation method for fungible items where the newest items are assumed to be used first. Means stocks will be valued at old prices. Not used much in the UK for tax reasons.

Limiting or key factor: a factor of production which is in limited supply and therefore constrains output.

Liquidation: the procedure whereby a company is wound up, its assets realised and the proceeds divided up amongst the creditors and shareholders.

Liquidity: the ease with which funds can be raised by the sale of assets.

Liquidity ratios: ratios which purport to indicate the liquidity of a business. They include the current ratio and the acid test ratio.

Listed companies: companies whose shares are traded on the stock exchange.

Machine hour rate: a method of absorption of the costs of a cost centre where the costs are shared out among the products which use the centre in proportion to the use of machine hours by the relevant products.

Management accounting: the provision and interpretation of information which assists management in planning, controlling, decision making, and appraising performance.

Management by exception: control and management of costs and revenues by concentrating on those instances where significant variances by actual from budgets have occurred.

Manufacturing accounts: financial statements which measure and demonstrate the total costs of manufacturing in a period. They are followed by Trading and Profit and Loss Accounts.

Marginal costing: a system of cost analysis which distinguishes fixed costs from variable costs.

Marginal cost: the additional cost incurred by the production of one extra unit.

Margin of safety: the excess of budgeted activity over breakeven activity. Usually expressed as a percentage of budgeted activity.

Mark-up: gross profit expressed as a percentage of cost of goods sold.

Matching convention: the idea that revenues and costs are accrued, matched with one another as far as possible so far as their relationship can be established or justifiably assumed, and dealt with in the Profit and Loss Account of the period in which they relate. An example is the matching of sales of a product with the development costs of that product. The appropriate periods would be when the sales occur.

Master budgets: the overall budgets of an enterprise comprising cash budget, forecast Profit and Loss Account and forecast Balance Sheet. They are made up from subsidiary budgets.

Materiality: the accounting convention that recognises that accounting is a summarising process. Some items and transactions are large (= material) enough to merit separate disclosure rather than inclusion with others in a lump sum. Examples are an exceptionally large bad debt or an exceptionally large loss on sale of a fixed asset.

Minority interest: the interests in the assets of a Group relating to shares in group companies not held by the holding company or other members of the group.

Modified accounts: financial statements which are shortened versions of full accounts. Small and medium sized companies can file these with the Registrar of Companies instead of full accounts.

Money measurement: the convention that requires that all assets, liabilities, revenues and expenses shall be expressed in money terms.

Net: usually means after deductions. For example net current assets = current assets less current liabilities and net cash flow means cash inflows less cash outflows. Contrast gross.

Net book value: the valuation on the Balance Sheet of an asset. Also known as the carrying value or written down value.

Net present value: the value obtained by discounting all cash inflows and outflows attributable to a proposed capital investment project by a selected discount rate.

Net realisable value: the actual or estimated selling price of an asset less all further costs to completion (e.g. cost of a repair if it needs to be repaired before sale) and all costs to be incurred before and on sale (e.g. commission).

NIFO: Next in first out – a pricing policy where costs are collected on the basis that the cost of materials and components is the next input price.

Nominal value: the face value of a share or debenture as stated in the official documents. Will not usually be the same as the issue price which may be at a premium and which will almost never correspond to actual value.

Objectivity: the convention of using reliable and verifiable facts (e.g. the input cost of an asset) rather than estimates of 'value' even if the latter is more realistic.

Operating cycle: the period of time it takes a firm to buy inputs, make or market a product and sell to and collect the cash from a customer.

Opportunity cost: the value of a benefit sacrificed in favour of an alternative course of action.

Ordinary shares: the equity capital of a company.

Out-sourcing: the obtaining of services (such as administration or computing) from separate outside firms instead of using the enterprise's own employees.

Overheads: indirect costs.

Overtrading: a paradoxical situation when a firm does so much business that stocks and debtors rise leading to working capital and liquidity difficulties.

Par value: the nominal sum imprinted on a share certificate and which appears in the Balance Sheet of a company as share capital. It has no significance as a value.

Payback: the number of years which will elapse before the total incoming cash receipts of a proposed project are forecast to exceed the initial outlays.

Periodicity: the convention that financial statements are produced at regular intervals usually at least annually.

Preference shares: shares in which holders are entitled to a fixed rate of dividend (if one is declared) in priority to the ordinary shareholders and to priority over ordinary shareholders in a winding up.

Planning variance: a variance arising because the budgeted cost is now seen as out of date. Examples are wage or price rises.

Premium: an amount paid in excess of par or nominal. Premiums can be on issues and redemptions of shares or debentures.

Prepayments: expenditure already made on goods or services but where the benefit will be felt after the Balance Sheet date. Examples are rent or rates or insurances paid in advance.

Price earnings ratio: an investor ratio calculated as – share price/ earnings per share.

Prime cost: the direct costs of production.

Private company: any company that is not a public company.

Profitability index: in investment appraisal, the Net Present Value of cash inflows/the initial outlays.

Profit and Loss Account: a financial statement which measures and reports the profit earned over a period of time.

Pro Rata: in proportion to.

Prospectus: a document being an advertisement offering shares for sale to the public. Must comply with the rules of the Companies Act and the Stock Exchange.

Provision: a charge in the Profit and Loss Account of a business for an expense which arose in the past but which will only give rise to a payment in the future. To be a provision the amount payable must be uncertain as to amount or as to payability or both. An examples is possible damages awardable by a court in a future action over a past incident (e.g. a libel).

Prudence (or conservatism): the convention whereby revenue and profits are not anticipated, but provision is made for all known liabilities (expenses and losses) whether the amount of these is known with certainty or is a best estimate. Essentially – future profit, wait until it happens – future loss, count it now.

Public company: a company which states that it is a public company, ends its name with the designation Public Limited Company (PLC) and has a minimum share capital of £50,000. All listed companies are PLCs but not all PLCs are listed.

Quick ratio: also known as acid test ratio, current assets (except stock)/ current liabilities.

Quoted company: also known as a listed company, a company whose shares are traded on the stock exchange.

Realisable value: the amount that an asset can be sold for.

Realisation: to sell an asset and hence turn it into cash.

Realisation convention: the concept that a profit is accounted for when a good is sold and not when the cash is received.

Receiver: an insolvency practitioner who is appointed by a debentureholder with a fixed or floating charge when a company defaults.

Redemption: repayment of shares, debentures or loans.

Redemption yield: the yield given by an investment expressed as a percentage and taking into account both income and capital gain or loss.

Reducing balance: a method of depreciation whereby the asset is expensed to the Profit and Loss Account over its useful life by applying a fixed percentage to the written down value.

Registrar of companies: a civil service agency situated in Cardiff where files are maintained on all companies. These are open to view by the public.

Relevant costs: costs that will only be incurred if a proposed course of action is actually taken. The only ones relevant to an actual decision.

Relevant range: the range of activity which is likely. Within it variable costs are expected to be linearly variable with output and fixed costs are expected to be unchanged.

Reporting: the process whereby a company or other institution seeks to inform shareholders and other interested parties of the results and position of the entity by means of financial statements.

Reserves: a technical term indicating that a company has total assets which exceed in amount the sum of liabilities and share capital. This excess arises from retained profits or from revaluations of assets.

Resource accounting and budgeting: the use of normal accruals accounting and Balance Sheets in central government departments and agencies. It is a new discovery for the civil service.

Retained profits: also known as retentions, the excess of profits over dividends.

Return on capital employed: a profitability ratio being income expressed as a percentage of the capital which produced the income. A difficult idea because of the problems of defining income and capital.

Return on sales: the ratio of profit to sales expressed as a percentage.

Returns: the income flowing from the ownership of assets. May include capital gains.

Revenue: amounts charged to customers for goods or services rendered.

Revenue expenditure: expenditure that benefits only the current period and which will therefore be charged in the Profit and Loss Account.

Rights issue: an invitation to existing shareholders to subscribe cash for new shares in the company in proportion to their holdings.

Salvage value: also known as residual value, the amount estimated to be recoverable from the sale of a fixed assets at the end of its useful life.

Secured liabilities: liabilities secured by a fixed or floating charge or by other operation of law such as hire purchase commitments.

Securities: financial assets such as shares, debentures and loan stocks.

Segmental reporting: the practice of breaking down turnover, profits and capital employed into sections to show the separate contributions of each to the overall picture. Segments can be distinct products, geographical areas, classes of customer etc.

Semi-variable costs: costs which have a fixed element and a variable element. Repairs to machinery and telephone are examples.

Settlement discount: a reduction in the amount payable given to a customer to induce rapid payment.

Shares: the division of a company into numerous equal parts. A shareholder may have one or many shares.

SSAPs (Statements of Standard Accounting Practice): accounting practices which are now mandatory in the UK. There are 22 SSAPs covering numerous subjects including depreciation, stock valuation, extraordinary items, segmental reporting.

Standard cost: a predetermined cost that management establishes with great care and uses as a basis for comparison with actual to measure variances.

Stepped fixed costs: fixed costs which are fixed within a specific range of outputs but which step up to a new level if the range is exceeded.

Stock turnover: a ratio which purports to measure the speed at which raw materials or stocks for sale are used up or sold. It is expressed as average time in which the relevant stocks are actually in stock.

Straight line: a depreciation method which allocates the cost of a depreciable asset (less salvage value) over the estimated useful life of the asset in equal instalments.

Subsidiary company: a company of which more than half of the equity capital is owned by another company.

Substance over form: an accounting convention whereby a transaction is accounted for in accordance with its substance or commercial reality in preference to its legal form. Examples are finance leases, hire purchase and group accounts.

Sum of digits: a depreciation method that allocates the cost (less salvage value) of a depreciable asset over its useful life by steadily diminishing instalments.

Sunk costs: costs which have already been incurred and therefore are irrelevant and are not considered in making a decision.

Total absorption cost: a system of costing where all costs (or just production costs) are ascribed to products. Thus the total absorption cost of a product is its direct cost + its fair share of shared overheads.

Trade discount: a reduction in invoiced price of a good given to favoured customers, special classes of customer or for bulk purchase.

Trading account: a financial statement which measures and demonstrates the gross profit earned in a period.

Transaction: any event or activity in a firm requiring an entry in the double entry bookkeeping system. Examples are sales and purchases of goods and services and the receipts and payments of cash.

Trial balance: a listing in two columns (debit and credit) of all the balances in a double entry bookkeeping system.

True and fair view: the view that the Companies Act requires all financial statements to give. It is a difficult concept which is usually discussed in auditing texts.

Turnover: another term for total sales in a period.

Unsecured creditors: those creditors, short or long term, who do not have the benefit of a fixed, floating or other charge over any assets.

Value: the difficult concept in accounting. There are values in use, book values, values to the firm, going concern values, realisable values, nominal values, par values, written down values and many others.

Variable cost: a cost which in the short term and over a relevant range tends to vary linearly following the level of activity.

Variance: the difference between a planned, budgeted or standard cost and the actual cost. Variances are generally referred to as adverse (= unfavourable) or favourable.

Wasting assets: assets which are used up in producing goods. Can be applied to all fixed assets but usually confined to mines, quarries, and mineral rights.

Winding up: the liquidation of a company by realising the assets and distributing the proceeds to the parties entitled.

Working capital: the excess of current assets over current liabilities.

Work in progress: the inventory of goods started but not completed at a Balance Sheet date.

Write-off: to write something off is to charge it to Profit and Loss Account as an expense.

Written down value: the cost of an asset less accumulated depreciation. Also known as net book value or carrying value.

Yield: the return on an investment usually expressed as a percentage.

Appendix C
Answers to tasks in the Martin Padlocks Ltd saga

Unit 1 Starting a new business

Task 1

See Scenario 3.

Tasks 2

1. Recast Cash Flow Forecast

	Jan	Feb	Mar	Apr	May	Jun	Total
Receipts:							
Customers			6,000	9,000	15,000	15,000	45,000
Capital	15,000						
Total	15,000		6,000	9,000	15,000	15,000	60,000
Payments:							
Suppliers			14,000	11,000	11,000	13,000	49,000
Anne			500				500
Computer	1,000						1,000
Van	200	200	200	200	200	200	1,200
Equipment	3,000						3,000
Rent	2,000						2,000
Rates					750		750
Electricity				220			220
Stationery	240						240
Advertising			600			600	1,200
Van expenses	200	200	200	200	200	200	1,200
Wages	1,500	1,500	1,500	1,500	1,500	1,500	9,000
Martin	700	700	700	700	700	700	4,200
Total	8,840	2,600	17,700	13,820	14,350	16,200	73,510
B/F(a)	0	6,160	3,560	−8,140	−12,960	−12,310	0
C/F(b)	6,160	3,560	−8,140	−12,960	−12,310	−13,510	−13,510

2. Martin's business intends to buy a computer, a van (but he might lease this), and some equipment. Capital expenditure is on fixed assets which are assets which cost more than a trivial amount and will last over more than one accounting year.

Tasks 3

1. Second six months

	Jly	Aug	Sep	Oct	Nov	Dec	Total
Receipts:							
Customers	18,000	18,000	18,000	18,000	18,000	18,000	108,000
Payments							
Suppliers	13,000	13,000	12,000	12,000	12,000	12,000	74,000
Van	200	200	200	200	200	200	1,200
Rent	2,000						2,000
Rates				500			500
Electricity	300			300			600
Stationery		200					200
Advertising			600			600	1,200
Van expenses	200	200	200	200	200	200	1,200
Wages	1,500	1,500	1,500	1,500	1,500	1,500	9,000
Martin	700	700	700	700	700	700	4,200
Total	17,900	15,800	15,200	15,400	14,600	15,200	94,100
b/f	−13,510	−13,410	−11,210	−8,410	−5,810	−2,410	−13,510
c/f	−13,410	−11,210	−8,410	−5,810	−2,410	390	390

2. Payments to suppliers precede receipts from customers, so when the business stabilises and presuming the business is profitable then the receipts will exceed payments. The overdraft may reduce again if there is expansion of sales, increases in stocks, capital expenditure or unprofitable trading. The balance is a function of many variables so that prediction can actually be done only by forecasting in detail.

3. The main point about a spreadsheet is to use formulae which add the separate receipts and payments columns and calculate the balances so that immediate recalculation of the balances follows any change in the detail of receipts or payments.

Unit 2 The Profit and Loss Account

Tasks 1

1. The business is trading — the buying and selling of goods. It is desirable to calculate the profit on this activity (the Gross Profit) before calculating overheads.

2. Yes — all sales in the period are included because of the realisation convention. Thus the profit on this sale is included in the profit for the year even though the cash was not received.

3. There is no opening stock because 'opening stock' is the stock left over from the previous year and this is the first year.

4. They are included in purchases and also in the stock at the year end. In effect they are included in the purchases in the trading account but taken out again because they are included in the stock.

   Stationery is not in purchases but in the overhead category — Printing and Stationery. Purchases in the trading account only includes goods for resale.

5. If the stock was included at selling price then the profit on sale would be included before the goods were sold. Try the effect of different stock values on the calculation of gross profit.

6. £370 only would be included as October, November and December are in this year but January, February and March are a next year expense. This is the accruals convention.

7. This is capital expenditure which means the cost of the computer is not just an expense of this year but also of all the years when it will be used. Accounting treatment is to include it on the Balance Sheet and to include a part of the cost in each year's Profit and Loss Account under the Depreciation process.

8. There are many reasons why the gross profit margin is not exactly 50%. Many items may have been sold at a lower mark-up perhaps because they were damaged or part of a special promotions. Some items may be included in cost of sales but without a corresponding sale as the goods were lost or destroyed. Accounting error (especially stocktaking) can also be part of the reason.

9. Profit is not cash. It is most important to realise this. The Profit and Loss Account includes sales and purchases where cash is received in the next or previous year. Expenses are subject to the accruals convention. Capital expenditure is in the Profit and Loss Account only through depreciation. Some cash flows (loans, drawings etc) are not in the Profit and Loss Account at all.

Tasks 2

Forecast Profit and Loss Account for 19x2

Sales		290,000
Less: Cost of Goods Sold:		
Opening Stock	14,730	
Purchases	206,270	
	221,000	
Less Closing Stock	21,000	200,000
Gross Profit		90,000
Less: Expenses		
Rent	4,000	
Rates	1,870	
Electricity	1,080	
Printing and Stationery	756	
Advertising	1,416	
Van Expenses	3,254	
Wages	23,400	
Director's Remuneration	19,200	
Employers' National Insurance	4,260	
Audit and Accountancy	1,600	
Sundries	1,000	
Lease on van	2,400	

Bank Interest and Charges	1,495	
Depreciation	1,100	
Redecoration	2,500	69,331
Net Profit		20,669

Note that if sales are £290,000, gross profit will be $45/145 \times £290,000 = £90,000$.

Cost of goods sold will thus be £200,000. Take £14,730 to give £185,270.

This is purchases less 10% of purchases and so stock is $1/9 \times £185,270$ or £21,000 to the nearest £'000.

2. We have already dealt with a.

   b. The problem is 'is the profit earned in 19x2 or 19x3?'. Strict observance of the realisation convention leads us to see the sale in 19x3 when it will be invoiced. Thus the accounting treatment is to include the goods in stock at £550 and put the sale through in 19x3.

3. It would not be included in expenses as it is capital expenditure. It will be subject to the depreciation process and thus £500 included in the Profit and Loss Account as Depreciation (assuming straight line method).

4. No effect on profit – in purchases but also in closing stock.

   Gross Profit would then be $50/150 \times £290,000 = £96,667$.

5. Suggestions may include: raising prices, changing products stocked, more advertising, appointing a rep, negotiating lower input prices, economies on overheads.

Tasks 3

1. I think you have grasped this now.

2. The entity is the company not Martin personally. The period is one year. The profit is measured in money terms. Gross profit is that earned on all sales in the year irrespective of cash flows. The sales in the year are matched against the cost of goods sold and the expenses of the year.

Tasks 4

1. £5,236

2. Profit £18,786

3. Note use of entity (the business), money, period, realisation (contract sales), accruals (materials and insurance). Only contentious issue is £320. I have charged all this to profit although part might be seen as relating also to later years.

4. Differences include debtors, stock of materials, insurance, capital expenditure and depreciation, drawings.

Unit 3 The Balance Sheet

Tasks 1

1. Fixed assets have a long life. Current assets are constantly being turned over or circulated.

2. Net book value is the original cost less arbitrary depreciation. A saleable value, if one can be found, is not used in Balance Sheets.

3. Persons or firms who owe money to Martin for goods supplies but not yet paid for.

4. That part of expense payments which extend into the following year.

5. Creditors are persons or firms who are owed money for goods already supplied but not yet paid for.

6. Current assets less current liabilities (= creditors: amounts falling due within one year). Net, in accounting, generally means 'after deducting something'.

7. It is legally repayable on demand.

8. Sums due for services or goods received or other obligations due (e.g. tax or dividends) not yet paid for.

9. The ANNUAL interest chargeable on a loan is expressed like this.

Task 2

Answer in Scenario 4.

Task 3

a. Include in debtors – realisation convention.

b. Exclude – goodwill can sometimes be included at its cost but only if it was purchased.

c. Exclude – they never belonged to the company.

d. Include – £250 in creditors.

Tasks 4

Balance Sheets do not measure the value of assets on the kind of prices that could be obtained if they were sold. Further the Balance Sheet does not measure the value of the business as a whole. The Balance Sheet does list the assets (but some e.g. goodwill may be omitted) and liabilities (but some e.g. potential redundancy pay are omitted) and gives values which can be understood and prove useful to those who understand these things – I hope you are beginning to!

Tasks 5

2. Salary and investment income?, mortgage (but some part is off the loan and some interest), food, heating, entertainment, holidays etc, assets — house, car appliances, investments etc, liabilities — mortgage, unpaid bills, HP. Capital expenditure — car, appliances etc.

3. Net worth? Your wealth? Amount left if you die?

Unit 4 Depreciation

Task 1

Salvage value is the estimated sale price at the end of the life of a fixed asset, depreciation policy means the choice of straight line, reducing balance etc.

Tasks 2

1. There is usually no clear reason or thinking behind a firm's policy on straight line or reducing balance. Perhaps computers are the type of asset which reduce in value more rapidly in early years or perhaps they give more 'utility' in earlier years.

2. i. Straight line (less in first year)
   ii. Hard to say!

Tasks 3

1. Second year Profit and Loss Account 250 + 900 + 2,100 + 400 = 3,650

2.

Computer	1,000	750	250
Stacking	3,000	1,800	1,200
Van	7,000	2,100	4,900
Machine	3,000	400	2,600
	14,000	5,050	8,950

3. New fixed assets are not an expense of the year of purchase but depreciation is an expense.

Task 4

a. Depreciation is an annual charge in the Profit and Loss Account. As it is charged it is added to (accumulates) year by year. In effect as depreciation accumulates the net book value declines.

b. Land does not usually lose value.

c. Not all the £185,000 was spent in the same year.

d. Just the difference between the 'net book value' and the actual sale proceeds.

e. Use of the cost convention and the depreciation process. Sometimes property is actually revalued up to its market price.

f. Resale value is not used and probably the plant still has use to the business. It thus has value to the business beyond the resale value.

Task 5

This is the nature of accounting. It is historical and is based on input costs. It is also usually based on existing circumstances. Hypothetical circumstances (e.g. a sale of the course) can be discussed in notes attached to the accounts but not usually in the accounts proper.

Unit 5 Costing and pricing a product

Tasks 1

1.

Direct Costs: Materials	0.50	(Indirect costs	Depr	2,400
Labour	0.30		Other	25,000
	0.80			27,400
Indirect costs	0.46		/ 60,000 = 0.46)	
Total	1.26			

2. Selling Price 1.26 × 1.3 = £1.64

Task 2

Price	1.8	1.75	1.69	1.65	1.55
Profit	13,300	20,450	26,000	11,750	19,050

Optimum is at £1.69 and 60,000 units.

Task 3

Cash flow forecast: new cash flows will be revenue from sales (delayed by slowness of customers to pay), payments for Machinery, materials, labour and overheads (some possible delays here as credit can be taken for many items). Net effect likely to be need for more bank borrowing.

Task 4

Breakeven sales calculated by: Fixed costs £25,300 + Variable costs 83.5p and sales at 1.70 a unit so breakeven sales are 29,249 units or £49,723.

Task 5

Materials	— more efficient use of bulk material at large outputs, quantity discounts.
Labour	— less time wasted on setting up at higher outputs, learning curve.
Rent and rates	— fixed.
Insurance	— mostly fixed but some premiums may change with output (e.g. EL and PL).
Repairs	— may rise with more use of factory and machinery.
Electricity	— semi-variable as we have seen.
Foreman	— fixed but tendency to overtime as output rises.

Unit 6 Future strategy and budgeting

Tasks 1

1. Probably the principal limitation is sales.

2. **Budgeted Profit and Loss Account for the fourth year**

Sales		300,000
Variable costs:		
Materials	90,000	
Labour	60,000	150,000
Contribution		150,000
Fixed Costs:		
Manager	20,000	
Rent	12,000	
Rates	7,000	
Factory Overheads	40,000	
Depreciation	11,000	90,000
Net Profit		60,000

Budgeted Balance Sheet as at the end of year four

Fixed Assets		
Cost		60,000
Depreciation		11,000
		49,000
Current Assets		
Debtors	50,000	
Cash at Bank	4,500	
	54,500	
Current Liabilities		
Creditors	15,000	39,500
		88,500
Capital at beginning of year		28,500
Net profit		60,000
		88,500

4. Budgets required, contents and actions might be:

Sales: quantity to be sold and price: set up sales force or engage agents, design and print literature etc

Material: type and quantity of material and prices to be paid: determine suppliers and place contracts (especially important if techniques such as just in time are to be adopted)

Labour: type, quantity and wage rates: engage staff

Overheads: list under appropriate headings with amounts expected: action depends on heading, may involve placing contracts for maintenance, cleaning, insurance etc. Note that many overheads are optional (e.g. insurance) and the budget is the process for deciding what should be afforded.

Capital Expenditure: purchases to be made and price to be paid: commission design and purchase.

Cash Budget: a cash flow forecast taking into account patterns of payment by customers: arranging bank overdraft or other forms of finance as necessary.

5. Coordinating: materials and labour must match projected output and sales, capital expenditure must be made to achieve output, necessary finance must be made available.

Communication: all staff are fully appraised of the hopes and aspirations of the firm so that they can play their part in fulfilling plans.

Motivation: causes staff to see budget as their property (assuming they were involved in its preparation), motivates them to fulfil budget, provides a challenge, fosters identification with the firm and its aspirations.

Control: Assume the budget represents a good plan. Deviations from the plan can be detected and action taken to return it on to course.

Evaluation: Staff are expected to conform to the budget and the budget represents a benchmark or standard against which actual performance can be measured.

Delegation: the budget represents a plan of action. Staff are expected to action the plan. Without it staff would continuously need to seek authority for action from senior management.

Tasks 2

1. Possibly building, maintenance, bar, social, fund-raising, membership, finance.

2. Preparation of budgets will force committee to express intentions in money terms. This can be changed to optimise it, make it feasible, and communicate it to members. Any needs (e.g. for finance) can be identified and necessary action taken.

3. Income and expenditure account and Balance Sheet, cash flow, capital expenditure, bar trading, fund-raising, maintenance.

4. See answer to task 6.1.5 above.

Unit 7 Marginal costing

Tasks 1

1. i. Contribution per item is $£4.00 - £2.50 - \dfrac{£100}{500} - £0.30 = £1$

   Fixed Costs are $\dfrac{£6,000}{5} + \dfrac{£1,000 - £200}{4} = £1,400$

   Thus break even is 1,400 units

   ii. Contribution per item is $£4 - £1 - £0.70 = £2.30$

   Fixed costs are $\dfrac{£20,000 - £2,000}{5} + £12,000 + £3,000 = £18,600$

   Thus break even is $\dfrac{£18,600}{£2.30} = £8,087$

2. Profits at 20,000 units:

	Buy	Make
Contribution	20,000	46,000
Fixed Costs	1,400	18,600
Net Profit	18,600	27,400

Thus make!

3. Let sales in units be x, then:

$x \times £1 - £1,400 = x \times £2.30 - £18,600$ then $x = 13,233$ units and profit = £11,831.

4. Other matters to consider are:

Continuity of supply (Taiwanese may sell to others in preference, long journey)

Price stability

Quality control

Risk (breakeven is high on manufacture)

Exchange rate risks

Tasks 2

1. Assume 5,000 a year for two years and ignore further years.

Costs will be $5,000 \times (£2 + £0.50 + £100/500) + £3,000/2 = £15,000$

Breakeven price is thus £15,000/5,000 = £3.

2. Saving will be 20p × 65,000 = £13,000.

Thus the French order of 5,000 would actually cost only £15,000 – £13,000 = £2,000, a price of 40p each would be breakeven!

3. Advantages are simply more profit as long as the acceptance of the order meant incremental inflows greater than incremental outflows.

Disadvantages include all customers wanting the preferential price, the French customer selling to UK customers, anti-dumping complaints from France.

Tasks 3

1.

	AM	PM
Selling Price	11.00	15.00
Costs	7.50	11.00
Contribution	3.50	4.00
Minutes of scarce item	10	20
Contribution/minute	35p	20p
Preference	1	2
Make	6,000	7,200b
Use	1,000 hours	2,400a

a = balance available and b = what can be made in the balance available.

2. To breakeven on PMs Machining cost cannot exceed £15.00 – £7 = £8

3 an hour can be made so £24 is the maximum.

Task 4

Currently profitability on a marginal basis looks like £5,600 - £2,560 - (£12,300 - £8,900) = £360 Loss. But this excludes uncosted benefits and costs such as those mentioned. You can see the problem of weighing up matters that are not expressed in the common term of £s. Is it possible to put these into money terms? E.g. what would cost be to clean up so school does not look scruffy in the mornings.

Unit 8 Working capital

Tasks 1

1. Data indicate:

    All of June sales are o/s

    74% of May sales are o/s so that it seems that 26% of customers settle in the month following the month of the sale

    47% of April sales are o/s so that it seems that 53% of the customers settle within two months of the end of the month of sale.

    These results are not dissimilar from those at the end of December

    May and June Purchase Accounts remain unpaid at the end of June

    Most of the April Purchases have been settled.

    This shows that Martin is now paying more slowly than in December.

    Stocks for resale are:

	Over 3 month	Over two month	Over 1 month	Less than 1 month
Dec	9.5%	21.4%	26.2%	42.9%
June	11.3%	23.6%	26%	39%

    Little change but stocks are larger (£123K against £84K)

    9/42 = 21% of the stock of materials has been in stock for more than three months, 17% for more than two months and 21% for more than one month. This is not dissimilar to the December position.

2.

	December Qtr	June Qtr	Increase
Sales	233,000	282,000	21%
Purchases	151,000	198,000	31%
	End December	End June	
Material Stocks	35,000	42,000	20%
Stocks for resale	84,000	123,000	46%

    Higher sales and stocks will require more WC but higher purchases will tend to reduce WC requirement. Net effect is an increase requirement for WC and if this is not met in full then an increase in Overdraft (or a more than proportional increase in creditors) would result.

3. i. Rapid paperwork, active pursuit of slow payers, targeting of sales on quick payers.

Tasks 2

1. Offering discounts is very expensive and the company is unlikely to gain a net benefit by doing so and taking settlement discounts from suppliers. Some other source of WC should be found (e.g. factoring, long term debt etc).

2. Some query on an invoice, 'its in the computer system', absence of cheque signers, – use your imagination!

3. Seems reasonable but doubtful ethics. Difficulties include changes in attitude by individual suppliers, higher input prices quoted by suppliers, poor supplier relationships, difficulty in getting supplies in times of scarcity.

4. Increased stock and debtors need financing. This need is reduced by increase in creditors.

Task 3

Points to make:

He prices himself too low (people who value themselves lowly are so valued by others)

Formal contracts with penalty clauses which both sides abide by

Instalment payments can be specified

Proper scheduling of work so that delays do not occur

Arranging for deliveries of supplies to be made when they can be used

Very rapid paperwork

All this seems obvious but most small contractors behave like Ted!

Unit 9 Stocks

Tasks 1

1. i.   Cost per box = £2 – 40p + 20p + 13p = 1.93 × 860 = £1,659.80
    ii. £4 each × 2,760 = £11,040
    iii. 10 at 3.5 + 200 at 4.25 = £885
    iv. 1,800 × 1.19 = £2,142

2. i.   Stock understated ii.   Stock understated
    iii. Stock understated iv.   Stock overstated
    v.   Stock overstated   vi.   Stock overstated
    vii. Stock overstated   viii. Stock understated
    ix. Stock understated x.   Stock overstated

Task 2

Economic order quantity minimises costs by balancing admin costs of ordering against storage costs etc. Guesses are mostly used and actual timing of sales and deliveries are erratic. Reorder levels assume uniform sales and purchases but the real world is more chaotic.

Task 3

Use of EOQ , establishment of re-order levels. Some system of perpetual inventory or frequent stock taking. Specials to avoid stocks reaching sell by dates and to sell off slow selling items (which should not be re-ordered). These measures should reduce stocks and make stocktaking easier. Perpetual inventory at cost seems feasible and would make pricing (at FIFO) easier. She will need to know the cost of making dishes — if this is too high then......

Unit 10 Investment appraisal

Tasks 1

1. Net Cash flows:

	0	1	2	3	4	5
Sales		100	200	200	150	100
Return at end						45
VC		68	136	136	102	68
FC		21	21	21	21	21
Initial	115					
Net	−115	11	43	43	27	56
Discounted	−115	9.46	31.82	27.52	14.85	26.88

a. The project pays back within 4 years – OK

b. Present Value = 110, NPV = –5 and Profitability index is 0.96

c. Average Capital employed = $\dfrac{80,000}{2}$ + 35,000 = 75,000

Average profits are $\dfrac{135 - \text{Depreciation of } 70}{5}$ = 13

Accounting rate of Return = 17%

2. The project is within the four year payback period. However the NPV is negative and on that ground should be rejected.

However the figures are all estimates and now the project has been set up as a financial model it is possible to review the situation and perhaps make changes which will make it viable. For example:

❐ Bargain hard with suppliers to reduce the £80,000 to £75,000 (which makes the project viable) or less.

❐ Consider raising the price to say £10.50 or reducing it to see if sales would rise.

❐ 5 year horizon may be unrealistic and modifications then may prolong the life.

 ❐ can costs be reduced?

The new product increases Martin's range and may improve the market for his other products. This entry into a new field may suggest other possibilities later.

Tasks 3

1. A suitable array:

	0	1	2	3	4	5
	–6,000	900	900	900	900	4,900
Discounted	–6,000	800	720	640	580	2,790

   NPV = – 470

2. Benefits include quietness, smaller maintenance costs (many softwood windows rot), a deterrence to burglars.

3. Personal opinion — it looks as if the financial + non-financial benefits add up to an acceptable package.

4. £6,000 is probably accurate, savings are very subjective — probably £400 — £1,000 may be a better bet than a point estimate. £4,000 is also very subjective. Cost of capital is probably right to + or – 2%.

   Time horizon is clearly just a guess.

5. Extra required is 470 which is the discounted figure at 12% after five years. This is £824

Unit 11 Manufacturing and construction

Task 1

a. Less than a month's supply – not known if this is much or little but it seems reasonable.

b.

	19x1	19x2	
Materials	34	31	marginally down
Labour	63	66	marginally up
Other	3	3	

c. Low tech — high labour costs relative to production overheads.

d. Has risen a lot at end of 19x2 — this may be natural variation.

   At £45,000 still only 20 days but this may be high for the industry.

e. Has risen substantially at end of 19x2. £143,000 represents 2 month's sales — seems high and may indicate difficulty in selling and overstocking.

f. Downward — 20% down in money terms — more in real terms.

g. 18.5% to 18.7 good!

h. Admin has been reduced by 13% but has gone from 9% of sales to 10% of sales.

   Selling etc reduced by 16% but has gone from 8.5% of sales to 8.9%.

i. This is one-off expense which occurs in 19x1 only. Including Production Overheads would distort comparisons (which we have made) between 19x1 and 19x2. Note that without it 19x1 would more or less have broken even.

j. Financial Charges have risen 50% presumably on borrowings to finance losses, extra stocks and work in progress but perhaps also to buy fixed assets. Note that the effect of lower turnover is to reduce debtors but also creditors.

k. Machinery — production overheads, computer — Administration, Van — Selling.

l. 821 + 105 = 926 not 924.

Tasks 2

1.

	A	B
Include in Turnover	19,450	34,762
Include in cost of sales	16,900	41,896
Thus profit (loss) taken	2,550	*(7,134)
Include in debtors	5,250	8,762
Include in current liabilities		**3,462

* = £34,762 – £38,434 – £3,462 (total loss)

** = £50,700 – £34,762 – £19,400 (total loss less loss so far)

2. Losses on contracts, negative cash flow caused thereby. False optimism, to keep the labour force occupied, to recover some overheads.

3. This year, *part* of the profit on contract A is matched with *total* loss on contract B. Next year (if there is one!) *part* of profit on contract A only. Conclusion — what do you think?

Tasks 3

1. Plant — at second hand prices, probably very low; Stocks — at auction prices, also very low; Redundancy pay — at amount payable; Long term loans — payable immediately.

2. Materiality — debtors as debtors £x not A Ltd £y + B Ltd £z +...., stocks — Stocks: raw materials £x, finished goods £y but not 200 widgets at £6 = £1,200 +........ Plant — I think you have the idea!

   Consistency — debtors with provision for doubtful debts calculated the same way each year. Stocks — all at FIFO (or *all* at AVCO), each item at lower of cost and NRV, inclusion (if any) of overheads on same basis each year. Plant — all at cost less depreciation on consistent basis (e.g. straight line and similar assumptions re salvage and economic life. Creditors — not especially affected.

Task 4

Research student and general research — in Profit and Loss Account as spent. Business: plant — include in plant at fair value and depreciate as usual, stocks — include in purchases at fair value, patents, trade marks and goodwill — write off to reserves immediately (can be capitalised and depreciated but not usual) — in Unit 14 you will see how this is affected in company accounting.

Unit 12 Total absorption costing

Tasks 1

Overhead apportionment and Allocation Schedule

Cost	Method	Machining	Assembly	Packing	Total
Rent	Area	3,200	2,400	3,200	8,800
Rates	Area	1,345	1,010	1,345	3,700
Fire Ins	Area	437	327	436	1,200
Super	Employees	4,937	5,925	4,938	15,800
Repairs	pro rata				
	Depreciation	2,308	266	426	3,000
Depreciation		13,000	1,500	2,400	16,900
Energy		2,600	350	600	3,550
Labour		12,200	9,150		21,350
		40,027	20,928	13,345	74,300

2. Machining — Machine hour rate — £4

   Assembly — Labour hour rate — £1.744

   Packing — Labour hour rate — £1.668

Tasks 2

1.

	VX	WY
Materials	2.40	2.60
Labour 1.80	3.30	
Machine time	1.33	2.00
Assembly Ohds	0.44	0.29
Packing Ohds	0.69	0.56
	6.66	8.75

2. 75% hours:

   Machining – £5.337, Assembly £2.325, Packing £2.224

	VX	WY
Materials	2.40	2.60
Labour 1.80	3.30	
Machine time	1.78	2.67
Assembly Ohds	0.58	0.39
Packing Ohds	0.93	0.74
	7.49	9.70

3. In 2, the overheads have to be recovered by a smaller output requiring fewer hours. Thus costs per item of output are higher.

4. The idea of using piecework is to turn all costs into linearly variable costs which are determinable in advance. Unfortunately all businesses have some fixed costs which have to be recovered and an obvious way to recover them is on hours.

5. Instead of three cost centres use 5.

6. The calculated costs are forecasts. Actual costs may be more.

   Number of hours (machine and labour) chargeable to production may be less than predicted.

Tasks 3

1.
	£
Cost of Manufacturing	2.80
Addition for non mfg ohds	0.80
Total cost	3.60
Profit 1/9	0.40
Selling Price	4.00

2. Prices are mostly dictated by market forces. Thus Martin may have to set a price below £4 to make any sales. Conversely he may be able to set a price above £4 and still sell the product.

Tasks 4

1. Marginal cost — almost free but with some extra costs (e.g. lab materials), most costs are fixed (e.g. teaching and admin salaries). Full cost — likely to be high: market rate.

2. Marginal cost — determine extra costs per student. Full cost — would require a large scale exercise in allocation and apportionment. Market rate: local charges from FE colleges, correspondence school rates, market survey etc.

Unit 13 Standard costing

Tasks 1

Materials: Price 11 × 80p = £8.80 ADV

Usage 1 × £5.20 = £5.20 ADV

Packaging 60p ADV

Labour:	Stamper	Rate 3.25 × 40p = £1.30 FAV
		Efficiency 1/4 hour × £4 = £1 ADV
	Polisher	Rate 2.75 × £1 = £2.75 ADV
		Efficiency 1/4 hour at £5 = £1.25 FAV
	Packer	Rate 4 × 30p = £1.20 ADV
		Efficiency 1/2 hour × £3.90 = £1.95 ADV

Reasons may be: Material – prices have gone up (standard is now wrong?), random variation in usage, inefficiency, excess wastage. Packaging – as materials. Labour – Stamper – lower cost and lower efficiency seem to suggest low grade labour used. Polisher is vice versa. Packer perhaps had an off day.

See explanations in Scenario 4!

Tasks 2

1. Planning: Material Price, Packaging Price, Stamper rate, Polisher Rate, Packer rate.

   The others are operating but it is arguable about all except the metal usage and stamper efficiency.

2. Change some standards, adjust the selling price of the product upwards, improve training.

Tasks 3

Variable Overheads: Assuming variable overheads are driven by Stamper and Polisher hours then variances are:

> *Efficiency:* $(15 + 5) \times 1.50 = £30$ ADV (more hours were used on production than standard so more variable overheads were spent)
>
> *Expenditure:* $(125 + 130) \times 1.50 = £382.50$ compared with actual of £402 so variance is £19.50 ADV

Fixed Overheads:

> *Expenditure:* £50 ADV
>
> *Volume:* Fixed Overheads are budgeted at £2,250 for an output of 375 standard hours = £6 an hour. As output fell short by $(375 - 340)$ Standard Hours the variance is $35 \times £6 = £210$ ADV

Tasks 4

This shows that the techniques of standard costing are useful but need to be adapted to the circumstances. In this case three variances seem relevant – volume, price and exchange rate:

Volume:	We can calculate that the sales price in £ is £29.52 giving a margin of £9.52. As the sales exceeded budget by 200 units the variance is $200 \times £9.52 = £1,904$ FAV
Margin:	The Margin budgeted is $4 or £1.90 less than budgeted so the variance is $2,200 \times £1.90 = £4,180$ ADV
Exchange Rate:	There is a gain here of:

$$\frac{2,200 \times 58}{2.1} - \frac{2,200 \times 58}{2.05} = £1,483 \text{ FAV}$$

£1,904 FAV + £4,180 ADV + £1,483 FAV = £793 ADV

Proof:	Budget $\dfrac{2,000 \times 62}{2.1} - (2,000 \times 20) = £19,047$
	Actual $\dfrac{2,200 \times 58}{2.05} - (2,200 \times 20) = £18,244$

Net £803 ADV which is subject to rounding differences.

Unit 14 Company accounting

Tasks 1

3.

Cost of sales	Dist Costs	Admin Exes
Goods for resale	Discounts	M/D Salary
Forklift	PR Costs	Auditor
		Computer

Some of these are arguable and need more detailed knowledge of circumstances!

4. 5 times

5. Debentures + Bank Overdraft

6. Corporation Tax

7. The investments were disposed of in 19x8.

8. 5 million at 19x7 plus 5 million actually issued in 19x8 so a total of 10 million at end of 19x8.

9. One penny

10. Profit and Loss Account figure includes an interim of 0.6p per share

11. £120,00010 million = 1.2p

13. Property, plant, vehicles etc

14. PAYE and NHI and VAT

15. 14% a year. They are redeemable any time (at the company's choice) in the years 1998 and 1999.

16. Some of the shares were bought from the company at more than the 'nominal' or face price.

17. To balance the Balance Sheet when fixed assets were revalued upward and thus to indicate the source of increase in net assets.

18. No! Reserve has a technical meaning. It is not a 'thing'.

19. Retained profits accumulate from year to year. The Profit and Loss Account only shows one year.

20. £4,818,000 or 48.18p a share.

21. Stock exchange prices vary according to demand and supply. They represent the price for a small parcel of shares. The Balance Sheet makes no attempt to value the whole company. It is just a list of assets and liabilities (with omissions) at stylised values.

Tasks 2

1. Points to make:

   Premises: substantial additions in the year, small surplus on revaluation in the year. Depreciation in the year (which is also accumulated as accumulated brought forward was eliminated in the revaluation) is at 2% of the valuation allowing for land at nil depreciation. Land is thus £1,042,000

Plant: considerable additions in the year, no disposals in the year, all plant at year end depreciated at 12 1/2% (i.e. no fully depreciated plant), NBV at under half cost so plant is more than half way through its life.

Tasks 3

1. Dividend will be £50 and the new shares will be worth £50 so no apparent difference. The matter is slightly complicated by capital gains tax. He might consider that he does not need the cash and would be better off adding to his capital by accepting the shares.

2. The company might consider that with 4% of the share capital it has a sufficient stake in the company and would therefore prefer the dividend. The company may also need cash to finance its outgoings although its cash flow considerations are unknown to us.

3. Some shareholders increase their stake and those accepting cash keep theirs at the same amount in an enlarged capital. In a normal bonus issue all shareholders receive new shares pro rata their holdings.

Tasks 4

1. The law and the stock exchange requires it. Also it is clearly desirable that the directors should account to the owners for their stewardship at regular intervals.

2. The accounts would be useless without such confidence.

3. Directors, if unconstrained, would present such figures as would please the shareholders whether true or not. The auditors prevent this. In Ruritania, a first duty of the auditor is to seek evidence that the books he sees are the true books of the company and not some books kept for the auditor or the taxman to see!

4. Auditors are required to make a report. If a true and fair view is not given or the accounts do not comply with the Companies Act then the auditor has to say so in his report and detail and quantify the difference. There are possible consequences for the payment of the dividend.

Task 5

Points to make:

Land values are not comparable

Building values are not comparable

Goodwill values are not comparable

As a consequence:

Net assets are not comparable, profits (different policies on depreciation and amortisation and different values to be depreciated) are not comparable, return on capital employed is not comparable.

Unit 15 Ratio analysis

Tasks 1

Percentages to sales:

Manufacturing Account	19x6	19x7	IFC
Materials	14.0	16.3	14.7
Labour	20.5	20.7	22.4
Prime cost	34.5	37.0	37.1
Works overheads	30.9	35.4	34.0
Finished Output	63.4	73.7	71.1
Gross profit	38.6	23.8	29.0
Admin Costs	10.4	8.0	5.1
Selling Costs	15.1	15.3	9.2
Dist. Costs	4.7	3.3	1.1
Net Profit	8.6	(2.8)	13.6
ROCE	17.1	(6.7)	30.0
Turnover/Fixed Assets	53.3	14.7	11.2
AUR	2.0	2.0	2.2
Stock (raw mat) days	155	153	114
Stock (wip)	53.4	35.9	27.7
Stock (Finished)	94.7	57.3	57.6
Debtors payment	87	90	77
Creditors –Materials	88	99	82

2. Materials have risen as a proportion of cost – above IFC

Labour is same proportion – better than IFC

Works overheads have risen to a higher proportion of selling price – just above IFC

Gross Profit ratio has gone from very good to very bad

Admin costs are reducing but are still too high

Selling Costs have not changed and are much too high

Distribution costs have improved but are much too high

AUR is not bad

Too large a stock of raw materials

Work in progress has improved but is still too high

Finished goods stock is much better and equates to IFC

Debtors have worsened and need reducing to IFC

Creditors payment is slower and longer than IFC.

Attention to: Materials costs and usage, works overhead costs, selling price, admin costs, selling costs, distribution costs, stock of raw materials, work in progress, plant still needs some modernising.

Tasks 2

1. and 2.   Turnover is up 23%, Gross profit steady at 36%, Overheads steady at 26% of turnover, Profit after tax up by 11% but has fallen as a percentage of sales from 7.3% to 6.6%, Dividend up 5% and has gone from a cover of 1.75 to 1.85.

   ROCE after tax 121% to 83% but as relatively low capitally intensive industry and a high volatility in capital employed this is not very relevant as a ratio.

   Capital employed has nearly doubled – relatively recent growth from a small base?

   Increase in Fixed Assets at cost of 58% is dramatic and mostly financed from within (from creditors?)

   Stock 60 days to 55 days – good

   Debtors 100 days to 91 days – good but could do better

   Purchases creditors 96 days to 110 days – not good enough.

   Gearing fairly high and overdraft is very high for a company with little security – directors' guarantees?

3. Raising turnover and heavy capital expenditure without any external or long term sources of funds and a high dividend.

4. When will Martin be paid – after 110 days on average.

   Will he be paid (i.e. will Stade survive)? Company is profitable and expanding. Liquidity problem needs solving but the company is a good one and this should be possible. If it does go bust assets will diminish and the bank and the receiver/liquidator will get it all. Creditors would get very little.

   On balance give credit but watch it very carefully!

Unit 16 Sources of finance

Tasks 1

1. Finance needed – £200,000 + £60,000 + increase in stock and debtors (£190,000) less increase in creditors (£74,000) + £75,000 = £451,000.

2. Factory – mortgage loan – long term, cheap, bank are secured, 100% Mortgage probably not available.

   Vans – HP – but this is very expensive.

   Debtors— factoring, flexible, since all debtors are included this will probably cover the whole 30% increase in debtors, some other benefits e.g. credit control and perhaps collection.

   Other assets – Overdraft, short term, can be withdrawn, not cheap, flexible (only current amount borrowed is paid for), short term for fixed assets not seen as good, very popular for stocks, secured.

   Loan from cousin – cheap, long term, not repayable, ultimately gives cousin a stake in the business diluting Martin's control.

   Venture Capital – part surrender of control, plenty of funds available for future expansion, loss of part of benefit if company floated, availability of advice.

3. Leasing, Martin himself (perhaps by second mortgaging his house), extended credit by suppliers.

Task 2

14.4%

Unit 17 The Stock Exchange

Task 1

He can sell some of his shares to give him personal liquid capital and enable him to buy his country estate. (Do all nouveau riche businessmen want to join the country gentry?)

His uncle can sell some of his shares to enable him to buy his farm.

The company can sell some new shares to enable it to expand without retaining all its profits.

Tasks 2

1. a. 3 million × £1.80   = £5,400,000

   b. 2 million × £1.80   = £3,600,000

   c. 600,000 × £1.80   = £1,080,000

   d. 400,000 × £1.80   = £720,000

   e. one half

2. Access to capital, ability to offer paper in a takeover, a higher public profile.

3. a. Loss of 100% control, smaller proportion of the dividend, constraints on his remuneration (although there seems to be very little restraint on PLC directors' remuneration!).

   b. Glare of public scrutiny, possibility of unwelcome takeover attempts, need to maintain performance and dividends. Compliance with Cadbury and Greenburg Codes.

4. Anybody – institutions and private citizens. There is a tendency for institutional investors to prefer the large company but conversely small PLCs are suggested as better left to sophisticated investors (are there any?). Local companies (like this) tend to attract local investors.

Tasks 3

1. Advantages to Oldee – Money (or securities which can be sold), no risk of his own company failing (e.g. if should have ill health), Leisure, a salary with probably a minimum of work (for one year), a chance to participate in a dynamic business.

   Disadvantages to Oldee – loss of power over others, loss of control over his own destiny, boredom, risk that Martin PLC may fail, loss of some of the perks of being a director (e.g. travel, company car etc).

   Cash – invest it how he likes, spend it, some CGT payable.

Shares — all his capital tied up in Martin PLC (some unit trusts will offer an exchange so he can spread his risk), no cash unless he sells some, on the plus side — no CGT unless sold, Martin PLC is a dynamic company.

Convertibles — reasonable interest (£48K Gross) although not indexed against the inevitable inflation, probably not all lost even if Martin PLC fails, possibility of capital gain of Martin PLC does well — shares have not got to rise much before conversion is worth doing.

2. This would be a reverse takeover with the effect that Martin would be taken over by Keen and Keen would become a PLC by the back door. Martin may lose his directorship but clearly such affairs are subject to much negotiation and regulation.

Task 4

For capital growth rather than income Martin can invest in real property, equities, chattels (such as antiques or paintings) or with profits life assurance. More adventurously he may try to find small businesses to invest in. Investment experts are eager to offer advice on what will rise in value in the future but investors are wise to realise that the future is unknown even to experts. The EMH applies to realty and chattels as well as to equities!

Task 5

This is price sensitive information. Correctly as soon as the information is available to the company it is announced to the public as is required by the Stock Exchange. As it is new information which enhances the value of the company, the shares rise in price as expected. Sligh is acting on the information as an insider with knowledge not available to the general investing public. This is illegal and if it can be proved may attract severe penalties including imprisonment. It may remain undetected by the authorities if her name is not Sligh (it may be if she is his father's sister). However this is a big deal (£400,000) and the matter may be suspicious enough to come to the attention of the authorities. Chance is a fine thing but is the game worth the candle!

Unit 18 Accounting in the not-for-profit sector

Tasks 1

1. Every item! Except perhaps insurance, rates and heat and light.
2. Note large changes and ask for explanations — make a plausible guess and then look at Scenario 3.

Tasks 2

1. No — approx break-even.
2. Bar profit — lower wages. Discos — inflation and perhaps even more discos. Subscriptions — increased rates. Catering — reducing charges to placate members or perhaps the club in general meeting some costs. Depreciation and fixed assets — major capital expenditure on equipment.

3. Yes! Either big deficits or higher subs. If higher subs, funds would probably be available for replacement. But cash flow and profits are not the same!

4. A total of £4,600 is due for prizes but cash is only £543 (at year end). In principle £1,500 is OK but to ensure cash is available, an amount equal to the fund should have been invested in separate assets. As it was not, the prize requirements have to be found from the assets generally which may not be liquid.

5. The matching convention means that life member subs should be credited to I and E account over the membership periods of life members (these need to be esti-mated!).

6. Not enough detail.

Tasks 3

1. See Unit 6 on budgeting.

2. If about the same number of subs were received each year then the credit would be about the same each year. However the Balance Sheet unappropriated surplus would be less.

3. A 20% rise would seem to be optimal. Gross profit would be £13,243. But in not-for-profit situations matters are never simple! Members who stop using the bar may resign and hence engender a loss in subs. There may be other knock-on effects and it is a social club after all.

4. Costs must be split into primarily hockey, primarily tennis and shared. Subs should reflect pattern of costs. However total must be as required and other factors may affect equity. For example members who play both sports may not think they should pay both section subs in full. Market considerations may suggest other subs than those dictated by costs. Side effects may mean poor members dropping out or dropping a sport. There may be non-players who provide support and bar profits. Should they be encouraged with low subs?

5. Can change providers more easily. Providers will work well to keep the contract. No redundancy pay, sick pay or holiday pay. Lack of control, possible lack of flexi-bility.

Unit 19 Cash flow statements and some international issues

Tasks 1

1. 15 x £176,000 = £2,640,000

2. Cash — may have to be borrowed and then paid back. Changes gearing. Equity — higher dividends, changes shareholding. Loan stock — interest, repayment and gearing. Convertibles — interest repayment or new equity. Combination of loan and equity. A degree of uncertainty.

3. Operating cash flows were positive — £340 less tax, interest on existing debt and taxation £225 = £115. But there is also a need for repayment of overdraft and for capital expenditure. Clearly cash flows are currently insufficient. Future may bring

higher profits and operating cash flows but also higher capital expenditure, repayment of existing finance and higher turnover involves higher working capital.

Tasks 2

2. £375 - (2,350 + 680) $\times$ 0.15 = - £79,500 — a residual loss!

Tasks 4

1. Building products — declining turnover, profits (now in loss), net assets. Currently (1995) building is in the doldrums and growth prospects look poor and risk of loss is high. But who can predict the future?

   Vehicle fabrics — growth in turnover and net assets and large growth in profit. Prospects seem good. By being in two markets, the company is able to hedge risk.

   Decline in UK and growth in EC. Again a hedging of risk by being in two areas.

   Turnover decline in UK and growth in all other markets.

2. Seems obvious to me.

3. This is a situation where the more information that is given, the more information one seeks. The main need is for the changes in location and geographical turnover to be analysed over the two product divisions.

Appendix D
Answers to Quick Answer Questions

Answers to QAQs 1.1

1. Martin has a total capital of £15,000. He may well have other possessions (accountants usually call possessions assets) such as a house on mortgage but all we know about is £15,000.

2. His capital of £15,000 is held in the form of

	£
Assets: Impeccable Building Society	5,000
Deposit Account Mudland Bank	10,000
Capital:	15,000

You will note that you can consider capital in two ways:

❐ the total amount

❐ the detailed way that the capital is held.

Accountants frequently look at capital in this dual way.

3. We will look at this again later but two points may give you an indication:

   a. He will need to acquire some equipment to store his stock of padlocks and also he will need to buy a van and a computer to keep records on.

   b. He will need to buy some padlocks to put into stock so that he can sell them. He will have to pay for these padlocks. In addition when he has sold them it may be some time before the customers actually pay for them.

   So, before the business receives any money it will have to make some payments. The amount needed will be put into the business by Martin as the initial capital of the business.

Answers to QAQs 1.2

1. The principal reasons why payments are greater than receipts in the first six months are:

   a. Martin will need to pay for some items as soon as he starts. These include the computer, the Van, the Equipment and Anne's fee.

   b. The company will need to build up a stock which has to be paid for before it is sold.

   c. The company will trade on credit. This means it will buy goods in one month and pay for them at an agreed later date. Most suppliers expect payment in the month following the purchase but frequently find that customers take longer to pay than the agreed time allowed. Similarly Martin has to give credit to his customers. The problem arises as Martin gives more credit to his customers than his suppliers give to him.

2. He would have to delay making them until money came in from customers but by then other payments may be due. Ultimately being unable to make payments when they fall due can cause a business to go into receivership or liquidation or, in a word, go bust.

Answers to QAQs 2.1

1. Sales are more than forecast.

   Rent, Electricity, Stationery, Van running, Wages and Director's Remuneration are more or less as forecast. Director's Remuneration and Rates are a little more and Advertising less than forecast.

2. Employers' National Insurance Contributions were not forecast. Remember that it cost more to employ people than the gross wages. The audit fee was not forecast but part of it was included in the preliminary costs. Bank Interest is a significant item but is hard to forecast as rates vary and the borrowing is up and down.

3. Stock is less than expected. Perhaps Martin found that a large stock was not necessary.

Answers to QAQs 3.1

1. 31 December 19x1. Balance Sheets are lists of assets and liabilities at a particular date which in this case is 31 December 19x1.

2. You may have recognised:

   ❏ the Fixed Assets: the Computer and the Stacking Equipment. You may recall the cost of these from the cash flow forecast and the depreciation from the Profit and Loss Account.

   ❏ the Stock.

   ❏ the Bank Overdraft. Well, at least you knew that the company had a bank overdraft. The balance is different from the forecast but forecasts are never quite right.

   ❏ the Share Capital: you know that Martin put £15,000 into the company.

   ❏ the Profit and Loss Account: you know that the company made a profit of this amount but it may surprise you to see it on the Balance Sheet.

3. You will see that these show the same amount. The figure in the Profit and Loss Account shows the profit made in the year and this results in an increase in net assets at the end of the year compared with the beginning. The figure in the Balance Sheet shows the source of the increase in net assets measured in the Balance Sheet.

4. The Fixed Assets and all the Current Assets are assets. The creditors: amounts falling due within one year and the Loan are all liabilities.

   You should have got these right but you may be surprised to know that the Share Capital and the Profit and Loss Account are also liabilities. They are liabilities to the shareholders.

5. The Profit and Loss Account measures the profit earned over a period of time – one year in this case.

   The Balance Sheet shows the assets and liabilities at the year end.

Answer to QAQ 3.2

Yes – most adjustments to the Profit and Loss Account will also affect the Balance Sheet and vice versa. If a liability had been omitted – say a van repair of £50, then:

- ❏ van expenses in the Profit and Loss Account would go up by £50 and consequently the net profit would go down.
- ❏ the creditors would go up by £50 in the Balance Sheet and consequently the assets less liabilities would go down by £50.
- ❏ the capital and reserves would go down by £50 as the Profit and Loss Account figure in the Balance Sheet would go down and consequently the capital and reserves total would still be the same as the net assets.

Answers to QAQs 4.1

1. Fixed Assets are long lasting and relatively valuable assets. They are owned to be used in the business to help make a profit. They are not expected to be sold except when they are no longer needed.

2. Cost means simply what they cost the company when they were bought. The idea of cost is simple but students often wonder whether the original or *historical* cost is relevant or useful information.

3. £1,100. This is based on the information which Martin gave to Anne about the useful economic lives of the fixed assets.

4. If three years had been chosen then the depreciation on the Stacking Equipment would have been £1,000 and the total depreciation would have been £1,500.

5. Yes. The profit would have been £400 less as depreciation directly affects the measurement of profit.

6. Yes. This year the assets have depreciated by £1,100 and this 'loss in value' is regarded as an expense and so the profit is reduced by this amount.

7. and 8.

   £2,900. This is called the net book value or sometimes the written down value. It is simply the original cost less the depreciation so far. It does not mean that the assets can be sold for this amount. Students wonder what it does mean and accountants usually say it represents the value of the assets *to the business* and not the value to some hypothetical buyer.

Answer to QAQ 4.2

		£
The computer:	Cost	1,000
	50% year 1	500
		500
	50% year 2	250
		250
	50% year 3	125
Salvage value at end of year 3		£125

Stacking Equipment: The cost was £3,000 and the salvage value is estimated at £300 so the expected loss is £2,700. Using the straight line method and assuming a three year life depreciation will be:

$$£2,700 \div 3 = £900 \text{ a year.}$$

The Balance Sheet values will be £2,100 at the end of year 1, £1,200 at the end of year 2 and £300 at the end of year three.

Answers to QAQs 4.3

1. As the Club House is depreciated over 50 years the annual depreciation will be

$$£90,000 \div 50 = £1,800.$$

Since the accumulated depreciation is now £54,000 Martin can assume that the Club House has been depreciated for

$$54,000 \div £1,800 = 30 \text{ years.}$$

2. The Golf Course is land and usually land is not depreciated. The reason is that land is assumed to have an infinite life. The Golf Club may also think, that as the Course has appreciated rather than depreciated in value, no depreciation is necessary. However *appreciation* in value is not considered a valid reason for not depreciating an asset with limited life.

Answers to QAQs 5.1

1. Annual Depreciation is (£15,000 – £3,0005) $\div$ 5 = £2,400

2.

	£
Depreciation	2,400
Rent etc	10,000
Other overheads	1,500
Electricity	3,000
Foreman	10,500
Labour 60,000 x 30p	18,000
Materials 60,000 x 50p	30,000
Total	75,400

3. £75,400 $\div$ 60,000 = £1.26

You will see that the cost of manufacture of one unit of a product depends on how many are made.

Answers to QAQs 5.2

1. We all have a tendency to prefer a product which is cheaper so more will be sold if the price is lowered. The relationship between sales quantity and price is very difficult to estimate in practice. Economists talk about *elasticity of demand* by which they mean that sales of some products are more *sensitive* to price differences than others.

2. Not certain at all. Management accounting is about what to do in the future and the future is simply uncertain. Bear in mind that the sophisticated techniques used in management accounting usually work on very uncertain forecasts!

3. We said that the factory could only produce 60,000 units in a year. If more can be sold Martin will have to buy them from another manufacturer or enlarge his own factory.

4. The cost of a single unit of output is:

Labour and Materials		80p
The rest of the costs divided by 60,000:		
$27,400 \div 60,000$		46p
		126p

If the £27,400 was divided by a different output (say 40,000 units) then the cost per unit would be more:

Labour and Materials		80p
$27,400 \div 40,000$		68p
		148p

We cannot make more than 60,000 a year so we will have to calculate the costs of a higher output later.

Answer to QAQ 5.3

Considerations that Martin might take into account include:

❐ some pricing strategies may be more risky

❐ the larger factory unit will be greater burden if things do not work out well – risk again

❐ a higher turnover may require more of Martin's time

❐ a higher turnover will involve a greater investment of cash and he may have other priorities for this scarce resource.

Answers to QAQs 6.1

1. Martin must prepare a summary of the *financial* effects of each alternative. This should be in the form of forecast Profit and Loss Accounts and Balance Sheets. In order to do this he will need to assess the costs of each alternative, the prices of property etc. He will also need to produce a *cash flow forecast* for each alternative to see what finance may be required. He will then have to determine if the finance will be available and what it will cost.

2. Consequence of a wrong choice:

   a. Loss of opportunity to make money, provide employment etc.

   b. Loss of opportunity in wholesaling but risk of failure if the manufacturing does not turn out as planned.

   c. Loss of opportunity in manufacturing and risk of failure if wholesaling does not work out as planned.

d. Risk of failure due to either activity failing. Loss of control by Martin as he cannot be in two places at once and more activity will require more of his limited time.

e. Risk of failure if either activity fails.

Purchasing will involve taking a mortgage and if the business fails and property prices fall then the company may fail.

Renting usually involves taking on a commitment to pay rent for a defined period of years. Failure of the business will still leave this requirement.

Answers to QAQs 6.2

1. Material and labour costs are variable. The remaining costs are fixed. However it is possible that some of the other factory overheads may be variable.

2.
Material cost	60p
Labour cost	40p
Prime cost	100p

Answers to QAQs 8.1

1. Stocks are basically valued at cost. However, some items may be valued at *below cost* and we will consider this in Unit 9.

2. Working capital is usually defined as current assets less current liabilities. Current liabilities are now described as in this extract, that is, as creditors: amounts falling due within one year. Current liabilities can include items such as corporation tax due and dividends payable but for most purposes, working capital can be defined as:

Current Assets less

Trade creditors and bank overdraft, and in this case amounts to:

£306,000 − £189,000 = £117,000.

Answers to QAQs 8.2

1. Debtors:

Within one month after sale $(76,000 − 61,000) \div 76,000 \times 100 = 20\%$

Within two months after sale $(73,000 − 31,000) \div 73,000 \times 100 = 57\%$

We can deduce from this that 37% (57% − 20%) is paid in the second month after the sale.

Three months or more (balance)   43%

This is a sample only and other month ends may yield a different view.

However it is probably a good indication.

2. Creditors:

Month after sale	approx 50%
Month after that	approx 50%

You will recall (see Unit 1) that Martin intended to pay in the month following the purchase. He does not do this but does pay half of his suppliers in the following month and the other half in the month after that. Presumably keeping to monthly payment would push his overdraft over the limit.

3. Debtors paying more quickly would reduce the overdraft

   Lower stocks would also reduce the overdraft

   Paying creditors more quickly would increase the overdraft.

Answers to QAQs 10.1

1. No! Martin has already spent the £5,000. Cost accountants call this a *sunk* or *dead* cost. What is done cannot be undone. In making decisions only the *future* costs and revenues should be considered.

2. Most products have a limited life. When a firm develop a new product which is good then, for a time, it will do very well. However good products inspire competition and probably the college think that by year 6 the competition may make it unprofitable for Martin's company.

3. Martin will have to build a stock of raw materials for manufacture and also maintain a stock of finished goods. This will cost money. In addition the money spent on finished goods will not be recovered immediately on sales but will have to await payment from the customer. Some mitigation of this will come as Martin will take credit from his suppliers. At the end of the project, money will come in as stocks are sold off without replacement and debtors pay without further debtors being created.

4. The Contribution is Sales price less marginal costs:

   £10.00 − £6.80 = £3.20.

5. No! 5,000 units sold will give a contribution of:

   5,000 x £3.20 = £16,000

   but fixed costs will be £21,000 so a loss would be made.

Answers to QAQs 11.1

1. In a wholesale company the typical transaction begins with the arrival of goods from a supplier. Perhaps the goods remain in stock for some four weeks and then are sold and delivered to a customer. The whole cycle of buying, stocking and selling is over in four weeks. The associated cash flows may be a little different. If the firm pay in the month following delivery and the customers two months after delivery then the cash cycle takes about two months.

   In a construction company the cycle is much longer. The time between commencement of a construction contract and completion may be many months or even years. The associated cash cycle may begin with the first payment of workers and sub-contractors in the first week of the contract and end with final payment of the retention money (some part of the contract price is held back for a period after completion to cover faults in construction) which may be years after.

The accounting problem is that dividing the life of a business over single years involves valuing and assessing the effects of contracts and transactions in progress. This is a bigger problem when the business cycle is long.

2. Companies generally fail when they find themselves unable to pay their creditors. Many of such companies have borrowed money from their banks (or other lenders) and when such lenders have taken a charge over the assets (this will be explained in Unit 14) and the company fails, the lenders appoint an administrative receiver (usually an accountant with a special qualification in insolvency). The receiver has the duty of taking charge of the company's affairs and selling its assets for the benefit of the lenders and other creditors. After the receiver has finished his duties, or where a company fails and no lender has a charge over the assets, the final winding up of the company is done by a liquidator. A liquidator is also usually an accountant with a qualification in insolvency.

Answers to QAQs 12.1

1. a. Materials: Materials and Components

   Labour: Outworkers and the supervisor

   Services: Licence, rent and rates

   b. Variable: Materials and components and the outworkers

   Fixed: Supervisor, Licence and rent and rates

   c. In this case, all the costs can be seen as direct in that they are all traceable to the particular product which is the only product made in this part of the factory. On the other hand, the supervisor, licence and rent and rates are shared by all the output and so they are overheads in that they are shared by each individual lock.

2. a. Total cost = $5,000 \times 4.20 + 19,000 = £40,000$

   Cost per unit $40,000 \div 5,000 = £8$

   b. Total cost = $10,000 \times 4.20 + 19,000 = £61,000$

   Cost per unit $61,000 \div 10,000 = £6.10$

   This example illustrates the point that costs per unit are lower if the fixed costs are shared among a larger number of products.

   It also raises the point that in valuing a product it is necessary to specify the output. 'What is the cost of making this product?' does not have a simple unequivocal answer!

Answer to QAQ 13.1

Direct: Materials and Labour

Indirect: The rest

Variable: Materials , labour and energy

Fixed: Depreciation and rent etc

Energy is clearly a variable cost as more energy will be used if more keys are made. However measuring the cost of energy for a batch of each type of key made is not economically feasible and so energy is regarded as a variable overhead.

Answer to QAQ 13.2

Standard Cost of one batch of type 501 Keys

			£
Materials:			
	6 Kilos of Metal at £4 a kilo		24.00
	Packaging		3.00
Labour:	Stamper:	2 hours at £4.00 an hour	8.00
	Polisher:	2.5 hours at £5.00 an hour	12.50
	Packer:	2 hours at £3.90 an hour	7.80
Variable Overheads:			
	4.5 hours at £1.50 per Stamper and Polisher hour		6.75
Fixed Overheads:			
	6.5 hours at £6 a direct labour hour		39.00
Total			101.05

Answer to QAQ 13.3

The material and labour costs are direct costs and variances are extracted for specific products or batches of single products. It is useful to know if the actual costs of making a product or a batch are as standard or more or less.

Overhead variances are shared by all products and driven by the total output for variable overheads and by time for fixed overheads. So overhead variances are extracted for total output and periods of time.

Answers to QAQs 14.1

1. You should recognise some of the following:

    Gross Profit, Profit, Interest, Fixed Assets, Current Assets, Stocks, Debtors, Creditors, Bank Overdrafts, Capital, Share Capital, Profit and Loss Account.

    You may well know some of the other words.

2. Fixed Assets are usually valued at cost less accumulated depreciation. However land is usually valued just at cost. In this case some of the fixed assets have been valued at a valuation above cost but we will look at this later.

3. Working capital is defined differently by different people but you have probably included Stock, Debtors, Creditors and the Overdraft.

Answer to QAQ 14.2

a. The directors own a total of 798,800 shares. Only Mr Smith and Mr Hare have large holdings. As each share is worth 80p, Mr Smith's holding is worth £480,000. During the last year Mr Smith has sold 200,000 shares and Mr Hare has bought 90,000 shares.

b. The total number of shares on the Balance Sheet is 10,000,000 so the directors (primarily Mr Smith) own only 8% of the company. In many public companies director shareholdings are negligible.

c. Mr Smith is the Chairman, Mr Crippen is the chief executive. Ms Burke, Ms Palmer and Ms Ripper are presumably full time executives of the company. Non-executive directors normally assist the company by attending Board Meetings and giving the company the benefit of their experience in a very part time way. Non-executive directors are thought to give some control over aberrant behaviour of executives.

d. The Chairman's emoluments are £20,000 which is modest so presumably he is part-time only. Probably the £85,000 refers to Mr Crippen. The three non-executive directors are presumably in the 0 to £5,000 band. The other three executive directors are in the band £55,000 to £65,000. Your author really does not see why the Companies Act should require this odd manner of disclosure but not a list of names with emoluments against each. (Note that the Greenbury Code does.)

Answers to QAQs 14.3

1. Only a small number of shareholders attend Annual General Meetings so that the hotel will be able to accommodate the hundred or so who will turn up.

2. AGMs take very little time and most are called for 12 noon so that those present can enjoy a lunch at the expense of the company.

3. In theory the Board of Directors of public companies are elected by the shareholders. In practice vacancies on the Board are filled by the Board and the new appointment ratified at the next AGM as in this case. One or more directors are required to resign each year but they are usually re-elected. On rare occasions a group of shareholders may attempt to unseat a director but these efforts are seldom successful. Shareholder democracy only really becomes a reality when a takeover bid is made for the company.

Answers to QAQs 14.4

1. The depreciation for a year reduces profit of the year and also reduces the carrying value of assets in the Balance Sheet. Remember that the carrying value (= net book value or written down value) is the cost (or revaluation) less accumulated depreciation.

2. Imagine a company with a Balance Sheet as:

(all figures in '000)

Fixed Assets	1,200	
Current Assets	900	
	2,100	
Current Liabilities	800	Detail
	1,300	
Debentures	500	
	800	

..... continued

Capital	200	
Profit and Loss Account	600	Total
	800	

Note that the 'Reserves' in this case is the Profit and Loss Account.

The company buys another company for £300,000 and borrows the money short term from the bank. The cost of the company £180,000 for net physical assets and £120,000 for goodwill.

The effect on the Balance Sheet is:

Fixed Assets (Investments)	+ £180,000
Current Liabilities (borrowing)	+ £300,000
Profit and Loss Account	– £120,000

So the Balance Sheet after acquisition is:

Fixed Assets	1,380	
Current Assets	900	
	2,280	
Current Liabilities	1,100	Detail
	1,180	
Debentures	500	
	680	
Capital	200	
Profit and Loss Account	480	Total
	680	

There will be no effect on the annual profit.

Answers to QAQs 15.1

1. Raw Materials consumed, Prime Cost, Factory inputs in the year, Works cost of finished goods output, Cost of goods sold, Gross Profit.

   Cost of Fixed Assets held at the year end, Net book value or written down value, Net current assets.

2. Increase for turnover and capital expenditure (up from £10,000 to £160,000).

   Decrease for work in progress, other overheads, and stocks.

3. Stocks in the Balance Sheet are at the end of 19x6 £548,000 consisting of materials £105,000, work in progress £163,000 and finished goods £280,000.

4. Depreciation in the Profit and Loss Account for 19x6 is £34,000 and in the Balance Sheet the same amount. I have charged all the depreciation to works overheads but as fixed assets are both plant and vehicles, depreciation should be split between works overheads and probably distribution costs. We will keep the problem simple!

Answers to QAQs 15.2

1. Gross Profit

   Net Profit before tax

   Net Profit after tax

   Retained Proft for the year

   Net Current Liabilities

2. The dividend per share is £2 in 19x7 and £2.10 in 19x8.

   Of this 60p in each year was an interim and the remainder are the final dividends.

3. The retained Profits for 19x8 are £89,000 and the Profit and Loss Account in the Balance Sheet has increased by that amount from £94,000 to £183,000.

Answers to QAQs 16.1

1. All the creditors: amounts falling due within one year (commonly known as current liabilities) and the capital and reserves are sources of finance. For example, buying on credit enables the company to obtain stock and pay for it only after a couple of months. It is more difficult to see that, for example, the corporation tax due is a source of finance. But if you consider that the profits are earned in say the year ending 31 December 19x1 and that the tax is not payable till 1 October 19x2, you may see that it is a source of finance.

2. External sources are all the current liabilities except perhaps the dividend. Internal sources are the share capital which was originally invested in the business at the foundation of the company plus the Profit and Loss Account.

   A profit is a source of finance in the sense that it is an increase in net assets without an increase in external liability. For example if Martin has £1 and buys a lock with it and then sells it for £1.50, he then has £1.50. He has acquired 50p by making a profit. The Profit and Loss figure is the aggregate profits made by the company since its foundation less corporation tax and dividends.

   It is, as it were, the total of all the 50p profits made. It is not cash as the money is mostly invested in stock, debtors and fixed assets as it becomes available.

Answers to QAQs 17.1

1. Forms of finance used include:

   Trade credit, Bank Overdraft, Leasing, Factoring, Hire Purchase, Bills of Exchange, Longer term bank loans, Mortgage loans from an insurance company, Shares sold to shareholders, Retained Profits.

2. £3,150,000 ÷ 400,000 = £7.875

   A share is worth more than this for many reasons including:

   ❏ The assets are valued by reference to cost and they include an asset (property) which is worth substantially more than book value.

   ❏ A principal asset of the company – goodwill – is omitted entirely from the Balance Sheet.

In practice share valuation is very difficult and depends on whether a minority or majority holding is being valued, the profits of the company and many other factors.

3. A creditor secured on a fixed charge has first access to the proceeds of sale of the property on which the loan is secured so he cannot lose if the property is sold for more than the loan.

   A creditor secured by a floating charge has first access to the proceeds of sale of all the assets (but ranks behind the fixed charge creditors) and so cannot lose if the assets are sold for more than the amount of the loans. Note that in practice there are some creditors (including staff) who take preference over floating charge creditors.

Answers to QAQs 17.2

1. The value, using PE, would be 12 x £650,000 = £7,800,000

2. A 4% yield means that the company is worth $25 \times (100 \div 4)$ times the dividend

$$= 25 \times £70,000 = £1,750,000.$$

3. The profits are what the company earns. They are the best the company can do and are objectively measured. The dividend is a matter of policy. Martin pays a small dividend (small as a proportion of profits) in order to expand the company. Most of the dividend comes to him and he prefers to pay himself very little. If the company were floated, a much larger dividend would need to be paid to satisfy the investors need for a 4% yield on a price calculated by reference to earnings.

Answers to QAQs 18.1

1. You may have recognised some accountancy words — profit, loss, depreciation, Balance Sheet, at cost, book value, stock, creditors, cash at bank. Many words are common English words with their ordinary meanings. Some you can guess at their meaning — deficit for example.

2. The Club does not exist to make a profit but to provide a service for its members. However it is desirable, and in the long term, essential that income exceeds expenditure. You will see that in 19x9, the Club had a deficit. This word tends to be used in Club accounts instead of 'loss'. The corresponding word used instead of profit is surplus.

3. No. As you will see the land and buildings are valued at cost on the Balance Sheet and there is no depreciation of land or buildings in the Income and Expenditure Account.

Answer to QAQ 19.1

There are several possibilities. Martin's company manufacture and sell in the UK. However they also sell in the EC and in other countries. Expansion of UK manufacturing facilities depends on obtaining more sales outside the UK but this is difficult without special knowledge of overseas markets. One way of acquiring this *special knowledge* is to take over a company which already has it. The takeover of a competing firm can give several benefits. *Duplicate activities* can be eliminated, efforts are no longer needed to compete with each other, each can contribute *ideas* and knowledge to the other, *economies of scale* can be introduced. It is said that the whole can be more than the sum of the parts. This effect can be called synergy (from the Greek — working together). Martin's company may wish to have international shareholders and having overseas subsidiaries may give more international credibility. Acquiring an overseas company may reduce overall risk to the combined group.

Appendix E Six assignments

Assignment 1 (to Unit 4)

Bingo Care Homes Ltd operate an up-market old peoples home and respite care centre. The company is owned by a consortium of business and professional people. The company was formed in 19x1 and with the newly subscribed capital the company purchased and converted a large Victorian residence. The company has been profitable and large dividends have been payable. It is now 19x8 and the chief executive Sister Nightingale is presenting the annual accounts to the Board. The Balance Sheet shows:

Balance Sheet as at 31 December 19x8

Fixed Assets	Land	Buildings	Equipment	Total
	£	£	£	£
Cost	50,000	146,000	24,800	220,800
Depreciation	–	23,360	13,630	36,990
Net Book Value	50,000	122,640	11,170	183,810
Current Assets				
Stocks			8,200	
Debtors			25,400	
Cash at Bank			1,290	
			34,890	
Creditors: less than one year				
Creditors			15,495	
Taxation			15,800	
			31,295	
Net Current Assets				3,595
Total assets less current liabilities				187,405
Liabilities: more than one year				
Bank Loan at 8%				50,000
c **Net Assets**				137,405
Capital and Reserves				
Share Capital in £1 shares				100,000
Profit and Loss Account				37,405
				137,405

Notes:

1. The bank loan is repayable in annual instalments of £10,000 in March each year.

2. The land and buildings have no additions or deletions since the company was formed.

3. The equipment is renewed at intervals and depreciation is 25% reducing balance.

4. The Profit and Loss Account is:

Balance at 31 December 19x7	£6,420
Profit after tax for 19x8	£30,985

Sister Nightingale reports that the company has made a profit of £30,985 after tax in 19x8 but that the company cannot afford to pay a dividend because:

❐ there is not enough money in the bank

❐ the bank loan instalment is due shortly

❐ the building needs complete redecoration and new washbasins and baths and some new fireproof doors.

She suggests instead that the company obtain some more money from the shareholders in the form of new share capital.

Required:

a. Explain why profit for the year may not equate with changes in cash balances over the year.

b. During 19x8 there was a change in the timing of payment of fees by the residents. As a result average debtors doubled. Explain the effect this would have had on profit and the cash balance.

c. What is the depreciation policy for the land and buildings? Assuming that the company regularly pays out 100% of its profits after tax in dividends, what would be the effect on dividends of changing the depreciation policy?

d. One of the directors, Dr Cash, suggests that the property should be revalued as it is worth substantially more, in fact about double, than it was in 19x1. What would be the effect of such a revaluation upwards on profits and dividends?

e. Another director, Mrs Grasp, suggests that her 1,000 shares are clearly worth £1,374 and she suggests that the whole company is sold so that the shareholders can realise their holdings. Explain how she arrived at the figure of £1,374 and why the company is not necessarily worth the figure she implies.

f. Another director, Ms Micawber, who is an accountant, suggests that the company is profitable but that a number of changes and new procedures are required if it is to continue. What might these changes be?

Assignment 2 (to Unit 7)

Sali runs the administrative unit connected with a local care organisation. She has charge of the unit's finances and obtains funding from the parent organisation and also from selling the unit's services to other organisations.

Her budget for 19x6 is:

Category	£
Rent	6,000
Insurance	1,500
Heating and lighting	2,300
Salaries	50,600
Depreciation of office equipment	3,000

Category	£
Telephone and postage	4,100
Stationery and sundries	3,800
Software	8,000
Travelling expenses	16,800
	96,100

She has calculated the budget on the basis of 90% capacity.

She reckons that any increase in activity over 100% of capacity will require additional premises at a cost of £1,000 a year together with extra insurance of £400 and extra telephone line rental of £800. Extra heating of £500 will also be required. Salaries are a fixed cost but any increase in work load above 100% will involve overtime at time and one third. Stationery and sundries and travelling expenses are a pure variable cost linearly changing with capacity utilisation. The office equipment and software should need no increase with more work.

Her parent organisation have told her that the budget will need to be revised as the level of activity will be 120% (including the sales of the unit's services to outside parties).

Required:

a. Revise her budget to 100% and 120%.

b. Install the problem on a spreadsheet so that budgeted costs can be calculated at any level of activity within the relevant range. Sali reckons that she could make up any shortfall of work below 90% by contracting more sales and that her staff and additional premises would take her to 140% of current capacity.

Sali has been approached by a sister organisation to do some work which will take the unit from 120% of capacity to 130%. The work will also require an additional computer at a cost of £1,000 and software at £400.

Required:

c. Calculate the cost on i. total absorption cost principles and ii. marginal cost principles.

d. The sister organisation have offered a maximum price which is only a little more than marginal cost. Discuss the factors which might make her accept or reject the work.

Assignment 3 (to Unit 10)

Pendil Clothing Ltd is a charity which manufactures clothing using homeless people as its labour force. It sells its products to retailers. It has no branch in a certain remote region of the UK but is considering opening one so that it can do business with local retailers.

The data required is:

❐ Annual rent (5 year lease), rates, and insurance of the branch £2,800.

❐ Annual staff salaries £13,600 plus free volunteers.

❐ Other branch costs £4,000 a year.

❐ Cost of fitting out the branch £15,000 + the cost of a vehicle £10,000. The fittings should just last the five years and the vehicle will have a salvage value of £1,000.

❐ Sales are expected to be £60,000 a year. These will be on credit and payments are expected as:

20% in one month, 50% in two months and the remainder in three months.

❐ All purchases are from head office who charge 50% of the selling price and give one month's credit.

❐ Stock will average £20,000 at cost.

Required:

a. Appraise the project assuming a cost of capital of 10%.

b. Set up the project on a spreadsheet and appraise it with different numbers — e.g. six years, cost of capital 8% or 12%, sales at £50,000 or £70,000 etc.

c. Pendil are considering offering a 5% discount to their customers. They reckon this will induce the customers to pay such that 50% will take the discount, 20% will take two months and 30% will take three months.What is the true interest rate cost of this proposal?

d. While considering the proposal the trustees of the charity revised the estimate of sales down to £50,000. They reviewed the project again and decided to go ahead despite the negative NPV. Why do you think they did this?

Assignment 4 (to Unit 13)

Tenbury's Stores PLC have a chain of supermarkets. They have decided to enter into the sale of financial products, marketing four standard life assurance products of the Importunate Life. To test the market they allocate a part of one store (1,000 square feet) to a desk with the salesman and his computer. It is essential that the venture is profitable so they initially assess the costs of the project. This consists of setting up the desk and computer £12,000 (life four years) and initial advertising £8,000, the salesman's salary and expenses £25,000 and the cost of the floor space.

The store has 600,000 square feet and Tenbury's pay rent, rates and insurances £1,000,000. Heat, light and repairs £350,000. The store has 100 full-time equivalent shopfloor staff costing £850,000. In addition they spend £300,000 on administration salaries and costs which they apportion to staff.

Required:

a. Calculate the annual cost of the salesman and his space in the store.

b. The salesman's pitch is a prime part of the store and it seems illogical to allocate the same proportion of costs to prime space as to space used for storage of goods awaiting transfer to the shop shelves. Suggest ways that can be used for assessing the per square foot profitability of the different areas in the store.

The first year's sales budget for the new venture is: 100 policy type A, 150 type B, 80 type C and 40 type D. The average commission on each sale is expected to be A £150, B £80, C £250 and D £300. The actual outcome was:

Type	A	B	C	D
Number sold	95	180	62	42
Average Commission	140	48	240	360

The space actually occupied by the salesman turned out to be 1,200 square feet and his salary and expenses cost £30,000 and the initial advertising had to be repeated after four months. In addition, the store manager complained that the administration of the venture took a disproportionate part of his own and his staff's time.

Required :

c.   Write a report on the venture's first year and make reasoned recommendations for the following year.

Assignment 5 (to Unit 17)

Kramik Tiles PLC manufacture, import and distribute decorative tiles. The company is an old one which went public in 1960. Most of the shares are held by the institutions and small investors but some 15% are still held by descendants of the founders. The directors are five ex-employees who have risen to board status and four non-executives. The company trades from factory premises which were constructed in the nineteenth century but which have been much altered and improved. There is a surplus of industrial land in their area.

The Profit and Loss Accounts for the two years ending 31 December 19x5 and 19x6 show:

	1995	1996 Continuing	1996 Acquisitions	1996 Total
	£	£	£	£
Turnover	4,600	4,308	1,200	5,508
Cost of sales	2,498	2,410	876	3,286
Gross profit	2,102	1,898	324	2,222
Distribution expenses	976	1,034	123	1,157
Administration expenses	772	660	65	725
Operating profit	354	374	136	510
Profit on disposal of fixed assets	54	26		26
Profit on ordinary activities	408	400	136	536
Interest payable	102			278
	306			274
Tax	101			72
Profit for the financial year	205			202
Dividends	156			156
Retained profit	49			46

Balance Sheets

	1995		1996
Fixed assets		6,200	6,160
Current assets			
Stocks	330		580
Debtors	540		723
	870		1,303

	1995		1996
Creditors under twelve months			
Overdrafts	380		420
Trade creditors	220		318
Taxes	247		256
Dividends	104		104
	951		1,098
Net current liabilities/assets		81	205
Total assets less current liabilities		6,119	6,365
Creditors more than twelve months		500	1,000
		5,619	5,365
Capital and reserves			
Called up share capital		1,000	1,800
Share premium		800	–
Profit and Loss Account		3,819	3,565
Equity shareholders funds		5,619	5,365

Notes:

1. Fixed Assets:

	Land and Buildings			Plant /vehicles		
	Cost £	Depr £	Wdv £	Cost £	Depr £	Wdv £
b/f	5,000	2,000	3,000	8,400	5,200	3,200
Sold				1,400	1,300	100
				7,000	3,900	3,100
Add Acquisition	200		200	400		400
Add cash				1,000		1,000
	5,200		3,200	8,400	3,900	4,500
Depreciation		140	140		1,400	1,400
	5,200	2,140	3,060	8,400	5,300	3,100

The plant and vehicles sold realised £250,000

Depreciation Policy is:
Land — No depreciation

Buildings — 2% on freehold and over period of lease for leaseholds

Plan/vehicles — Straight line over 6 years

2. The share capital is in 25p shares which are quoted presently at 45p.

3. The business acquired was a tile distribution network with several branches. Its assets were:

Goodwill	300	Consideration:	
Short leases	200	Cash	650
Plant/vehicles	400	Loan Stock	500
			1,150
Stock	200		
Debtors	230		
	1,330		
Creditors	180		
	1,150		

The business was acquired on July 1st so only six months' trading is included in the Profit and Loss Account.

4. Creditors: more than twelve months are:

£500,000 10% Convertible loan stock, convertible at the option of the holders in June 19x9 at the rate of one share per £1 of stock. If not redeemed the stock is repayable at par in December 19x9.

£500,000 15% Convertible loan stock, convertible ten years after the acquisition at the rate of 1 share per £1 of stock or repayable at par the following year. This stock was issued as part consideration for the acquired business.

Required:

a. Comment on the company's performance and achievements over the two years.

b. What are the problems which face the company? The directors see manufacture as declining and intend to increase importation and distribution.

c. Comment on the share price.

A good approach to these requirements is to consider the accounts line by line. Ratios can be used where these are useful or relevant.

Assignment 6 (the whole book)

Albert Ltd have a wholesale clothing business in Uffington. The financial statements for 19x6 (all figures in £'000) showed:

Profit and Loss Account

Sales	2,389
Cost of sales	1,465
Gross profit	924
Wages	254
Other overheads	196

Balance Sheet

	Cost	Depr	NBV
Land	200	–	200
Buildings	253	120	133
Equipment, vehicles etc	481	243	238
	934	363	571

				Depr	NBV
Depreciation	84	Stock		244	
Operating profit	390	Debtors		398	
Overdraft interest	75			642	
Net profit before tax	315	Creditors		366	
Taxation	85	Overdraft		490	
Net profit after tax	230	Taxation		85	
Dividends	150	Dividends		70	
Retained	80			1,011	(369)
					202
		Share capital 20p shares			50
		Profit and Loss Account			152
					202

Note: Stocks at the beginning and the end of the year were the same.

The board are considering the budget for next year. Their thoughts turn on:

Sales up 10%

Stocks increased to three months purchases

Debtors collection period as 19x6
Creditors payment period as 19x6

Wages down 20% but redundancy payment of £20,000

Other overheads up 5% (but see below) etc.

Depreciation policy: Buildings over 50 years; Equipment 15% reducing balance

Overdraft interest about £60,000

Taxation 20% of net profit

Dividends the same as 19x6

Gross Profit ratio 40%

They intend to buy a vehicle. They estimate this will cost £18,000 to buy, will last four years and then be sold for £2,000, will cost £10,000 a year to run but save £16,000 of the projected overheads. They will only go ahead with the purchase if the net present value of the project is positive at 12%.

They have received an enquiry from a company in Belgium to supply 10,000 of their silk T shirts at a price of £6 each. Albert Ltd print the designs themselves and they estimate the cost of supply at: shirts £4 each; transport cost £1,000 the lot; wrapping £0.50 each; printing cost: materials £300 in total, labour £0.20 each and overheads at fixed £8,000 and variable £4,000. The Belgians will pay cash on delivery. Albert Ltd decide to go ahead with the sale.

Required:

a. Evaluate the project to buy the vehicle.

b. Evaluate the Belgian deal and discuss whether the company should have accepted the order.

c. Prepare budgeted Trading and Profit and Loss Account, Balance Sheet and Cash Flow Statement.

d. The bank have said that they are looking for substantial reductions in the overdraft in the short term. They see no more than £300,000 and falling as their limit. Suggest and review possible sources of finance for the company. The managing director Victoria has 20% of the shares but no private resources. The other shareholders are all wealthy.

e. Discuss with figures what the company as a whole may be worth.

Index